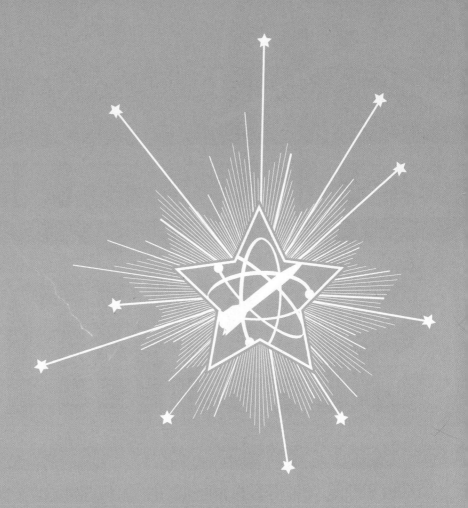

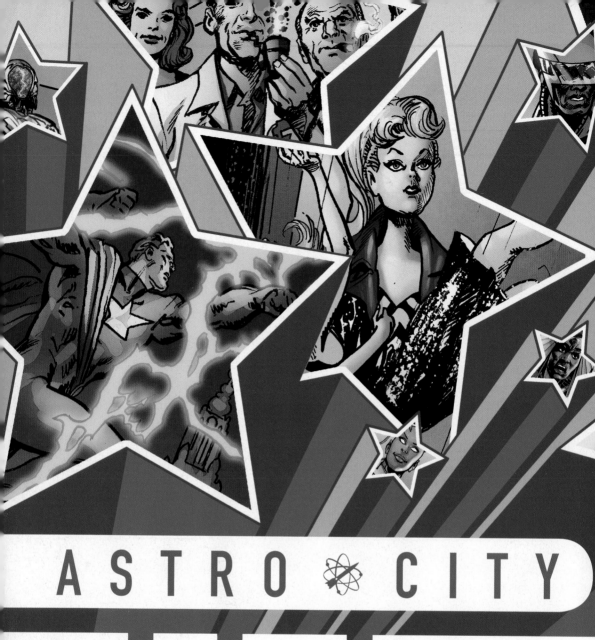

ASTRO ✷ CITY
shining

KURT BUSIEK
writer

BRENT ERIC ANDERSON
artist

ALEX SINCLAIR & WENDY BROOME
colors

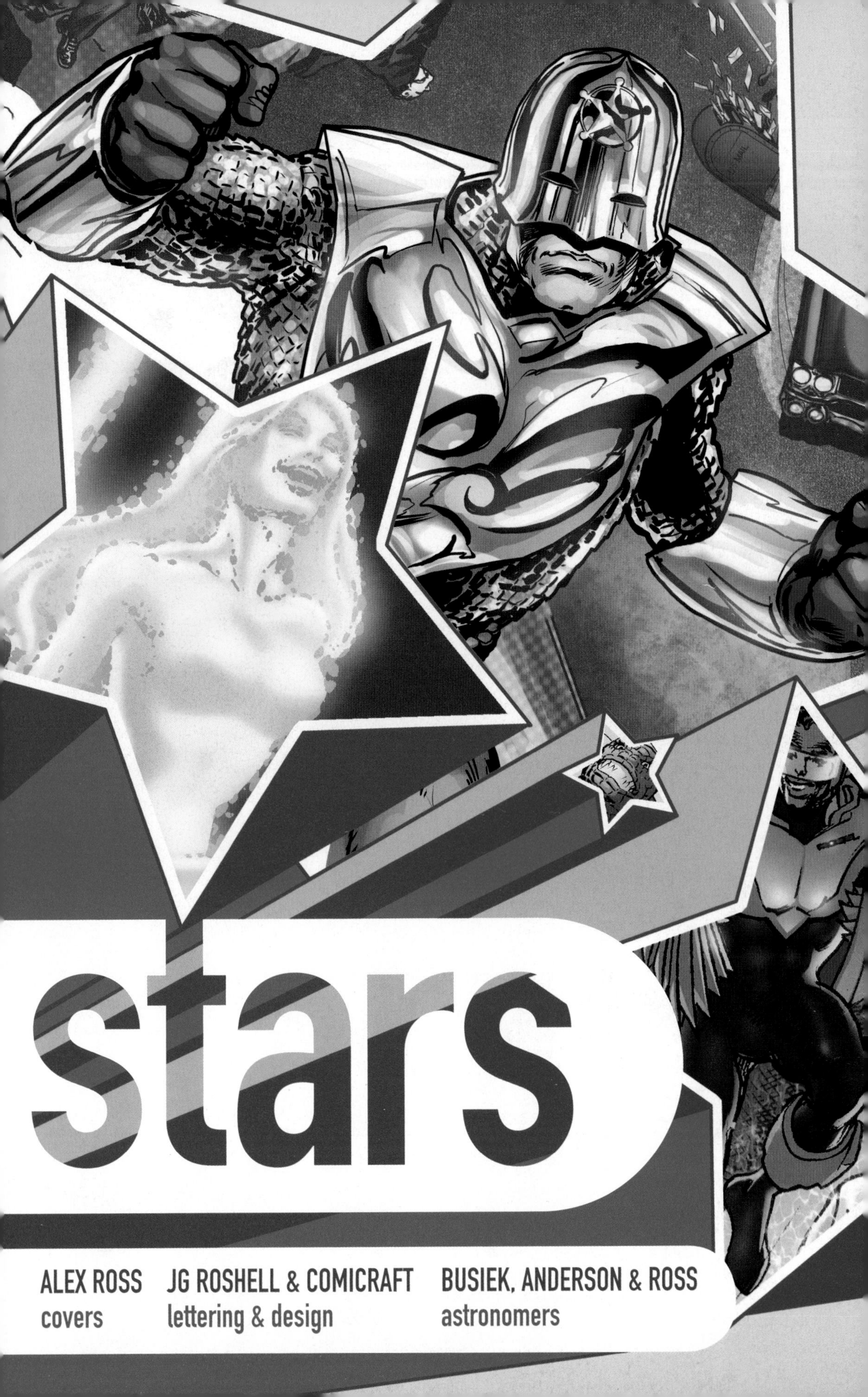

stars

ALEX ROSS
covers

JG ROSHELL & COMICRAFT
lettering & design

BUSIEK, ANDERSON & ROSS
astronomers

ANN HUNTINGTON BUSIEK
Managing Editor

RICHARD STARKINGS
Art Director

DEDICATIONS

VERTIGO

Ben Abernathy — Editors-Original Series
Scott Peterson
Kristy Quinn — Editor
Robbin Brosterman — Design Director – Books
Shelly Bond — Executive Editor – Vertigo
Hank Kanalz — Senior VP – Vertigo & Integrated Publishing

Diane Nelson — President
Dan DiDio and Jim Lee — Co-Publishers
Geoff Johns — Chief Creative Officer
John Rood — Executive VP – Sales, Marketing & Business Development
Amy Genkins — Senior VP – Business & Legal Affairs
Nairi Gardiner — Senior VP – Finance
Jeff Boison — VP – Publishing Planning
Mark Chiarello — VP – Art Direction & Design
John Cunningham — VP – Marketing
Terri Cunningham — VP – Editorial Administration
Alison Gill — Senior VP – Manufacturing & Operations
Jay Kogan — VP – Business & Legal Affairs, Publishing
Jack Mahan — VP – Business Affairs, Talent
Nick Napolitano — VP – Manufacturing Administration
Sue Pohja — VP – Book Sales
Courtney Simmons — Senior VP – Publicity
Bob Wayne — Senior VP – Sales

For Katie, who missed out on an earlier dedication by not being born yet.
— KURT

For Bryce, in thanks for all the monsters, hive warriors, otherworld omnicrats and other cool visual ideas he's gifted me. Born the same year as ASTRO CITY, he is fast becoming a shining star himself.
— BRENT

To all puppies everywhere.
— ALEX

Printed by RR Donnelley, Salem, VA . 3/7/2014.

DC Comics, a Warner Bros. Entertainment Company.

ISBN: 978-1-4012-2991-7

ASTRO CITY: SHINING STARS includes ASTRO CITY: SAMARITAN © 2006, ASTRO CITY: BEAUTIE © 2008, ASTRO CITY: ASTRA 1 & 2 © 2009, and ASTRO CITY: SILVER AGENT 1 & 2 © 2010.

contents

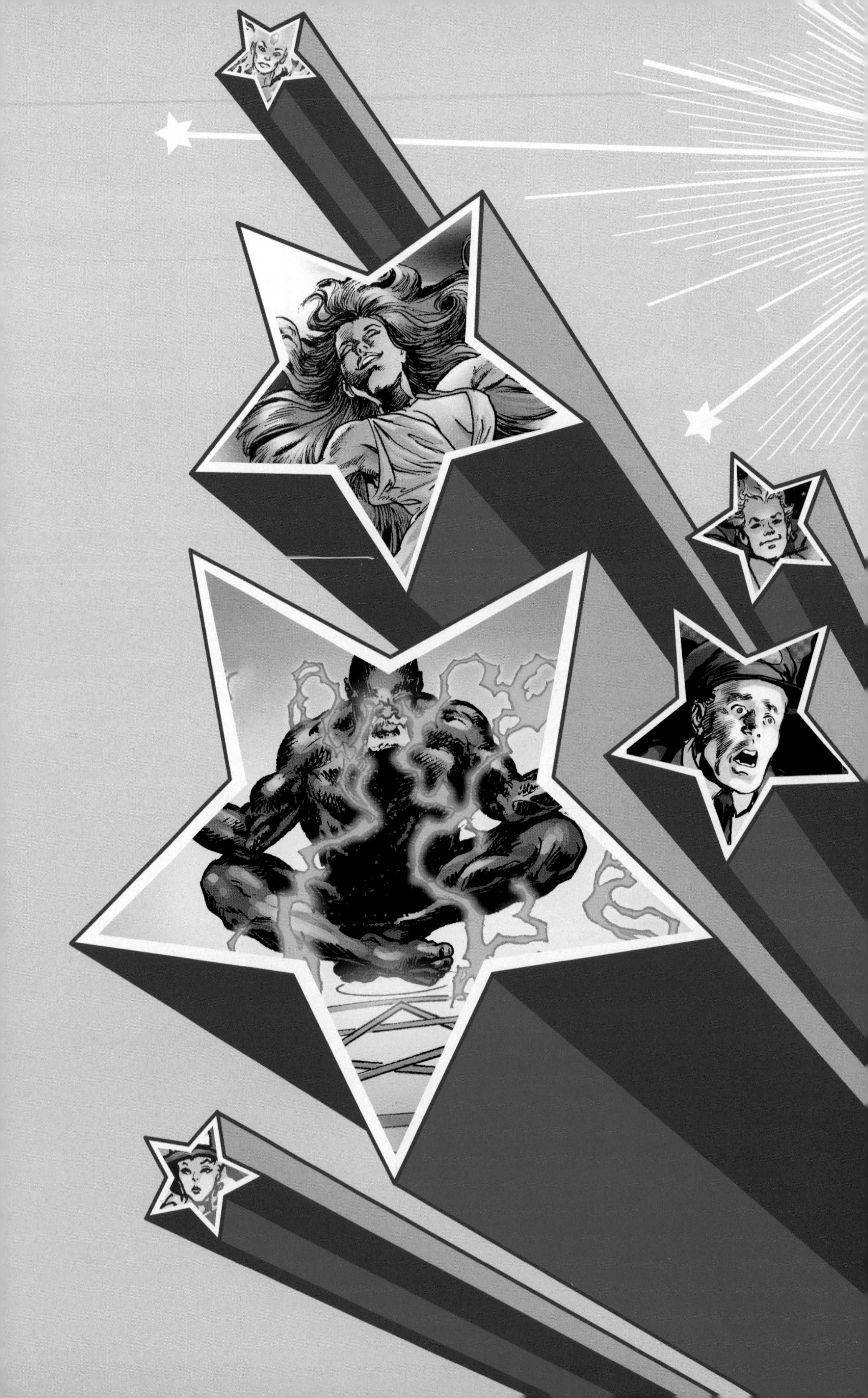

introduction

by MARK WAID

My history with Kurt Busiek, whom I have known now for over two decades, basically consists of a long chain of regrettable moments which follow this invariable pattern: (1) I misinterpret something Kurt says or does, (2) I mouth off about it in a mocking and/or overemotional fashion, and (3) Kurt sits back patiently to watch the truth, however long it takes, eventually catch up to me while (4) I come to wonder why he puts up with me at all.

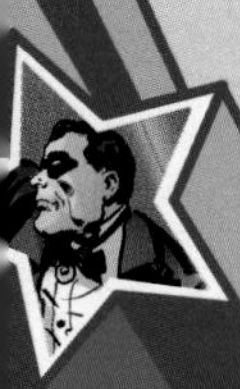

My initial reaction to ASTRO CITY is an excellent example, and since I have never, ever admitted this to Kurt before this moment, it will come as a surprise to him when he sees it here, or it would, except (goto=1): When I read the very first ASTRO CITY story, "In Dreams," I rolled my eyes so hard you'd think I was a slot machine.

"Pastiche," I said to my friends with that tone of voice and hand-wave of smug dismissal first perfected by composer Antonio Salieri. "Big deal. It's just a Superman story with the names changed. How original is that? Man, this thing is overrated."

Yes, yes (goto=4).

I kept reading, though, issue after issue. I really liked the art by Brent Anderson, and I certainly appreciated the craftsmanship of Kurt's scripts, but because I was impatiently oblivious to the art of what Kurt was doing, it took me a while to come around...and once I did, the revelation of what he was up to forever changed my own approach to writing.

See, Neil Gaiman's fond of saying that the comic book is not a genre, it's a medium, which is true, and I wish I'd said it first. Just like the detective story, just like the Western, that which comic books best capitalize on—superheroes—that's a genre, at least to most writers. But what I slowly began to see once I stopped regarding ASTRO CITY as simple fan-fiction was that Kurt had pulled off a gracefully subtle reversal, sui generis and brilliant in its invention. Kurt approaches the superhero as a medium, not a genre.

Probably moreso than anyone else working in comics thus far this century, Kurt uses the lens of the superhuman to tell tales that are so unrelentingly human that they seem almost gentle. No, scratch that; they are gentle, especially for stories about superheroes, because despite first appearances, they aren't about superheroes. They're about you and me and the guy down the street. Kurt's sorcery is that he uses the very specific tropes of superheroes to tell universal tales. Any competent author can write a story featuring a cowboy that tells you something about cowboys, but it takes a very special talent to write a series featuring superheroes where the first and foremost purpose of every installment is to tell you something about yourself.

The tale of the Samaritan and the Infidel isn't about a strongman battling with his arch-villain, it's about the insidious nature of temptation. The chapter on Beautie isn't about beating the crap out of an evil genius, it's about the price of being a lousy parent or an ignored child. The Silver Agent story is about personal redemption. And the Astra piece——by far my favorite in this book and, I'll bet, yours as well——is about how hard it is to find our identity and follow our passions when challenged by the expectations of our loved ones and the world around us. There is an emotional resonance to the Astra story in particular that so transcends the...the... the superheroness of it all that I am in awe.

I'm not saying that Kurt invented the technique of commenting on the human condition. He's good, but he's not that good. But what he has done with the ASTRO CITY series is to retro-engineer the metaphors of the superhero into commonly relatable experiences and thus ground them without making them seem mundane. My own instinct as a writer is to use the wonderful impossibilities inherent in the genre to amplify drama into melodrama, but in ASTRO CITY, Kurt does the opposite. He takes the operatic grandeur of the superhero world and all its larger-than-life trappings and simmers it into drama. Simple, quiet drama. How original is that?

It's not just original. It's unique. And I'm just sorry I didn't catch on from the start. But to his credit, Kurt's never given me a hard time about it.

(goto=3).

Welcome to Astro City. Enjoy your stay. You'll like it here. It's very familiar...but with a purpose and in a most unexpected way.

Mark Waid
Fortress of Solitude, 2010

Born in Hueytown, Alabama at the height of the Silver Age, MARK WAID began reading comics at the age of four, and has never looked back. Breaking into the comics field in his early twenties, he has worked as a journalist, an editor and a writer, and is best known for his work on such series as FLASH, FANTASTIC FOUR, CAPTAIN AMERICA, the Eisner award-winning KINGDOM COME and his own creation, IRREDEEMABLE. From 2007 to 2010, he was editor in chief at Boom! Studios, but has recently returned to full-time freelancing, looking to chart new courses for comics in the digital age.

THE FINEST STORIES of the FINEST HEROES
Astro City
STORIES
Samaritan
in
"The EAGLE and the MOUNTAIN"
by Kurt Busiek & Brent Anderson

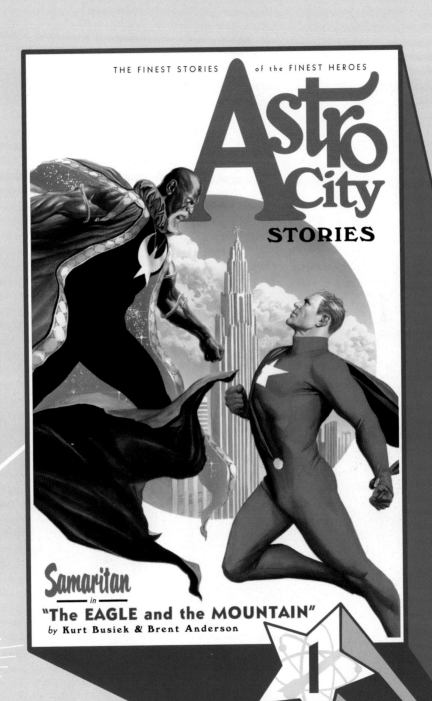

THE EAGLE AND THE MOUNTAIN

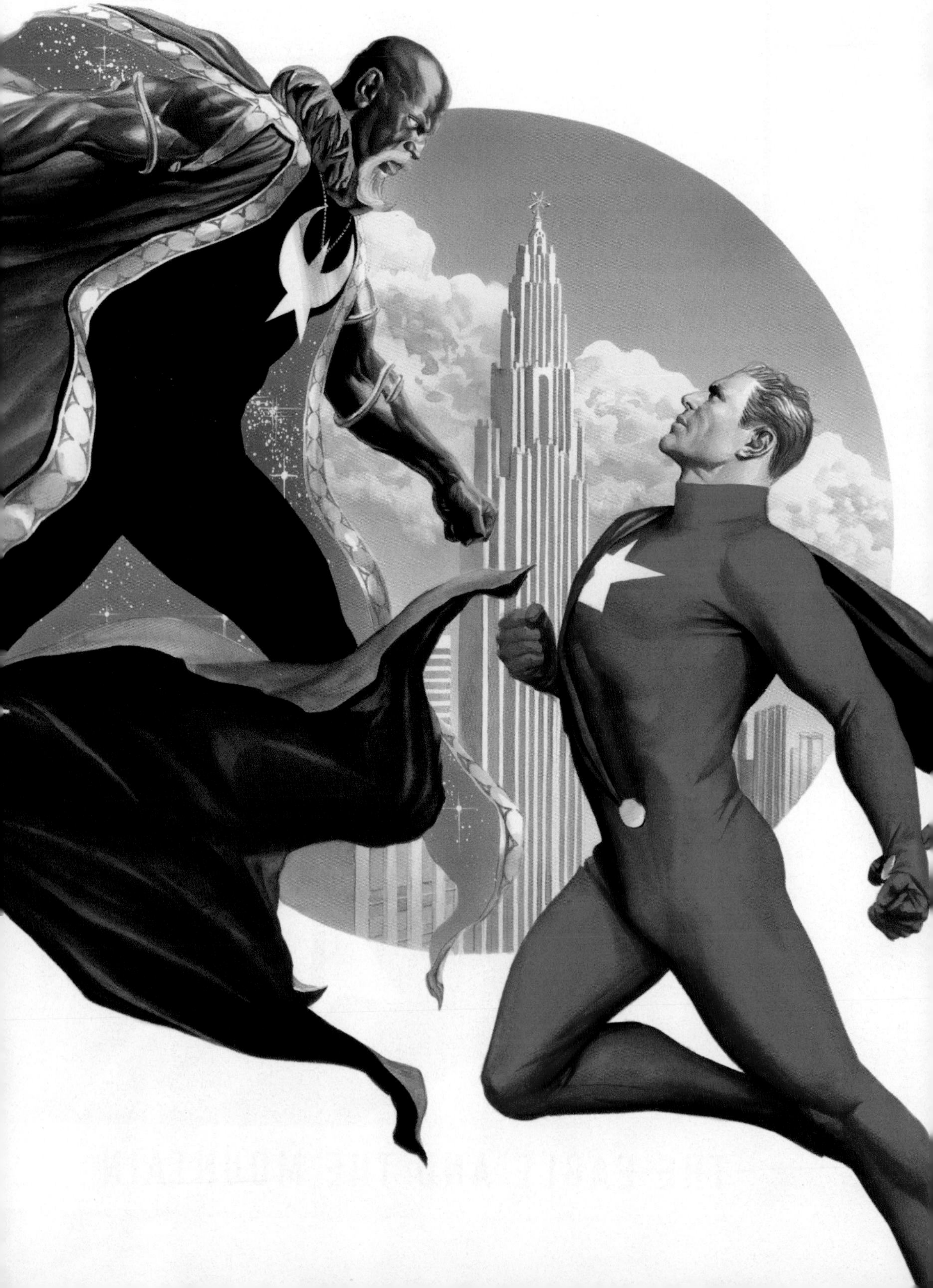

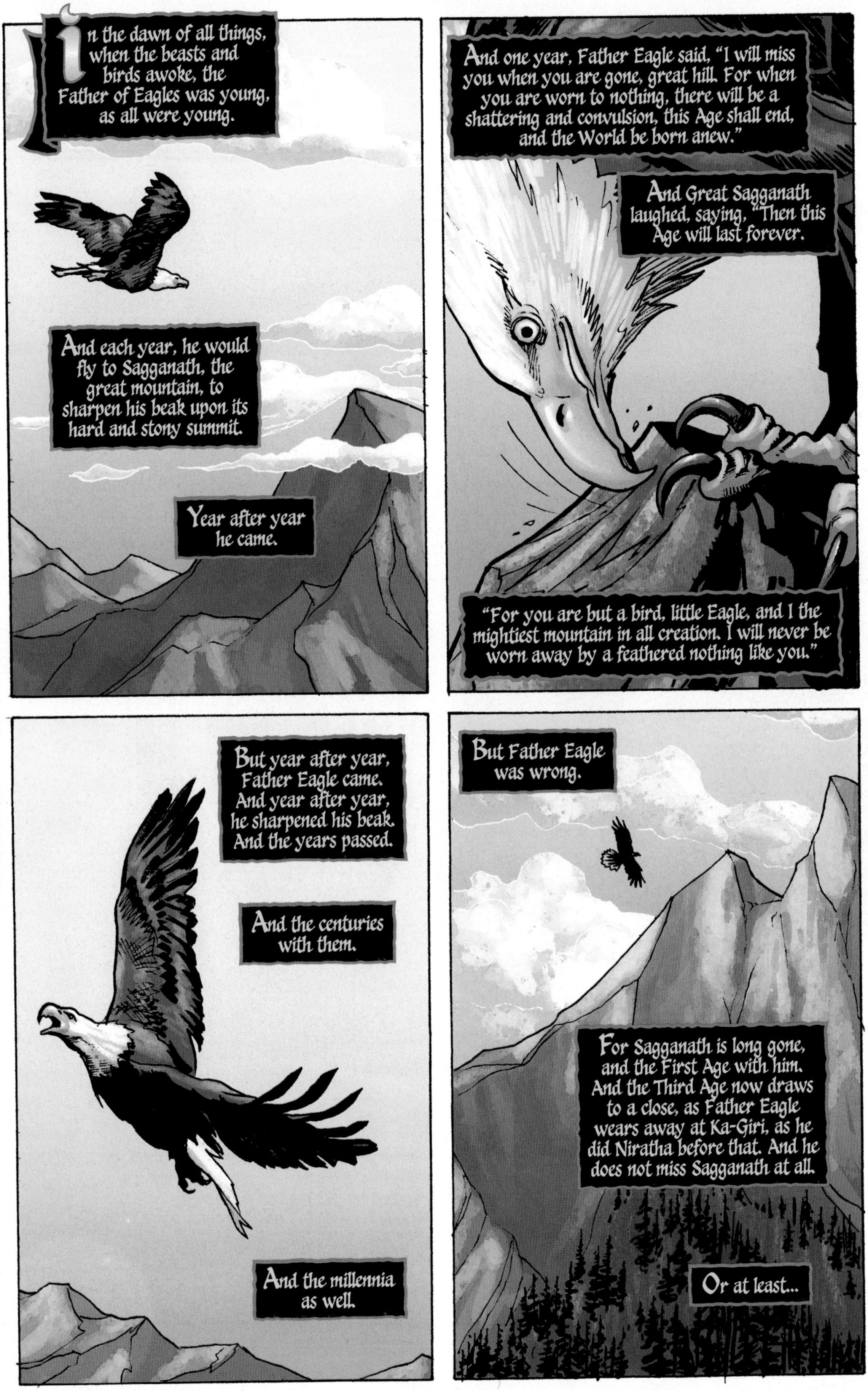
In the dawn of all things, when the beasts and birds awoke, the Father of Eagles was young, as all were young.
And each year, he would fly to Sagganath, the great mountain, to sharpen his beak upon its hard and stony summit.
Year after year he came.
And one year, Father Eagle said, "I will miss you when you are gone, great hill. For when you are worn to nothing, there will be a shattering and convulsion, this Age shall end, and the World be born anew."
And Great Sagganath laughed, saying, "Then this Age will last forever.
"For you are but a bird, little Eagle, and I the mightiest mountain in all creation. I will never be worn away by a feathered nothing like you."
But year after year, Father Eagle came. And year after year, he sharpened his beak. And the years passed.
And the centuries with them.
And the millennia as well.
But Father Eagle was wrong.
For Sagganath is long gone, and the First Age with him. And the Third Age now draws to a close, as Father Eagle wears away at Ka-Giri, as he did Niratha before that. And he does not miss Sagganath at all.
Or at least...

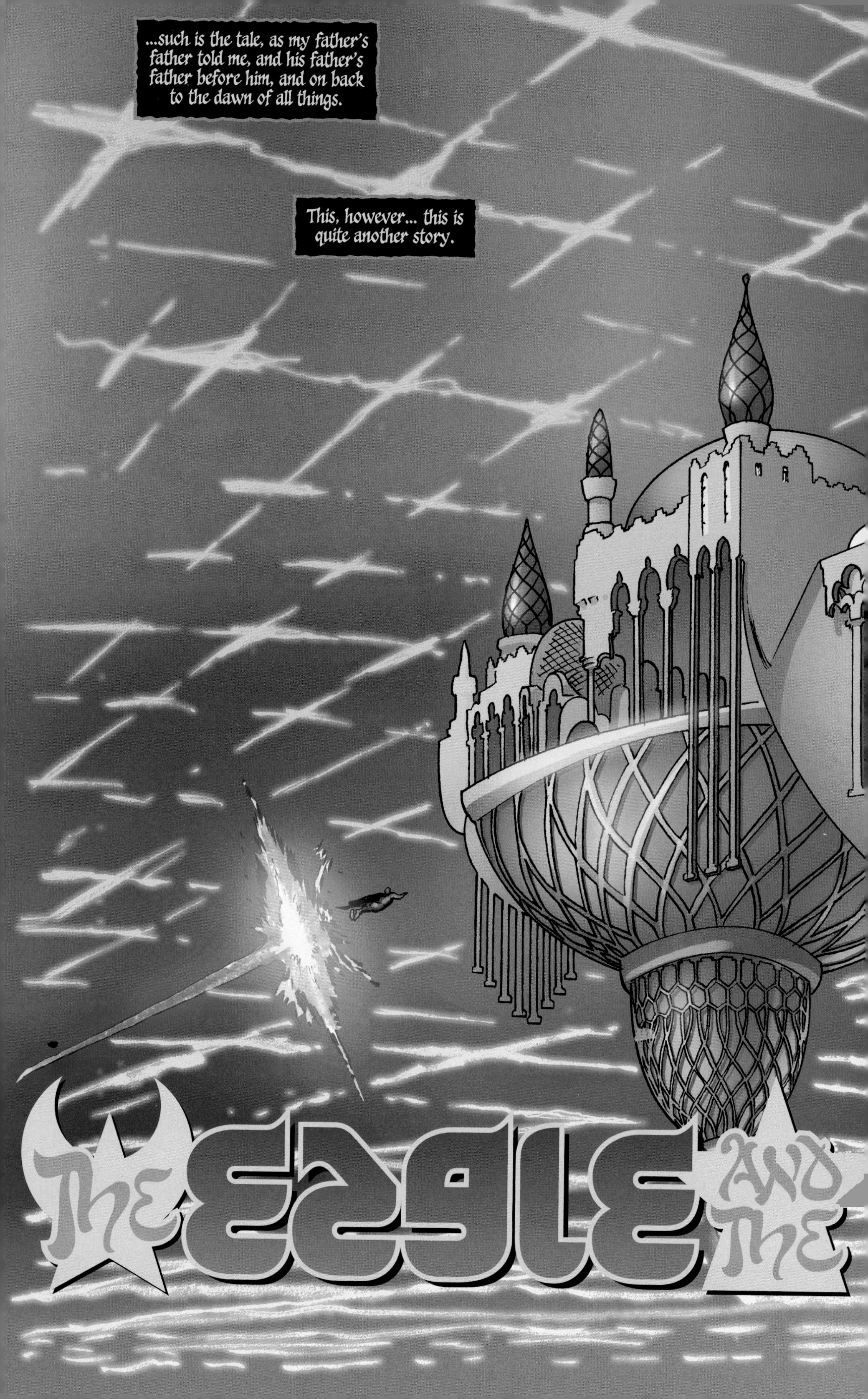
...such is the tale, as my father's father told me, and his father's father before him, and on back to the dawn of all things.
This, however... this is quite another story.
The Eagle and the

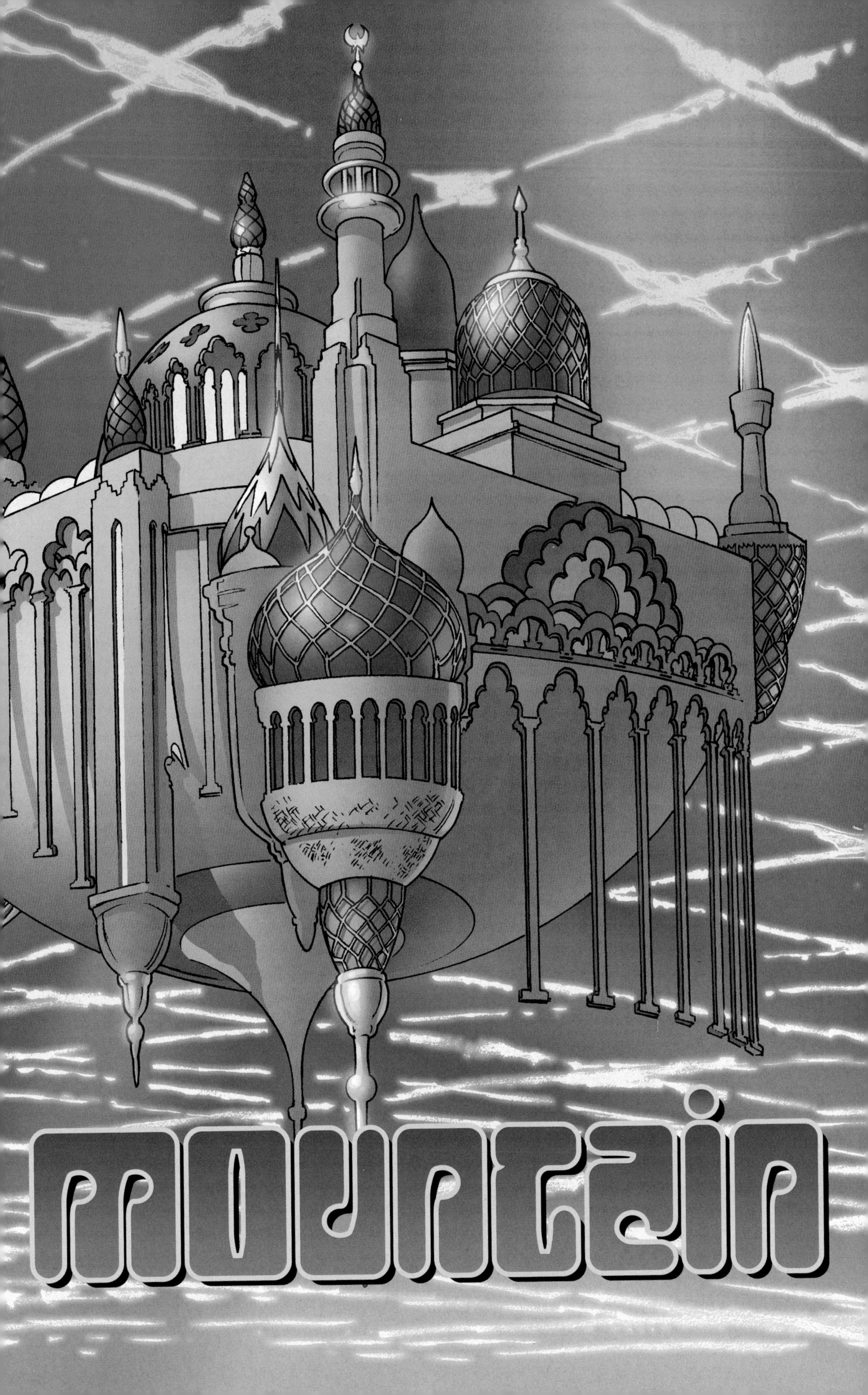
MOUNTAIN

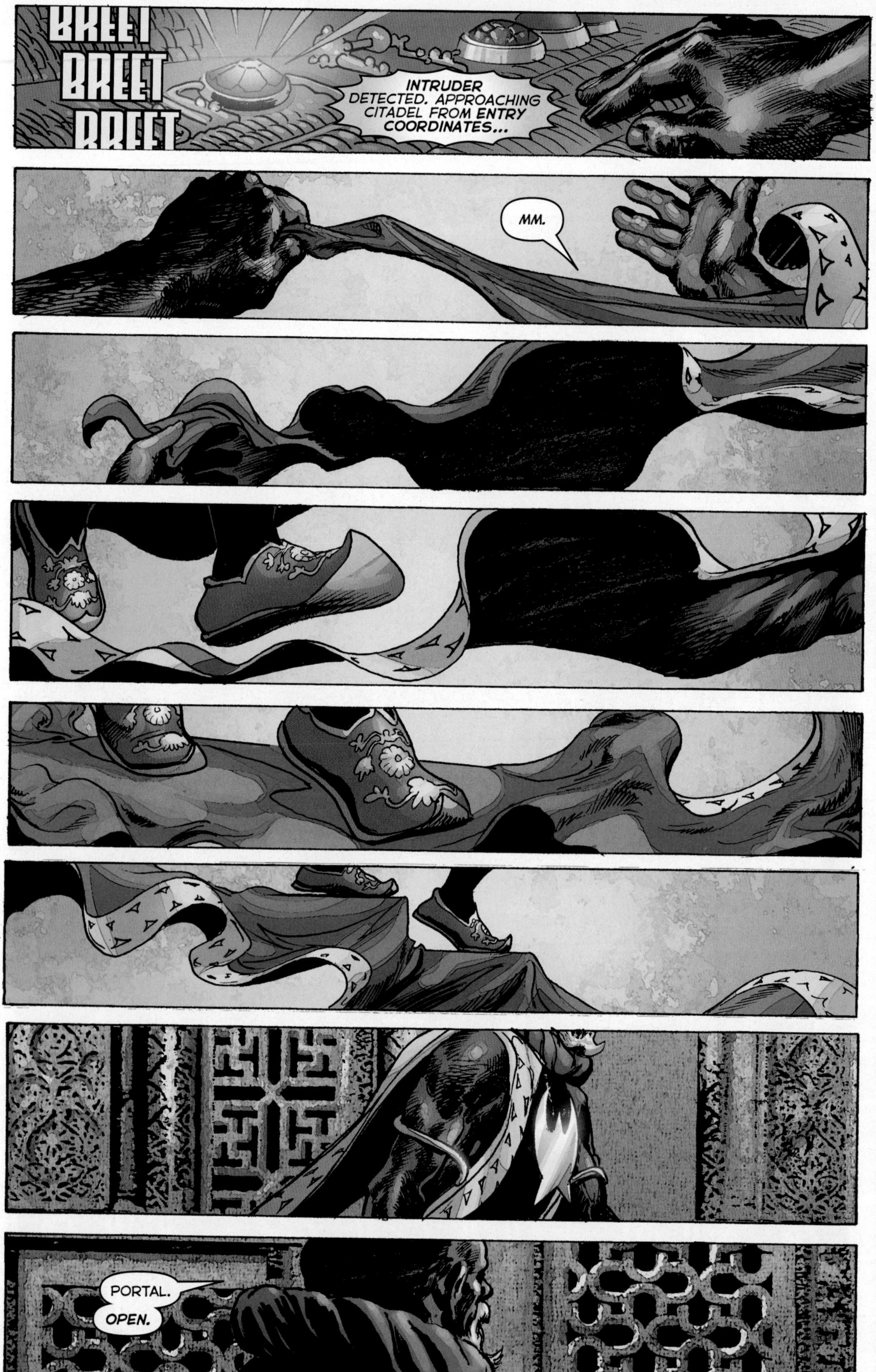
BREET BREET BREET
INTRUDER DETECTED. APPROACHING CITADEL FROM ENTRY COORDINATES...
MM.
PORTAL.
OPEN.

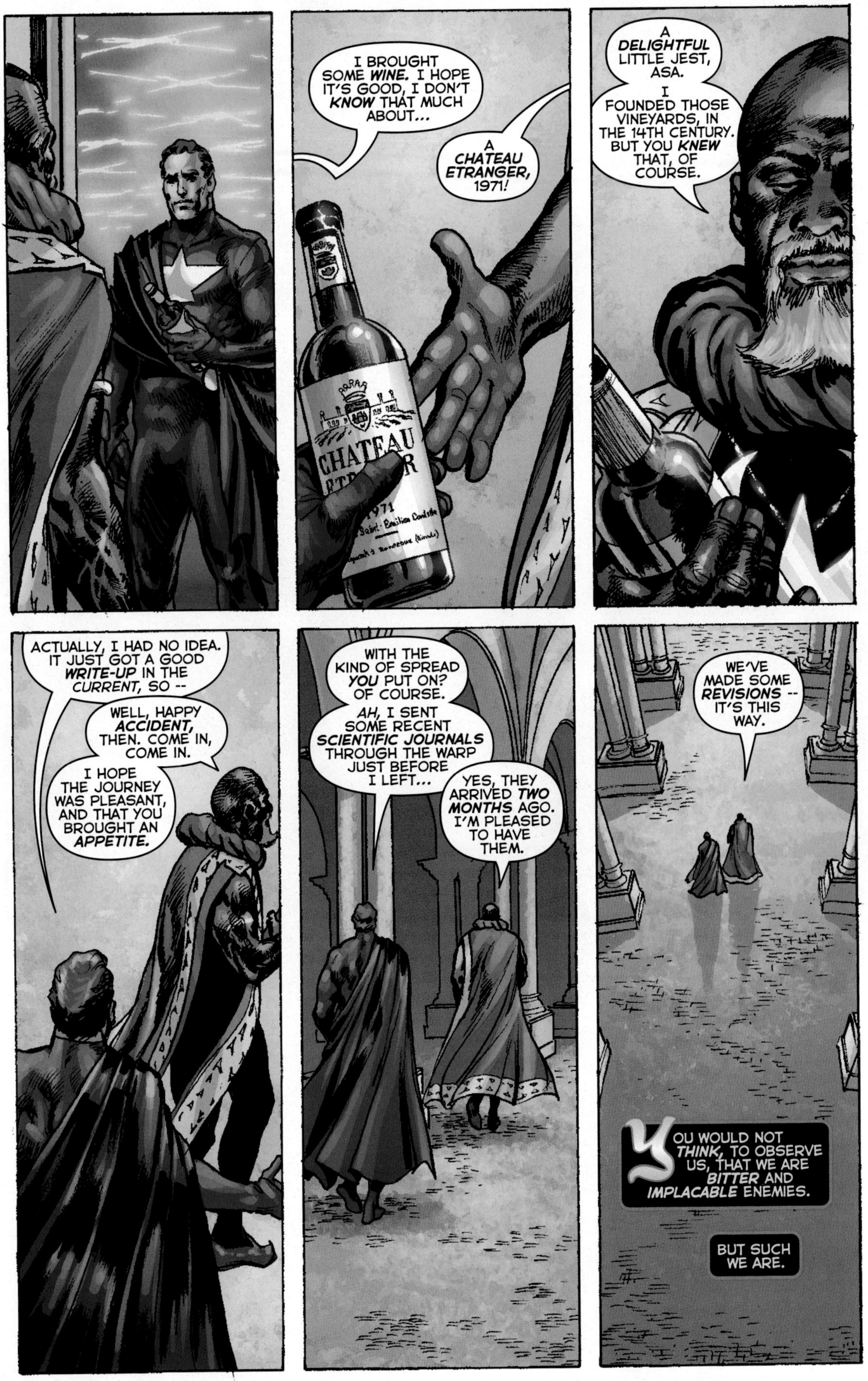
I BROUGHT SOME WINE. I HOPE IT'S GOOD, I DON'T KNOW THAT MUCH ABOUT...
A CHATEAU ETRANGER, 1971!
A DELIGHTFUL LITTLE JEST, ASA.
I FOUNDED THOSE VINEYARDS, IN THE 14TH CENTURY. BUT YOU KNEW THAT, OF COURSE.
ACTUALLY, I HAD NO IDEA. IT JUST GOT A GOOD WRITE-UP IN THE CURRENT, SO --
WELL, HAPPY ACCIDENT, THEN. COME IN, COME IN.
I HOPE THE JOURNEY WAS PLEASANT, AND THAT YOU BROUGHT AN APPETITE.
WITH THE KIND OF SPREAD YOU PUT ON? OF COURSE.
AH, I SENT SOME RECENT SCIENTIFIC JOURNALS THROUGH THE WARP JUST BEFORE I LEFT...
YES, THEY ARRIVED TWO MONTHS AGO. I'M PLEASED TO HAVE THEM.
WE'VE MADE SOME REVISIONS -- IT'S THIS WAY.
YOU WOULD NOT THINK, TO OBSERVE US, THAT WE ARE BITTER AND IMPLACABLE ENEMIES.
BUT SUCH WE ARE.

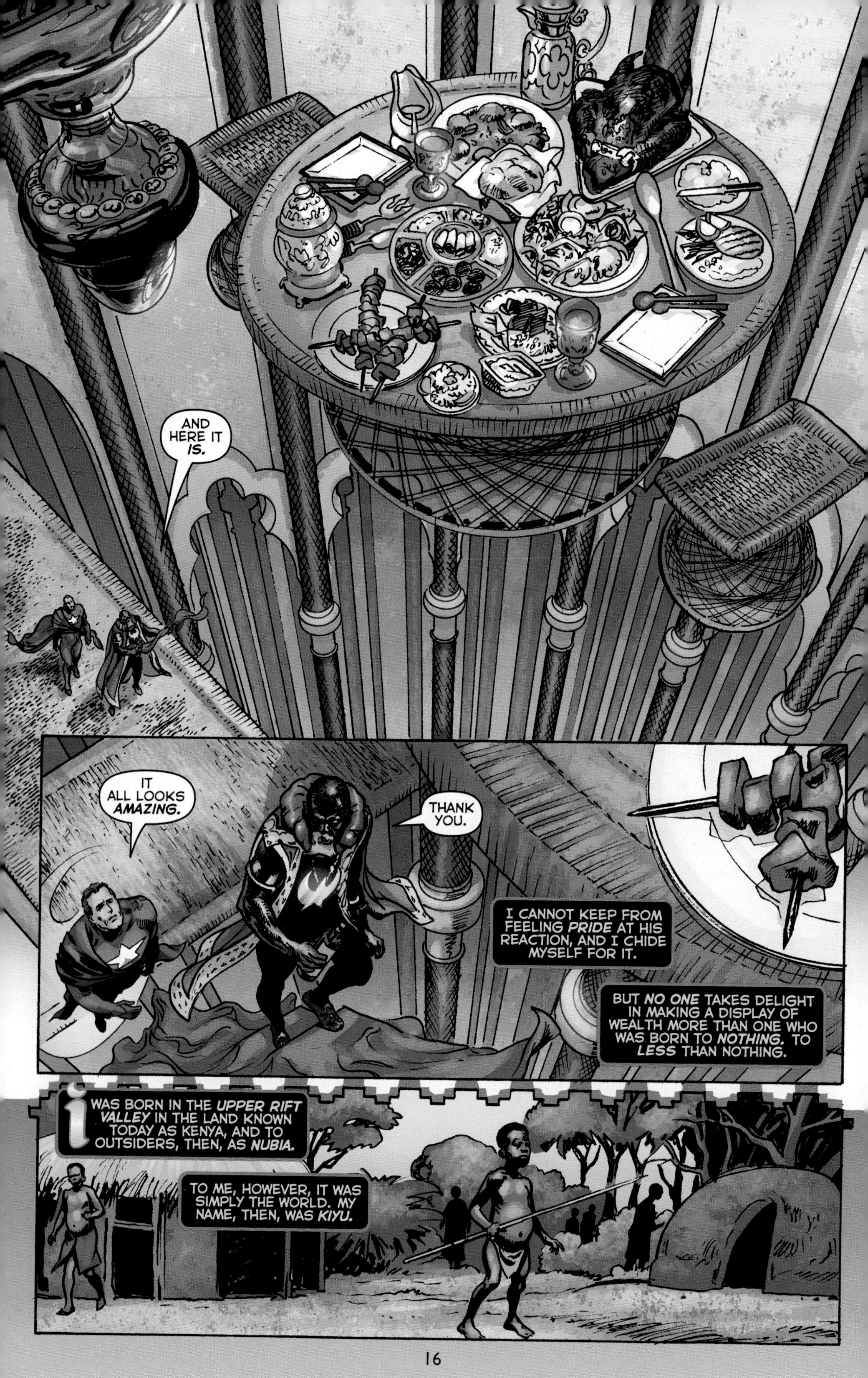
AND HERE IT IS.
IT ALL LOOKS AMAZING.
THANK YOU.
I CANNOT KEEP FROM FEELING PRIDE AT HIS REACTION, AND I CHIDE MYSELF FOR IT.
BUT NO ONE TAKES DELIGHT IN MAKING A DISPLAY OF WEALTH MORE THAN ONE WHO WAS BORN TO NOTHING. TO LESS THAN NOTHING.
I WAS BORN IN THE UPPER RIFT VALLEY IN THE LAND KNOWN TODAY AS KENYA, AND TO OUTSIDERS, THEN, AS NUBIA.
TO ME, HOWEVER, IT WAS SIMPLY THE WORLD. MY NAME, THEN, WAS KIYU.

WHERE DO THE *RAINS* COME FROM?

WHY DO THE GODS MAKE *STORMS?*

WHERE *ARE* THE GODS?

Even then, I wanted nothing more than to know the *HOW* and the *WHY* of everything in the world. But my people could not *TELL* me all I wished to know...

...AND IN TIME, I DECIDED TO *TRAVEL.* IF I COULD NOT FIND THE ANSWERS I SOUGHT AMONG MY PEOPLE...

...I WOULD FIND SOMEWHERE THAT I *COULD.*

BUT I FOUND *NONE* WHO COULD TELL ME MORE THAN MERE *TALES.*

I SOUGHT *FURTHER.*

AND WHEN I HEARD OF A *GREAT CENTER OF LEARNING* ON THE ISLAND OF ZANZIBAR, I MADE MY WAY THERE SWIFTLY...

...AND FOUND WHY THOSE WHO TOLD ME OF IT *LAUGHED* AS THEY DID SO.

FOR ZANZIBAR WAS HOME TO *SLAVERS* AS WELL AS SCHOLARS.

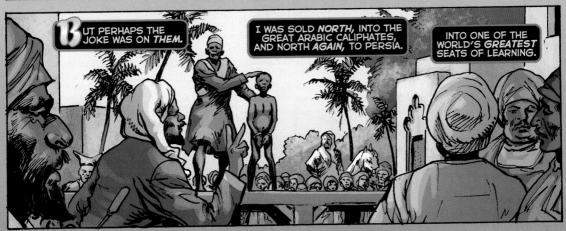

But PERHAPS THE JOKE WAS ON *THEM.*

I WAS SOLD *NORTH,* INTO THE GREAT ARABIC CALIPHATES, AND NORTH *AGAIN,* TO PERSIA.

INTO ONE OF THE WORLD'S *GREATEST* SEATS OF LEARNING.

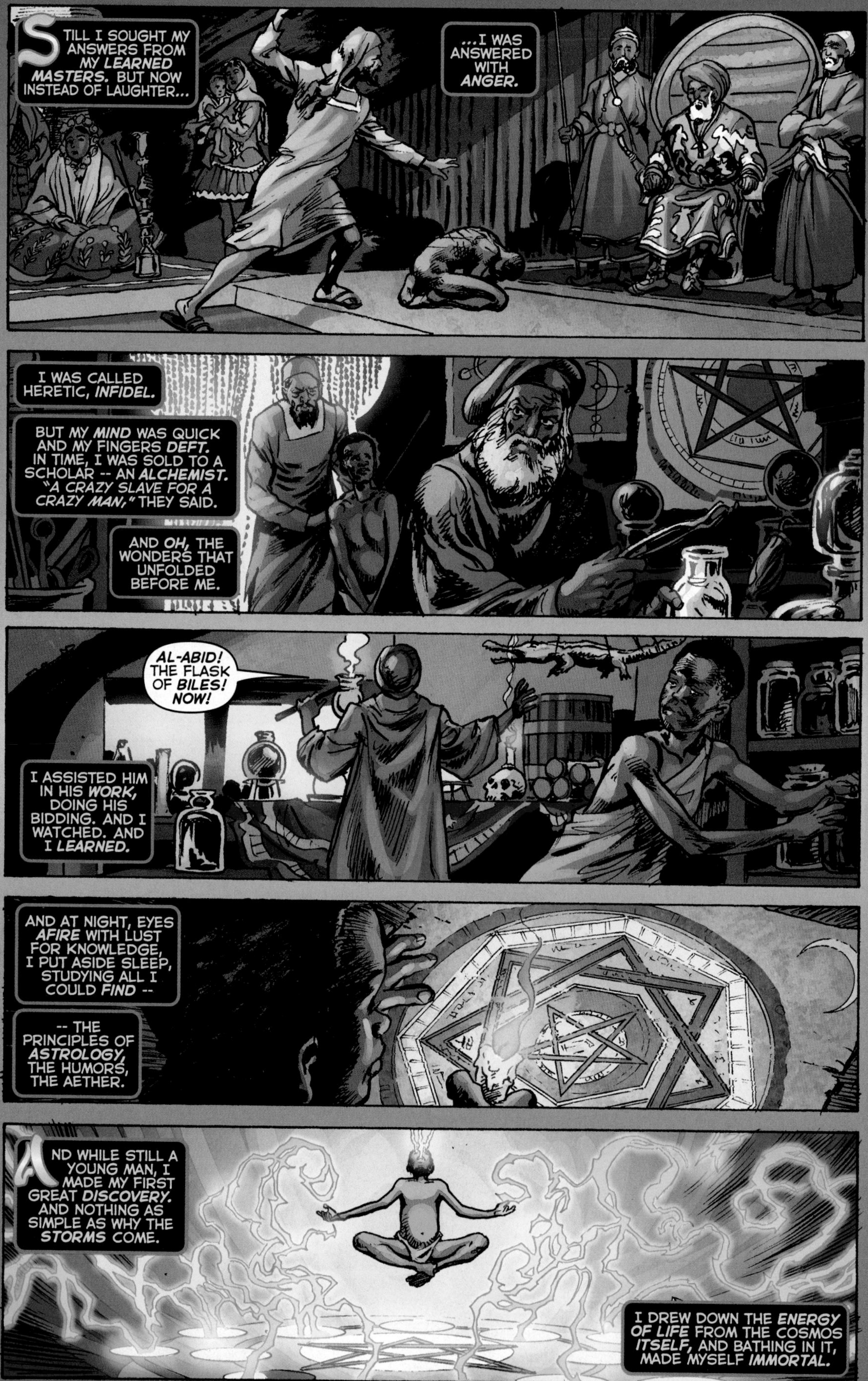
STILL I SOUGHT MY ANSWERS FROM MY LEARNED MASTERS. BUT NOW INSTEAD OF LAUGHTER...
...I WAS ANSWERED WITH ANGER.
I WAS CALLED HERETIC, INFIDEL.
BUT MY MIND WAS QUICK AND MY FINGERS DEFT. IN TIME, I WAS SOLD TO A SCHOLAR -- AN ALCHEMIST. "A CRAZY SLAVE FOR A CRAZY MAN," THEY SAID.
AND OH, THE WONDERS THAT UNFOLDED BEFORE ME.
AL-ABID! THE FLASK OF BILES! NOW!
I ASSISTED HIM IN HIS WORK, DOING HIS BIDDING. AND I WATCHED. AND I LEARNED.
AND AT NIGHT, EYES AFIRE WITH LUST FOR KNOWLEDGE, I PUT ASIDE SLEEP, STUDYING ALL I COULD FIND --
-- THE PRINCIPLES OF ASTROLOGY, THE HUMORS, THE AETHER.
AND WHILE STILL A YOUNG MAN, I MADE MY FIRST GREAT DISCOVERY. AND NOTHING AS SIMPLE AS WHY THE STORMS COME.
I DREW DOWN THE ENERGY OF LIFE FROM THE COSMOS ITSELF, AND BATHING IN IT, MADE MYSELF IMMORTAL.

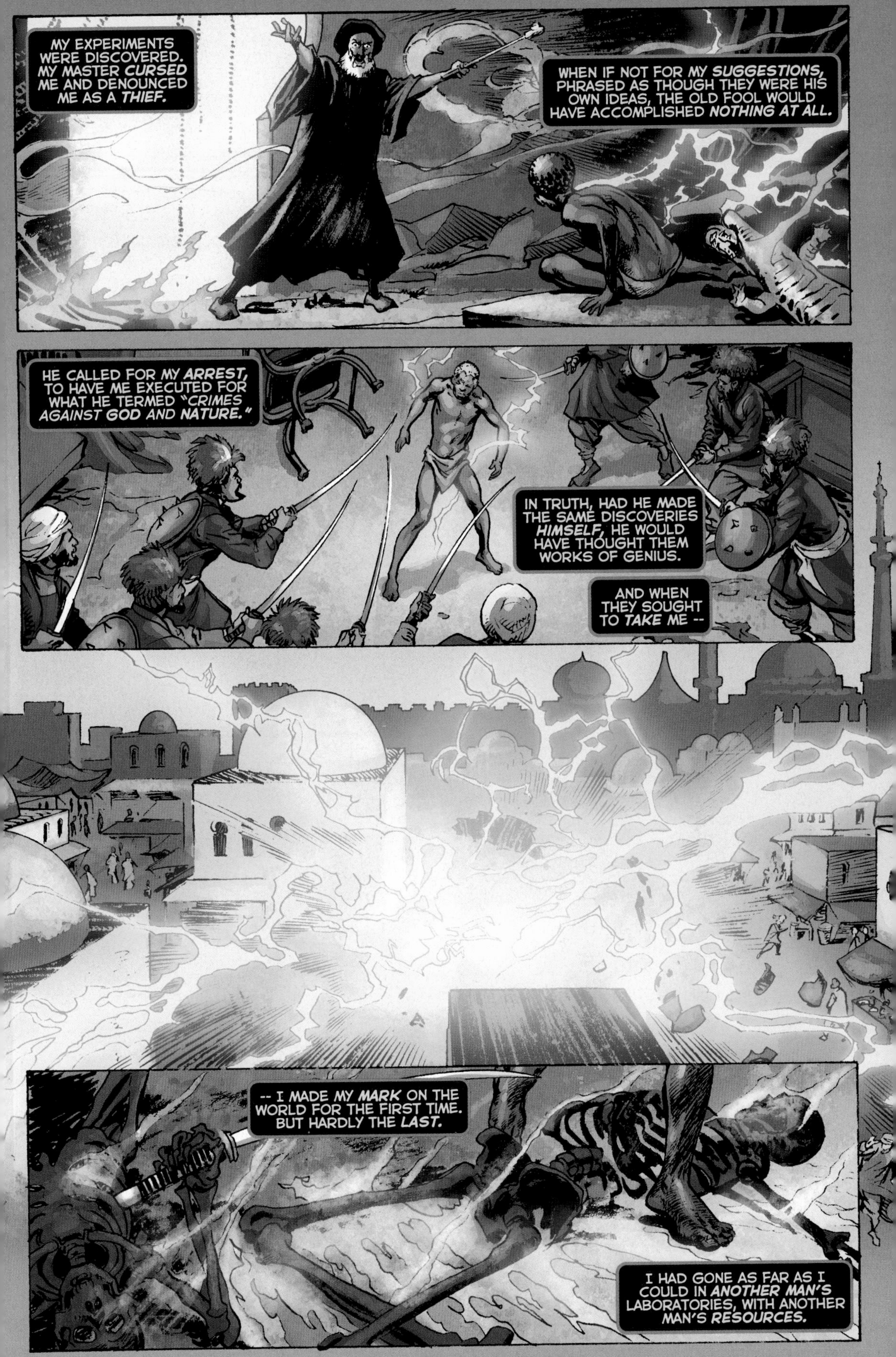
MY EXPERIMENTS WERE DISCOVERED. MY MASTER CURSED ME AND DENOUNCED ME AS A THIEF.
WHEN IF NOT FOR MY SUGGESTIONS, PHRASED AS THOUGH THEY WERE HIS OWN IDEAS, THE OLD FOOL WOULD HAVE ACCOMPLISHED NOTHING AT ALL.
HE CALLED FOR MY ARREST, TO HAVE ME EXECUTED FOR WHAT HE TERMED "CRIMES AGAINST GOD AND NATURE."
IN TRUTH, HAD HE MADE THE SAME DISCOVERIES HIMSELF, HE WOULD HAVE THOUGHT THEM WORKS OF GENIUS.
AND WHEN THEY SOUGHT TO TAKE ME --
-- I MADE MY MARK ON THE WORLD FOR THE FIRST TIME. BUT HARDLY THE LAST.
I HAD GONE AS FAR AS I COULD IN ANOTHER MAN'S LABORATORIES, WITH ANOTHER MAN'S RESOURCES.

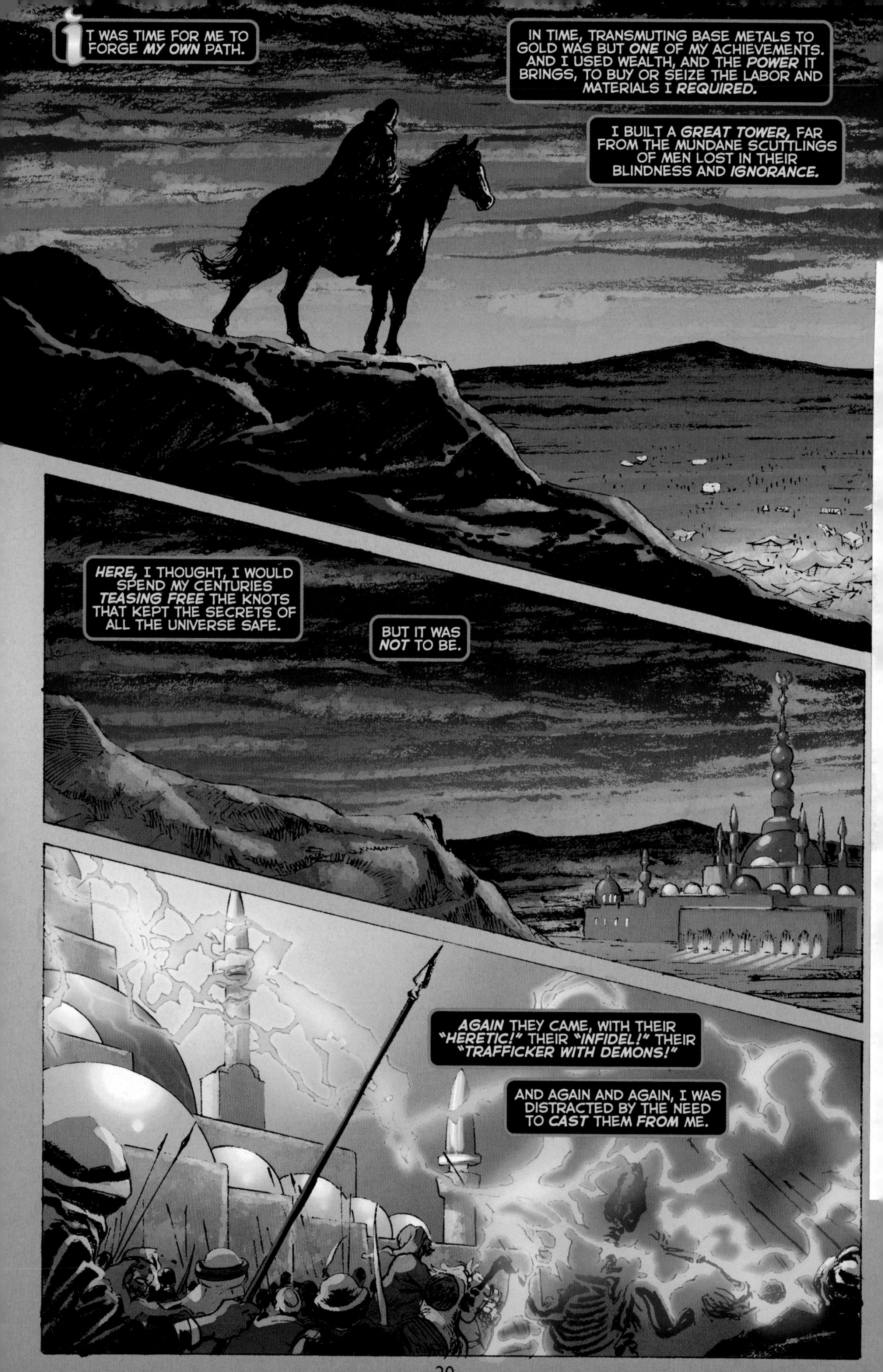
IT WAS TIME FOR ME TO FORGE MY OWN PATH.
IN TIME, TRANSMUTING BASE METALS TO GOLD WAS BUT ONE OF MY ACHIEVEMENTS. AND I USED WEALTH, AND THE POWER IT BRINGS, TO BUY OR SEIZE THE LABOR AND MATERIALS I REQUIRED.
I BUILT A GREAT TOWER, FAR FROM THE MUNDANE SCUTTLINGS OF MEN LOST IN THEIR BLINDNESS AND IGNORANCE.
HERE, I THOUGHT, I WOULD SPEND MY CENTURIES TEASING FREE THE KNOTS THAT KEPT THE SECRETS OF ALL THE UNIVERSE SAFE.
BUT IT WAS NOT TO BE.
AGAIN THEY CAME, WITH THEIR "HERETIC!" THEIR "INFIDEL!" THEIR "TRAFFICKER WITH DEMONS!"
AND AGAIN AND AGAIN, I WAS DISTRACTED BY THE NEED TO CAST THEM FROM ME.

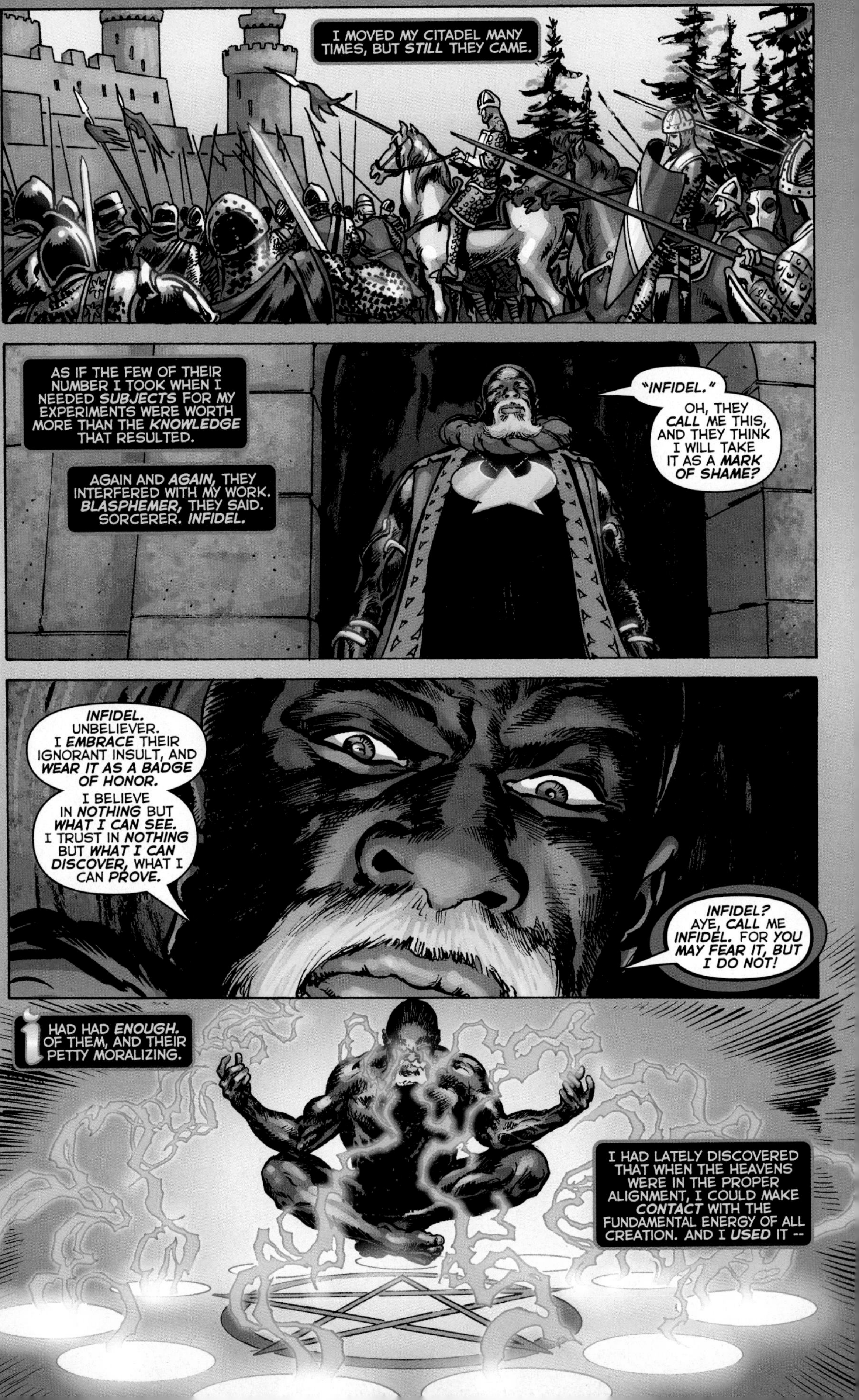

I MOVED MY CITADEL MANY TIMES, BUT STILL THEY CAME.
AS IF THE FEW OF THEIR NUMBER I TOOK WHEN I NEEDED SUBJECTS FOR MY EXPERIMENTS WERE WORTH MORE THAN THE KNOWLEDGE THAT RESULTED.
AGAIN AND AGAIN, THEY INTERFERED WITH MY WORK. BLASPHEMER, THEY SAID. SORCERER. INFIDEL.
"INFIDEL." OH, THEY CALL ME THIS, AND THEY THINK I WILL TAKE IT AS A MARK OF SHAME?
INFIDEL. UNBELIEVER. I EMBRACE THEIR IGNORANT INSULT, AND WEAR IT AS A BADGE OF HONOR.
I BELIEVE IN NOTHING BUT WHAT I CAN SEE. I TRUST IN NOTHING BUT WHAT I CAN DISCOVER, WHAT I CAN PROVE.
INFIDEL? AYE, CALL ME INFIDEL. FOR YOU MAY FEAR IT, BUT I DO NOT!
I HAD HAD ENOUGH. OF THEM, AND THEIR PETTY MORALIZING.
I HAD LATELY DISCOVERED THAT WHEN THE HEAVENS WERE IN THE PROPER ALIGNMENT, I COULD MAKE CONTACT WITH THE FUNDAMENTAL ENERGY OF ALL CREATION. AND I USED IT --

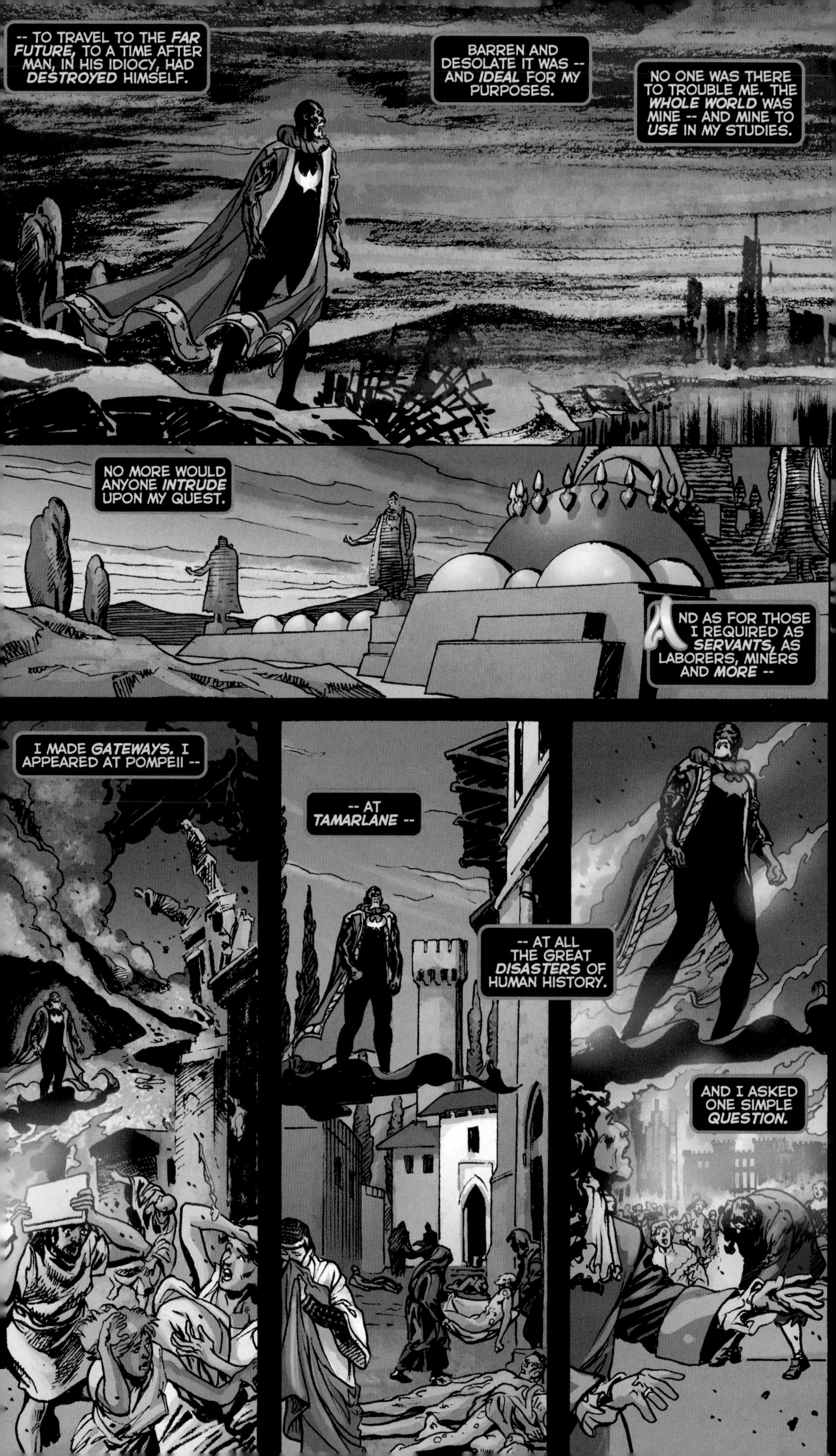
-- TO TRAVEL TO THE FAR FUTURE, TO A TIME AFTER MAN, IN HIS IDIOCY, HAD DESTROYED HIMSELF.
BARREN AND DESOLATE IT WAS -- AND IDEAL FOR MY PURPOSES.
NO ONE WAS THERE TO TROUBLE ME. THE WHOLE WORLD WAS MINE -- AND MINE TO USE IN MY STUDIES.
NO MORE WOULD ANYONE INTRUDE UPON MY QUEST.
AND AS FOR THOSE I REQUIRED AS SERVANTS, AS LABORERS, MINERS AND MORE --
I MADE GATEWAYS. I APPEARED AT POMPEII --
-- AT TAMARLANE --
-- AT ALL THE GREAT DISASTERS OF HUMAN HISTORY.
AND I ASKED ONE SIMPLE QUESTION.

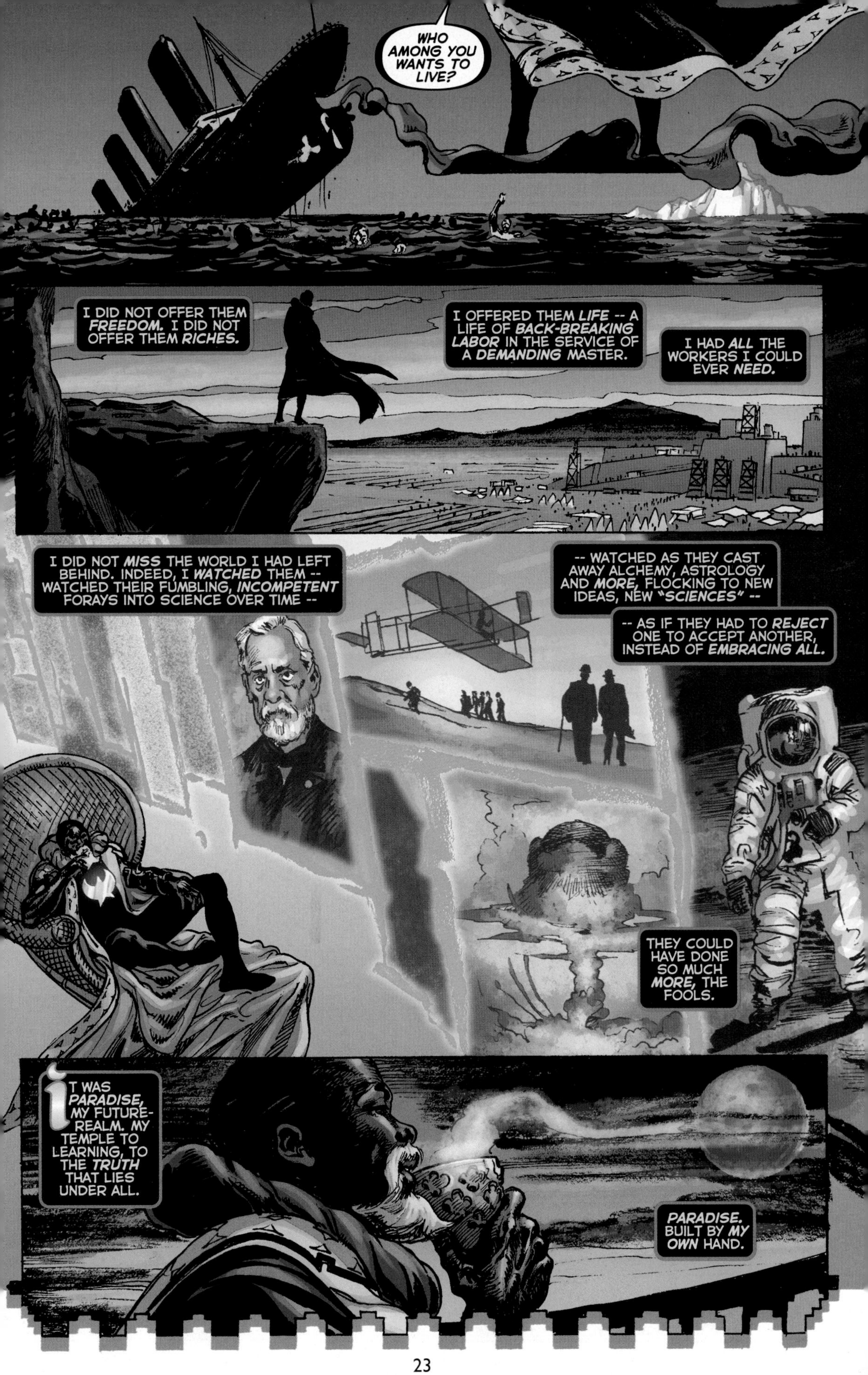
WHO AMONG YOU WANTS TO LIVE?
I DID NOT OFFER THEM FREEDOM. I DID NOT OFFER THEM RICHES.
I OFFERED THEM LIFE -- A LIFE OF BACK-BREAKING LABOR IN THE SERVICE OF A DEMANDING MASTER.
I HAD ALL THE WORKERS I COULD EVER NEED.
I DID NOT MISS THE WORLD I HAD LEFT BEHIND. INDEED, I WATCHED THEM -- WATCHED THEIR FUMBLING, INCOMPETENT FORAYS INTO SCIENCE OVER TIME --
-- WATCHED AS THEY CAST AWAY ALCHEMY, ASTROLOGY AND MORE, FLOCKING TO NEW IDEAS, NEW "SCIENCES" --
-- AS IF THEY HAD TO REJECT ONE TO ACCEPT ANOTHER, INSTEAD OF EMBRACING ALL.
THEY COULD HAVE DONE SO MUCH MORE, THE FOOLS.
IT WAS PARADISE, MY FUTURE-REALM. MY TEMPLE TO LEARNING, TO THE TRUTH THAT LIES UNDER ALL.
PARADISE. BUILT BY MY OWN HAND.

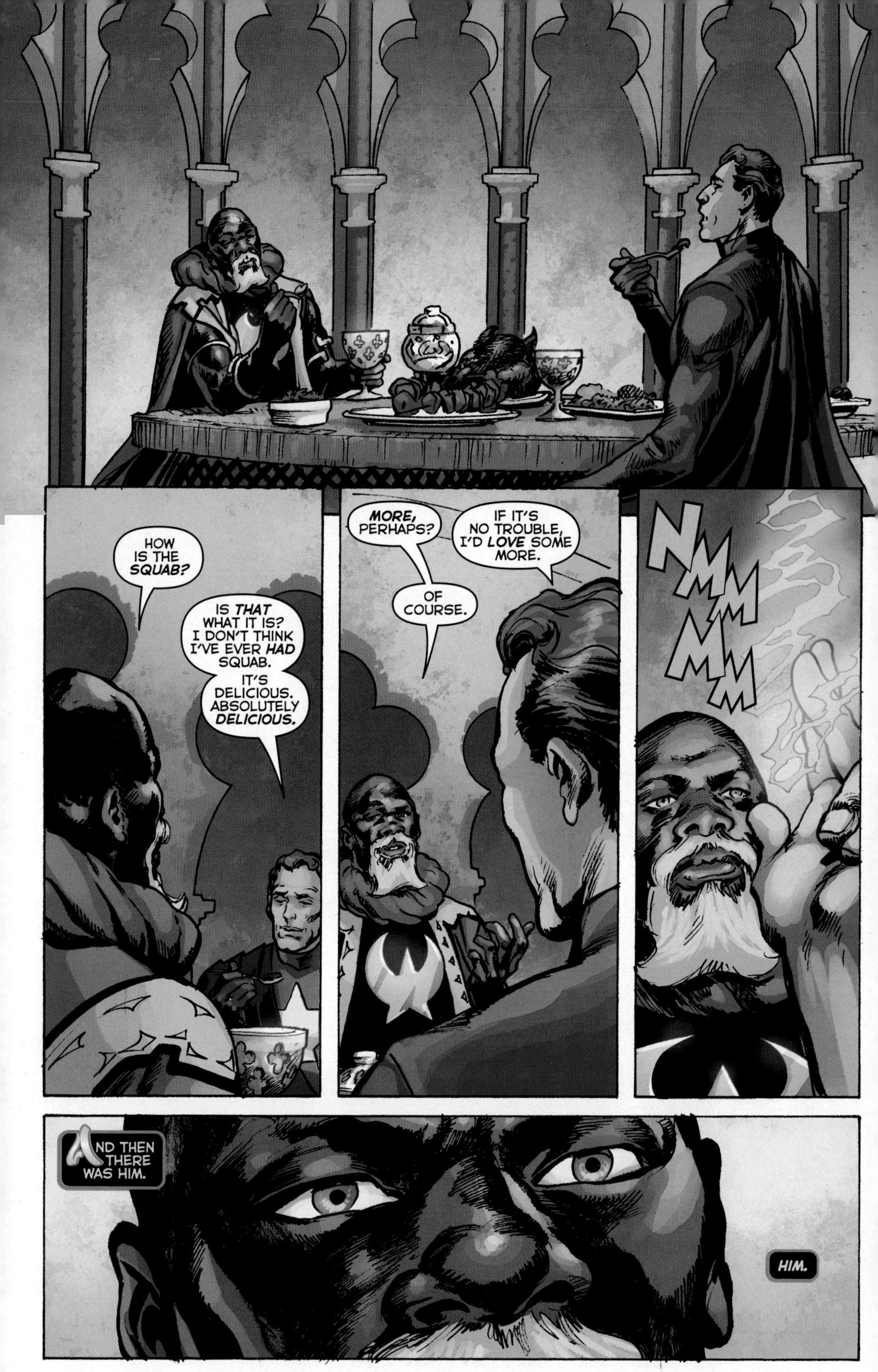
HOW IS THE SQUAB?
IS THAT WHAT IT IS? I DON'T THINK I'VE EVER HAD SQUAB.
IT'S DELICIOUS. ABSOLUTELY DELICIOUS.
MORE, PERHAPS?
IF IT'S NO TROUBLE, I'D LOVE SOME MORE.
OF COURSE.
NMMMMMMM
AND THEN THERE WAS HIM.
HIM.

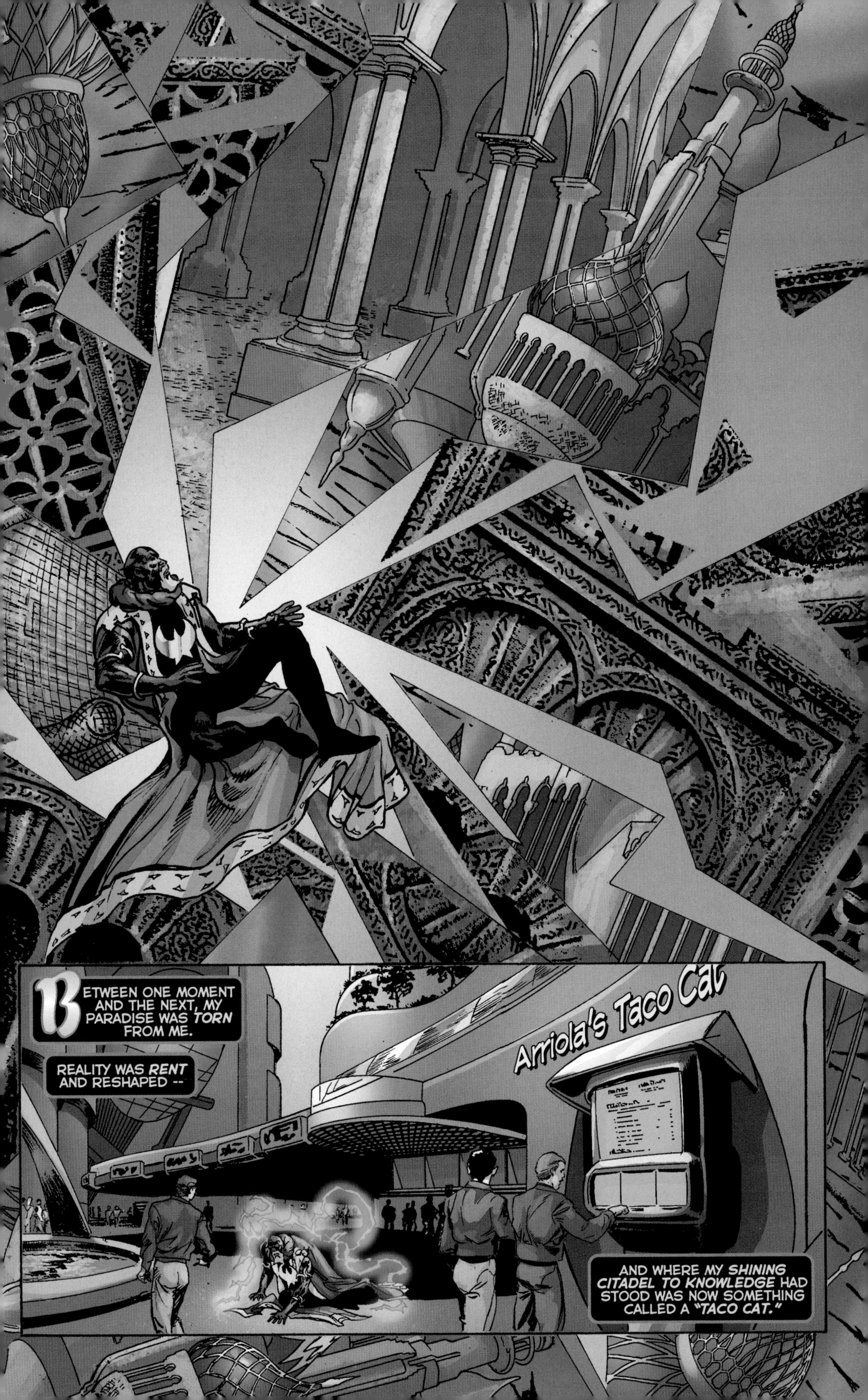
BETWEEN ONE MOMENT AND THE NEXT, MY PARADISE WAS TORN FROM ME.
REALITY WAS RENT AND RESHAPED --
Arriola's Taco Cat
AND WHERE MY SHINING CITADEL TO KNOWLEDGE HAD STOOD WAS NOW SOMETHING CALLED A "TACO CAT."

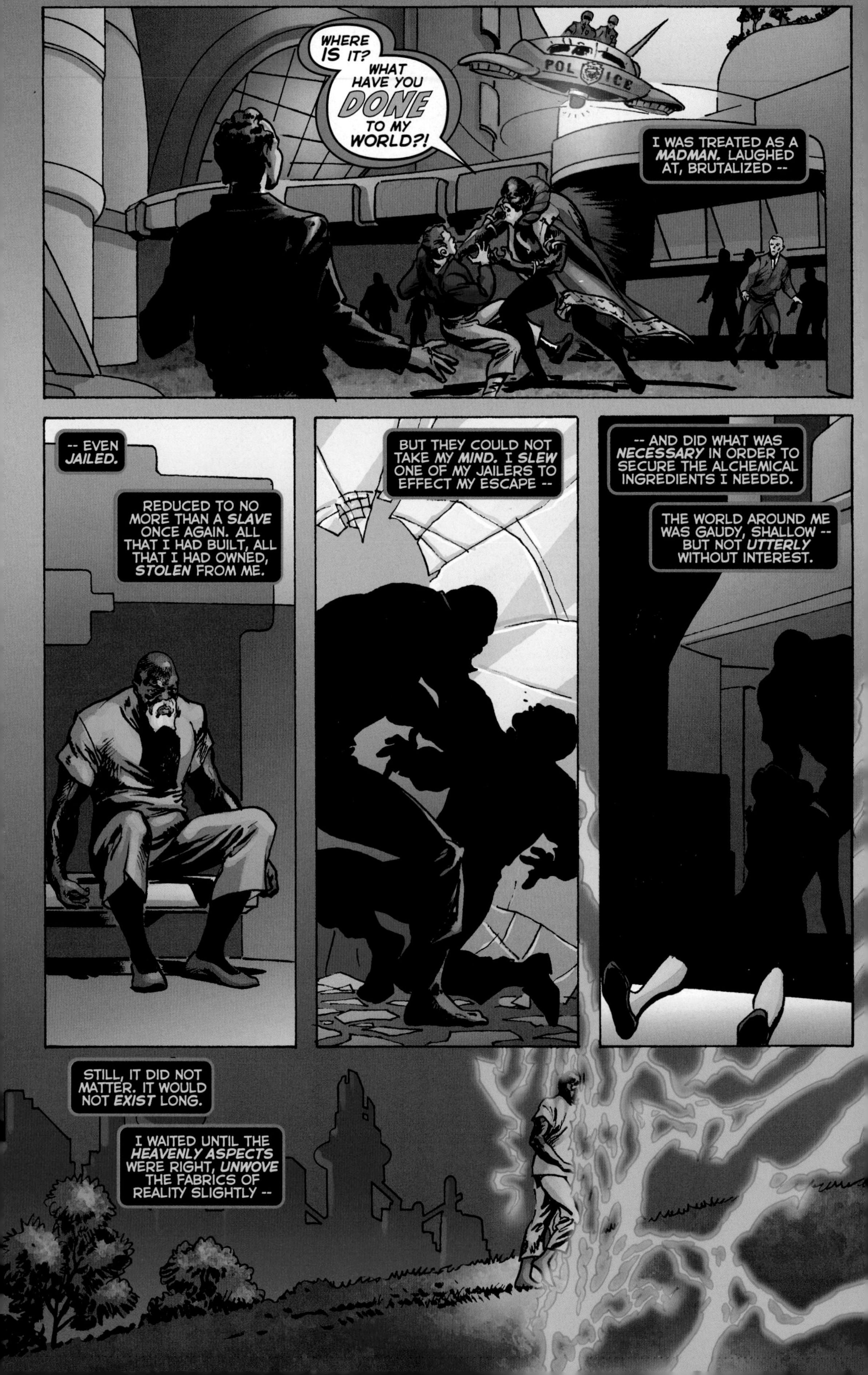
WHERE IS IT? WHAT HAVE YOU DONE TO MY WORLD?!
POL ICE
I WAS TREATED AS A MADMAN. LAUGHED AT, BRUTALIZED --
-- EVEN JAILED.
REDUCED TO NO MORE THAN A SLAVE ONCE AGAIN. ALL THAT I HAD BUILT, ALL THAT I HAD OWNED, STOLEN FROM ME.
BUT THEY COULD NOT TAKE MY MIND. I SLEW ONE OF MY JAILERS TO EFFECT MY ESCAPE --
-- AND DID WHAT WAS NECESSARY IN ORDER TO SECURE THE ALCHEMICAL INGREDIENTS I NEEDED.
THE WORLD AROUND ME WAS GAUDY, SHALLOW -- BUT NOT UTTERLY WITHOUT INTEREST.
STILL, IT DID NOT MATTER. IT WOULD NOT EXIST LONG.
I WAITED UNTIL THE HEAVENLY ASPECTS WERE RIGHT, UNWOVE THE FABRICS OF REALITY SLIGHTLY --

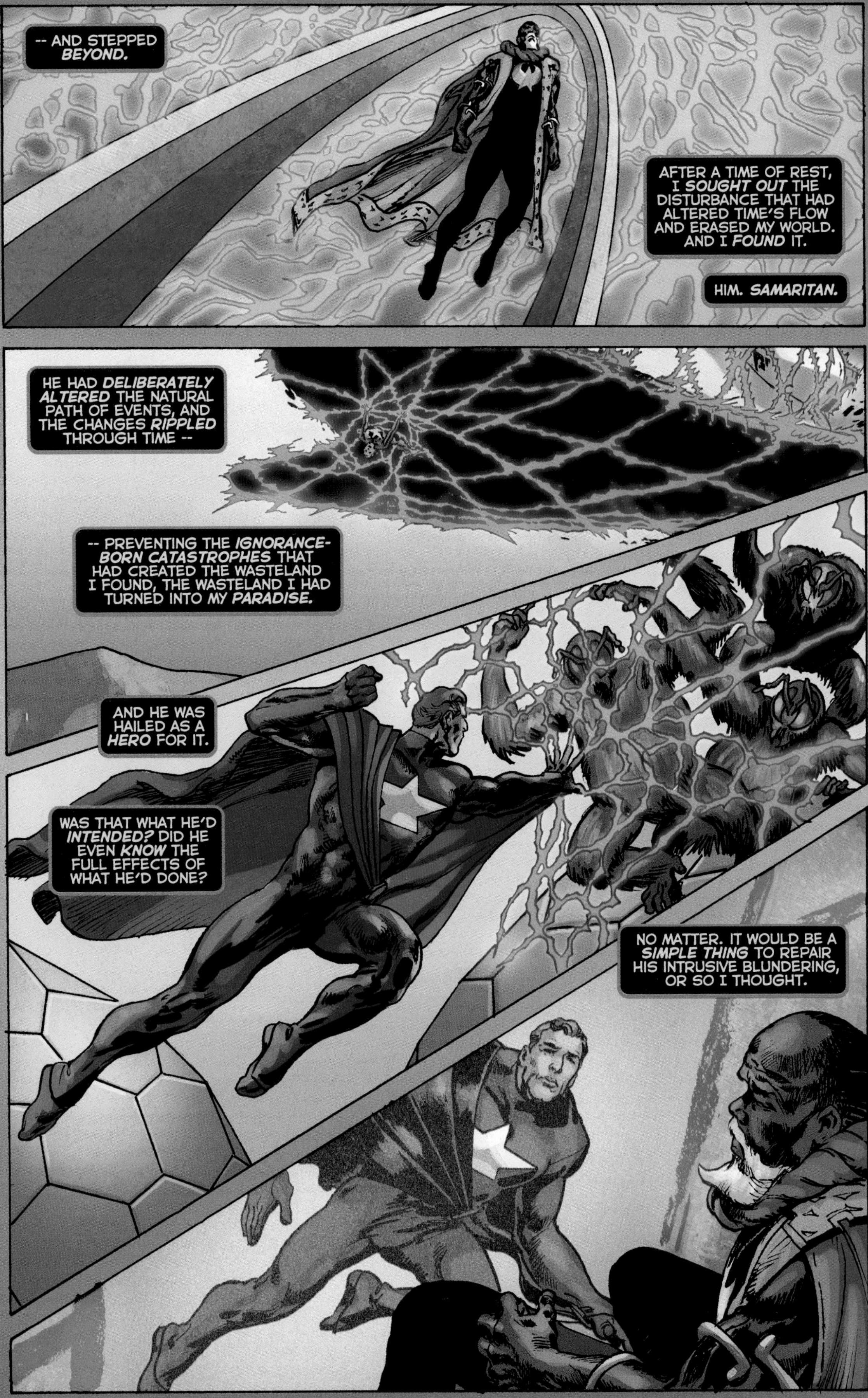

-- AND STEPPED BEYOND.
AFTER A TIME OF REST, I SOUGHT OUT THE DISTURBANCE THAT HAD ALTERED TIME'S FLOW AND ERASED MY WORLD. AND I FOUND IT.
HIM. SAMARITAN.
HE HAD DELIBERATELY ALTERED THE NATURAL PATH OF EVENTS, AND THE CHANGES RIPPLED THROUGH TIME --
-- PREVENTING THE IGNORANCE-BORN CATASTROPHES THAT HAD CREATED THE WASTELAND I FOUND, THE WASTELAND I HAD TURNED INTO MY PARADISE.
AND HE WAS HAILED AS A HERO FOR IT.
WAS THAT WHAT HE'D INTENDED? DID HE EVEN KNOW THE FULL EFFECTS OF WHAT HE'D DONE?
NO MATTER. IT WOULD BE A SIMPLE THING TO REPAIR HIS INTRUSIVE BLUNDERING, OR SO I THOUGHT.

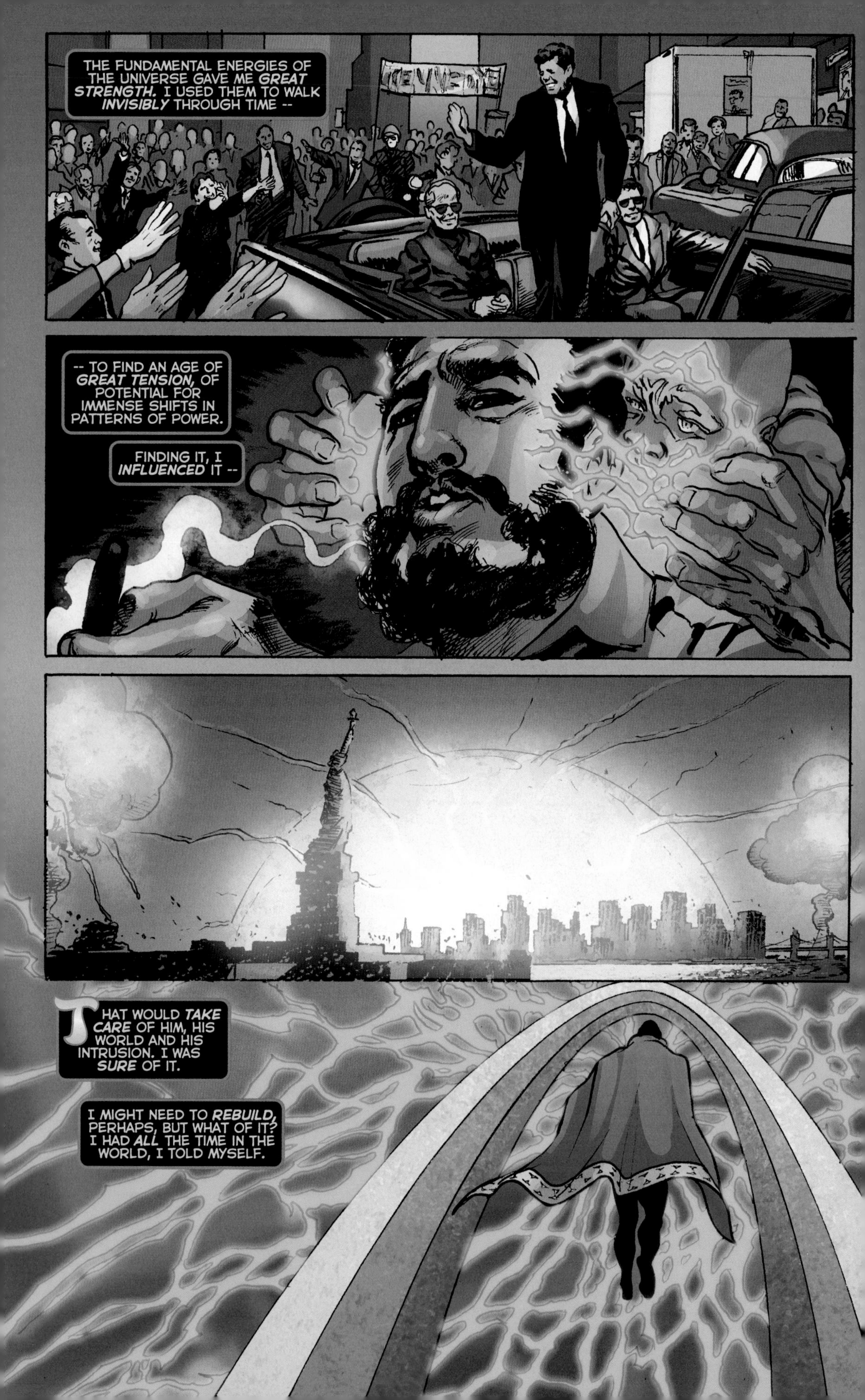
THE FUNDAMENTAL ENERGIES OF THE UNIVERSE GAVE ME GREAT STRENGTH. I USED THEM TO WALK INVISIBLY THROUGH TIME --
-- TO FIND AN AGE OF GREAT TENSION, OF POTENTIAL FOR IMMENSE SHIFTS IN PATTERNS OF POWER.
FINDING IT, I INFLUENCED IT --
THAT WOULD TAKE CARE OF HIM, HIS WORLD AND HIS INTRUSION. I WAS SURE OF IT.
I MIGHT NEED TO REBUILD, PERHAPS, BUT WHAT OF IT? I HAD ALL THE TIME IN THE WORLD, I TOLD MYSELF.

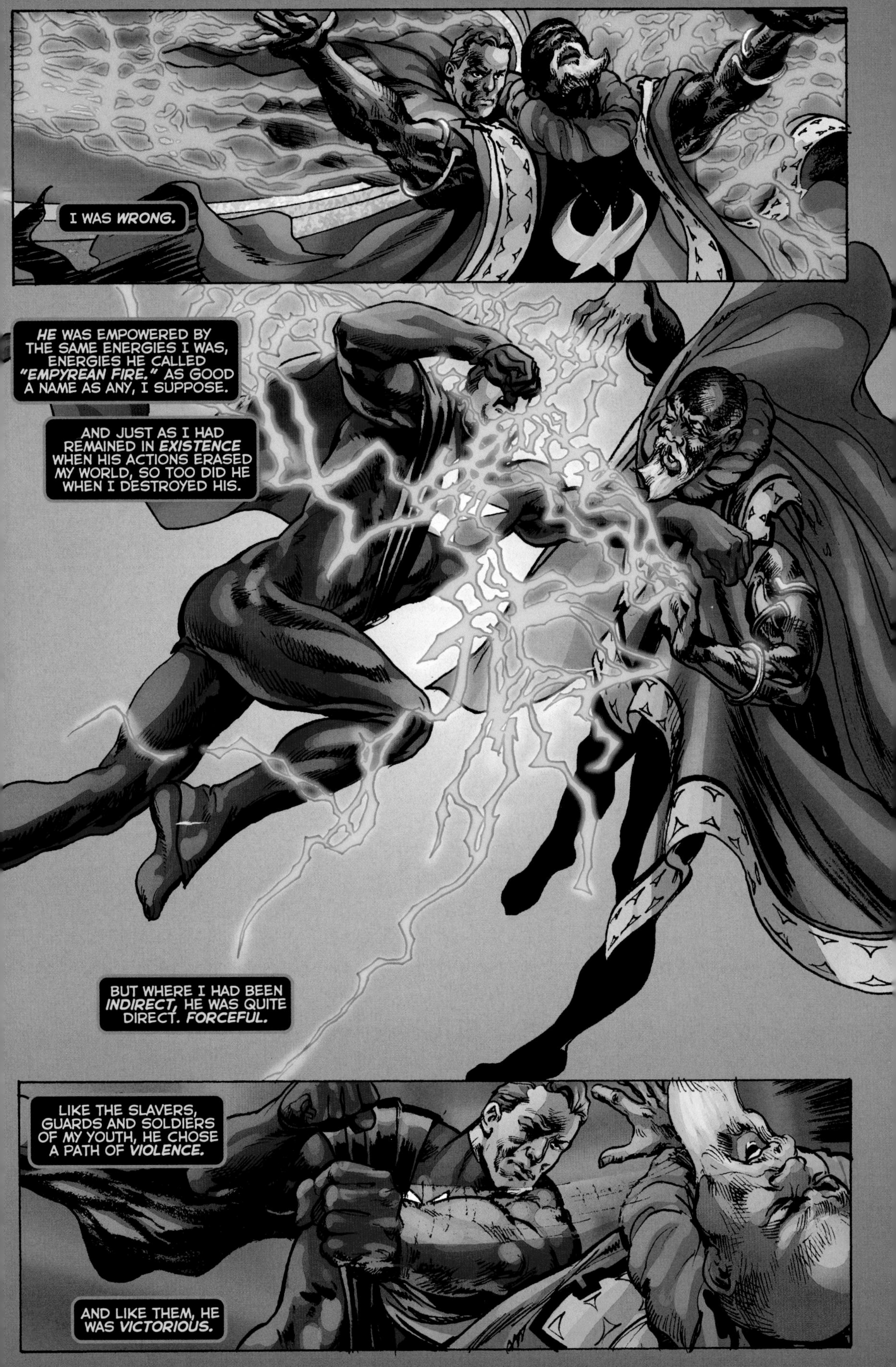
I WAS WRONG.
HE WAS EMPOWERED BY THE SAME ENERGIES I WAS, ENERGIES HE CALLED "EMPYREAN FIRE." AS GOOD A NAME AS ANY, I SUPPOSE.
AND JUST AS I HAD REMAINED IN EXISTENCE WHEN HIS ACTIONS ERASED MY WORLD, SO TOO DID HE WHEN I DESTROYED HIS.
BUT WHERE I HAD BEEN INDIRECT, HE WAS QUITE DIRECT. FORCEFUL.
LIKE THE SLAVERS, GUARDS AND SOLDIERS OF MY YOUTH, HE CHOSE A PATH OF VIOLENCE.
AND LIKE THEM, HE WAS VICTORIOUS.

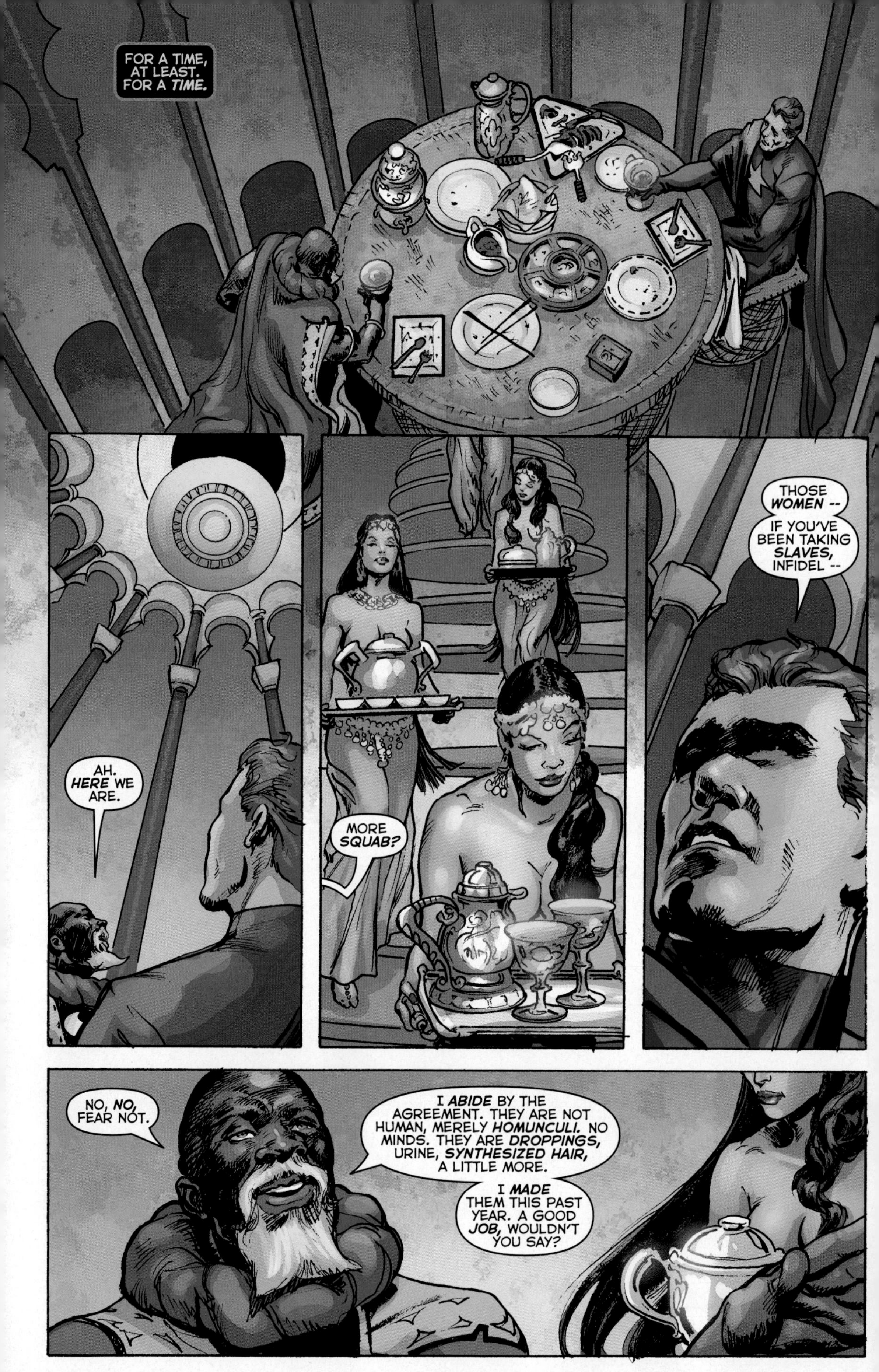
FOR A TIME, AT LEAST. FOR A *TIME.*
AH. *HERE* WE ARE.
MORE *SQUAB?*
THOSE *WOMEN* -- IF YOU'VE BEEN TAKING *SLAVES,* INFIDEL --
NO, *NO,* FEAR NOT.
I *ABIDE* BY THE AGREEMENT. THEY ARE NOT HUMAN, MERELY *HOMUNCULI.* NO MINDS. THEY ARE *DROPPINGS,* URINE, *SYNTHESIZED HAIR,* A LITTLE MORE.
I *MADE* THEM THIS PAST YEAR. A GOOD *JOB,* WOULDN'T YOU SAY?

I -- DON'T KNOW IF I'M **COMFORTABLE** WITH THAT --

WITH ALL DUE RESPECT, ASA, YOU ARE A **GUEST** IN MY HOME. WHAT **FURNISHINGS** I CREATE TO SERVE MY NEEDS AND WARM MY NIGHTS ARE NOT **SUBJECT** TO YOUR APPROVAL.

WERE THEY MERE **ROBOTS** CREATED BY SCIENCE YOU **UNDERSTAND**, WOULD YOU HAVE **SIMILAR** UNEASE?

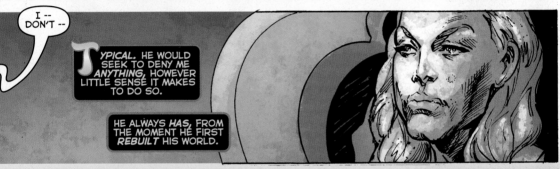

I -- DON'T --

TYPICAL. HE WOULD SEEK TO DENY ME **ANYTHING**, HOWEVER LITTLE SENSE IT MAKES TO DO SO.

HE ALWAYS **HAS**, FROM THE MOMENT HE FIRST **REBUILT** HIS WORLD.

WE FOUGHT SO **OFTEN**.

HE PUT SUCH **ENORMOUS** EFFORT INTO SAVING THE FOOLS AROUND HIM FROM THEIR OWN FOOLISHNESS. AS IF THEY'D LEARN ANYTHING FROM THAT BUT THAT **MISTAKES** HAD NO CONSEQUENCES.

I, HOWEVER, KNOW THAT SHEEP MUST BE **HERDED**.

THERE WAS A **WOMAN** -- WAS HER NAME ANDREA? ALLISON? -- WHO TREATED ME WITH **APPALLING** DISRESPECT.

NGAAA--

THERE! **FALL**, YOU BASTARD!

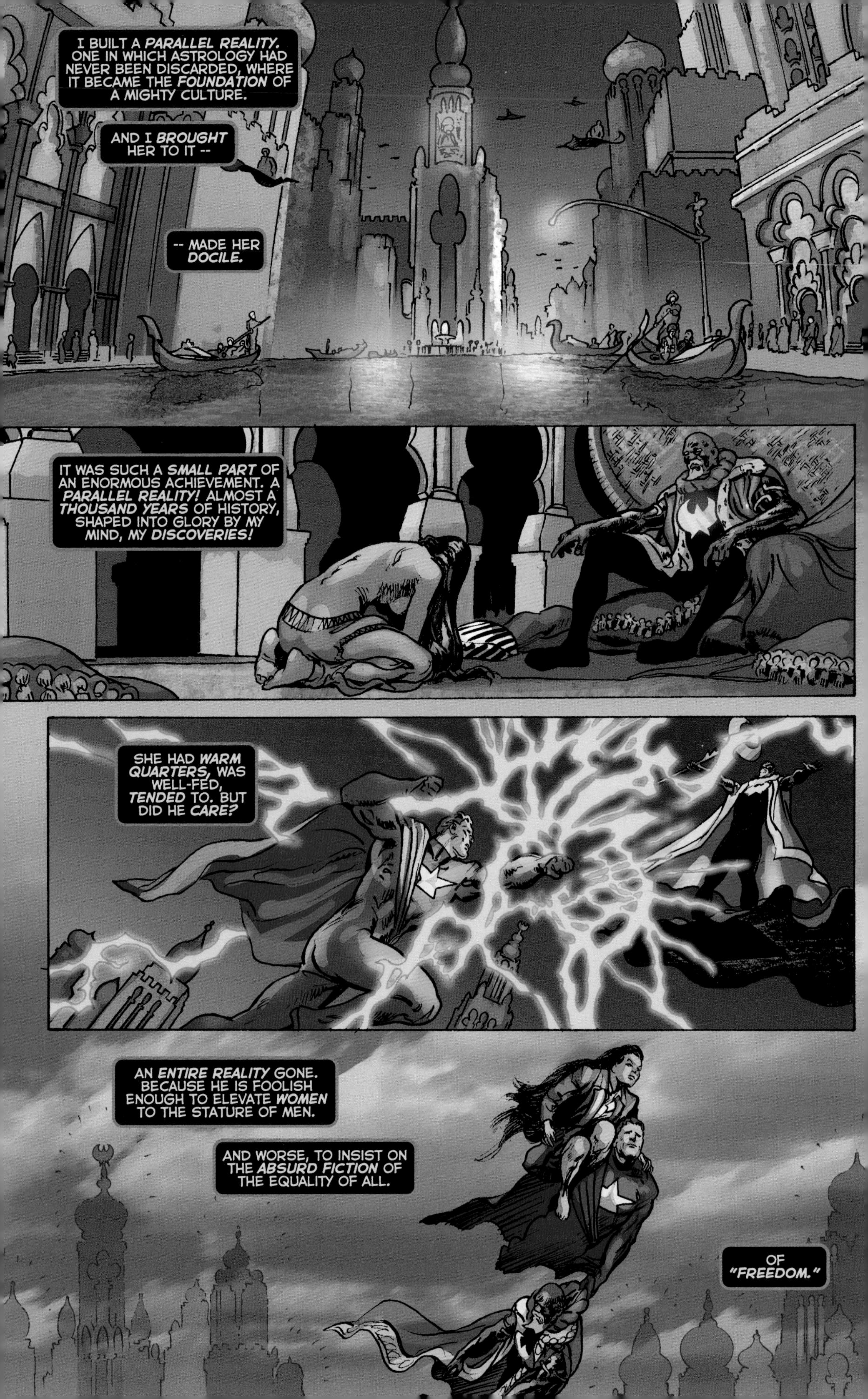
I BUILT A PARALLEL REALITY. ONE IN WHICH ASTROLOGY HAD NEVER BEEN DISCARDED, WHERE IT BECAME THE FOUNDATION OF A MIGHTY CULTURE.
AND I BROUGHT HER TO IT --
-- MADE HER DOCILE.
IT WAS SUCH A SMALL PART OF AN ENORMOUS ACHIEVEMENT. A PARALLEL REALITY! ALMOST A THOUSAND YEARS OF HISTORY, SHAPED INTO GLORY BY MY MIND, MY DISCOVERIES!
SHE HAD WARM QUARTERS, WAS WELL-FED, TENDED TO. BUT DID HE CARE?
AN ENTIRE REALITY GONE. BECAUSE HE IS FOOLISH ENOUGH TO ELEVATE WOMEN TO THE STATURE OF MEN.
AND WORSE, TO INSIST ON THE ABSURD FICTION OF THE EQUALITY OF ALL.
OF "FREEDOM."

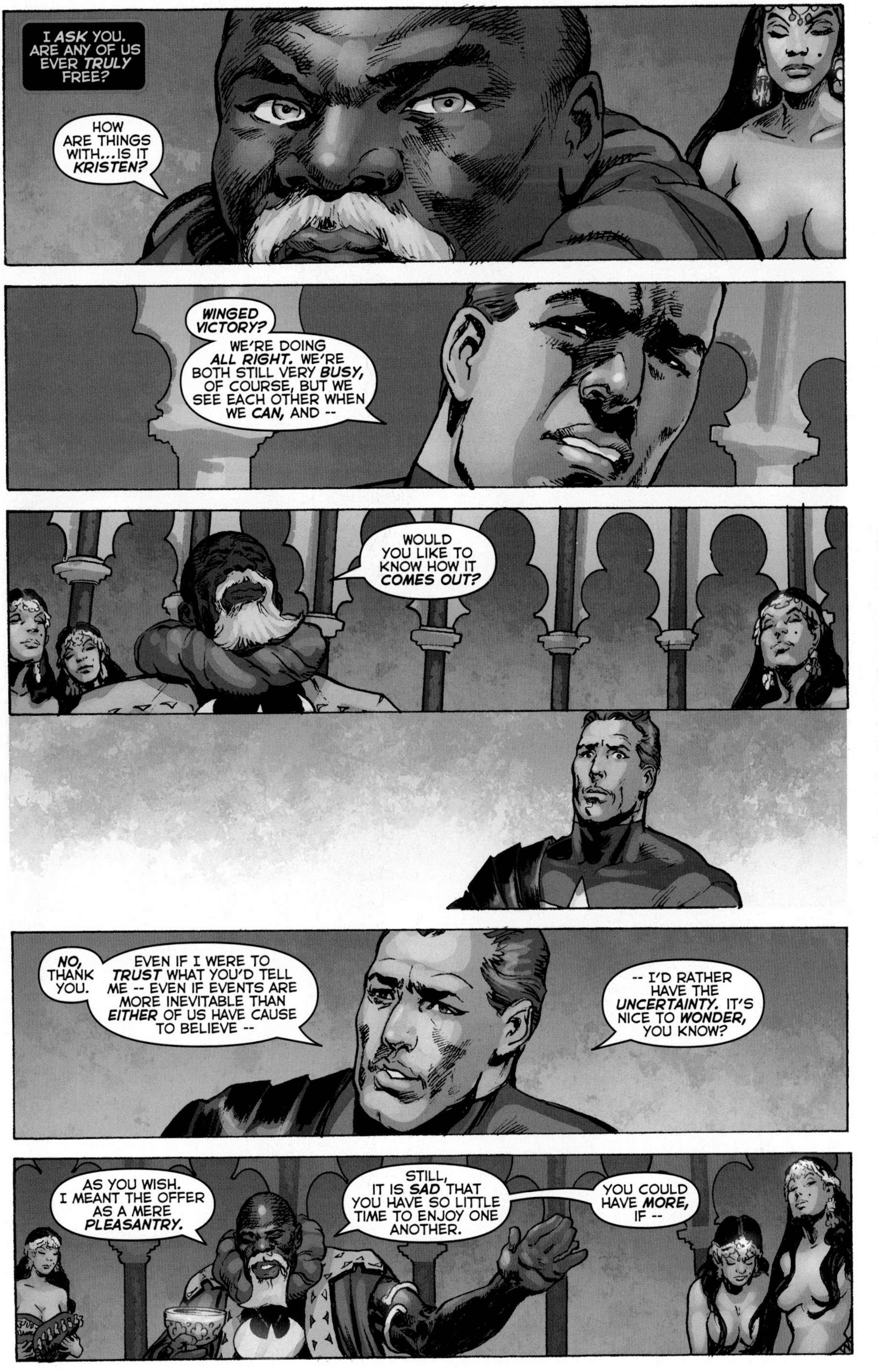
I ASK YOU. ARE ANY OF US EVER TRULY FREE?
HOW ARE THINGS WITH...IS IT KRISTEN?
WINGED VICTORY?
WE'RE DOING ALL RIGHT. WE'RE BOTH STILL VERY BUSY, OF COURSE, BUT WE SEE EACH OTHER WHEN WE CAN, AND --
WOULD YOU LIKE TO KNOW HOW IT COMES OUT?
NO, THANK YOU.
EVEN IF I WERE TO TRUST WHAT YOU'D TELL ME -- EVEN IF EVENTS ARE MORE INEVITABLE THAN EITHER OF US HAVE CAUSE TO BELIEVE --
-- I'D RATHER HAVE THE UNCERTAINTY. IT'S NICE TO WONDER, YOU KNOW?
AS YOU WISH. I MEANT THE OFFER AS A MERE PLEASANTRY.
STILL, IT IS SAD THAT YOU HAVE SO LITTLE TIME TO ENJOY ONE ANOTHER.
YOU COULD HAVE MORE, IF --

IF I *RULED THE WORLD?*

THE CHANCE TO *REST* WOULD BE NICE, I'M SURE. BUT NOT AT THAT *COST.*

NO, NO, *NOT* RULING THE *WORLD.*

BY THE *SWIRLING HEAVENS,* IMAGINE THE HEADACHES *THAT* RESPONSIBILITY WOULD BRING! I MEANT MERELY... *REORDERING* IT, A BIT. *CHANGING* THINGS SO THAT IT WORKS MORE SMOOTHLY, CLEANLY. NEEDS LESS... *CARETAKING.*

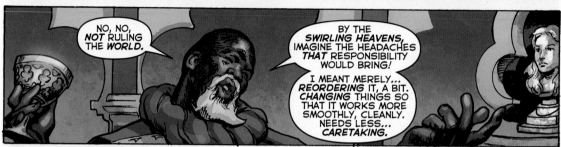

⊰SIGH⊱

NICE TO *THINK* ABOUT, I SUPPOSE.

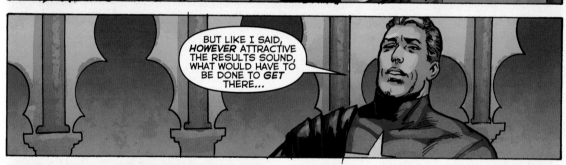

BUT LIKE I SAID, *HOWEVER* ATTRACTIVE THE RESULTS SOUND, WHAT WOULD HAVE TO BE DONE TO *GET* THERE...

OF COURSE.

JUST A *THOUGHT.*

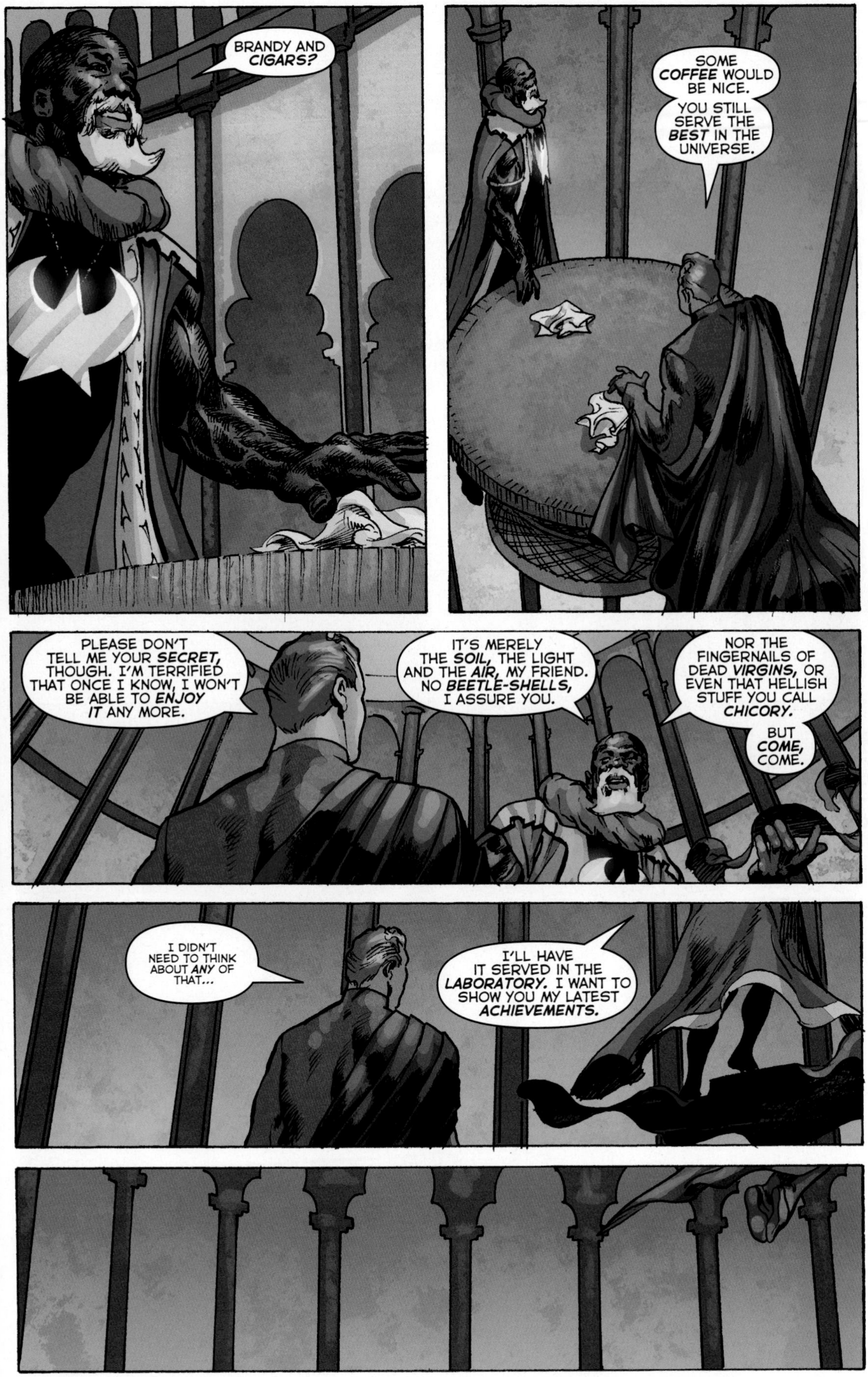
BRANDY AND *CIGARS?*
SOME *COFFEE* WOULD BE NICE.
YOU STILL SERVE THE *BEST* IN THE UNIVERSE.
PLEASE DON'T TELL ME YOUR *SECRET,* THOUGH. I'M TERRIFIED THAT ONCE I KNOW, I WON'T BE ABLE TO *ENJOY IT* ANY MORE.
IT'S MERELY THE *SOIL,* THE LIGHT AND THE *AIR,* MY FRIEND. NO *BEETLE-SHELLS,* I ASSURE YOU.
NOR THE FINGERNAILS OF DEAD *VIRGINS,* OR EVEN THAT HELLISH STUFF YOU CALL *CHICORY.*
BUT *COME,* COME.
I DIDN'T NEED TO THINK ABOUT *ANY* OF THAT...
I'LL HAVE IT SERVED IN THE *LABORATORY.* I WANT TO SHOW YOU MY LATEST *ACHIEVEMENTS.*

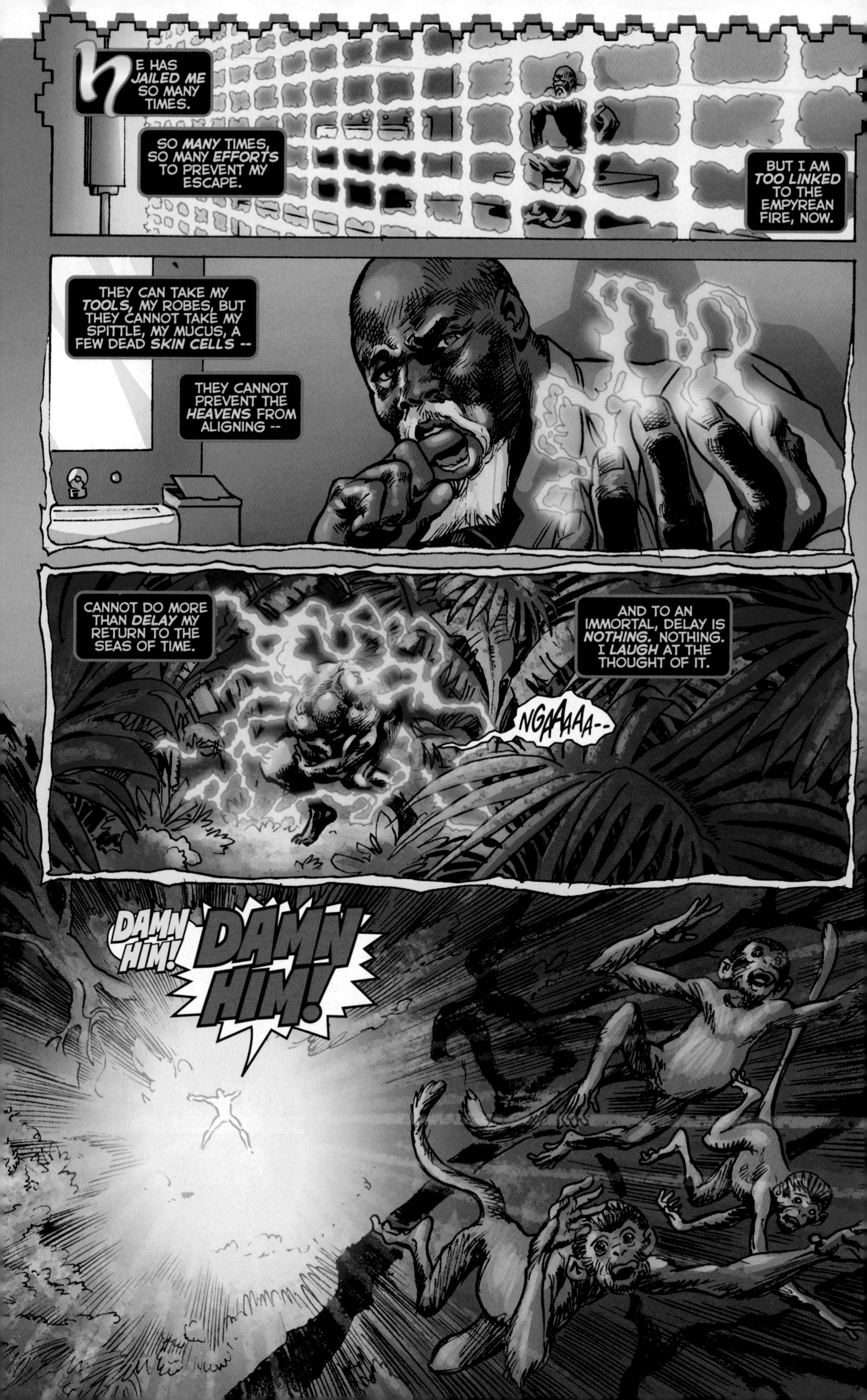
HE HAS JAILED ME SO MANY TIMES.
SO MANY TIMES, SO MANY EFFORTS TO PREVENT MY ESCAPE.
BUT I AM TOO LINKED TO THE EMPYREAN FIRE, NOW.
THEY CAN TAKE MY TOOLS, MY ROBES, BUT THEY CANNOT TAKE MY SPITTLE, MY MUCUS, A FEW DEAD SKIN CELLS --
THEY CANNOT PREVENT THE HEAVENS FROM ALIGNING --
CANNOT DO MORE THAN DELAY MY RETURN TO THE SEAS OF TIME.
AND TO AN IMMORTAL, DELAY IS NOTHING. NOTHING. I LAUGH AT THE THOUGHT OF IT.
NGAAAAA--
DAMN HIM! DAMN HIM!

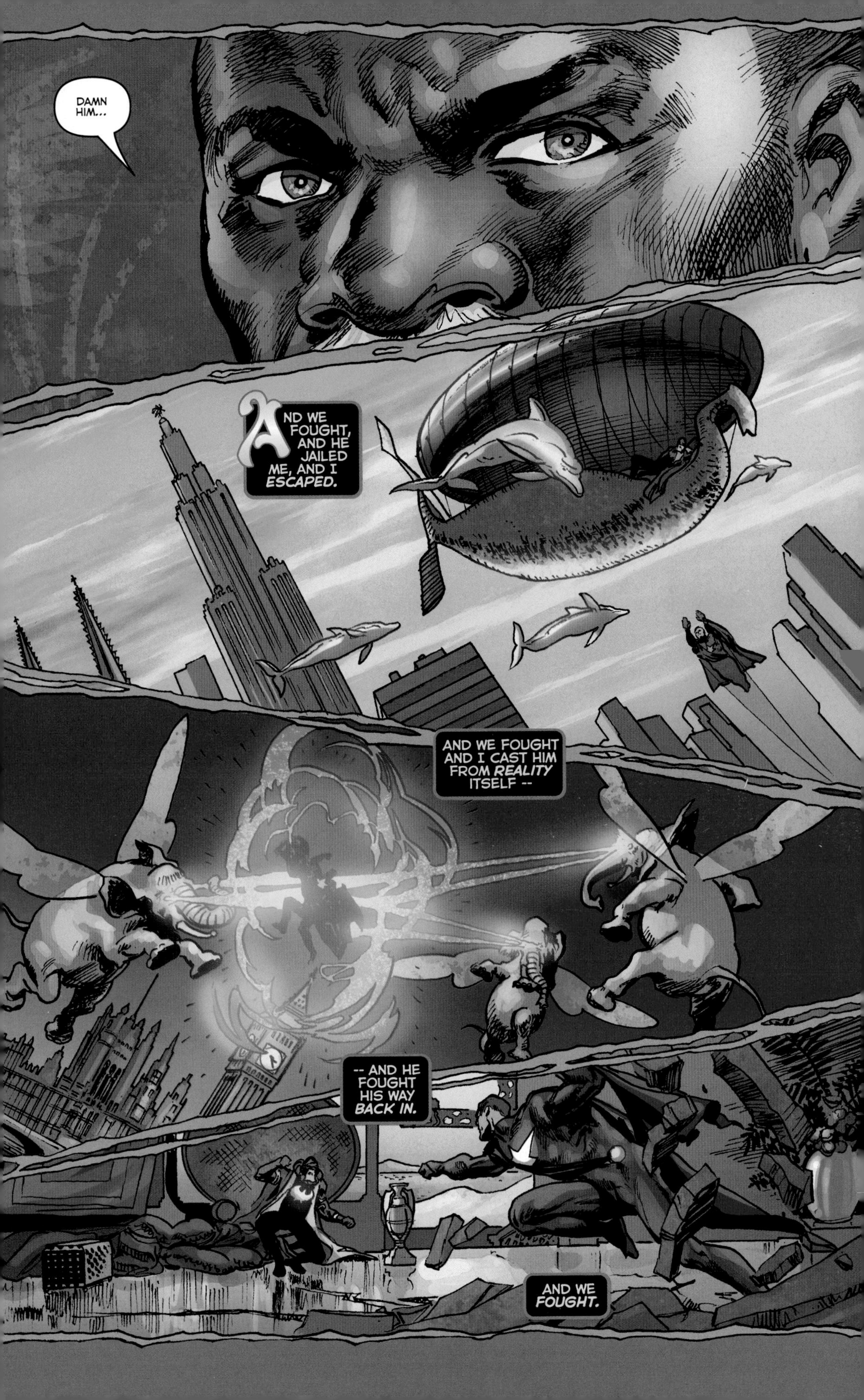

DAMN HIM...
AND WE FOUGHT, AND HE JAILED ME, AND I ESCAPED.
AND WE FOUGHT AND I CAST HIM FROM REALITY ITSELF --
-- AND HE FOUGHT HIS WAY BACK IN.
AND WE FOUGHT.

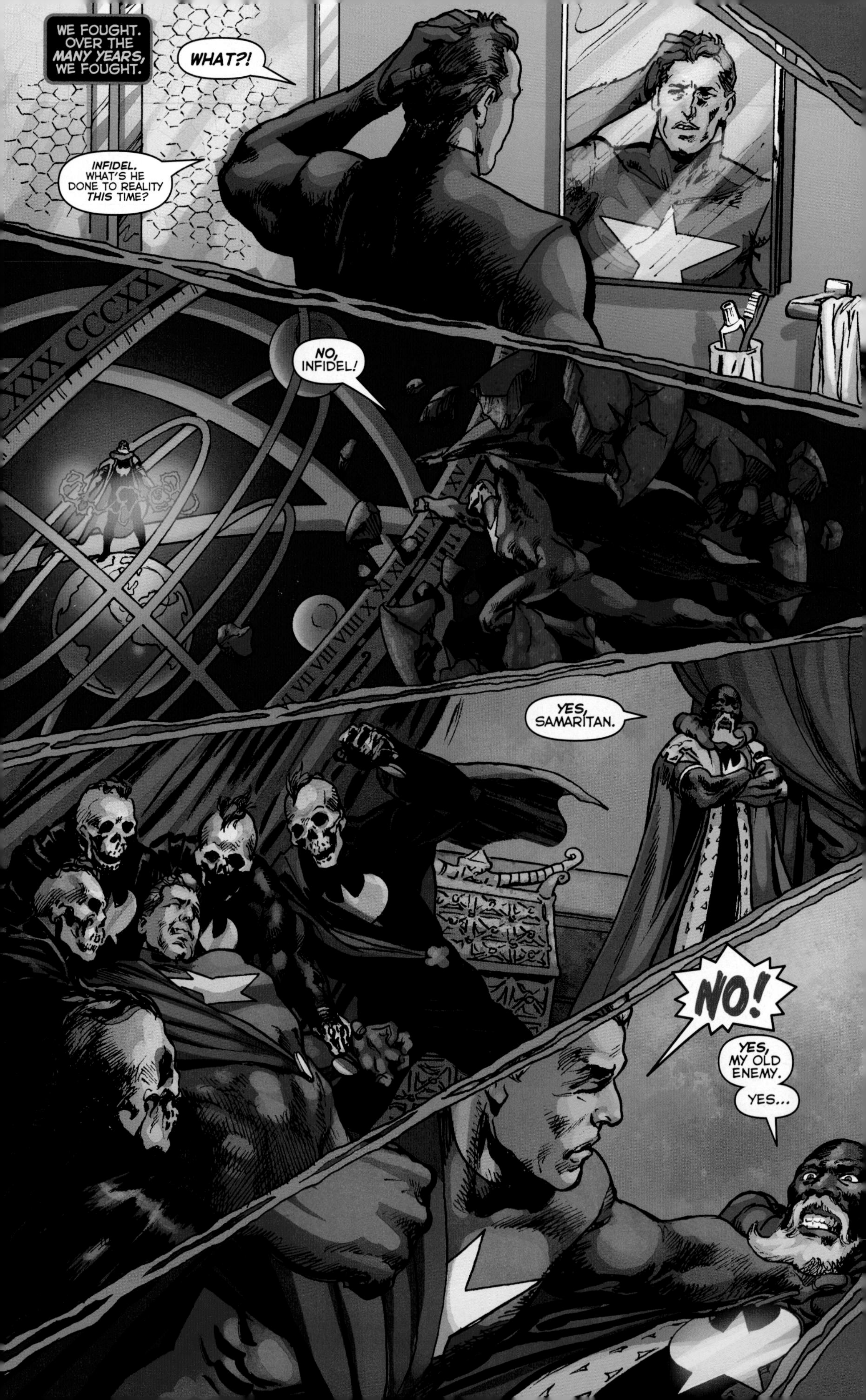
WE FOUGHT. OVER THE *MANY YEARS,* WE FOUGHT.
WHAT?!
INFIDEL. WHAT'S HE DONE TO REALITY *THIS* TIME?
NO, INFIDEL!
YES, SAMARITAN.
NO!
YES, MY OLD ENEMY.
YES...

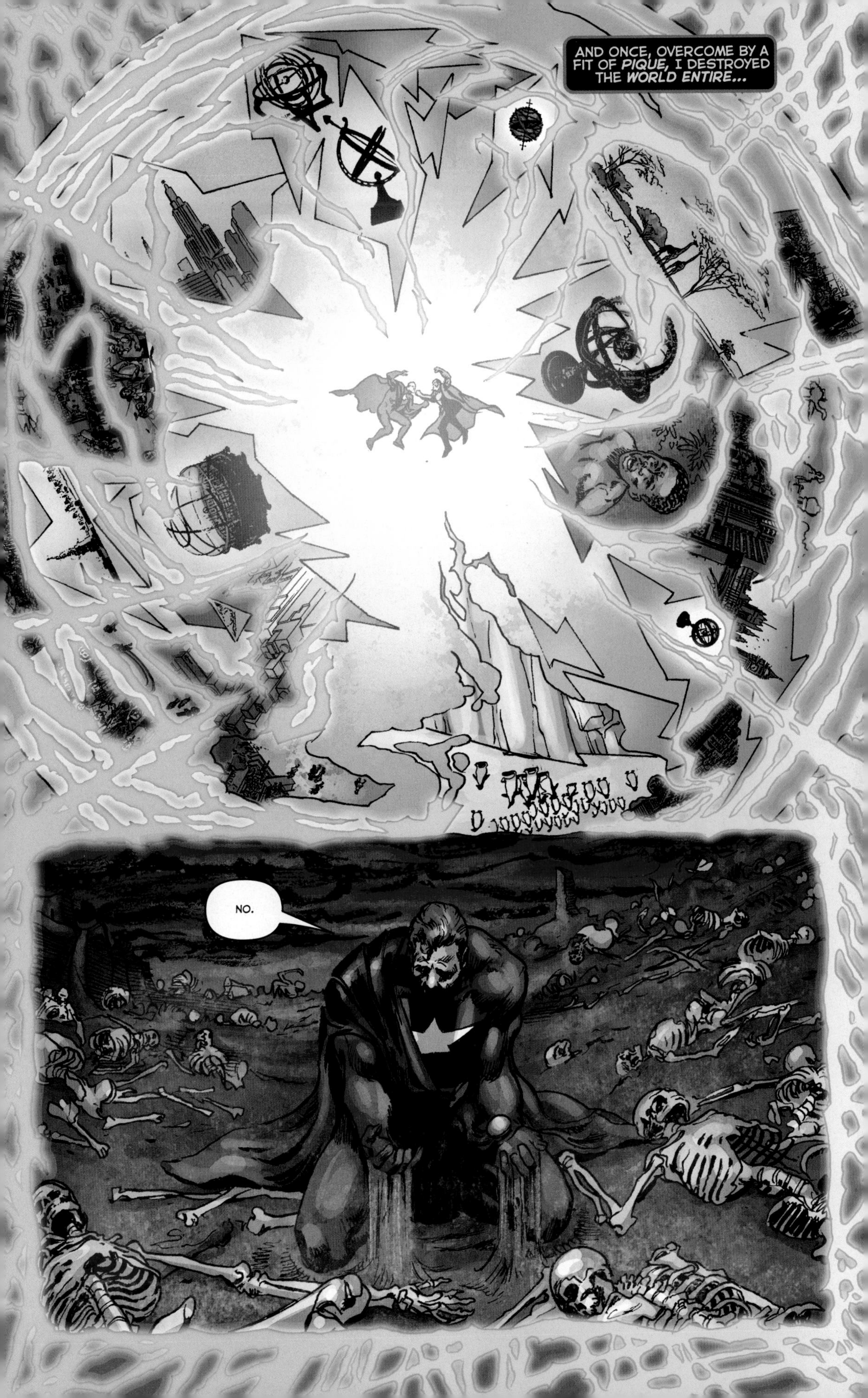
AND ONCE, OVERCOME BY A FIT OF PIQUE, I DESTROYED THE WORLD ENTIRE...
NO.

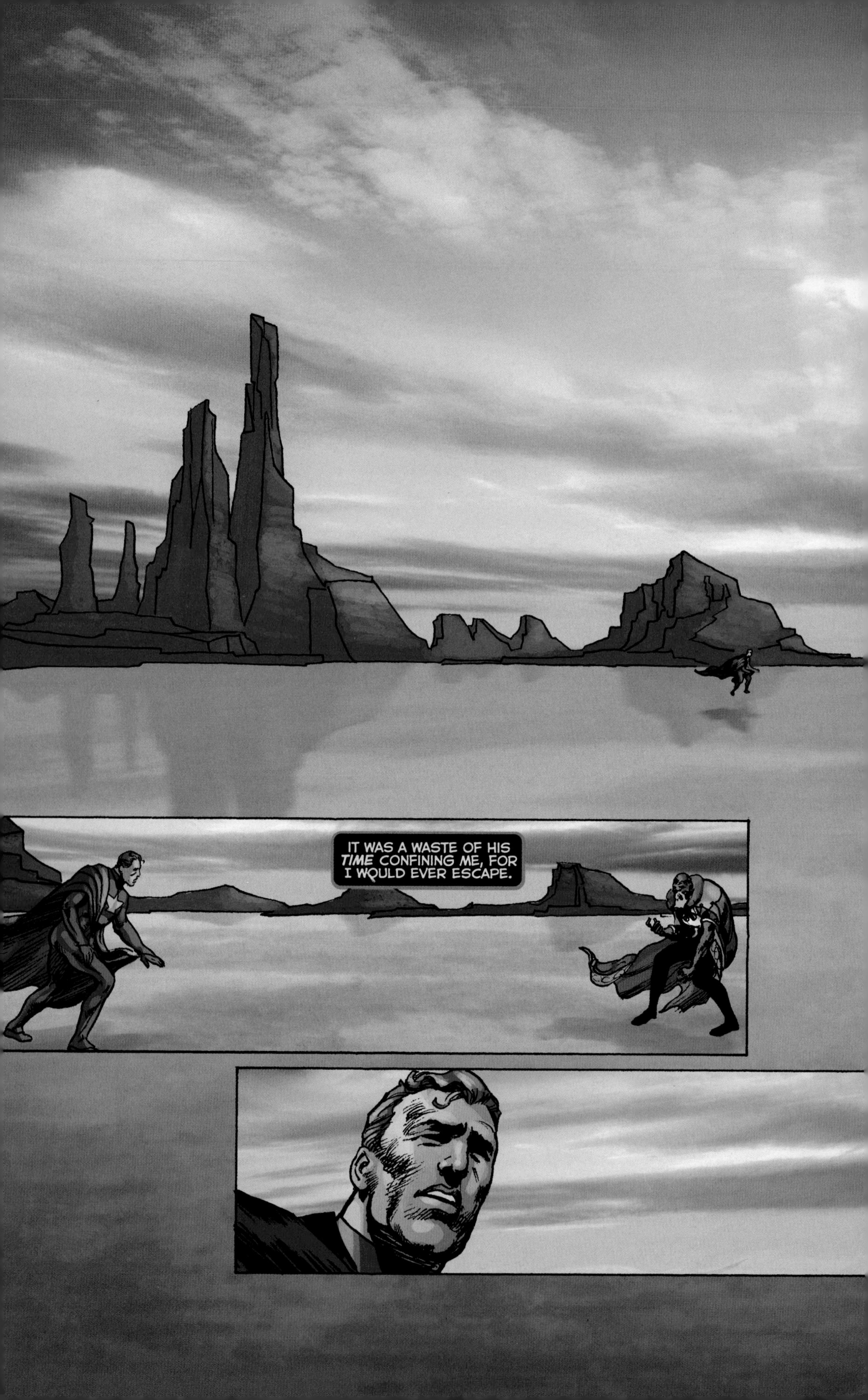
IT WAS A WASTE OF HIS *TIME* CONFINING ME, FOR I WOULD EVER ESCAPE.

AND IN THE LANDS THAT LIE *BENEATH* REALITY, THE LANDS THAT THE *SCHOLARS OF LEUGINA* CALL THE PLAINS OF *GETH*...

WE FACED EACH OTHER. AND WE *KNEW.*

IT WAS A WASTE OF *MY* TIME TO FIGHT HIM, FOR I COULD NO MORE DESTROY HIM THAN HE COULD DESTROY ME.

AND SO WE *ASKED* OURSELVES. SILENTLY, WITHOUT WORDS. IT WAS IN THE SET OF HIS *SHOULDERS.* THE LOOK IN *MY EYES,* PERHAPS.

WHAT *NOW?*

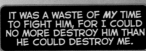

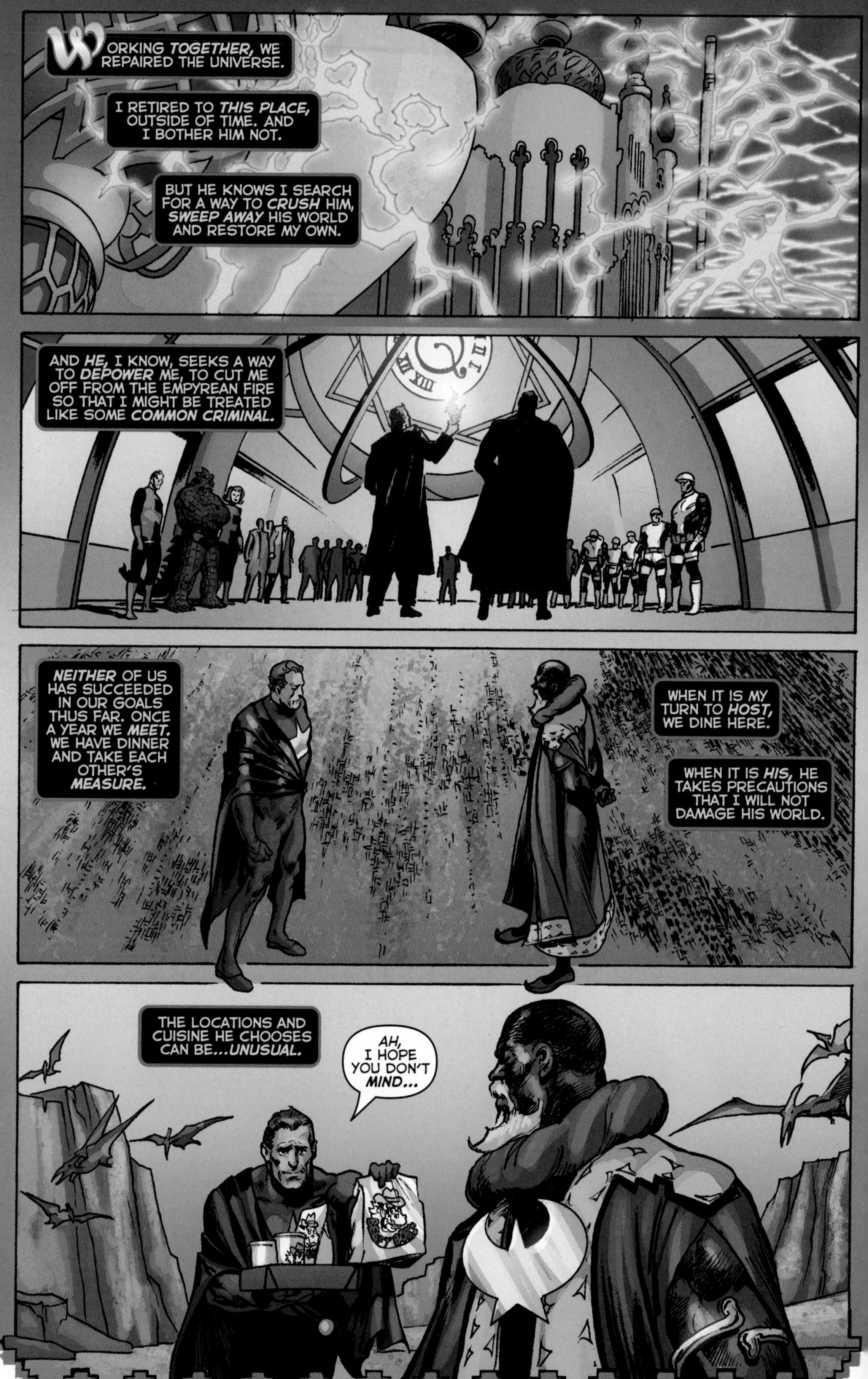
WORKING TOGETHER, WE REPAIRED THE UNIVERSE.
I RETIRED TO THIS PLACE, OUTSIDE OF TIME. AND I BOTHER HIM NOT.
BUT HE KNOWS I SEARCH FOR A WAY TO CRUSH HIM, SWEEP AWAY HIS WORLD AND RESTORE MY OWN.
AND HE, I KNOW, SEEKS A WAY TO DEPOWER ME, TO CUT ME OFF FROM THE EMPYREAN FIRE SO THAT I MIGHT BE TREATED LIKE SOME COMMON CRIMINAL.
NEITHER OF US HAS SUCCEEDED IN OUR GOALS THUS FAR. ONCE A YEAR WE MEET. WE HAVE DINNER AND TAKE EACH OTHER'S MEASURE.
WHEN IT IS MY TURN TO HOST, WE DINE HERE.
WHEN IT IS HIS, HE TAKES PRECAUTIONS THAT I WILL NOT DAMAGE HIS WORLD.
THE LOCATIONS AND CUISINE HE CHOOSES CAN BE...UNUSUAL.
AH, I HOPE YOU DON'T MIND...

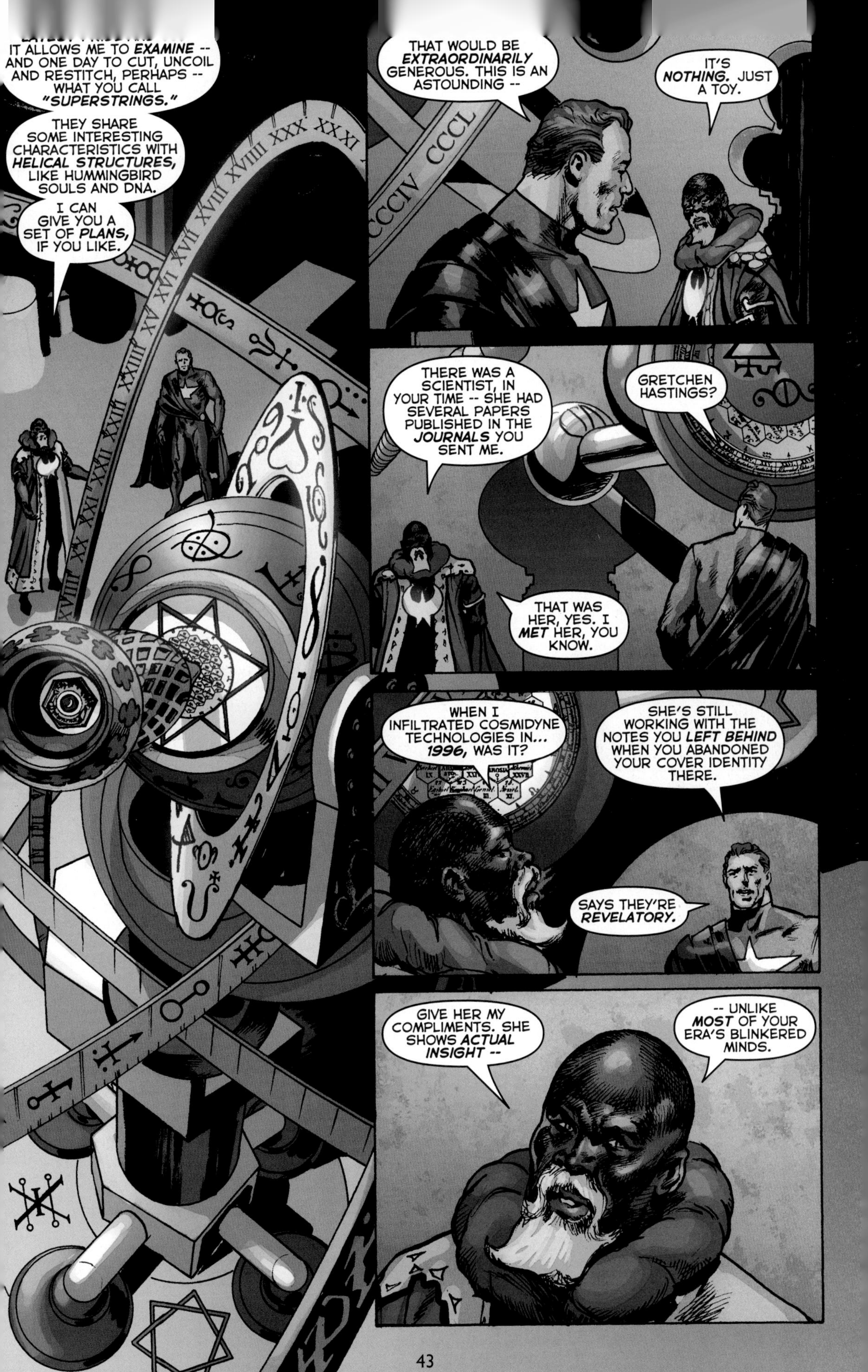

IT ALLOWS ME TO EXAMINE -- AND ONE DAY TO CUT, UNCOIL AND RESTITCH, PERHAPS -- WHAT YOU CALL "SUPERSTRINGS."
THEY SHARE SOME INTERESTING CHARACTERISTICS WITH HELICAL STRUCTURES, LIKE HUMMINGBIRD SOULS AND DNA.
I CAN GIVE YOU A SET OF PLANS, IF YOU LIKE.
THAT WOULD BE EXTRAORDINARILY GENEROUS. THIS IS AN ASTOUNDING --
IT'S NOTHING. JUST A TOY.
THERE WAS A SCIENTIST, IN YOUR TIME -- SHE HAD SEVERAL PAPERS PUBLISHED IN THE JOURNALS YOU SENT ME.
GRETCHEN HASTINGS?
THAT WAS HER, YES. I MET HER, YOU KNOW.
WHEN I INFILTRATED COSMIDYNE TECHNOLOGIES IN... 1996, WAS IT?
SHE'S STILL WORKING WITH THE NOTES YOU LEFT BEHIND WHEN YOU ABANDONED YOUR COVER IDENTITY THERE.
SAYS THEY'RE REVELATORY.
GIVE HER MY COMPLIMENTS. SHE SHOWS ACTUAL INSIGHT --
-- UNLIKE MOST OF YOUR ERA'S BLINKERED MINDS.

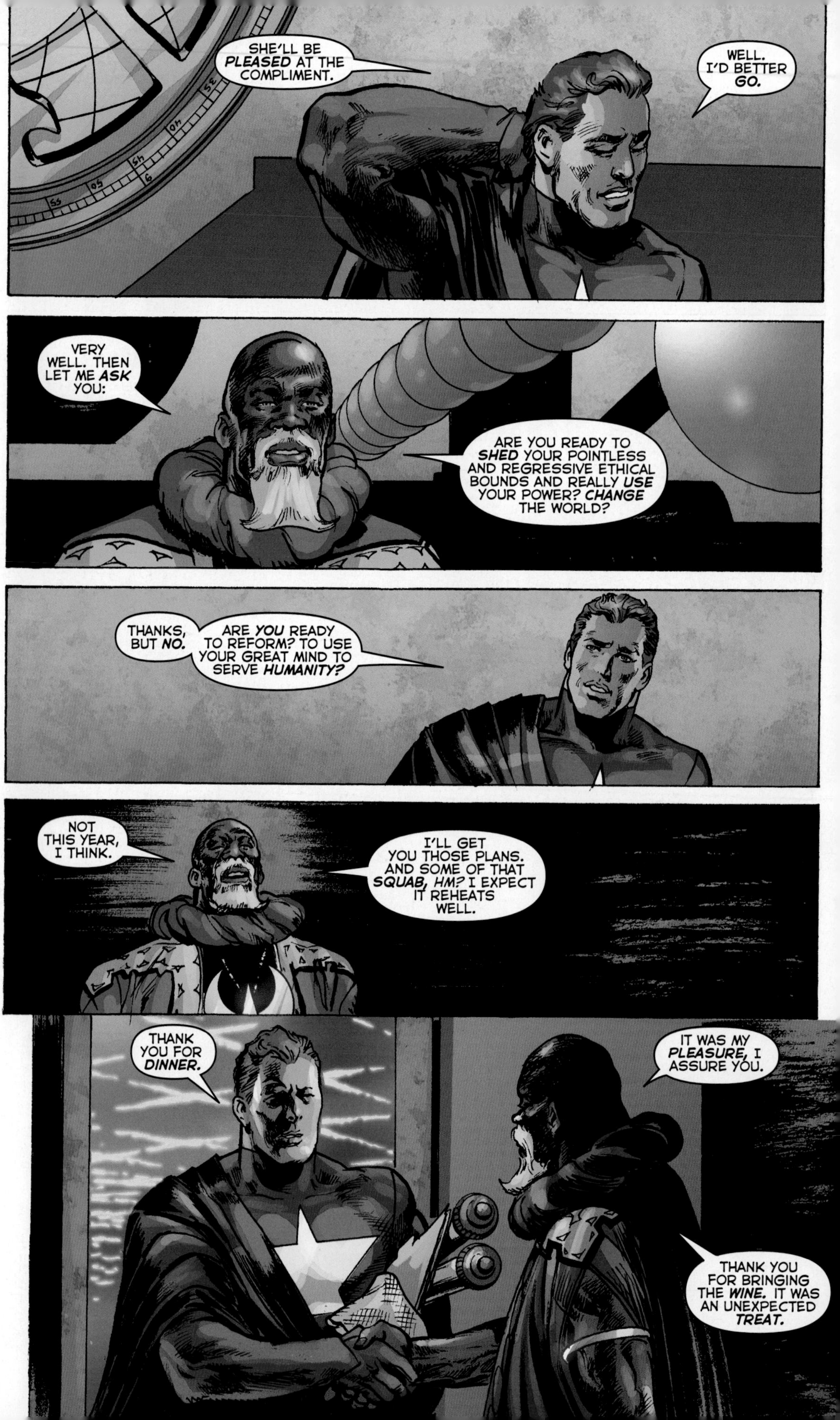
SHE'LL BE PLEASED AT THE COMPLIMENT.
WELL. I'D BETTER GO.
VERY WELL. THEN LET ME ASK YOU:
ARE YOU READY TO SHED YOUR POINTLESS AND REGRESSIVE ETHICAL BOUNDS AND REALLY USE YOUR POWER? CHANGE THE WORLD?
THANKS, BUT NO.
ARE YOU READY TO REFORM? TO USE YOUR GREAT MIND TO SERVE HUMANITY?
NOT THIS YEAR, I THINK.
I'LL GET YOU THOSE PLANS. AND SOME OF THAT SQUAB, HM? I EXPECT IT REHEATS WELL.
THANK YOU FOR DINNER.
IT WAS MY PLEASURE, I ASSURE YOU.
THANK YOU FOR BRINGING THE WINE. IT WAS AN UNEXPECTED TREAT.

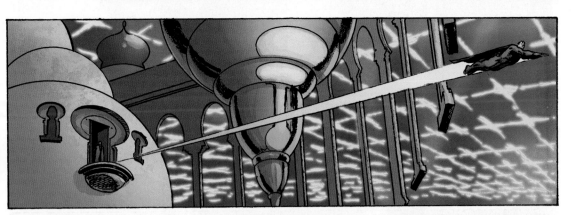

HE AND HIS ALLIES WILL SUBJECT THOSE SCHEMATICS TO EVERY TEST THEY CAN *MUSTER,* TO MAKE SURE THEY CONTAIN NO *HIDDEN TRAPS.*

JUST AS I EXAMINE THE *JOURNALS* AND *NOTES* HE SUPPLIES ME WITH FOR CONTACT POISONS, *NEURON-DEADENING INK,* AND MORE.

AS IF *EITHER* OF US WOULD STOOP TO SUCH INFANTILE TRICKERY.

ONCE HE IS OUT OF SIGHT, I CALL FOR THE *RECORDINGS* I MADE OF THE EVENING.

THEY WILL HAVE CAPTURED EVERY INSTANT, EVERY *NUANCE.* EVERY MOMENTARILY TIGHTENED JAW MUSCLE, OR FLICKERED *EYELID.*

I WILL REVIEW THEM IN DETAIL AT *MY LEISURE,* OF COURSE, BUT THERE IS ONE MOMENT I WISH TO SEE *IMMEDIATELY* --

FORWARD. THE END OF THE MEAL.

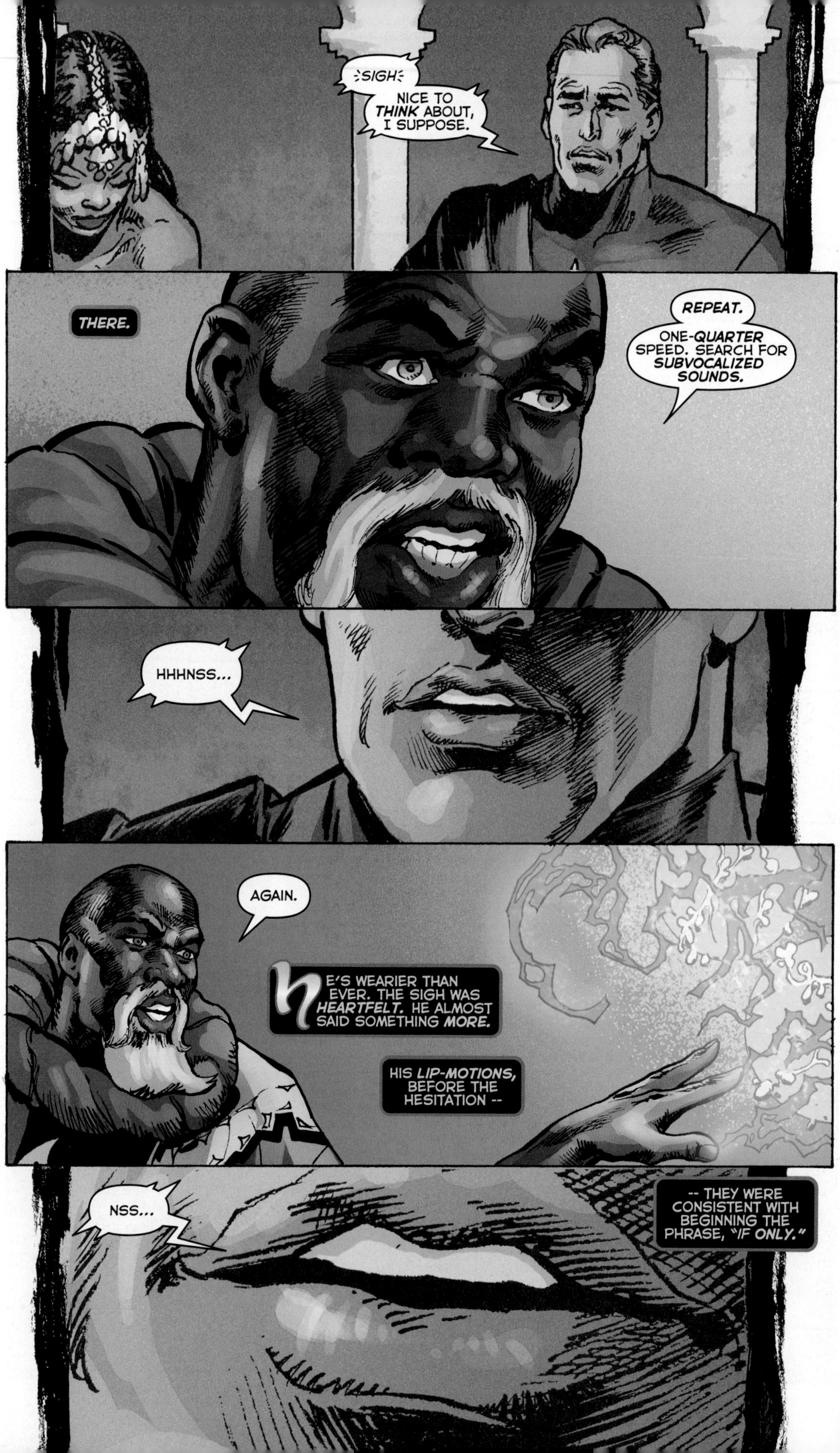
SIGH
NICE TO THINK ABOUT, I SUPPOSE.
THERE.
REPEAT.
ONE-QUARTER SPEED. SEARCH FOR SUBVOCALIZED SOUNDS.
HHHNSS...
AGAIN.
HE'S WEARIER THAN EVER. THE SIGH WAS HEARTFELT. HE ALMOST SAID SOMETHING MORE.
HIS LIP-MOTIONS, BEFORE THE HESITATION --
NSS...
-- THEY WERE CONSISTENT WITH BEGINNING THE PHRASE, "IF ONLY."

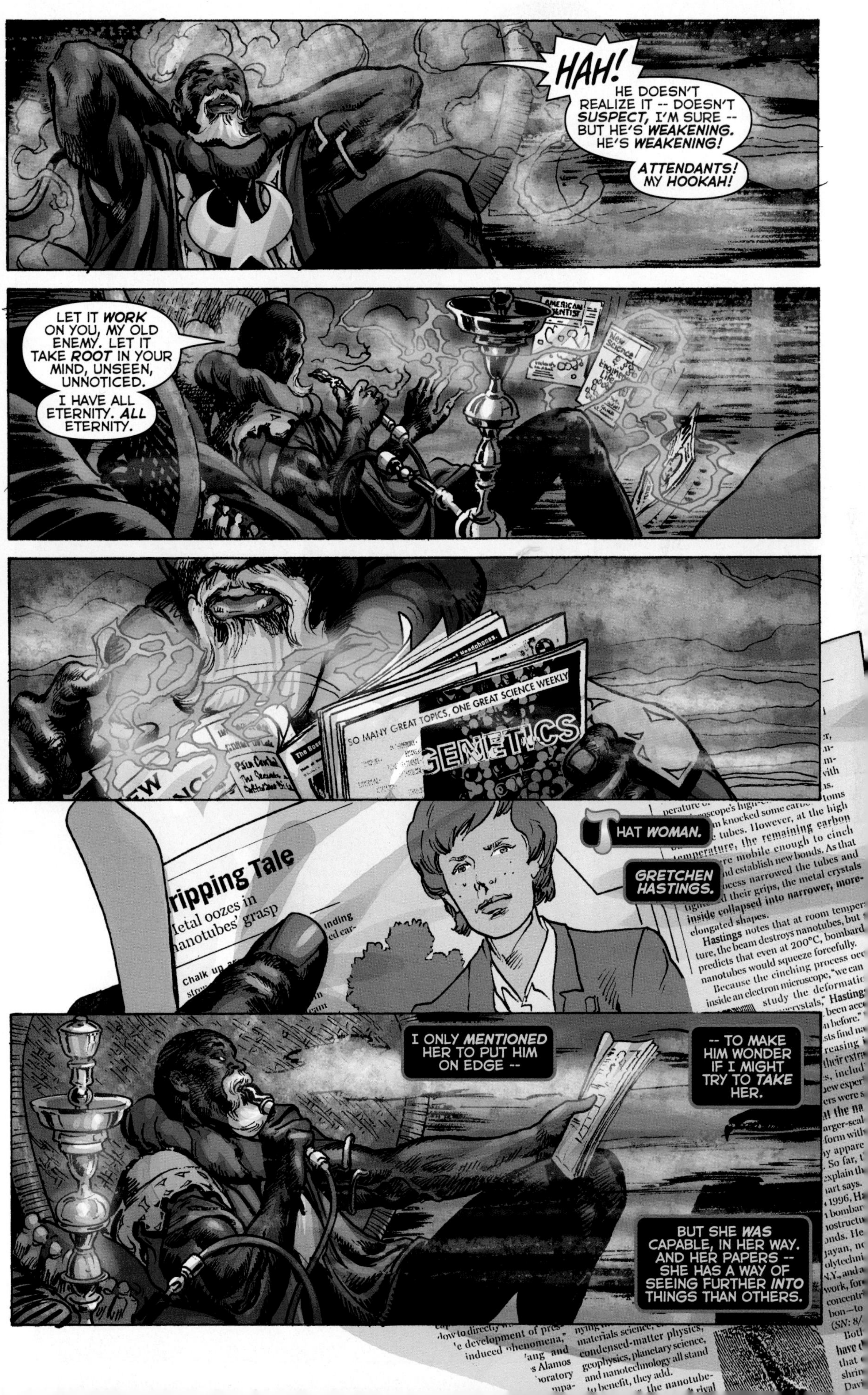
HAH!
HE DOESN'T REALIZE IT -- DOESN'T SUSPECT, I'M SURE -- BUT HE'S WEAKENING. HE'S WEAKENING!
ATTENDANTS! MY HOOKAH!
LET IT WORK ON YOU, MY OLD ENEMY. LET IT TAKE ROOT IN YOUR MIND, UNSEEN, UNNOTICED.
I HAVE ALL ETERNITY. ALL ETERNITY.
SO MANY GREAT TOPICS, ONE GREAT SCIENCE WEEKLY
GENETICS
THAT WOMAN.
GRETCHEN HASTINGS.
I ONLY MENTIONED HER TO PUT HIM ON EDGE --
-- TO MAKE HIM WONDER IF I MIGHT TRY TO TAKE HER.
BUT SHE WAS CAPABLE, IN HER WAY. AND HER PAPERS -- SHE HAS A WAY OF SEEING FURTHER INTO THINGS THAN OTHERS.

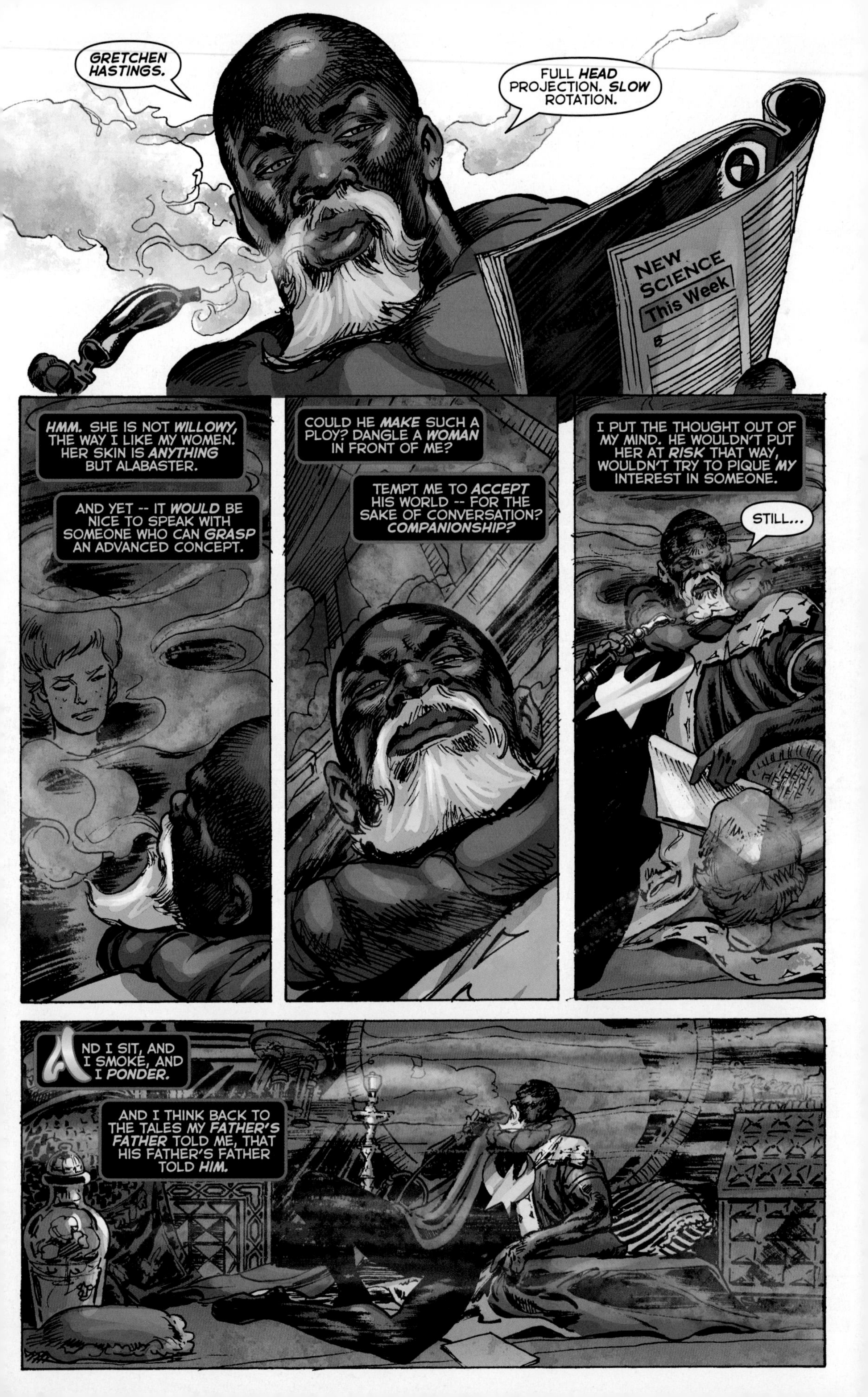
GRETCHEN HASTINGS.
FULL HEAD PROJECTION. SLOW ROTATION.
NEW SCIENCE This Week
HMM. SHE IS NOT WILLOWY, THE WAY I LIKE MY WOMEN. HER SKIN IS ANYTHING BUT ALABASTER.
AND YET -- IT WOULD BE NICE TO SPEAK WITH SOMEONE WHO CAN GRASP AN ADVANCED CONCEPT.
COULD HE MAKE SUCH A PLOY? DANGLE A WOMAN IN FRONT OF ME?
TEMPT ME TO ACCEPT HIS WORLD -- FOR THE SAKE OF CONVERSATION? COMPANIONSHIP?
I PUT THE THOUGHT OUT OF MY MIND. HE WOULDN'T PUT HER AT RISK THAT WAY, WOULDN'T TRY TO PIQUE MY INTEREST IN SOMEONE.
STILL...
AND I SIT, AND I SMOKE, AND I PONDER.
AND I THINK BACK TO THE TALES MY FATHER'S FATHER TOLD ME, THAT HIS FATHER'S FATHER TOLD HIM.

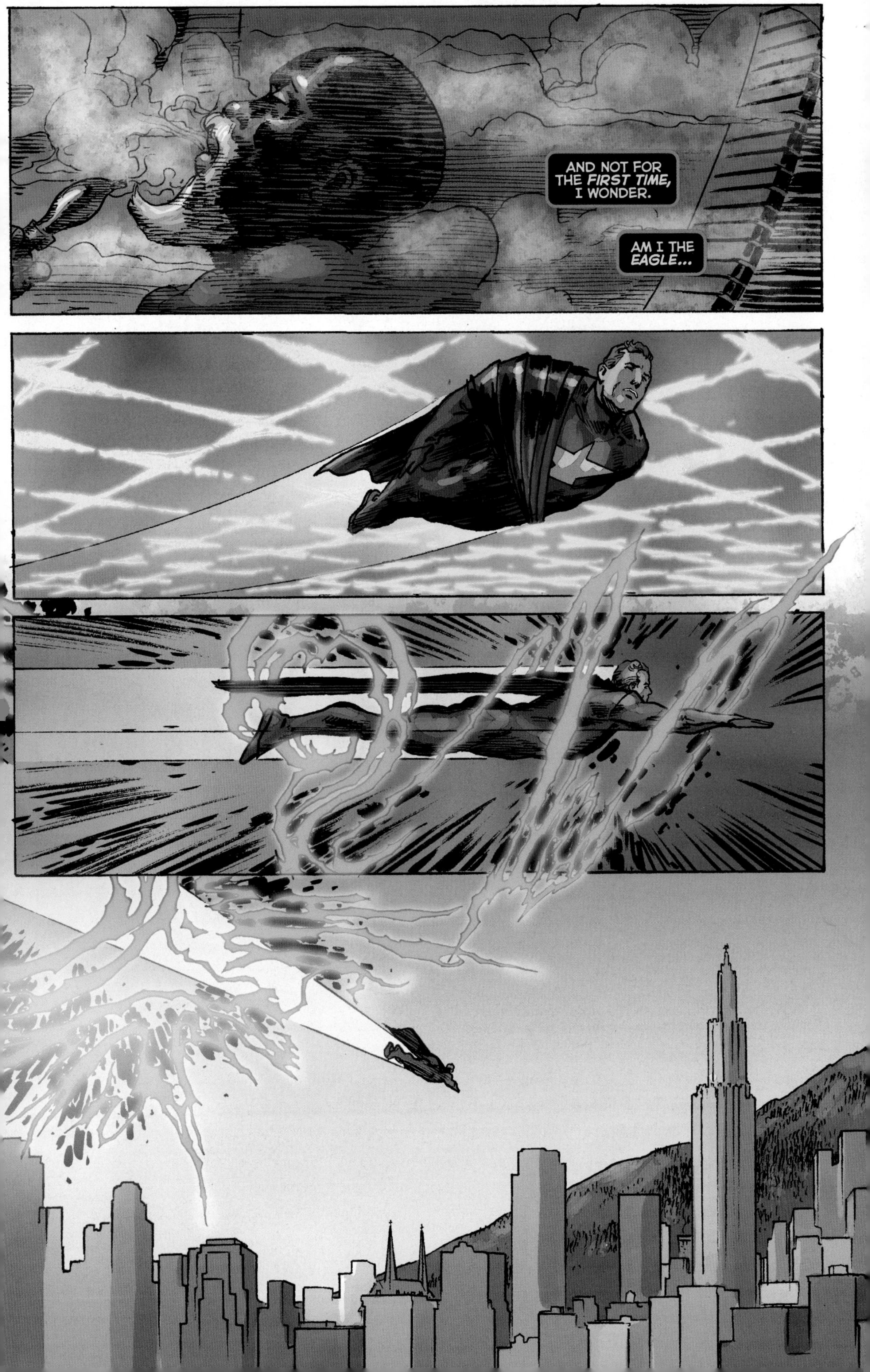
AND NOT FOR THE *FIRST TIME,* I WONDER.
AM I THE *EAGLE...*

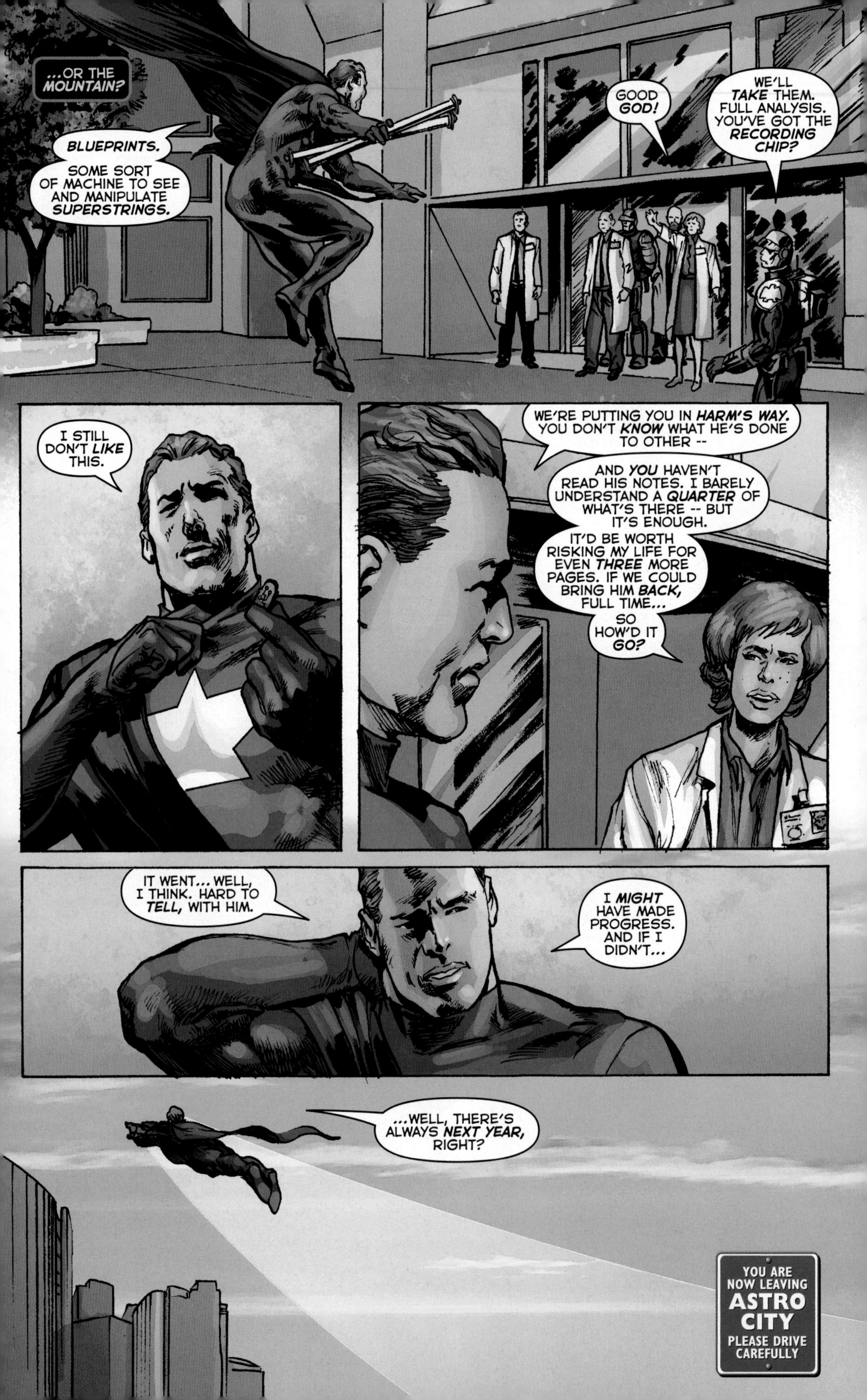
...OR THE MOUNTAIN?
BLUEPRINTS.
SOME SORT OF MACHINE TO SEE AND MANIPULATE SUPERSTRINGS.
GOOD GOD!
WE'LL TAKE THEM. FULL ANALYSIS. YOU'VE GOT THE RECORDING CHIP?
I STILL DON'T LIKE THIS.
WE'RE PUTTING YOU IN HARM'S WAY. YOU DON'T KNOW WHAT HE'S DONE TO OTHER --
AND YOU HAVEN'T READ HIS NOTES. I BARELY UNDERSTAND A QUARTER OF WHAT'S THERE -- BUT IT'S ENOUGH.
IT'D BE WORTH RISKING MY LIFE FOR EVEN THREE MORE PAGES. IF WE COULD BRING HIM BACK, FULL TIME...
SO HOW'D IT GO?
IT WENT... WELL, I THINK. HARD TO TELL, WITH HIM.
I MIGHT HAVE MADE PROGRESS. AND IF I DIDN'T...
...WELL, THERE'S ALWAYS NEXT YEAR, RIGHT?
YOU ARE NOW LEAVING ASTRO CITY PLEASE DRIVE CAREFULLY

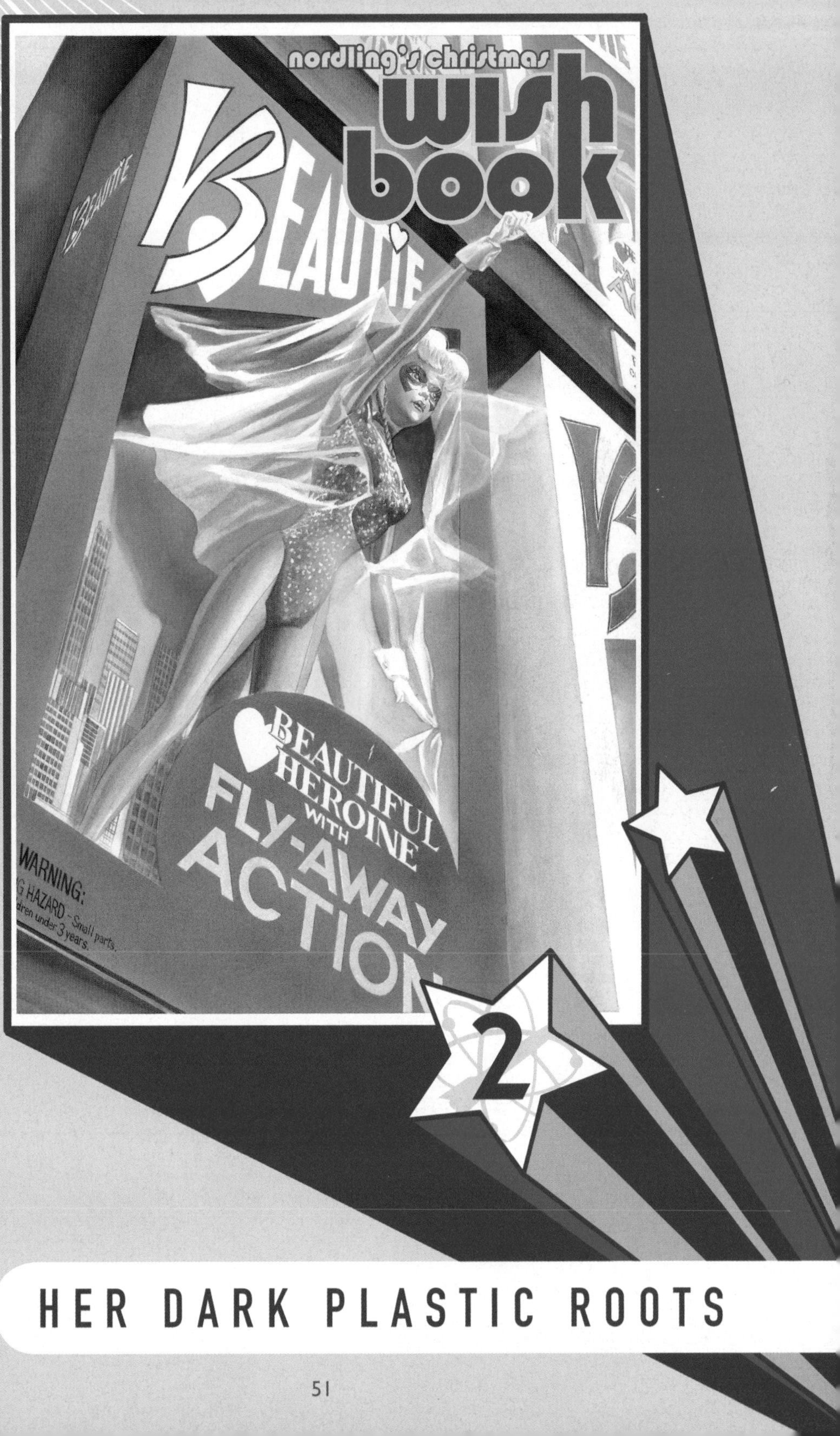
nordling's christmas
wish book
BEAUTIE
BEAUTIFUL HEROINE WITH
FLY-AWAY ACTION
WARNING:
2

HER DARK PLASTIC ROOTS

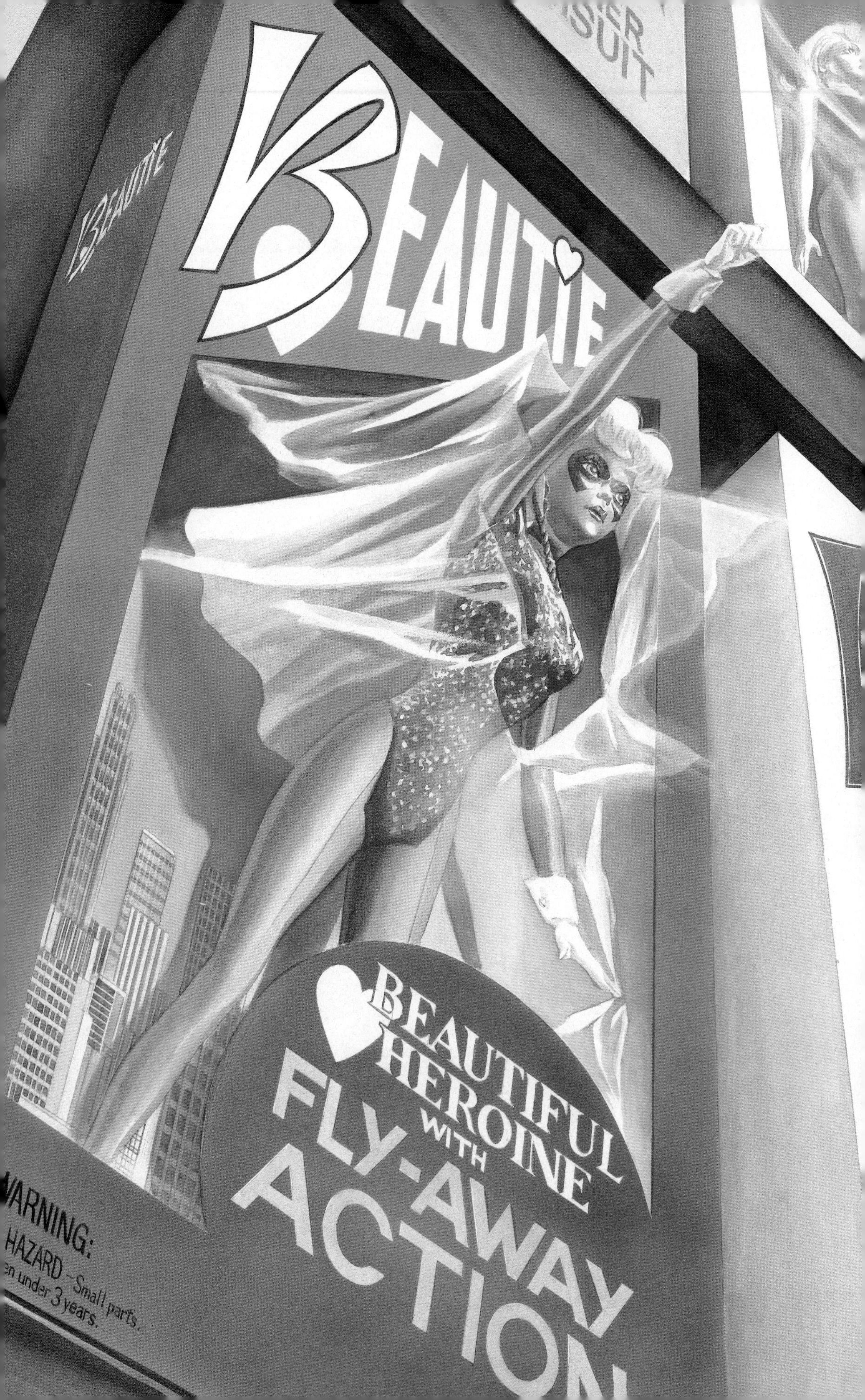

BEAUTIE
BEAUTIE
BEAUTIFUL HEROINE WITH FLY-AWAY ACTION
ARNING:
HAZARD – Small parts.
en under 3 years.

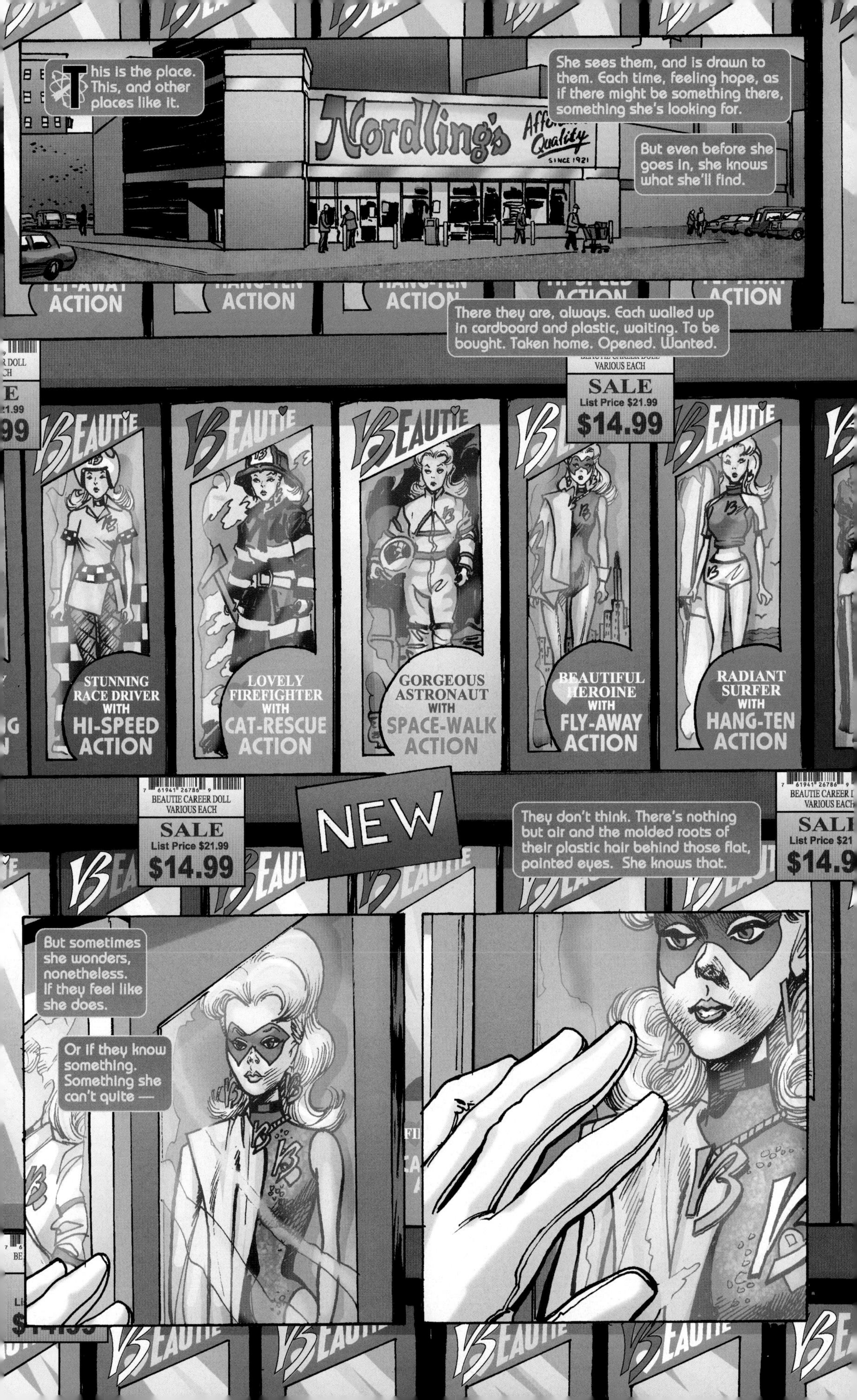
This is the place. This, and other places like it.
Nordling's
Quality
SINCE 1921
She sees them, and is drawn to them. Each time, feeling hope, as if there might be something there, something she's looking for.
But even before she goes in, she knows what she'll find.
There they are, always. Each walled up in cardboard and plastic, waiting. To be bought. Taken home. Opened. Wanted.
VARIOUS EACH
SALE
List Price $21.99
$14.99
BEAUTIE
STUNNING RACE DRIVER WITH HI-SPEED ACTION
LOVELY FIREFIGHTER WITH CAT-RESCUE ACTION
GORGEOUS ASTRONAUT WITH SPACE-WALK ACTION
BEAUTIFUL HEROINE WITH FLY-AWAY ACTION
RADIANT SURFER WITH HANG-TEN ACTION
7 61941 26786 9
BEAUTIE CAREER DOLL
VARIOUS EACH
SALE
List Price $21.99
$14.99
NEW
They don't think. There's nothing but air and the molded roots of their plastic hair behind those flat, painted eyes. She knows that.
But sometimes she wonders, nonetheless. If they feel like she does.
Or if they know something. Something she can't quite —

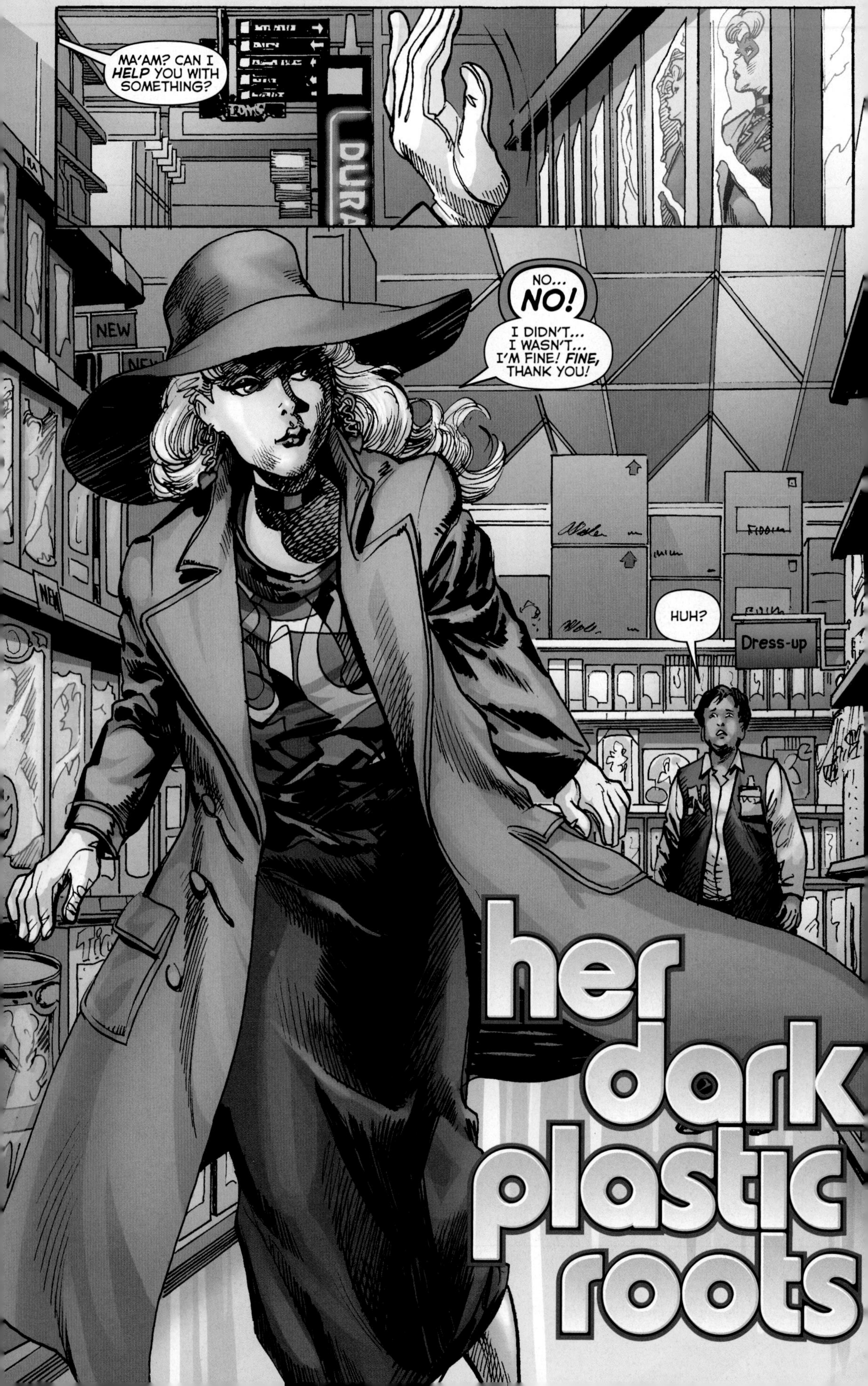
MA'AM? CAN I HELP YOU WITH SOMETHING?
DURA
NEW
NO... NO!
I DIDN'T... I WASN'T... I'M FINE! FINE, THANK YOU!
HUH?
Dress-up
her dark plastic roots

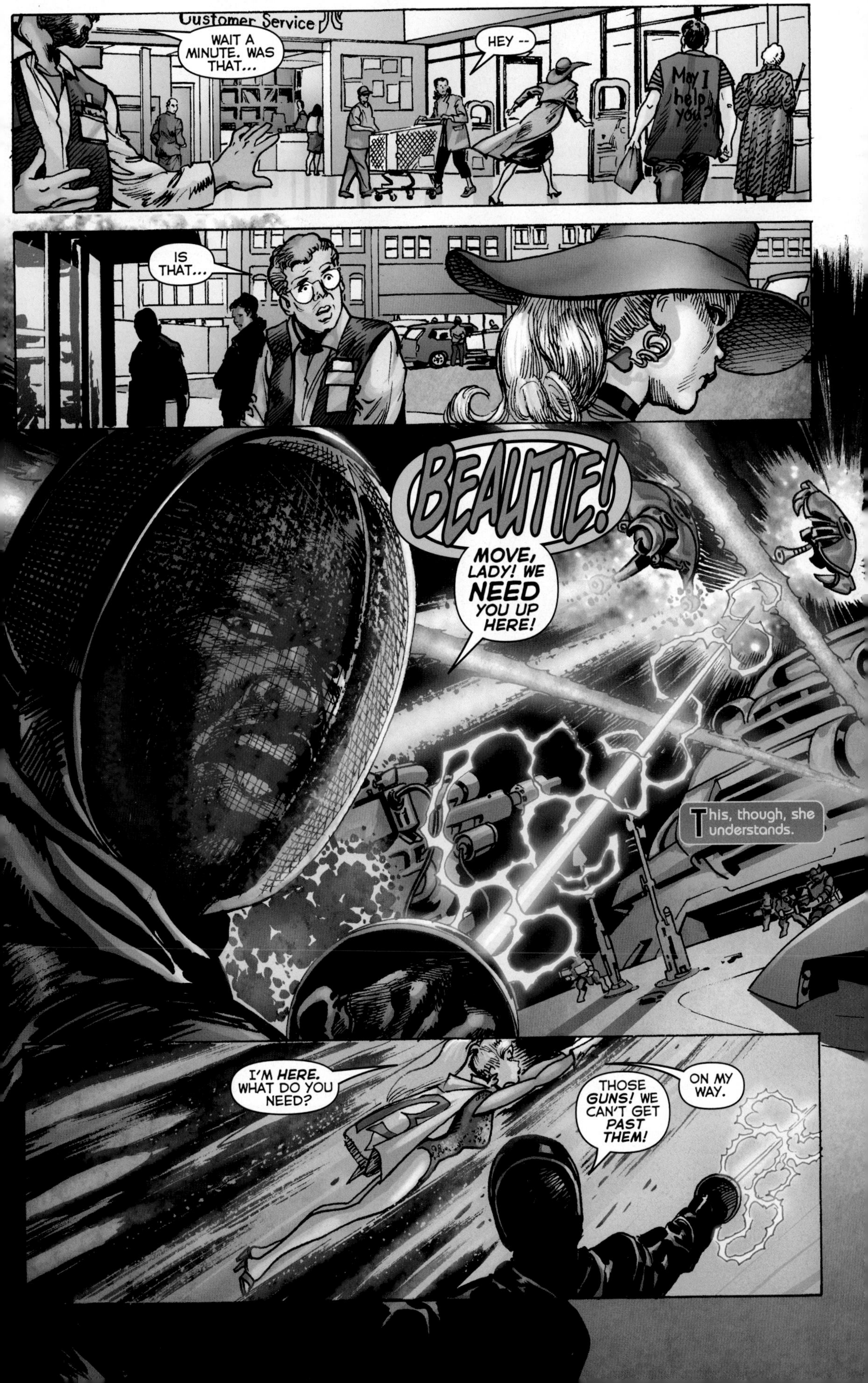
Customer Service
WAIT A MINUTE. WAS THAT...
HEY --
May I help you?
IS THAT...
BEAUTIE!
MOVE, LADY! WE NEED YOU UP HERE!
This, though, she understands.
I'M HERE. WHAT DO YOU NEED?
THOSE GUNS! WE CAN'T GET PAST THEM!
ON MY WAY.

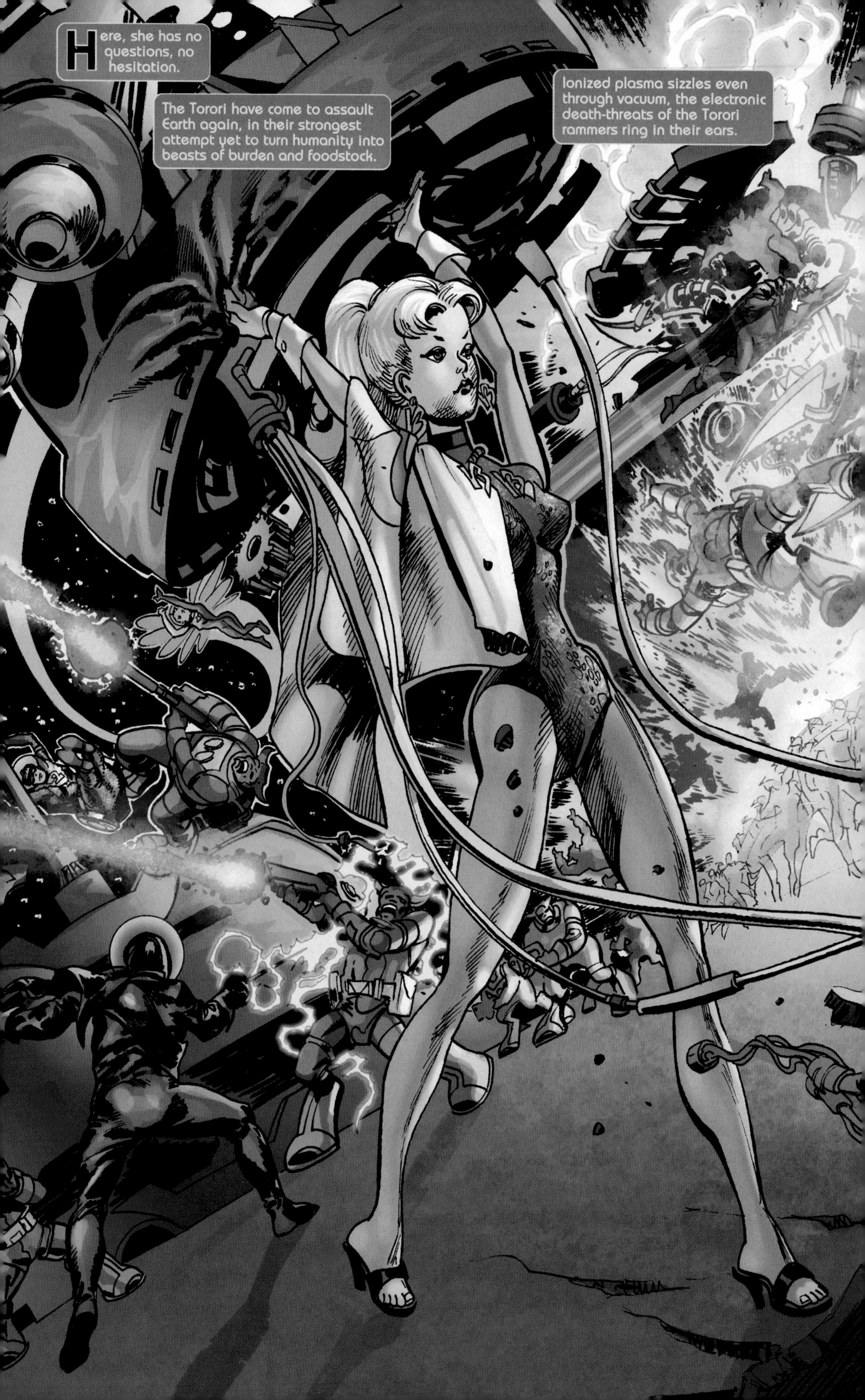
Here, she has no questions, no hesitation.
The Torori have come to assault Earth again, in their strongest attempt yet to turn humanity into beasts of burden and foodstock.
Ionized plasma sizzles even through vacuum, the electronic death-threats of the Torori rammers ring in their ears.

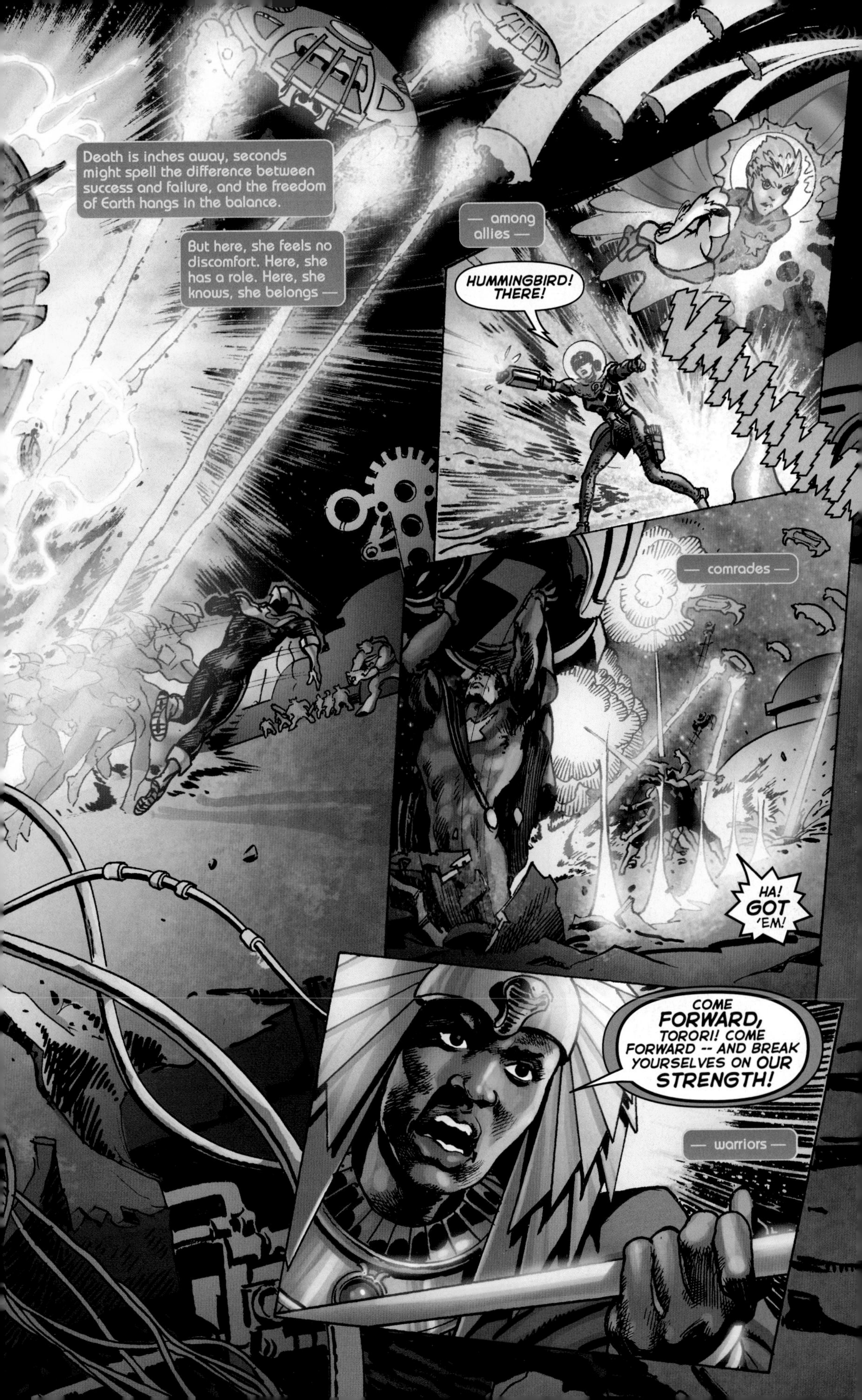
Death is inches away, seconds might spell the difference between success and failure, and the freedom of Earth hangs in the balance.
But here, she feels no discomfort. Here, she has a role. Here, she knows, she belongs —
— among allies —
HUMMINGBIRD! THERE!
VMMMMMM
— comrades —
HA! GOT 'EM!
COME FORWARD, TORORI! COME FORWARD -- AND BREAK YOURSELVES ON OUR STRENGTH!
— warriors —

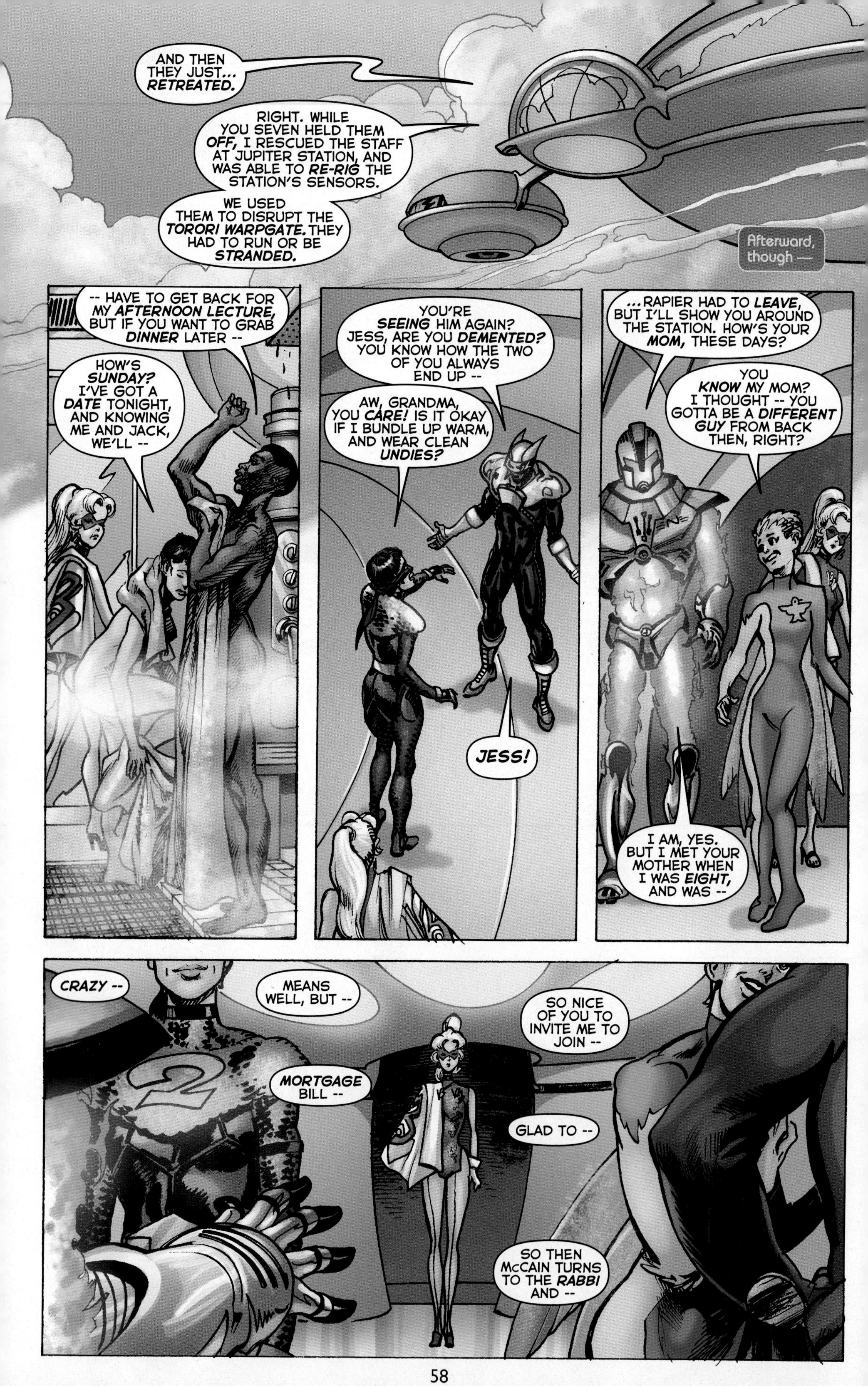
AND THEN THEY JUST... RETREATED.
RIGHT. WHILE YOU SEVEN HELD THEM OFF, I RESCUED THE STAFF AT JUPITER STATION, AND WAS ABLE TO RE-RIG THE STATION'S SENSORS.
WE USED THEM TO DISRUPT THE TORORI WARPGATE. THEY HAD TO RUN OR BE STRANDED.
Afterward, though —
-- HAVE TO GET BACK FOR MY AFTERNOON LECTURE, BUT IF YOU WANT TO GRAB DINNER LATER --
HOW'S SUNDAY? I'VE GOT A DATE TONIGHT, AND KNOWING ME AND JACK, WE'LL --
YOU'RE SEEING HIM AGAIN? JESS, ARE YOU DEMENTED? YOU KNOW HOW THE TWO OF YOU ALWAYS END UP --
AW, GRANDMA, YOU CARE! IS IT OKAY IF I BUNDLE UP WARM, AND WEAR CLEAN UNDIES?
JESS!
...RAPIER HAD TO LEAVE, BUT I'LL SHOW YOU AROUND THE STATION. HOW'S YOUR MOM, THESE DAYS?
YOU KNOW MY MOM? I THOUGHT -- YOU GOTTA BE A DIFFERENT GUY FROM BACK THEN, RIGHT?
I AM, YES. BUT I MET YOUR MOTHER WHEN I WAS EIGHT, AND WAS --
CRAZY --
MEANS WELL, BUT --
SO NICE OF YOU TO INVITE ME TO JOIN --
MORTGAGE BILL --
GLAD TO --
SO THEN McCAIN TURNS TO THE RABBI AND --

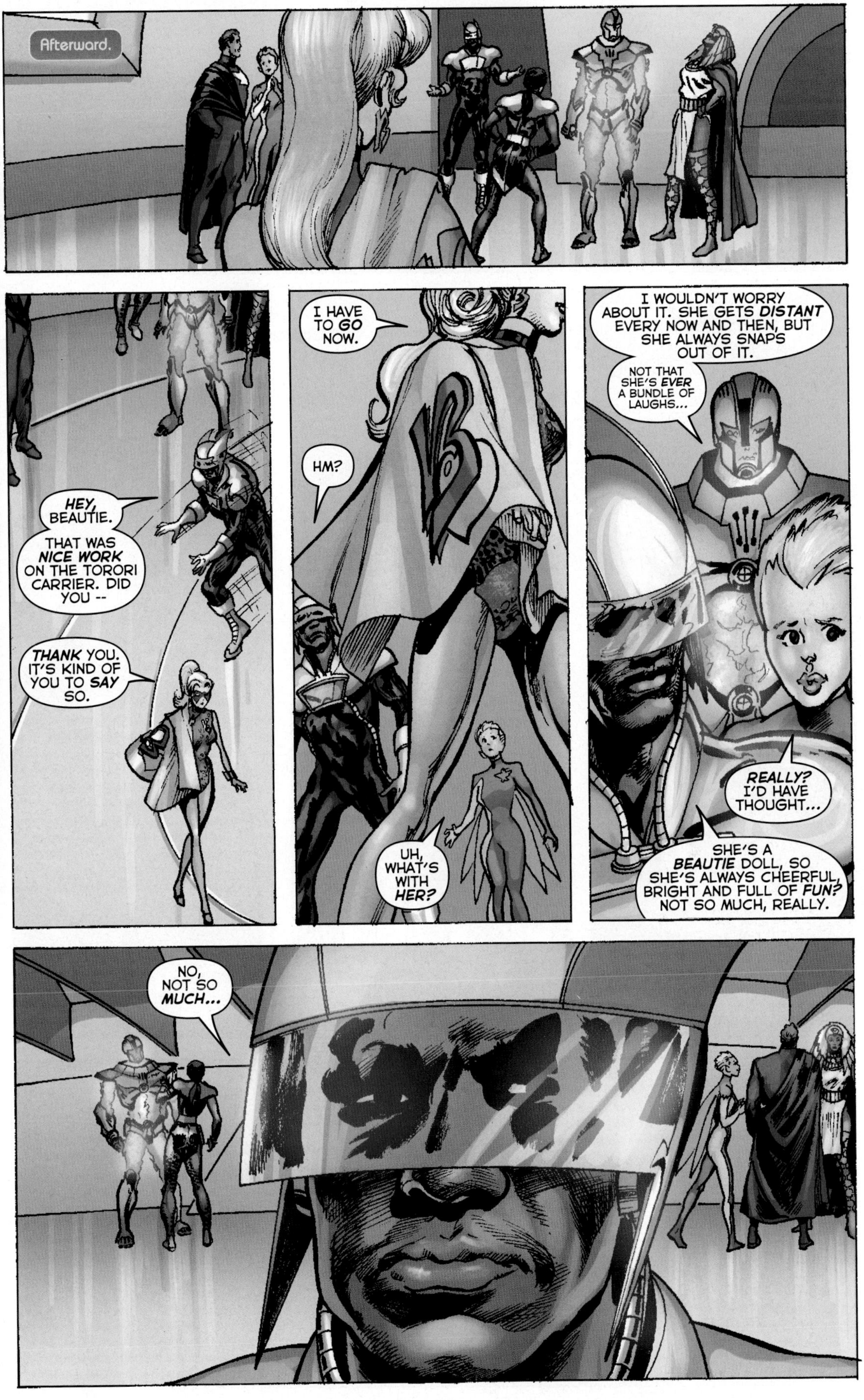
Afterward.
HEY, BEAUTIE.
THAT WAS NICE WORK ON THE TORORI CARRIER. DID YOU --
THANK YOU. IT'S KIND OF YOU TO SAY SO.
I HAVE TO GO NOW.
HM?
UH, WHAT'S WITH HER?
I WOULDN'T WORRY ABOUT IT. SHE GETS DISTANT EVERY NOW AND THEN, BUT SHE ALWAYS SNAPS OUT OF IT.
NOT THAT SHE'S EVER A BUNDLE OF LAUGHS...
REALLY? I'D HAVE THOUGHT...
SHE'S A BEAUTIE DOLL, SO SHE'S ALWAYS CHEERFUL, BRIGHT AND FULL OF FUN? NOT SO MUCH, REALLY.
NO, NOT SO MUCH...

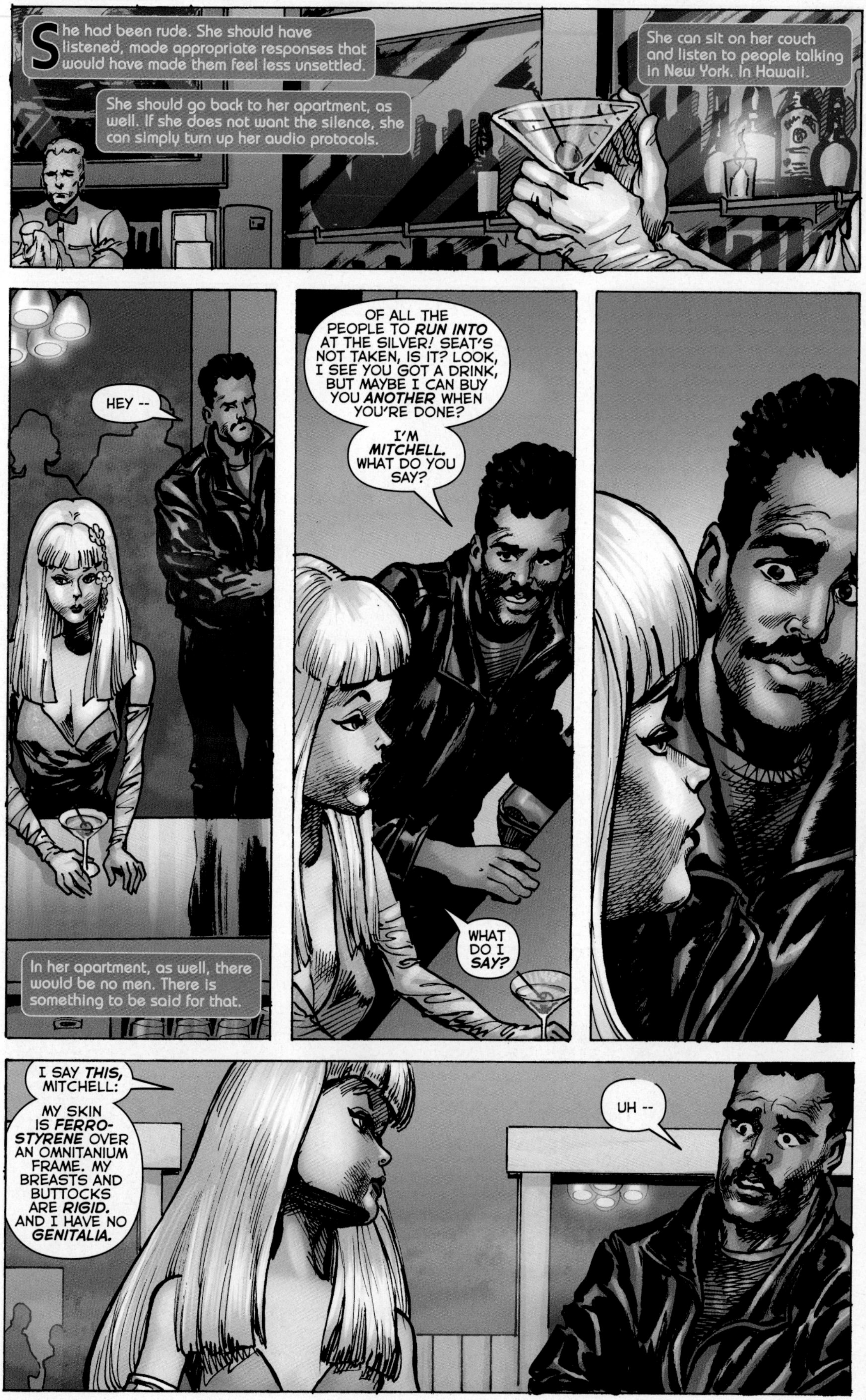
She had been rude. She should have listened, made appropriate responses that would have made them feel less unsettled.
She should go back to her apartment, as well. If she does not want the silence, she can simply turn up her audio protocols.
She can sit on her couch and listen to people talking in New York. In Hawaii.
HEY --
In her apartment, as well, there would be no men. There is something to be said for that.
OF ALL THE PEOPLE TO RUN INTO AT THE SILVER! SEAT'S NOT TAKEN, IS IT? LOOK, I SEE YOU GOT A DRINK, BUT MAYBE I CAN BUY YOU ANOTHER WHEN YOU'RE DONE?
I'M MITCHELL. WHAT DO YOU SAY?
WHAT DO I SAY?
I SAY THIS, MITCHELL:
MY SKIN IS FERRO-STYRENE OVER AN OMNITANIUM FRAME. MY BREASTS AND BUTTOCKS ARE RIGID. AND I HAVE NO GENITALIA.
UH --

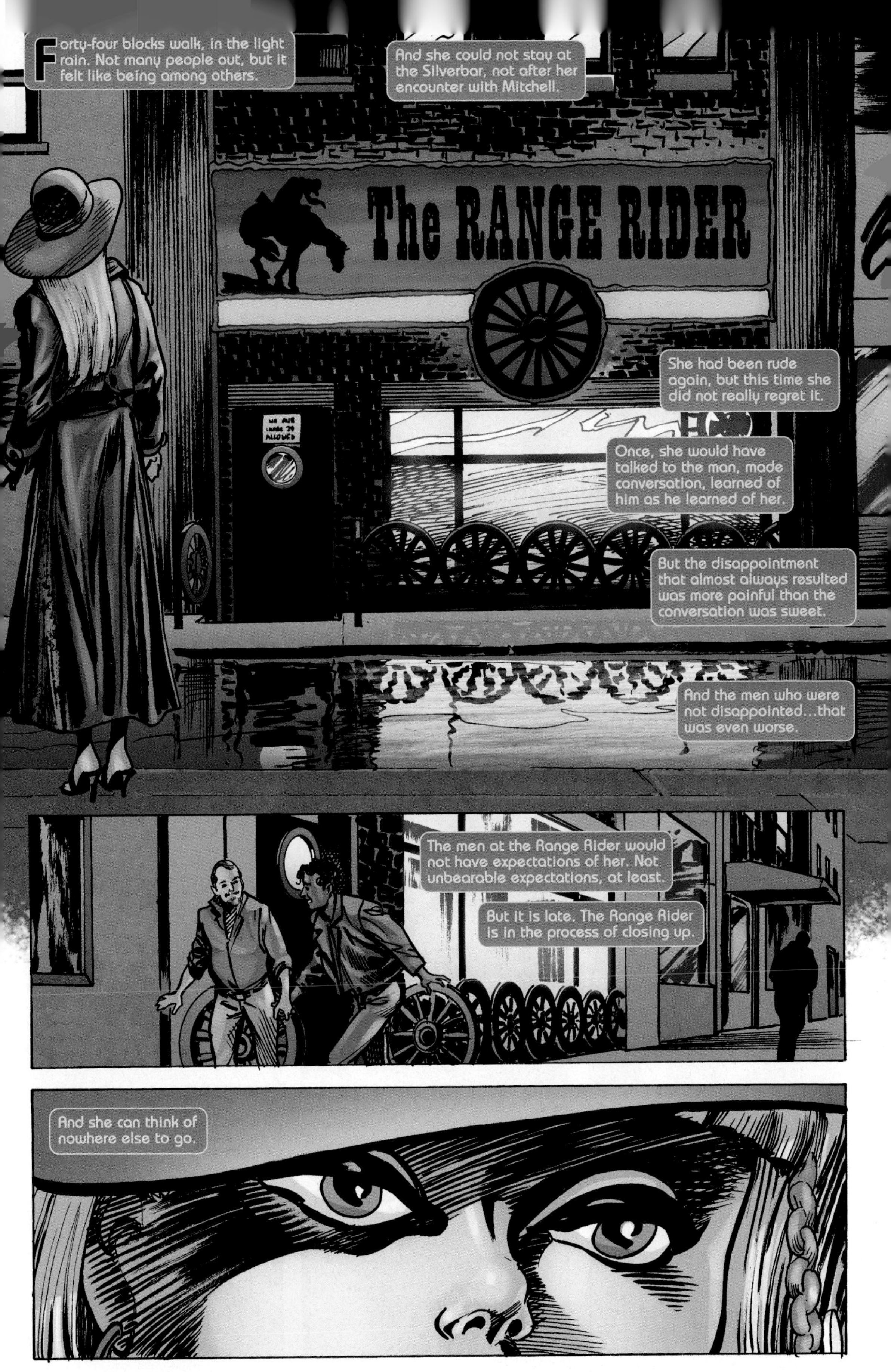

Forty-four blocks walk, in the light rain. Not many people out, but it felt like being among others.
And she could not stay at the Silverbar, not after her encounter with Mitchell.
The RANGE RIDER
She had been rude again, but this time she did not really regret it.
Once, she would have talked to the man, made conversation, learned of him as he learned of her.
But the disappointment that almost always resulted was more painful than the conversation was sweet.
And the men who were not disappointed...that was even worse.
The men at the Range Rider would not have expectations of her. Not unbearable expectations, at least.
But it is late. The Range Rider is in the process of closing up.
And she can think of nowhere else to go.

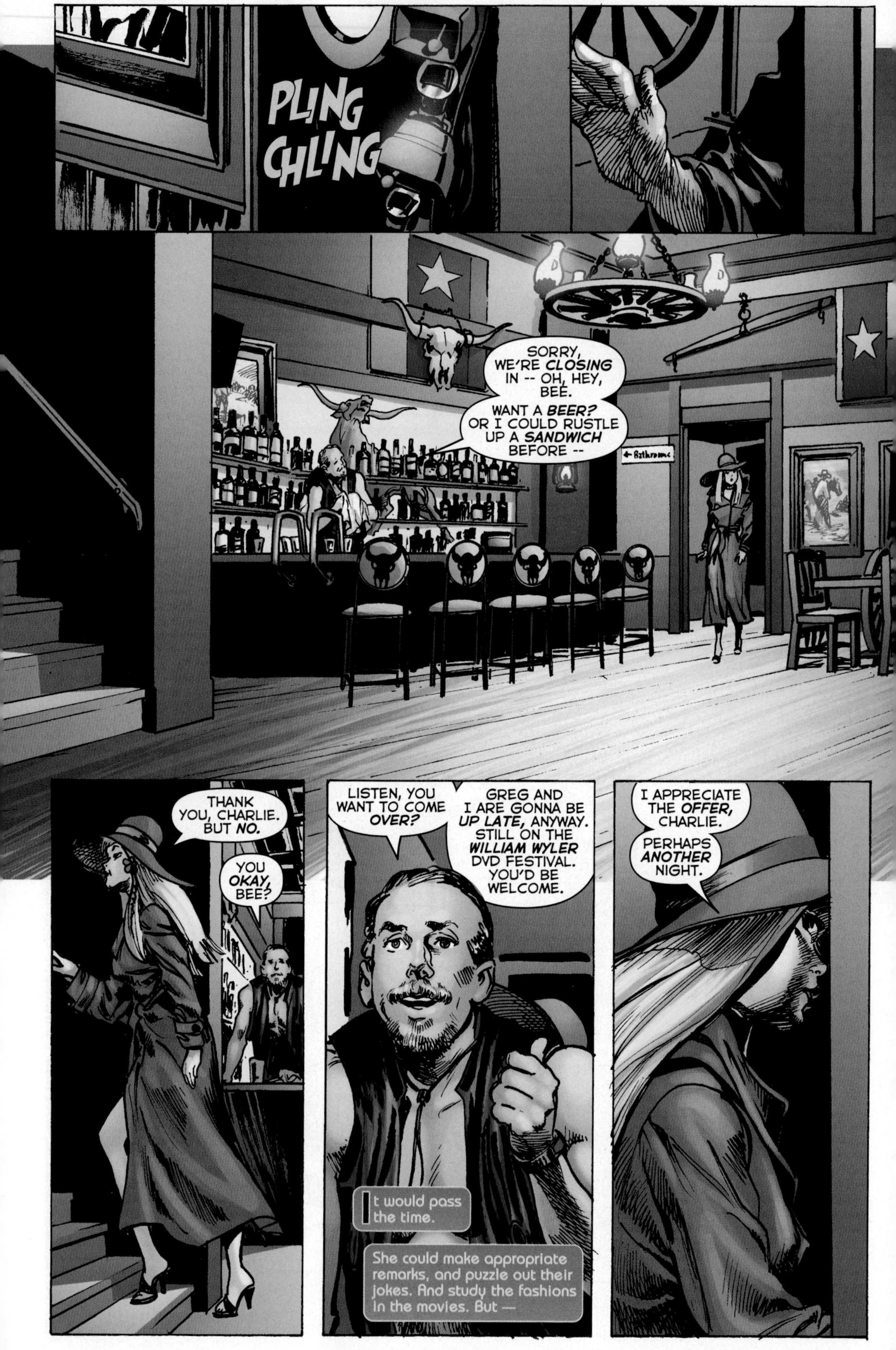
PLING
CHLING
SORRY, WE'RE CLOSING IN -- OH, HEY, BEE.
WANT A BEER? OR I COULD RUSTLE UP A SANDWICH BEFORE --
THANK YOU, CHARLIE. BUT NO.
YOU OKAY, BEE?
LISTEN, YOU WANT TO COME OVER?
GREG AND I ARE GONNA BE UP LATE, ANYWAY. STILL ON THE WILLIAM WYLER DVD FESTIVAL. YOU'D BE WELCOME.
It would pass the time.
She could make appropriate remarks, and puzzle out their jokes. And study the fashions in the movies. But —
I APPRECIATE THE OFFER, CHARLIE.
PERHAPS ANOTHER NIGHT.

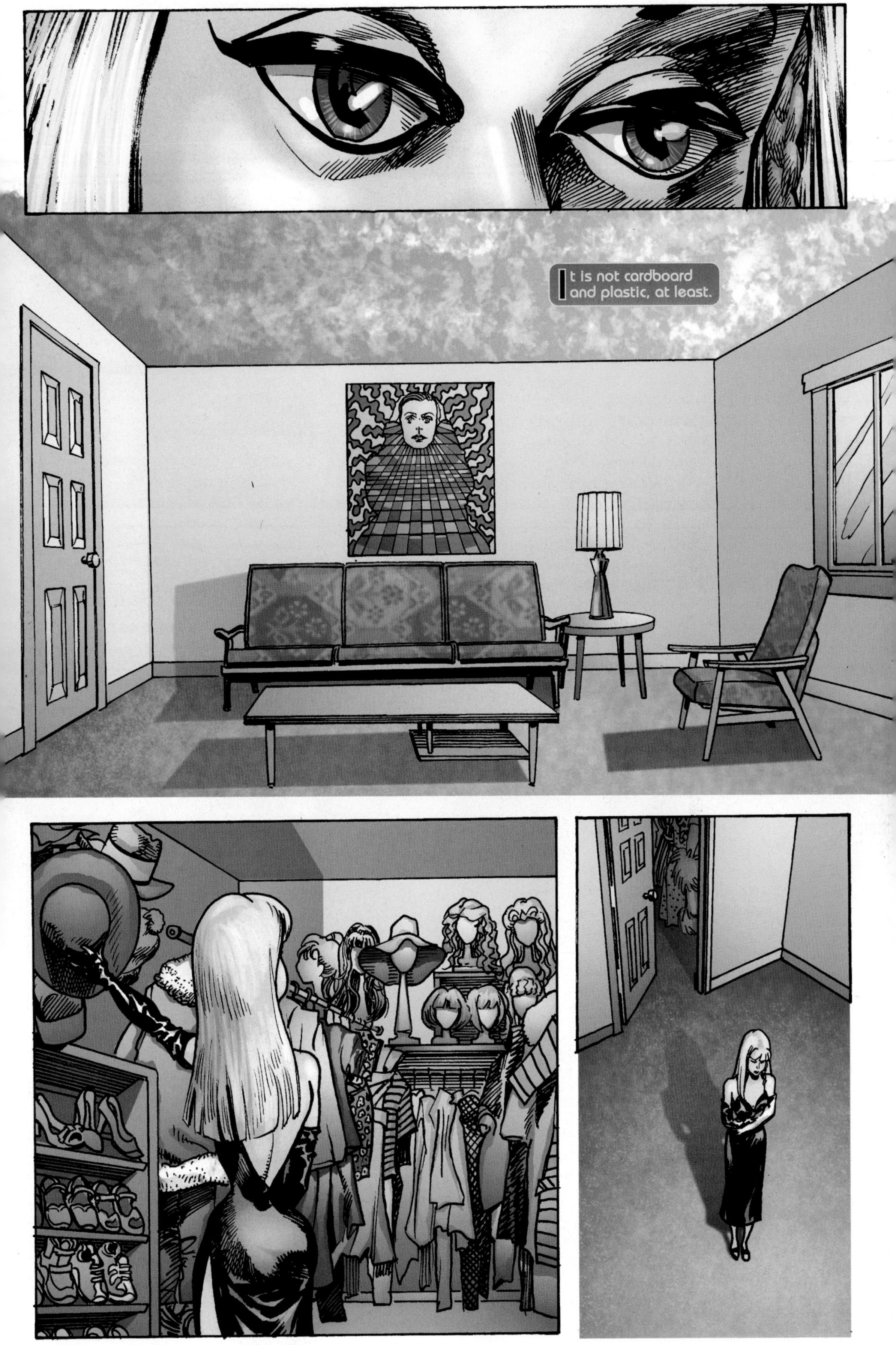
It is not cardboard and plastic, at least.

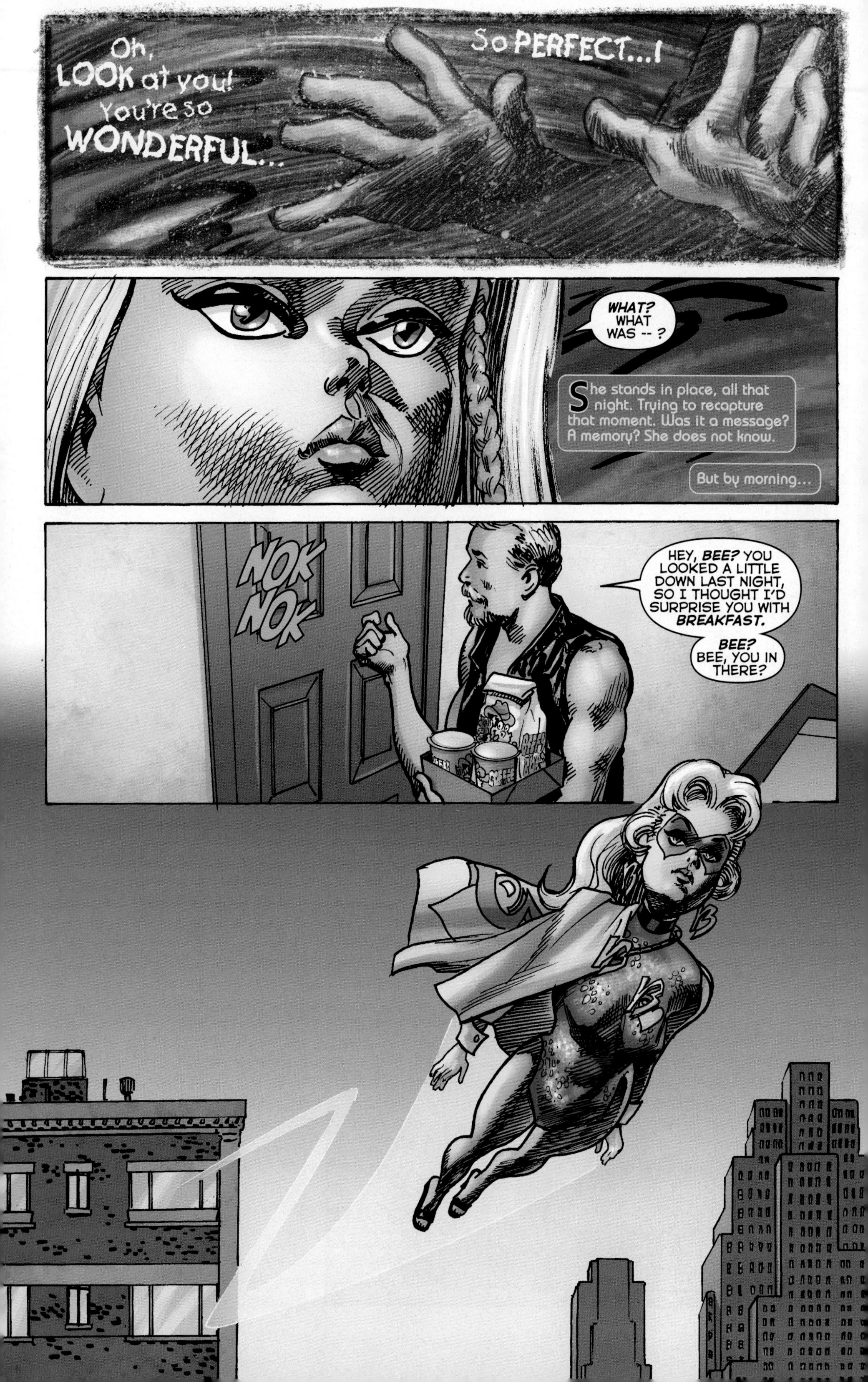
Oh, LOOK at you! You're so WONDERFUL...
So PERFECT...!
WHAT? WHAT WAS -- ?
She stands in place, all that night. Trying to recapture that moment. Was it a message? A memory? She does not know.
But by morning...
NOK NOK
HEY, BEE? YOU LOOKED A LITTLE DOWN LAST NIGHT, SO I THOUGHT I'D SURPRISE YOU WITH BREAKFAST.
BEE? BEE, YOU IN THERE?

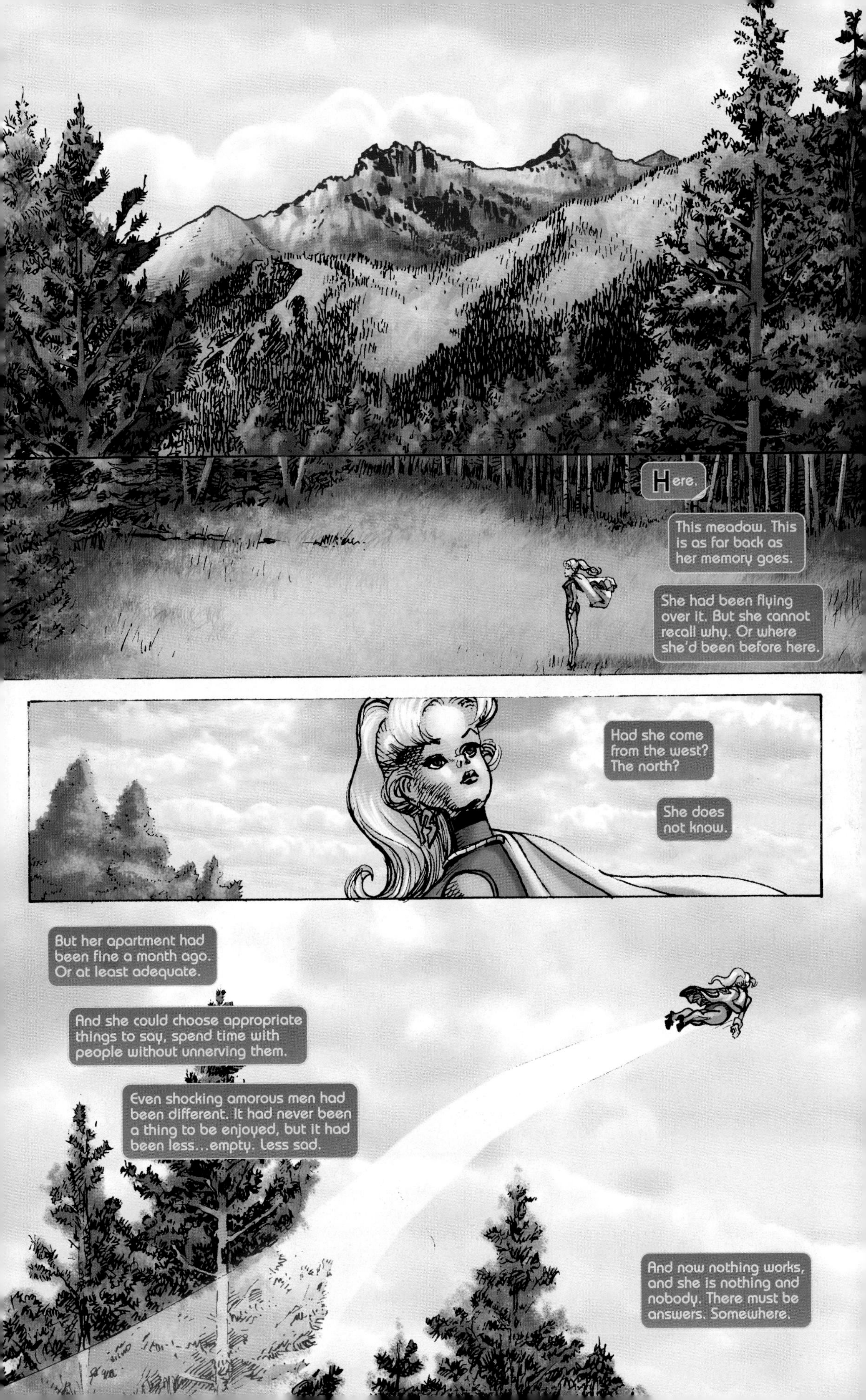
Here.
This meadow. This is as far back as her memory goes.
She had been flying over it. But she cannot recall why. Or where she'd been before here.
Had she come from the west? The north?
She does not know.
But her apartment had been fine a month ago. Or at least adequate.
And she could choose appropriate things to say, spend time with people without unnerving them.
Even shocking amorous men had been different. It had never been a thing to be enjoyed, but it had been less...empty. Less sad.
And now nothing works, and she is nothing and nobody. There must be answers. Somewhere.

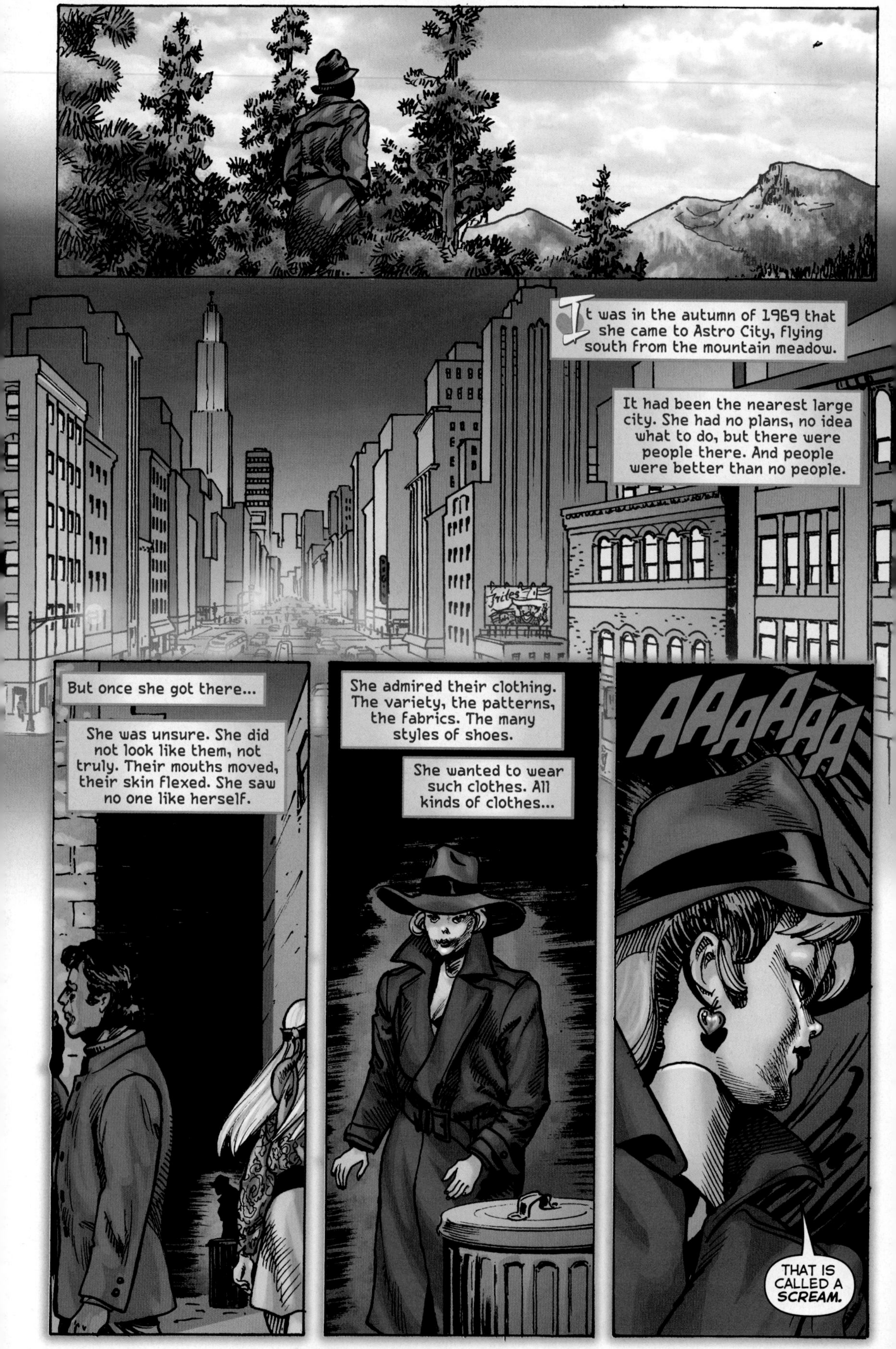
It was in the autumn of 1969 that she came to Astro City, flying south from the mountain meadow.
It had been the nearest large city. She had no plans, no idea what to do, but there were people there. And people were better than no people.
But once she got there...
She was unsure. She did not look like them, not truly. Their mouths moved, their skin flexed. She saw no one like herself.
She admired their clothing. The variety, the patterns, the fabrics. The many styles of shoes.
She wanted to wear such clothes. All kinds of clothes...
AAAAAA
THAT IS CALLED A SCREAM.

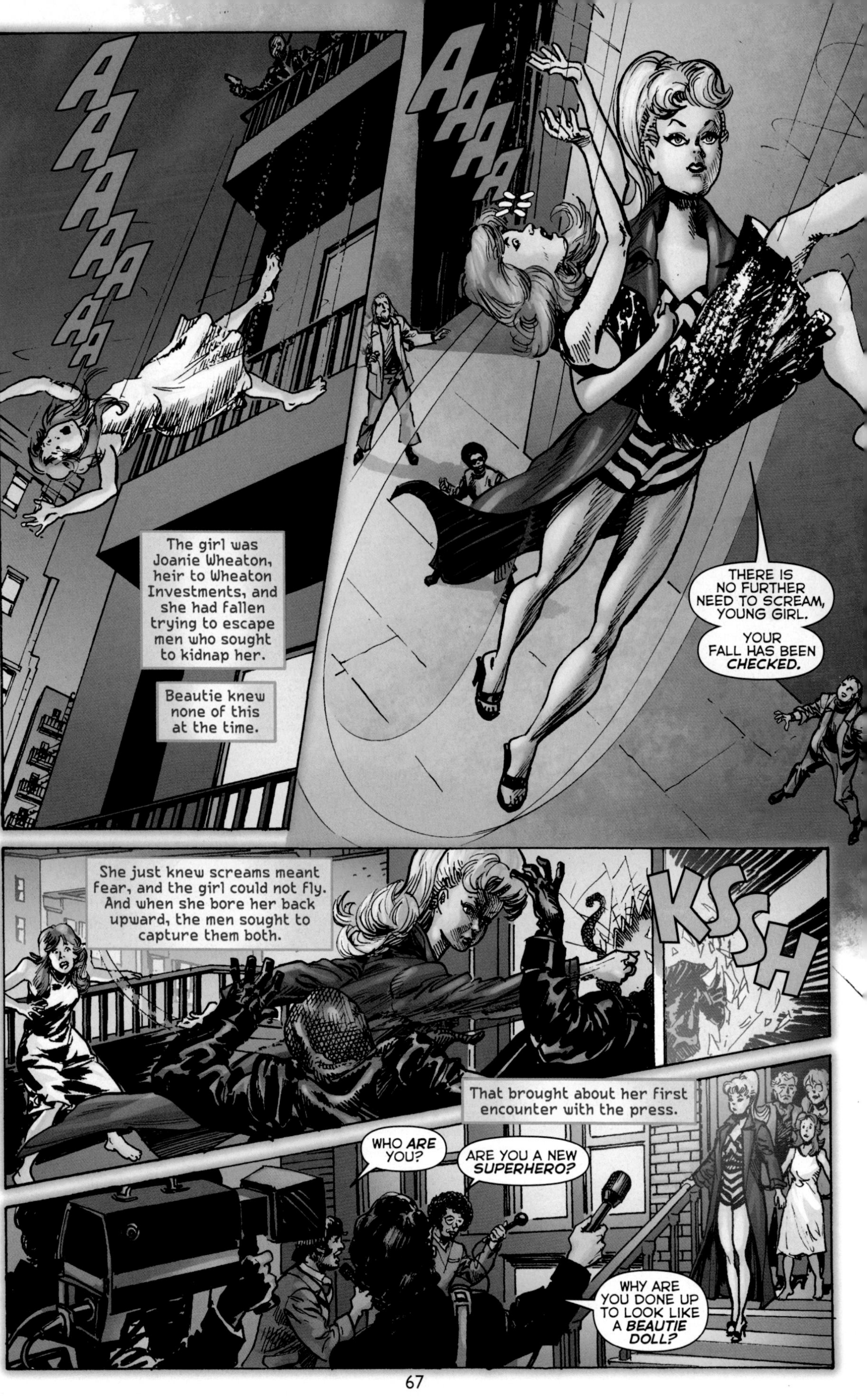
AAAAAAAAAA
AAAAA
The girl was Joanie Wheaton, heir to Wheaton Investments, and she had fallen trying to escape men who sought to kidnap her.
Beautie knew none of this at the time.
THERE IS NO FURTHER NEED TO SCREAM, YOUNG GIRL.
YOUR FALL HAS BEEN *CHECKED.*
She just knew screams meant fear, and the girl could not fly. And when she bore her back upward, the men sought to capture them both.
KSSH
That brought about her first encounter with the press.
WHO *ARE* YOU?
ARE YOU A NEW *SUPERHERO?*
WHY ARE YOU DONE UP TO LOOK LIKE A *BEAUTIE DOLL?*

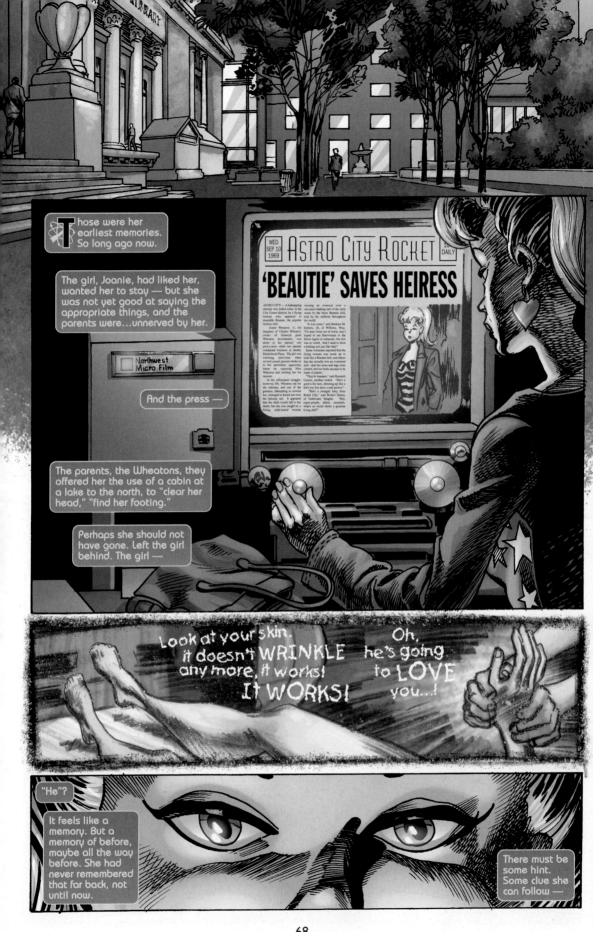

Those were her earliest memories. So long ago now.

The girl, Joanie, had liked her, wanted her to stay — but she was not yet good at saying the appropriate things, and the parents were...unnerved by her.

And the press —

The parents, the Wheatons, they offered her the use of a cabin at a lake to the north, to "clear her head," "find her footing."

Perhaps she should not have gone. Left the girl behind. The girl —

Northwest Micro Film

WED SEP 10 1969

ASTRO CITY ROCKET

10¢ DAILY

'BEAUTIE' SAVES HEIRESS

ASTRO CITY — A kidnapping attempt was foiled today in the City Center district, by a flying woman who appeared to resemble Beautie, the popular fashion doll.

Joanie Wheaton, 11, the daughter of financial giant Charles Wheaton, owner of financial giant Wheaton Investments, was alone in her parents' city pied-a-terre while her parents conducted business in nearby Binderbeck Plaza. The girl was watching television when several armed gunmen broke in to the apartment, apparently intent on capturing Miss Wheaton and holding her for ransom.

In the subsequent struggle, however, Ms. Wheaton ran for the balcony, and one of the gunmen, attempting to restrain her, managed to knock her over the balcony rail. It appeared that the child would fall to her death, but she was caught by a flying, pink-haired woman

wearing an overcoat over a one-piece bathing suit of the style worn by the basic Beautie doll, sold by the millions throughout the world.

"It was crazy," said Barbara M. Roberts, 26, of Willows, Wisc. "I'm here from out of town, and I hoped to see Starwoman or the Silver Agent or someone, but this was so weird. And I used to have a bathing suit just like that!"

Some witnesses reported that the flying woman was made up to look like a Beautie doll, and others that she actually was an oversized doll—that her arms and legs were jointed, and her body seemed to be made of plastic.

"They're humans," said Kenneth Carota, another tourist. "She's good-for her son, dressing up like a kid's toy, but she's a real person."

"She's a swingin' kitty from Robot City," said Robert Henry, of Goldwater Heights. "Hey, super-people, aliens, monsters, what's so weird about a genuine living doll?"

"He"?

It feels like a memory. But a memory of before, maybe all the way before. She had never remembered that far back, not until now.

Look at your skin. It doesn't WRINKLE any more, it works! It WORKS!

Oh, he's going to LOVE you...!

There must be some hint. Some clue she can follow —

68

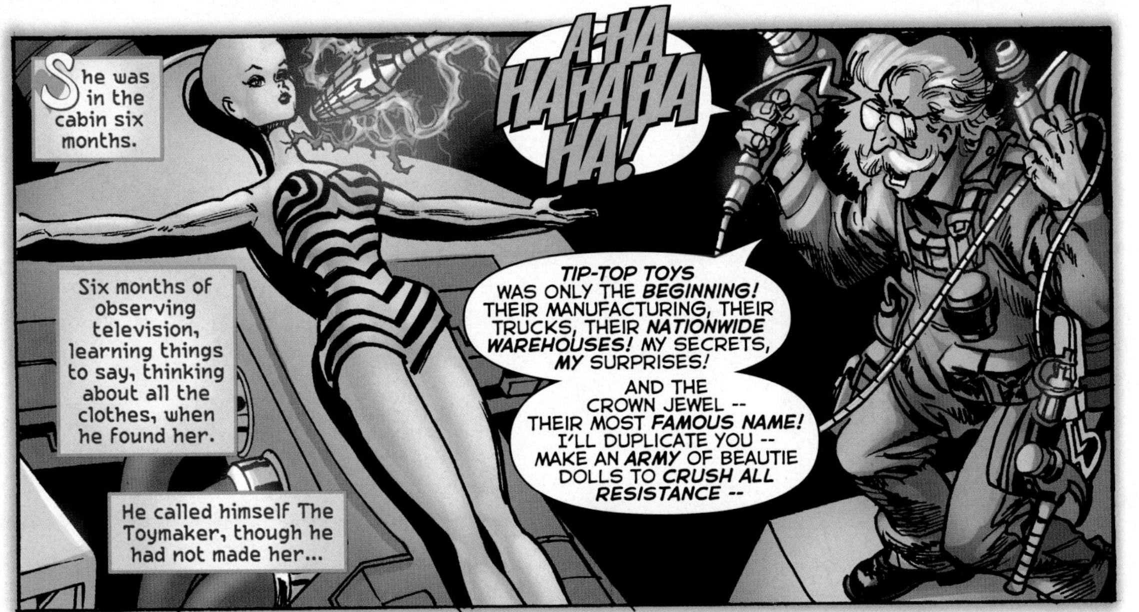
She was in the cabin six months.
A-HA HAHAHAHA HA!
Six months of observing television, learning things to say, thinking about all the clothes, when he found her.
TIP-TOP TOYS WAS ONLY THE BEGINNING! THEIR MANUFACTURING, THEIR TRUCKS, THEIR NATIONWIDE WAREHOUSES! MY SECRETS, MY SURPRISES!
AND THE CROWN JEWEL -- THEIR MOST FAMOUS NAME! I'LL DUPLICATE YOU -- MAKE AN ARMY OF BEAUTIE DOLLS TO CRUSH ALL RESISTANCE --
He called himself The Toymaker, though he had not made her...

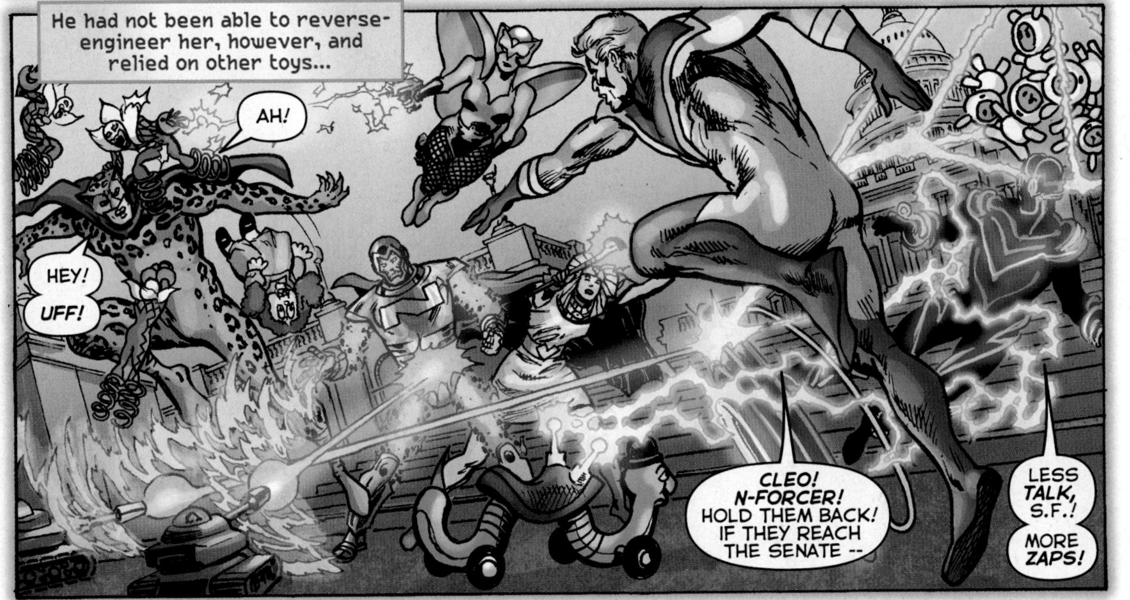
He had not been able to reverse-engineer her, however, and relied on other toys...
AH!
HEY!
UFF!
CLEO! N-FORCER! HOLD THEM BACK! IF THEY REACH THE SENATE --
LESS TALK, S.F.!
MORE ZAPS!

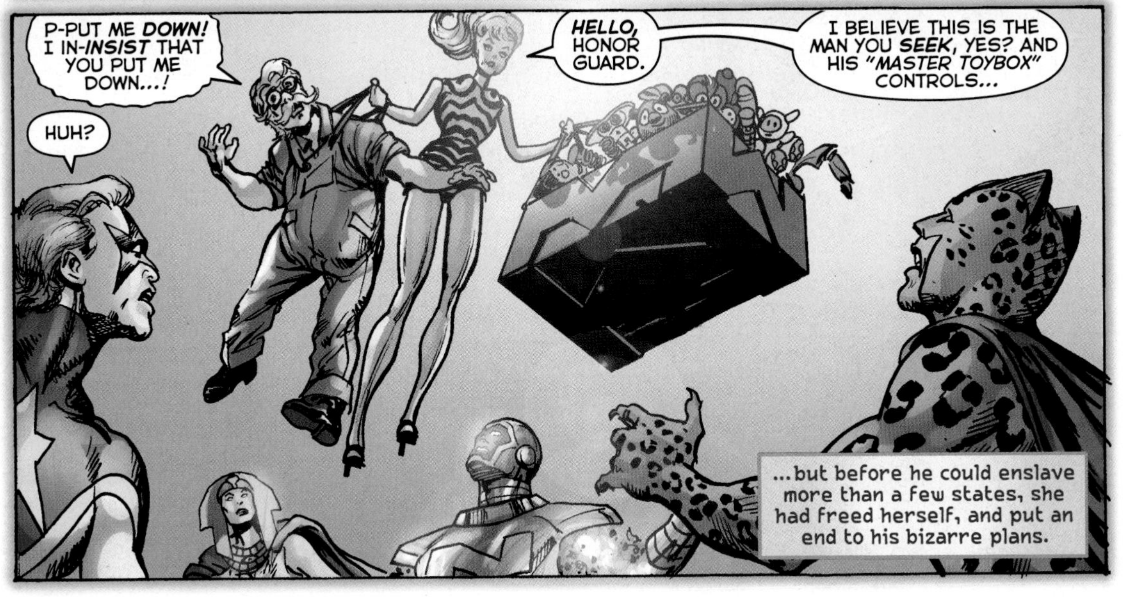
P-PUT ME DOWN! I IN-INSIST THAT YOU PUT ME DOWN...!
HUH?
HELLO, HONOR GUARD.
I BELIEVE THIS IS THE MAN YOU SEEK, YES? AND HIS "MASTER TOYBOX" CONTROLS...
...but before he could enslave more than a few states, she had freed herself, and put an end to his bizarre plans.

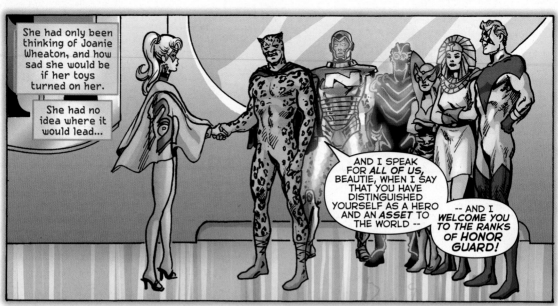

She had only been thinking of Joanie Wheaton, and how sad she would be if her toys turned on her.

She had no idea where it would lead...

AND I SPEAK FOR *ALL OF US*, BEAUTIE, WHEN I SAY THAT YOU HAVE *DISTINGUISHED* YOURSELF AS A HERO AND AN *ASSET* TO THE WORLD --

-- AND I *WELCOME YOU* TO THE RANKS OF *HONOR GUARD!*

...or how deep...

...PRECEDENT SET BY *LOONEY LEO V. FAGO'S FUNNY FEATURES*...

I *SEE.*

COUNSELOR? DOES TIP-TOP TOYS HAVE ANY *OBJECTION* TO THE RECOGNITION OF THIS BEING AS A *FREE PERSON* AND *CITIZEN?*

NONE WHATSOEVER, YOUR HONOR -- *PARTICULARLY* IN RECOGNITION OF HER HELP IN SAVING OUR COMPANY FROM A MADMAN.

WE DO HAVE SOME *TRADEMARK* CONCERNS, HOWEVER, AS WELL AS AN *OFFER* WE'D LIKE TO MAKE TO THE ARTIFICIAL YOUNG LADY...

...or how... loud.

AND SO WE'RE PLEASED TO INTRODUCE OUR NEW *COMPANY SYMBOL* AND *SPOKESMAN* -- THE *WORLD'S* ONLY LIVING, BREATHING BEAUTIE DOLL!

CLAP CLAP CLAP CLAP CLAP CLAP CLAP

I, AH, DO NOT ACTUALLY *BREATHE*...

The duties of the position were reasonably light. But it allowed her to keep the only name she knew.

And it paid enough for an apartment. For clothes.

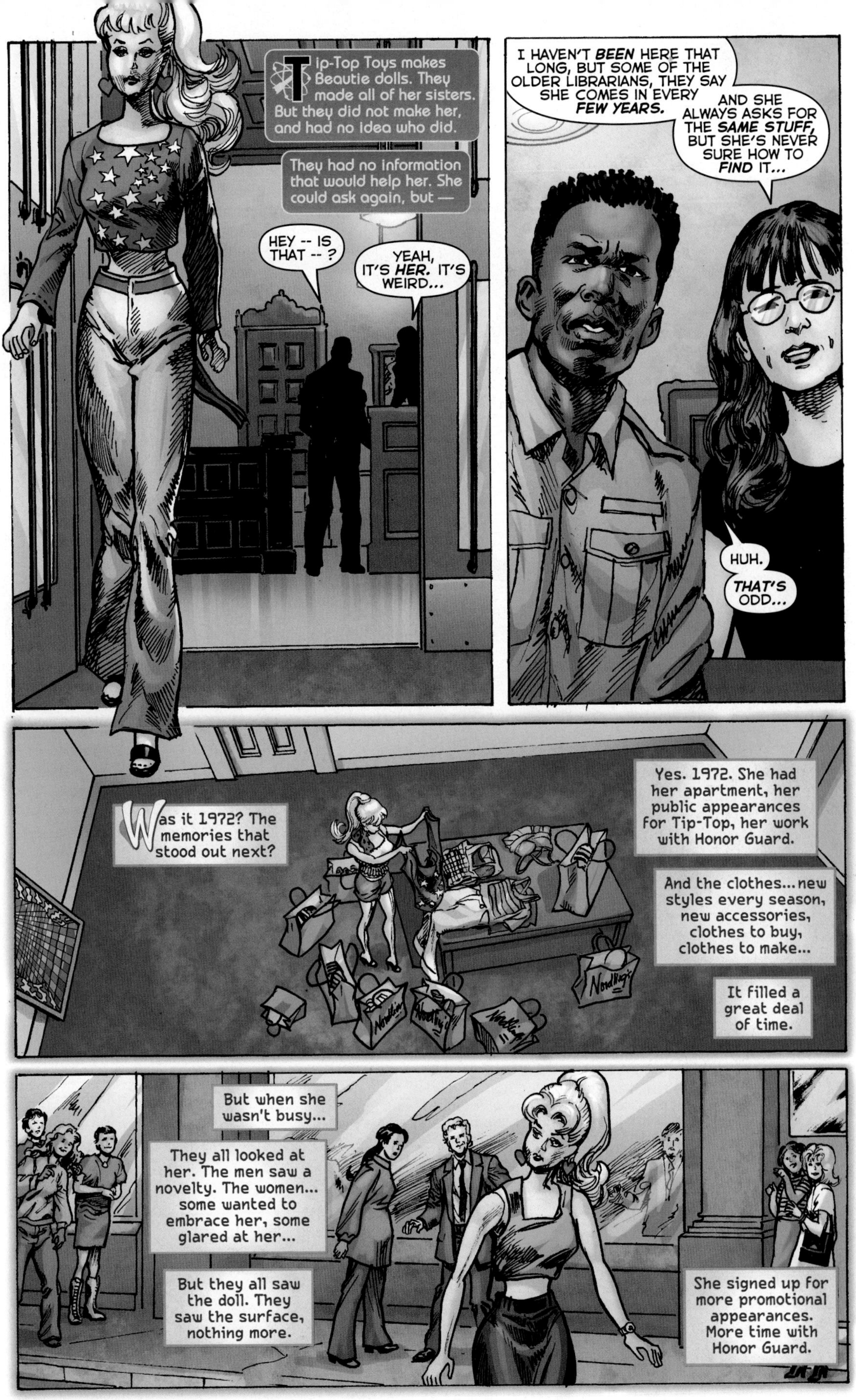
Tip-Top Toys makes Beautie dolls. They made all of her sisters. But they did not make her, and had no idea who did.
They had no information that would help her. She could ask again, but —
HEY -- IS THAT -- ?
YEAH, IT'S HER. IT'S WEIRD...
I HAVEN'T BEEN HERE THAT LONG, BUT SOME OF THE OLDER LIBRARIANS, THEY SAY SHE COMES IN EVERY FEW YEARS.
AND SHE ALWAYS ASKS FOR THE SAME STUFF, BUT SHE'S NEVER SURE HOW TO FIND IT...
HUH. THAT'S ODD...
Was it 1972? The memories that stood out next?
Yes. 1972. She had her apartment, her public appearances for Tip-Top, her work with Honor Guard.
And the clothes... new styles every season, new accessories, clothes to buy, clothes to make...
It filled a great deal of time.
But when she wasn't busy...
They all looked at her. The men saw a novelty. The women... some wanted to embrace her, some glared at her...
But they all saw the doll. They saw the surface, nothing more.
She signed up for more promotional appearances. More time with Honor Guard.

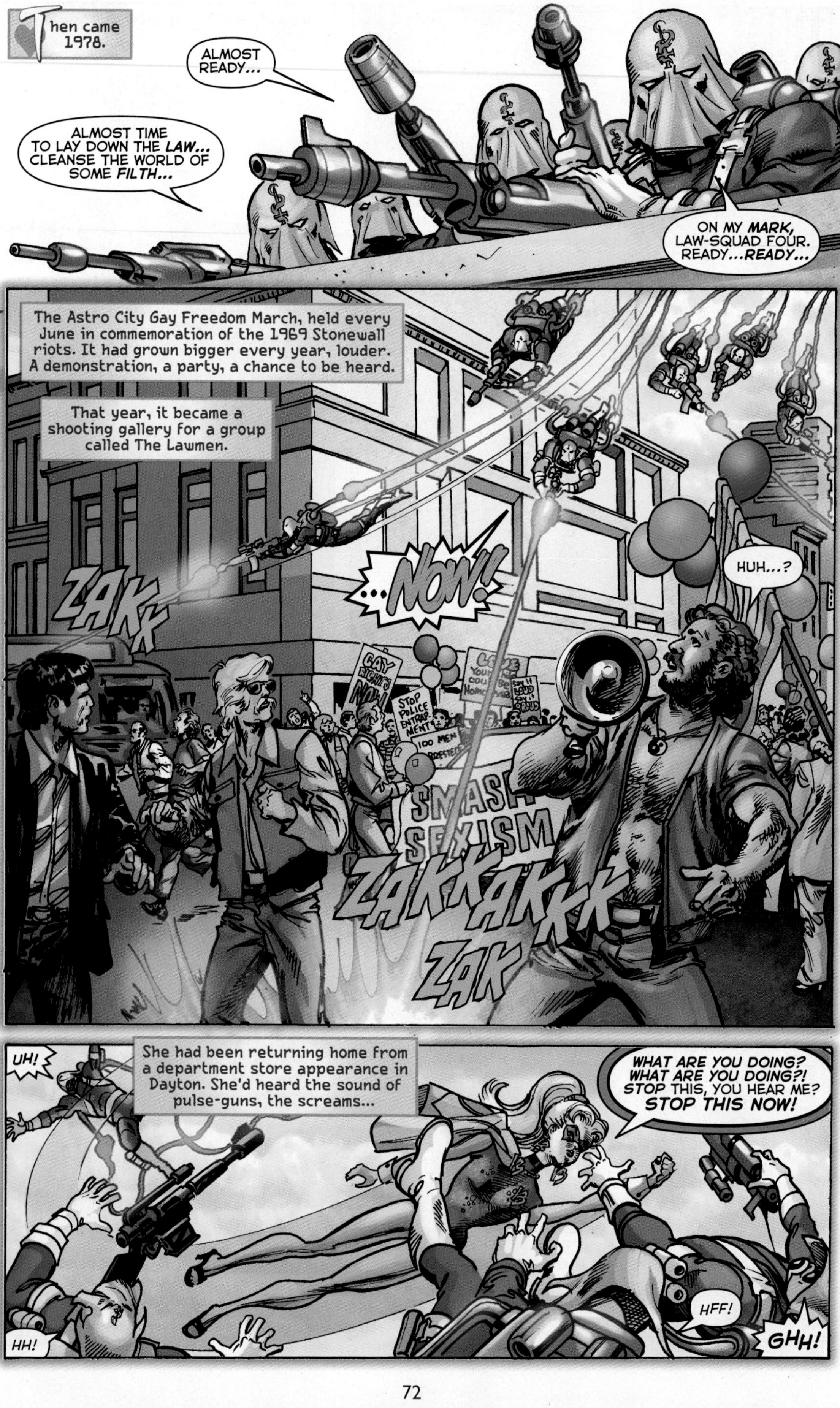
Then came 1978.
ALMOST READY...
ALMOST TIME TO LAY DOWN THE *LAW*... CLEANSE THE WORLD OF SOME *FILTH*...
ON MY *MARK*, LAW-SQUAD FOUR. READY... *READY*...
The Astro City Gay Freedom March, held every June in commemoration of the 1969 Stonewall riots. It had grown bigger every year, louder. A demonstration, a party, a chance to be heard.
That year, it became a shooting gallery for a group called The Lawmen.
ZAKK
...NOW!
HUH...?
GAY RIGHTS NOW!
STOP POLICE ENTRAPMENT
100 MEN
SMASH SEXISM
ZAKKAKKK
ZAK
She had been returning home from a department store appearance in Dayton. She'd heard the sound of pulse-guns, the screams...
UH!
WHAT ARE YOU DOING? WHAT ARE YOU DOING?! STOP THIS, YOU HEAR ME? **STOP THIS NOW!**
HFF!
HH!
GHH!

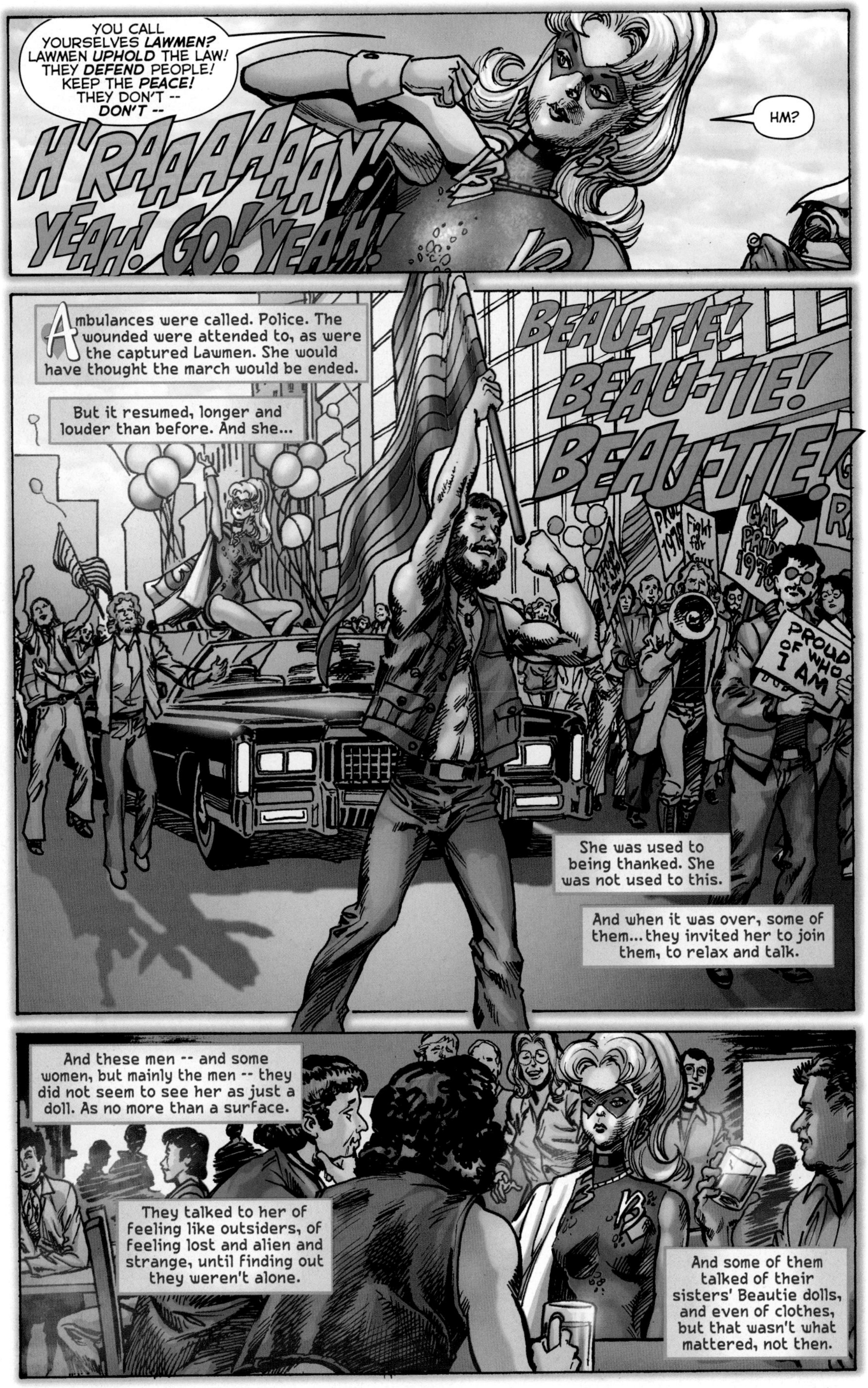
YOU CALL YOURSELVES LAWMEN? LAWMEN UPHOLD THE LAW! THEY DEFEND PEOPLE! KEEP THE PEACE! THEY DON'T -- DON'T --
HM?
H'RAAAAAAY! YEAH! GO! YEAH!
Ambulances were called. Police. The wounded were attended to, as were the captured Lawmen. She would have thought the march would be ended.
But it resumed, longer and louder than before. And she...
BEAU-TIE! BEAU-TIE! BEAU-TIE!
Fight for Your
GAY PRIDE 1978
PROUD OF WHO I AM
She was used to being thanked. She was not used to this.
And when it was over, some of them... they invited her to join them, to relax and talk.
And these men -- and some women, but mainly the men -- they did not seem to see her as just a doll. As no more than a surface.
They talked to her of feeling like outsiders, of feeling lost and alien and strange, until finding out they weren't alone.
And some of them talked of their sisters' Beautie dolls, and even of clothes, but that wasn't what mattered, not then.

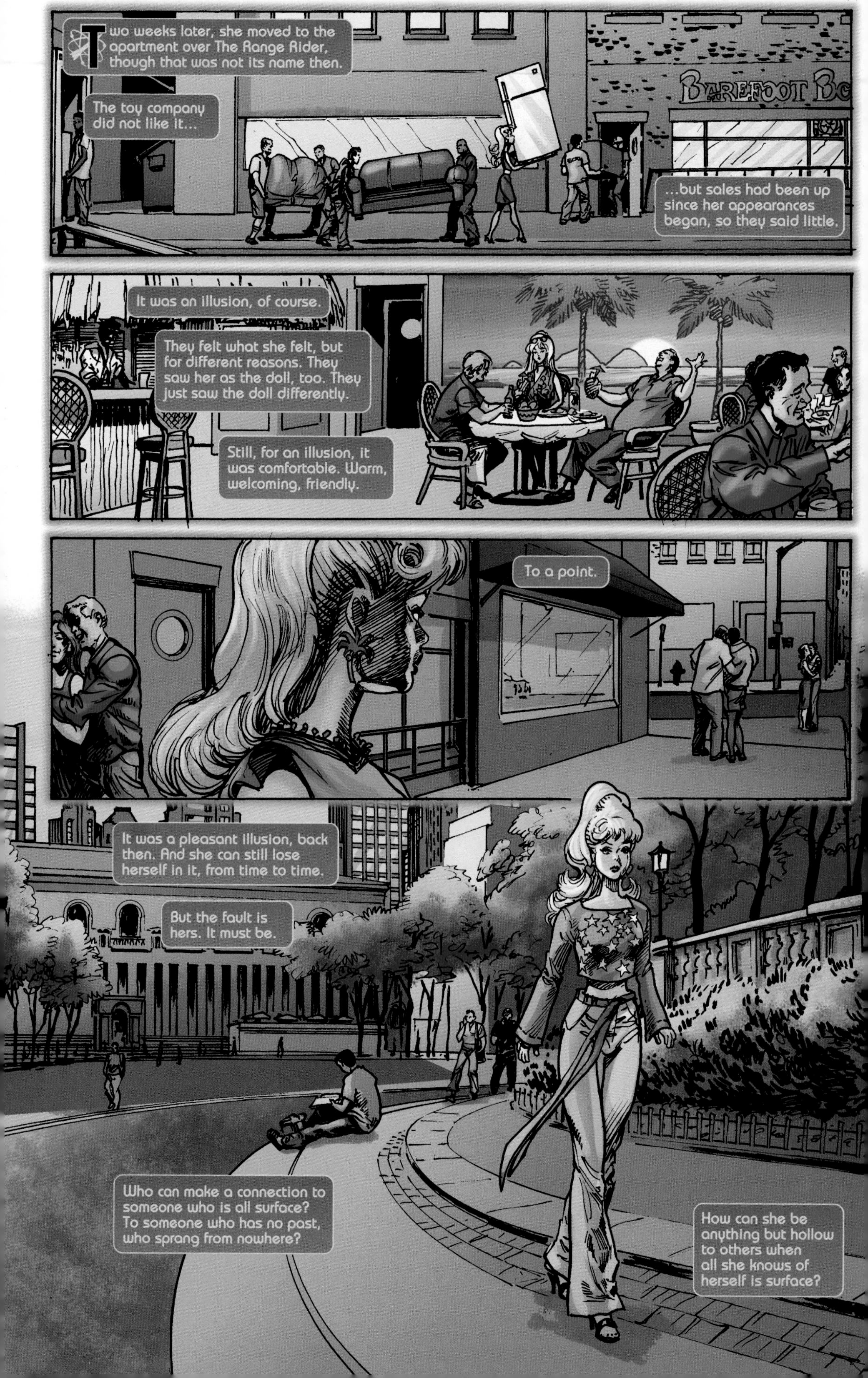
Two weeks later, she moved to the apartment over The Range Rider, though that was not its name then.
The toy company did not like it...
BAREFOOT BO
...but sales had been up since her appearances began, so they said little.
It was an illusion, of course.
They felt what she felt, but for different reasons. They saw her as the doll, too. They just saw the doll differently.
Still, for an illusion, it was comfortable. Warm, welcoming, friendly.
To a point.
It was a pleasant illusion, back then. And she can still lose herself in it, from time to time.
But the fault is hers. It must be.
Who can make a connection to someone who is all surface? To someone who has no past, who sprang from nowhere?
How can she be anything but hollow to others when all she knows of herself is surface?

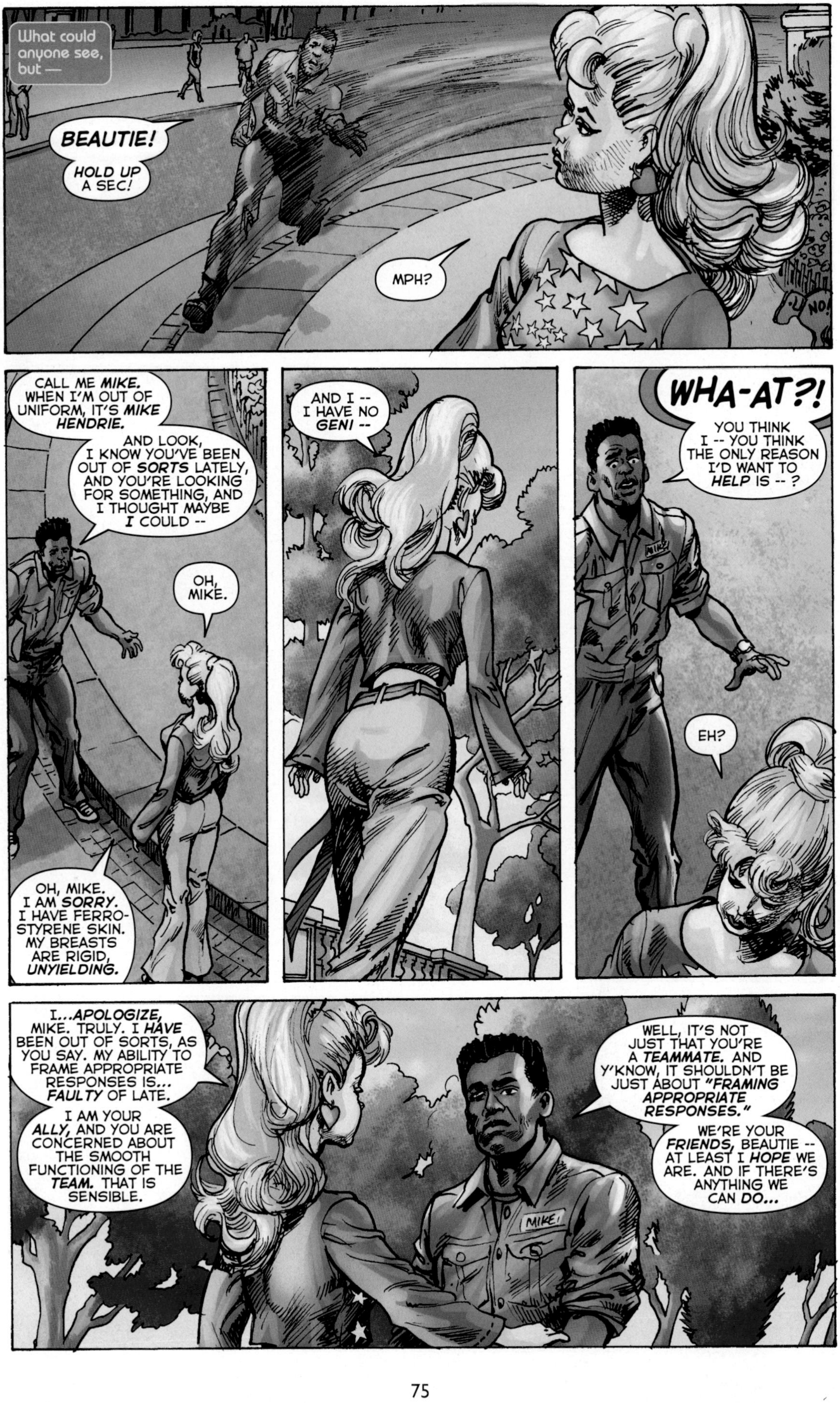
What could anyone see, but —
BEAUTIE!
HOLD UP A SEC!
MPH?
CALL ME MIKE. WHEN I'M OUT OF UNIFORM, IT'S MIKE HENDRIE.
AND LOOK, I KNOW YOU'VE BEEN OUT OF SORTS LATELY, AND YOU'RE LOOKING FOR SOMETHING, AND I THOUGHT MAYBE I COULD --
OH, MIKE.
OH, MIKE. I AM SORRY. I HAVE FERRO-STYRENE SKIN. MY BREASTS ARE RIGID, UNYIELDING.
AND I -- I HAVE NO GENI --
WHA-AT?!
YOU THINK I -- YOU THINK THE ONLY REASON I'D WANT TO HELP IS -- ?
EH?
I...APOLOGIZE, MIKE. TRULY. I HAVE BEEN OUT OF SORTS, AS YOU SAY. MY ABILITY TO FRAME APPROPRIATE RESPONSES IS... FAULTY OF LATE.
I AM YOUR ALLY, AND YOU ARE CONCERNED ABOUT THE SMOOTH FUNCTIONING OF THE TEAM. THAT IS SENSIBLE.
WELL, IT'S NOT JUST THAT YOU'RE A TEAMMATE. AND Y'KNOW, IT SHOULDN'T BE JUST ABOUT "FRAMING APPROPRIATE RESPONSES."
WE'RE YOUR FRIENDS, BEAUTIE -- AT LEAST I HOPE WE ARE. AND IF THERE'S ANYTHING WE CAN DO...
MIKE

DO YOU... KNOW WHO I AM? WHERE I CAME FROM? WHO...CREATED ME?

NO, I...I DON'T. BUT IF THAT'S WHAT YOU'RE TRYING TO FIND OUT...

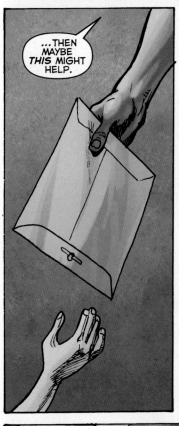

...THEN MAYBE THIS MIGHT HELP.

IT'S JUST SOME STUFF I CULLED FROM THE TEAM'S FILES. IT MIGHT GIVE YOU A STARTING POINT.

AND IF YOU NEED A HAND, OR JUST SOMEONE TO RIDE ALONG, SO YOU'RE NOT DOING THIS ALONE...

THANK YOU, BUT NO...

I...DO NOT UNDERSTAND HOW TO SAY THIS, BUT...

I AM GLAD YOU DID NOT KNOW THE ANSWER. I DON'T WANT TO BE TOLD, I WANT TO FIND OUT. NOT DATA, NOT WORDS. BUT FEELINGS. REALITY.

YOU HAVE KNOWN WHERE YOU COME FROM SINCE YOU WERE BORN. I HAVE NO IDEA.

AND I WANT TO FIND OUT FOR MYSELF. TO DO IT MYSELF. DO YOU UNDERSTAND?

SURE, I GUESS THAT MAKES SENSE. BUT IF YOU NEED ANYTHING, HOLLER. AND IF YOU'RE EVER OUT IN DETROIT, SALLY AND I WOULD BE GLAD TO HAVE YOU DROP BY.

THANK YOU AGAIN, MIKE HENDRIE. YOU ARE A KIND AND GENEROUS MAN.

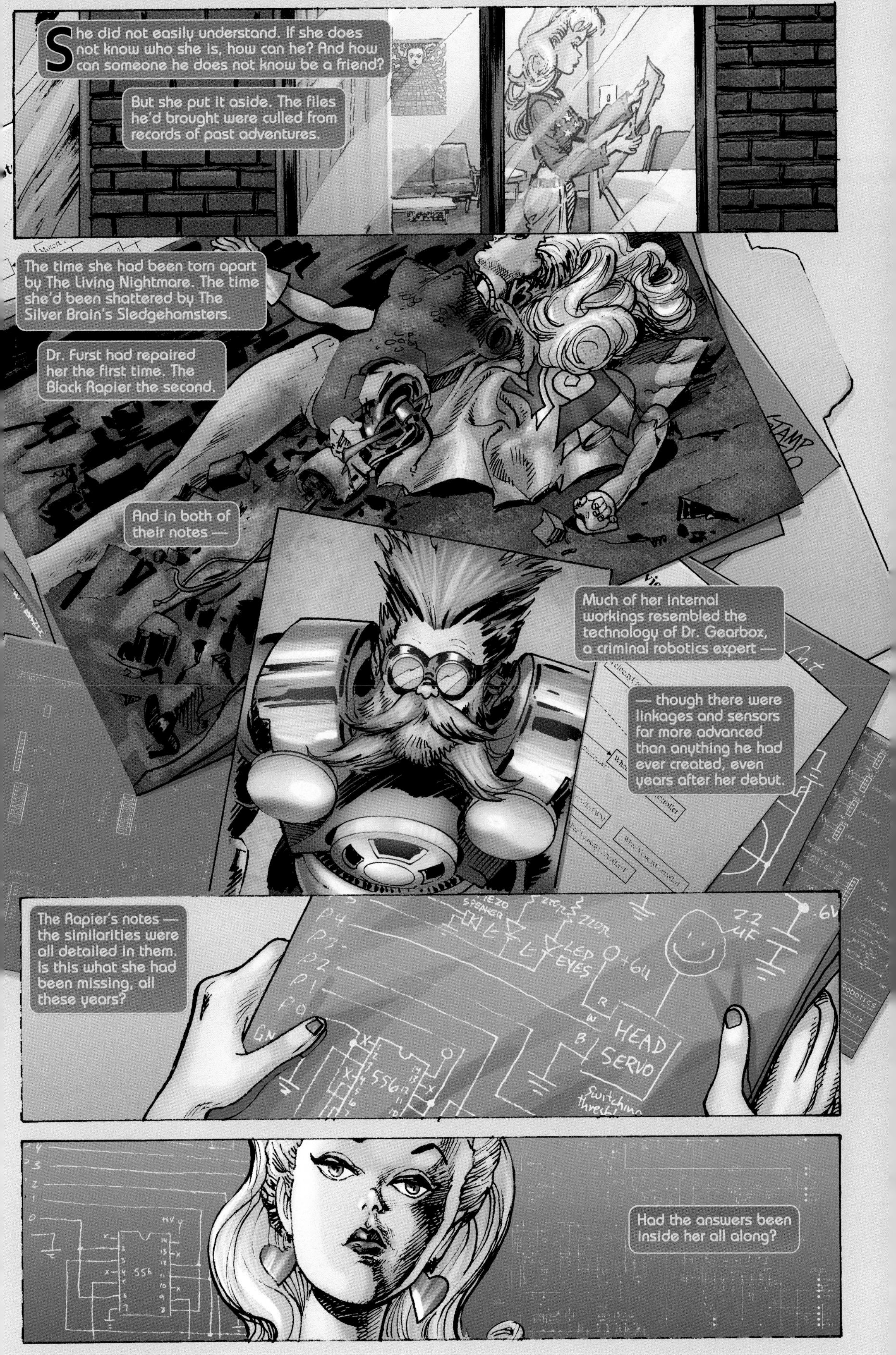
She did not easily understand. If she does not know who she is, how can he? And how can someone he does not know be a friend?
But she put it aside. The files he'd brought were culled from records of past adventures.
The time she had been torn apart by The Living Nightmare. The time she'd been shattered by The Silver Brain's Sledgehamsters.
Dr. Furst had repaired her the first time. The Black Rapier the second.
And in both of their notes —
Much of her internal workings resembled the technology of Dr. Gearbox, a criminal robotics expert —
— though there were linkages and sensors far more advanced than anything he had ever created, even years after her debut.
The Rapier's notes — the similarities were all detailed in them. Is this what she had been missing, all these years?
SPEAKER
LED EYES
HEAD SERVO
556
Had the answers been inside her all along?

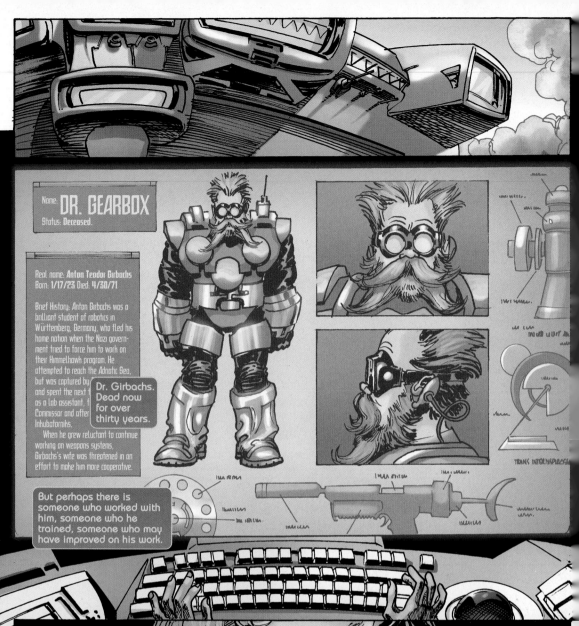

Name: DR. GEARBOX
Status: Deceased.

Real name: Anton Teodor Girbachs
Born: 1/17/23 Died: 4/30/71

Brief History: Anton Girbachs was a brilliant student of robotics in Württemberg, Germany, who fled his home nation when the Nazi government tried to force him to work on their Himmelhawk program. He attempted to reach the Adriatic Sea, but was captured by [...] and spent the next [...] as a lab assistant, f[...] Commissar and after [...] Inkubatornihs.

When he grew reluctant to continue working on weapons systems, Girbachs's wife was threatened in an effort to make him more cooperative.

Dr. Girbachs. Dead now for over thirty years.

But perhaps there is someone who worked with him, someone who he trained, someone who may have improved on his work.

There is no record. He did not trust assistants. He had clients, but no partners.

He had a daughter, however.

She would have been very young when Beautie was made, but perhaps she knows something the files do not.

He's going to be so SURPRISED, isn't he? HA! But he'll LOVE you. I know he will. He'll LOVE YOU...

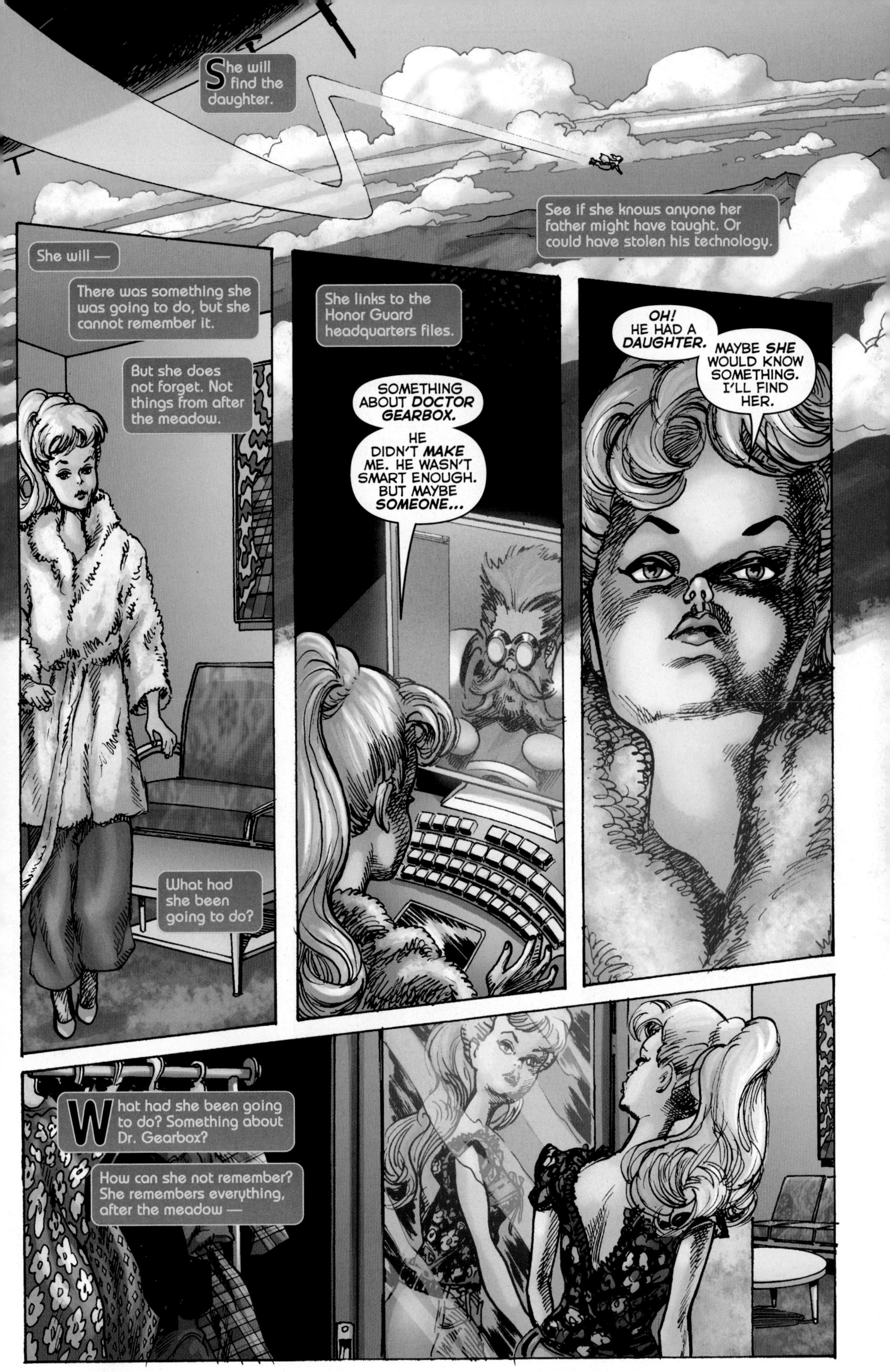
She will find the daughter.
See if she knows anyone her father might have taught. Or could have stolen his technology.
She will —
There was something she was going to do, but she cannot remember it.
But she does not forget. Not things from after the meadow.
What had she been going to do?
She links to the Honor Guard headquarters files.
SOMETHING ABOUT DOCTOR GEARBOX.
HE DIDN'T MAKE ME. HE WASN'T SMART ENOUGH. BUT MAYBE SOMEONE...
OH! HE HAD A DAUGHTER.
MAYBE SHE WOULD KNOW SOMETHING. I'LL FIND HER.
What had she been going to do? Something about Dr. Gearbox?
How can she not remember? She remembers everything, after the meadow —

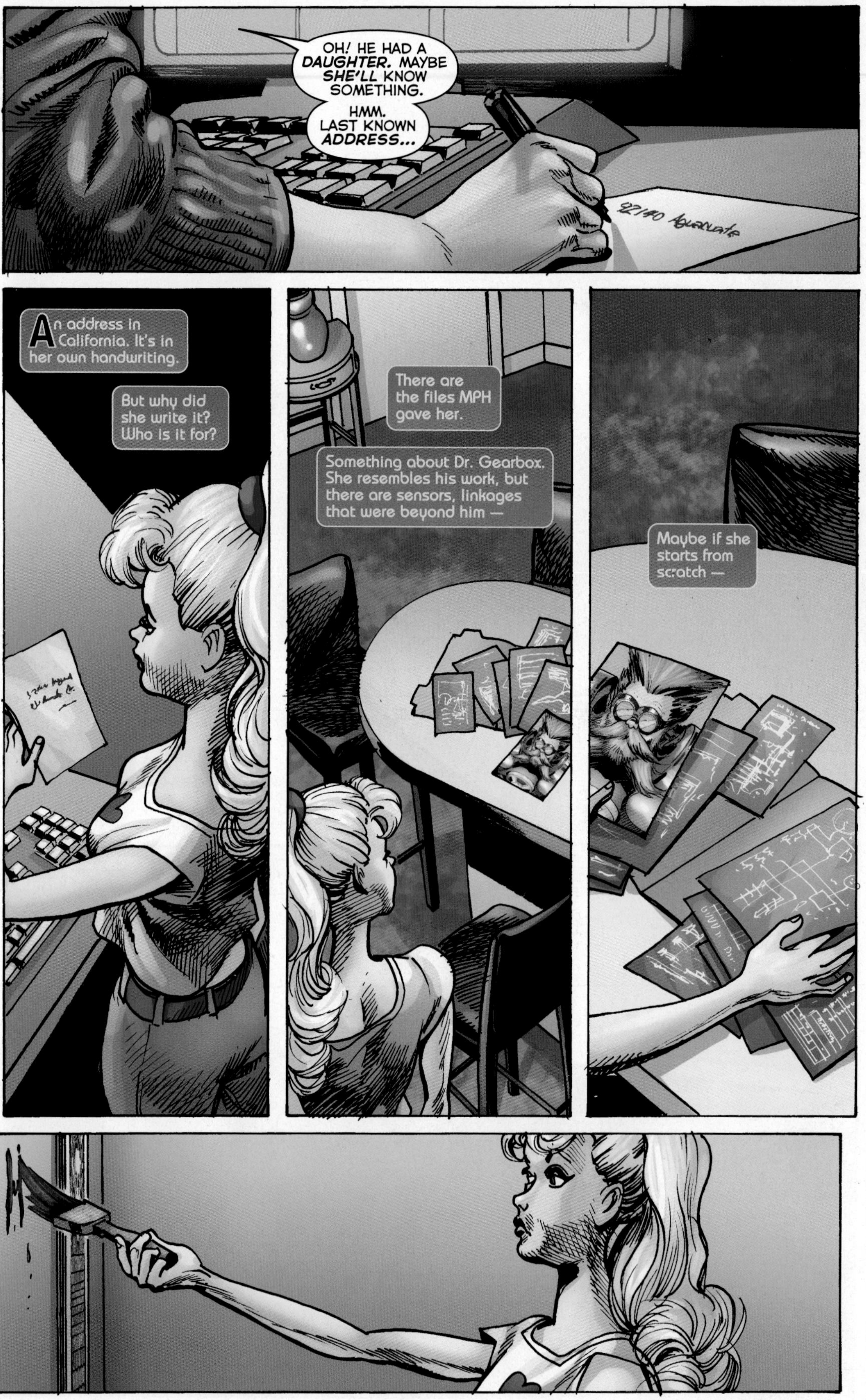
OH! HE HAD A DAUGHTER. MAYBE SHE'LL KNOW SOMETHING.
HMM. LAST KNOWN ADDRESS...
92140 Aguacate
An address in California. It's in her own handwriting.
But why did she write it? Who is it for?
There are the files MPH gave her.
Something about Dr. Gearbox. She resembles his work, but there are sensors, linkages that were beyond him —
Maybe if she starts from scratch —

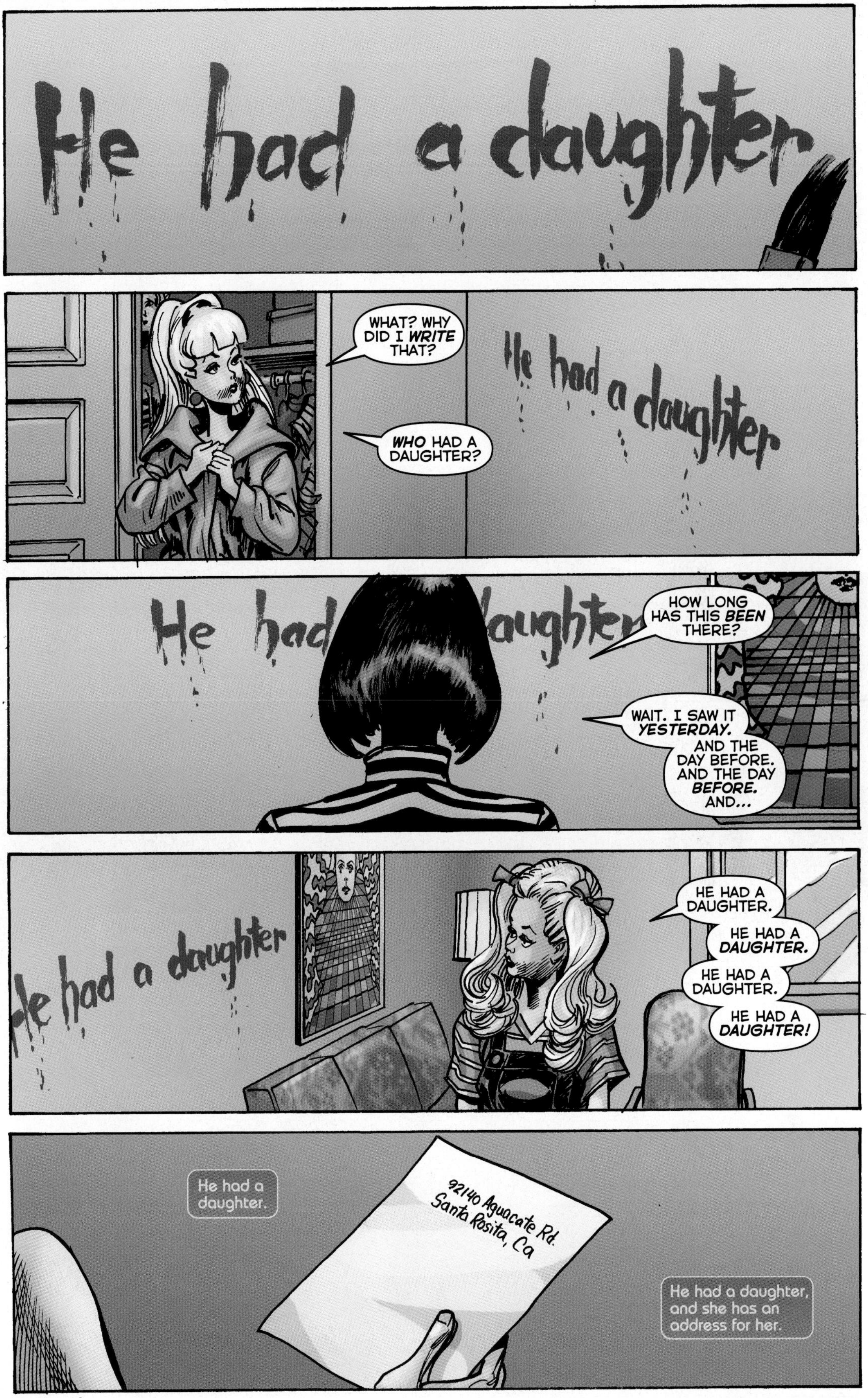
He had a daughter
WHAT? WHY DID I WRITE THAT?
WHO HAD A DAUGHTER?
He had a daughter
HOW LONG HAS THIS BEEN THERE?
WAIT. I SAW IT YESTERDAY.
AND THE DAY BEFORE. AND THE DAY BEFORE. AND...
HE HAD A DAUGHTER.
HE HAD A DAUGHTER.
HE HAD A DAUGHTER.
HE HAD A DAUGHTER!
He had a daughter.
92140 Aguacate Rd.
Santa Rosita, Ca
He had a daughter, and she has an address for her.

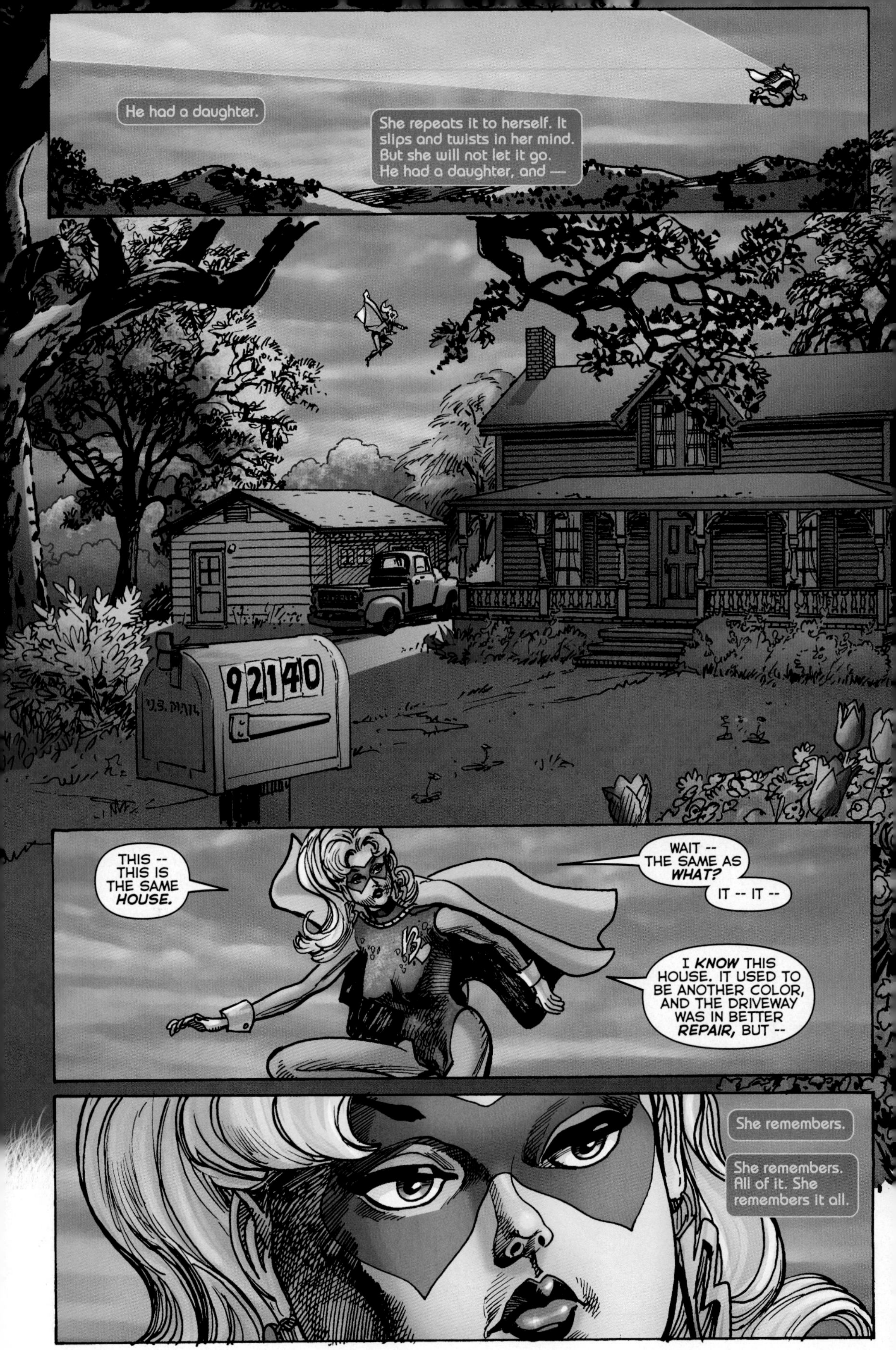
He had a daughter.
She repeats it to herself. It slips and twists in her mind. But she will not let it go. He had a daughter, and —
92140
U.S. MAIL
THIS -- THIS IS THE SAME HOUSE.
WAIT -- THE SAME AS WHAT?
IT -- IT --
I KNOW THIS HOUSE. IT USED TO BE ANOTHER COLOR, AND THE DRIVEWAY WAS IN BETTER REPAIR, BUT --
She remembers.
She remembers. All of it. She remembers it all.

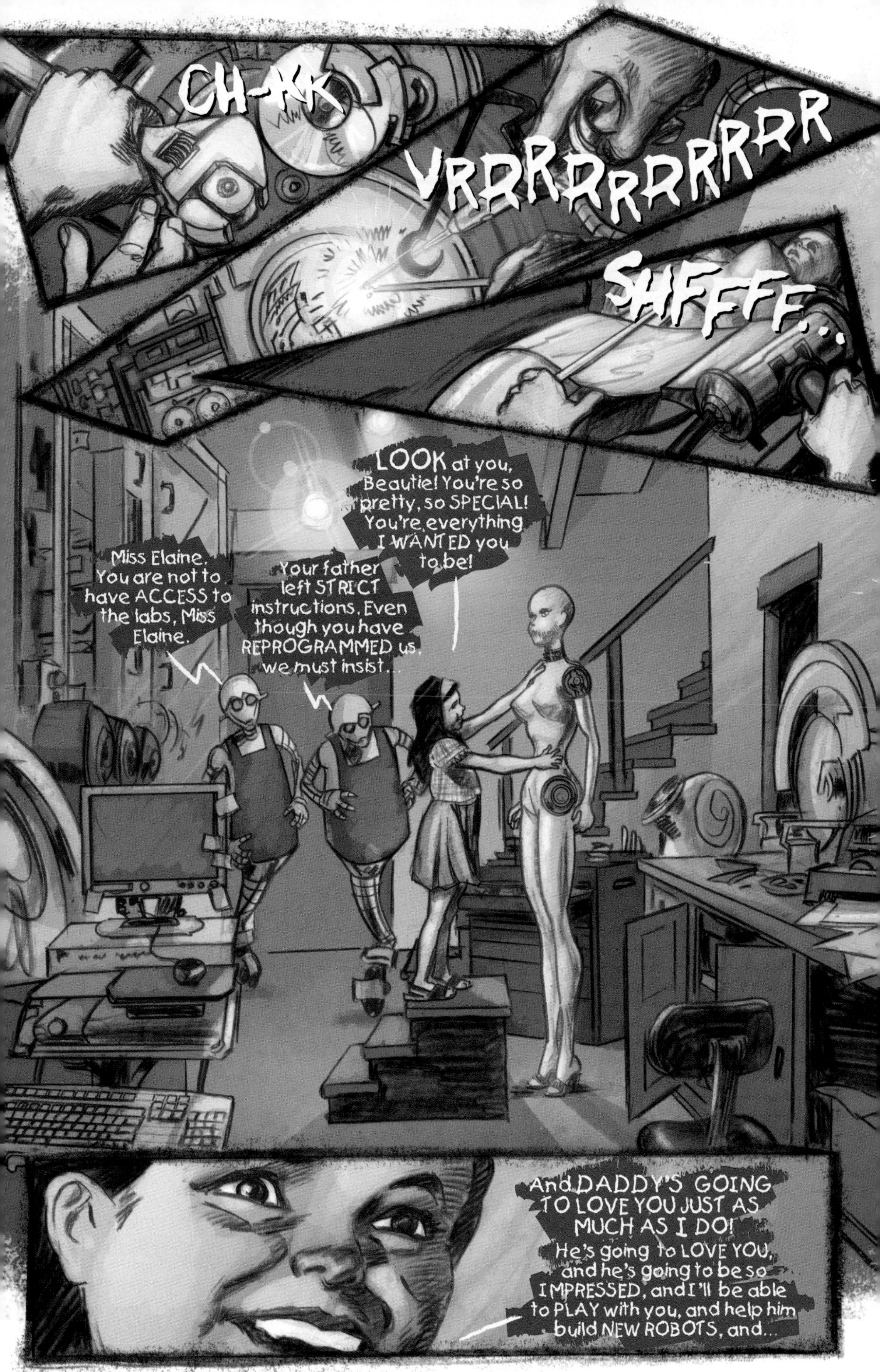
CH-KK
VRRRRRRRRRR
SHFFFF...
Miss Elaine. You are not to have ACCESS to the labs, Miss Elaine.
Your father left STRICT instructions. Even though you have REPROGRAMMED us, we must insist...
LOOK at you, Beautie! You're so pretty, so SPECIAL! You're everything I WANTED you to be!
And DADDY'S GOING TO LOVE YOU JUST AS MUCH AS I DO!
He's going to LOVE YOU, and he's going to be so IMPRESSED, and I'll be able to PLAY with you, and help him build NEW ROBOTS, and...

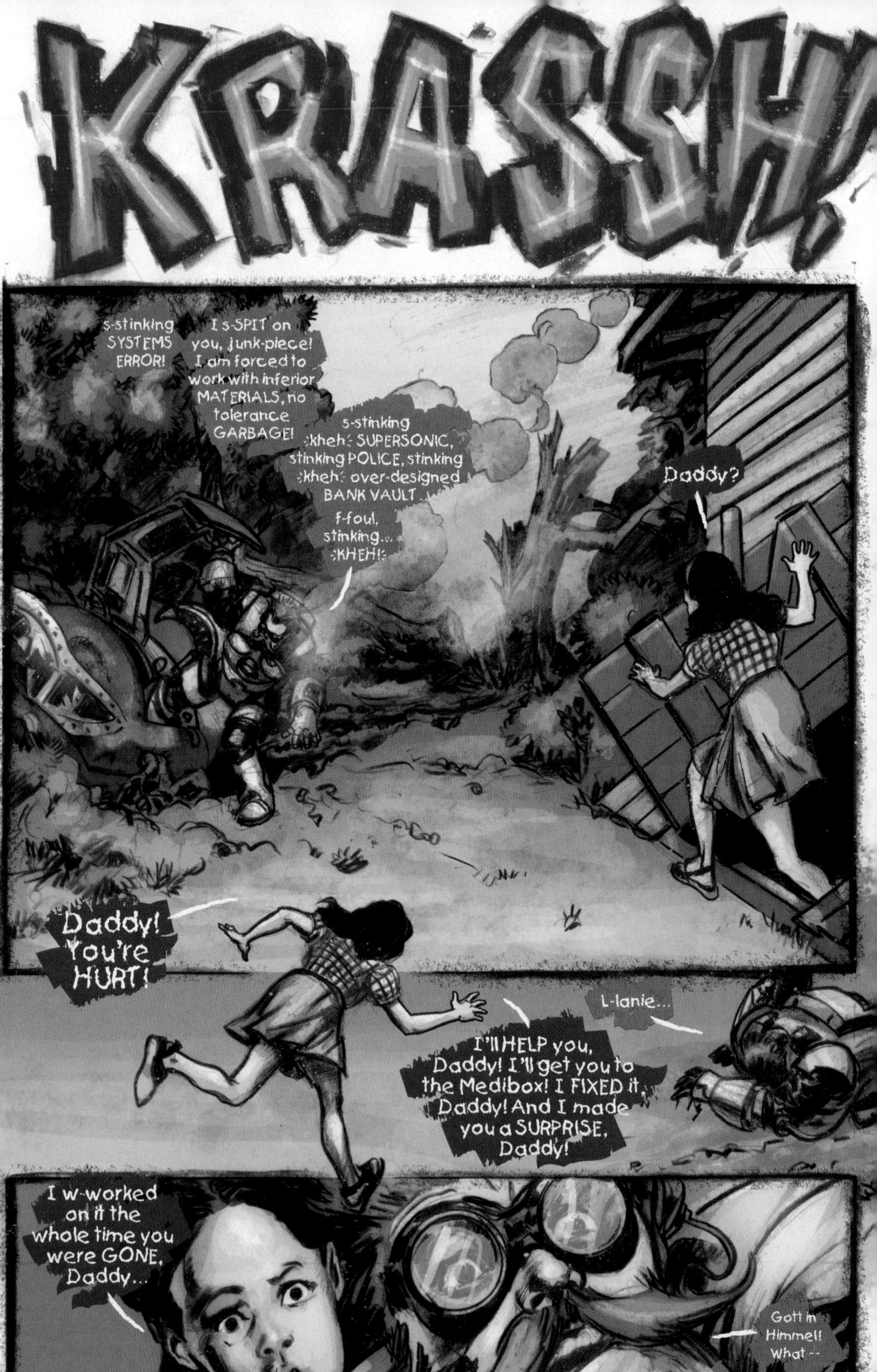
KRASSH!
s-stinking SYSTEMS ERROR!
I s-SPIT on you, junk-piece! I am forced to work with inferior MATERIALS, no tolerance GARBAGE!
s-stinking :kheh: SUPERSONIC, stinking POLICE, stinking :kheh: over-designed BANK VAULT...
f-foul, stinking... :KHEH!:
Daddy?
Daddy! You're HURT!
L-lanie...
I'll HELP you, Daddy! I'll get you to the Medibox! I FIXED it, Daddy! And I made you a SURPRISE, Daddy!
I w-worked on it the whole time you were GONE, Daddy...
Gott im Himmel! What --

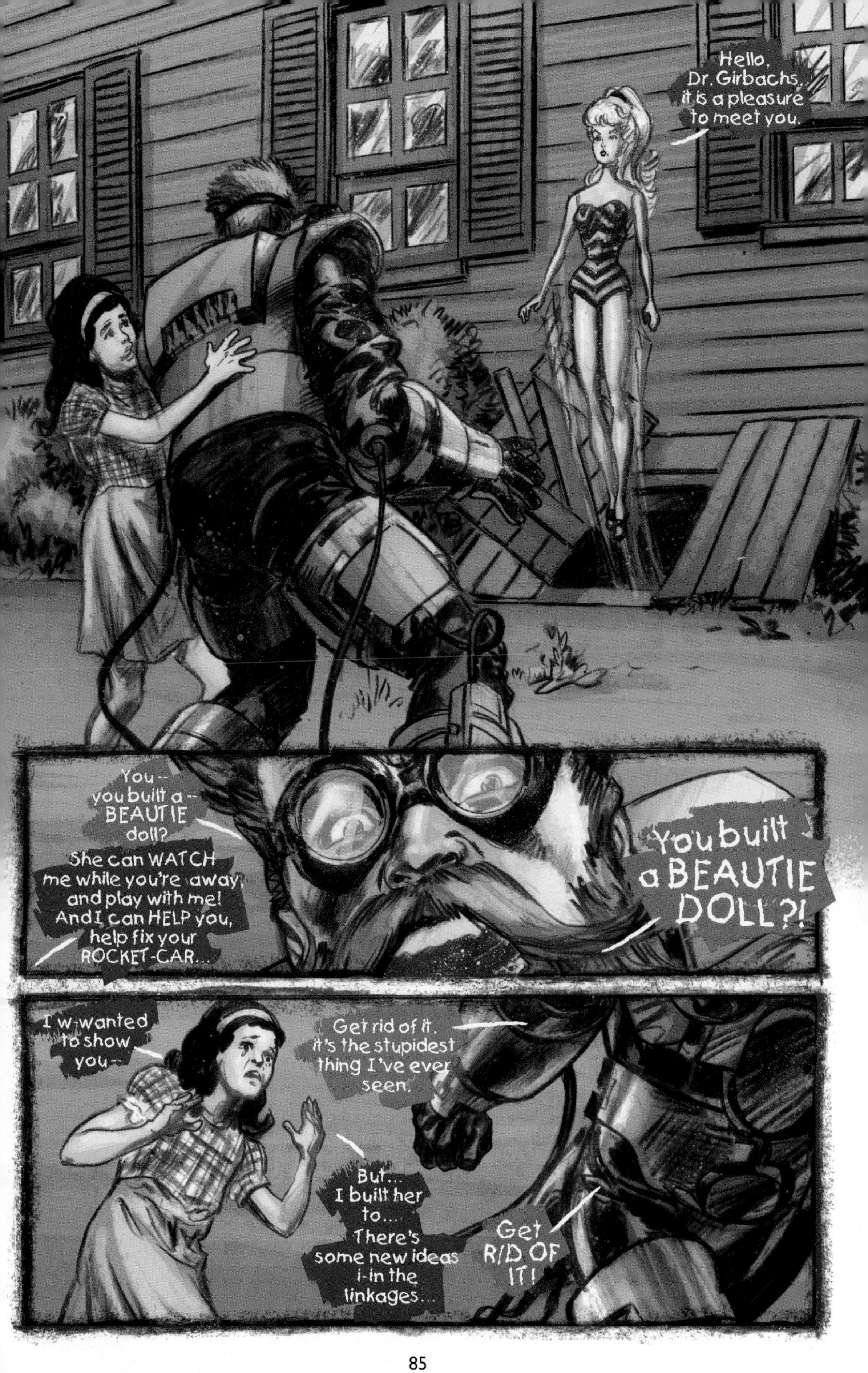
Hello, Dr. Girbachs, it is a pleasure to meet you.
You-- you built a-- BEAUTIE doll?
She can WATCH me while you're away, and play with me! And I can HELP you, help fix your ROCKET-CAR...
You built a BEAUTIE DOLL?!
I w-wanted to show you--
Get rid of it. it's the stupidest thing I've ever seen.
But... I built her to... There's some new ideas i-in the linkages...
Get RID OF IT!

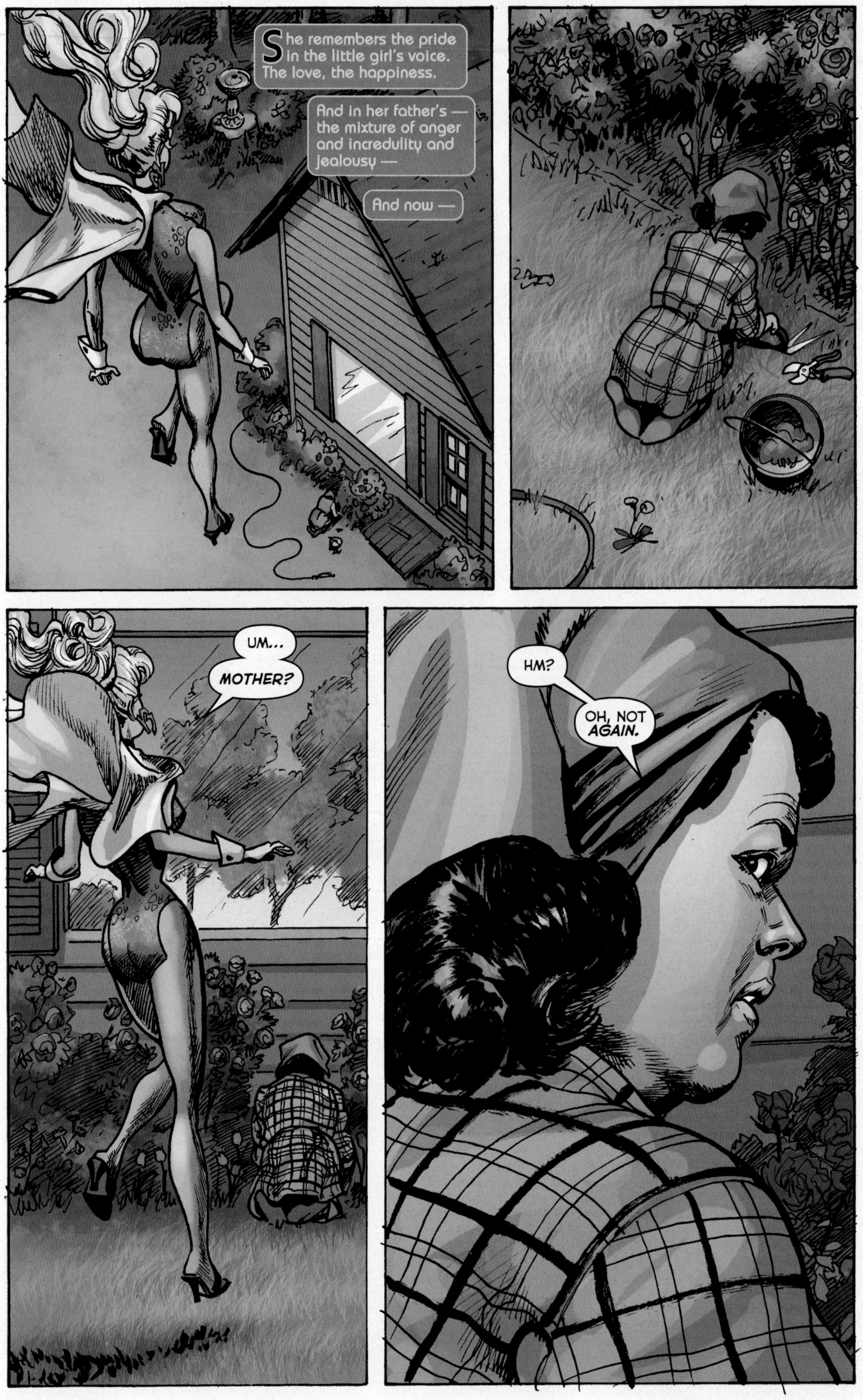
She remembers the pride in the little girl's voice. The love, the happiness.
And in her father's — the mixture of anger and incredulity and jealousy —
And now —
UM... MOTHER?
HM?
OH, NOT AGAIN.

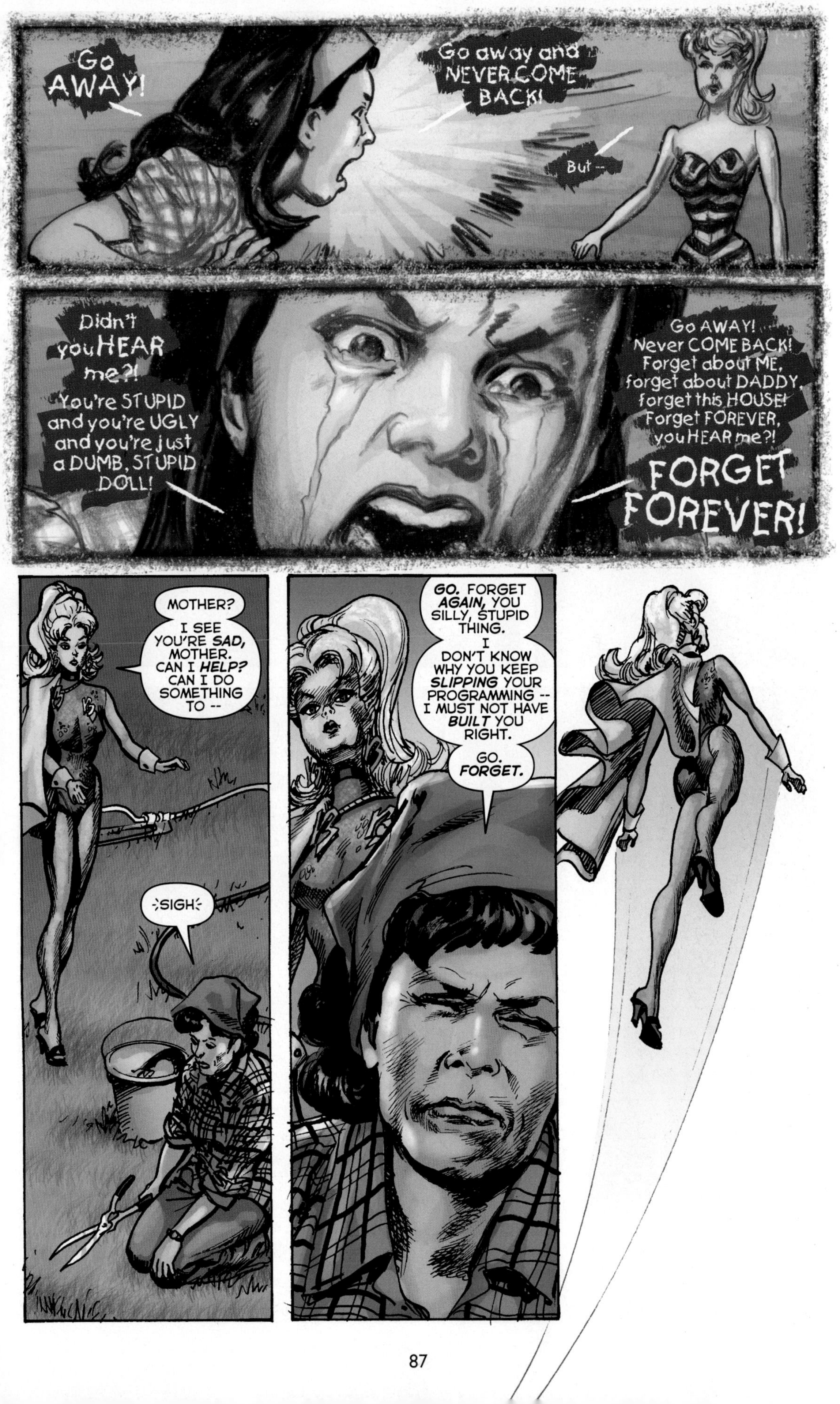
Go AWAY!
Go away and NEVER COME BACK!
But --
Didn't you HEAR me?! You're STUPID and you're UGLY and you're just a DUMB, STUPID DOLL!
Go AWAY! Never COME BACK! Forget about ME, forget about DADDY, forget this HOUSE! Forget FOREVER, you HEAR me?!
FORGET FOREVER!
MOTHER?
I SEE YOU'RE SAD, MOTHER. CAN I HELP? CAN I DO SOMETHING TO --
SIGH
GO. FORGET AGAIN, YOU SILLY, STUPID THING.
I DON'T KNOW WHY YOU KEEP SLIPPING YOUR PROGRAMMING -- I MUST NOT HAVE BUILT YOU RIGHT.
GO. FORGET.

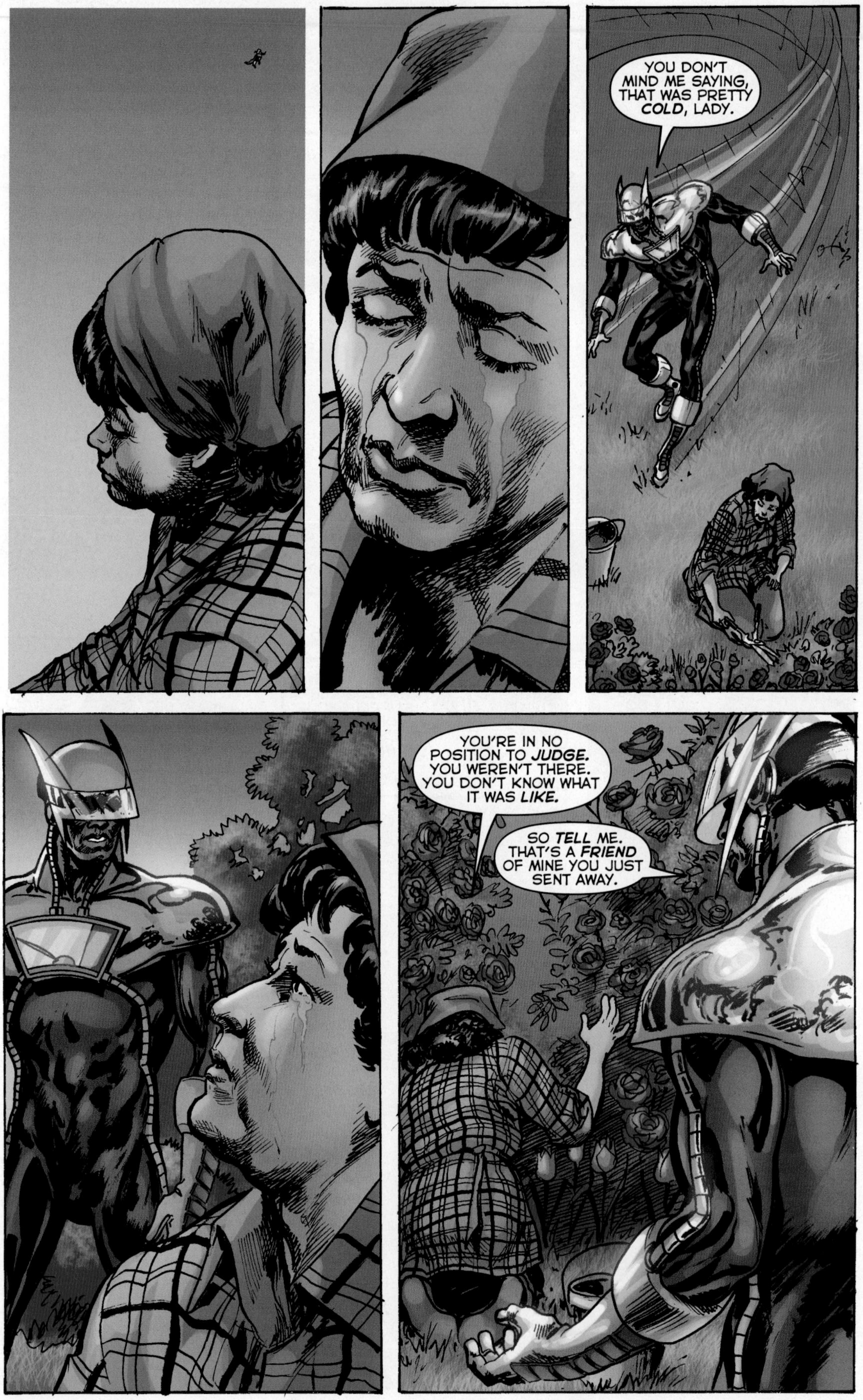
YOU DON'T MIND ME SAYING, THAT WAS PRETTY COLD, LADY.
YOU'RE IN NO POSITION TO JUDGE. YOU WEREN'T THERE. YOU DON'T KNOW WHAT IT WAS LIKE.
SO TELL ME. THAT'S A FRIEND OF MINE YOU JUST SENT AWAY.

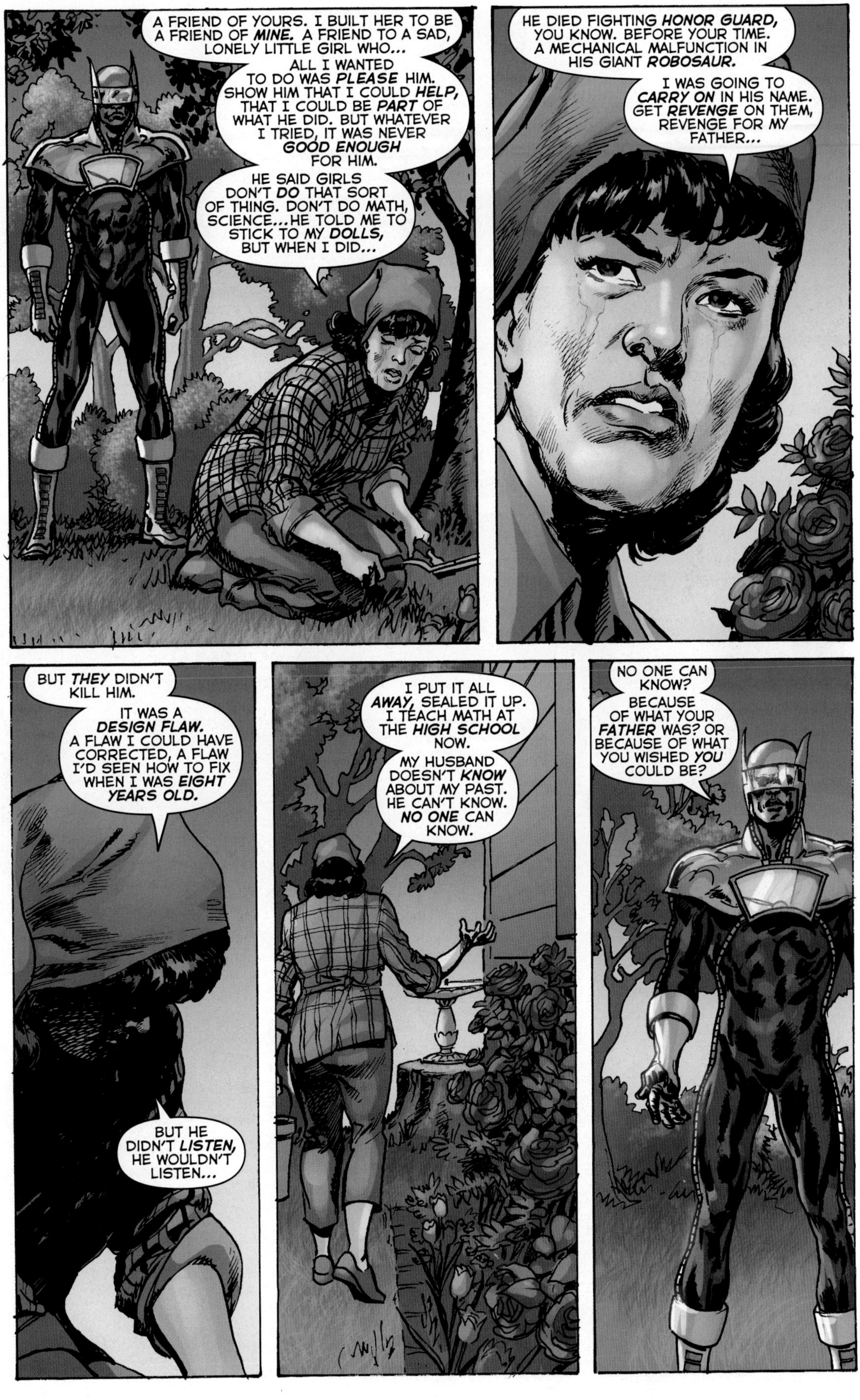
A FRIEND OF YOURS. I BUILT HER TO BE A FRIEND OF *MINE.* A FRIEND TO A SAD, LONELY LITTLE GIRL WHO...
ALL I WANTED TO DO WAS *PLEASE* HIM. SHOW HIM THAT I COULD *HELP,* THAT I COULD BE *PART* OF WHAT HE DID. BUT WHATEVER I TRIED, IT WAS NEVER *GOOD ENOUGH* FOR HIM.
HE SAID GIRLS DON'T *DO* THAT SORT OF THING. DON'T DO MATH, SCIENCE...HE TOLD ME TO STICK TO MY *DOLLS,* BUT WHEN I DID...
HE DIED FIGHTING *HONOR GUARD,* YOU KNOW. BEFORE YOUR TIME. A MECHANICAL MALFUNCTION IN HIS GIANT *ROBOSAUR.*
I WAS GOING TO *CARRY ON* IN HIS NAME. GET *REVENGE* ON THEM, REVENGE FOR MY FATHER...
BUT *THEY* DIDN'T KILL HIM.
IT WAS A *DESIGN FLAW.* A FLAW I COULD HAVE CORRECTED, A FLAW I'D SEEN HOW TO FIX WHEN I WAS *EIGHT YEARS OLD.*
BUT HE DIDN'T *LISTEN,* HE WOULDN'T LISTEN...
I PUT IT ALL *AWAY,* SEALED IT UP. I TEACH MATH AT THE *HIGH SCHOOL* NOW.
MY HUSBAND DOESN'T *KNOW* ABOUT MY PAST. HE CAN'T KNOW. *NO ONE* CAN KNOW.
NO ONE CAN KNOW?
BECAUSE OF WHAT YOUR *FATHER* WAS? OR BECAUSE OF WHAT YOU WISHED *YOU* COULD BE?

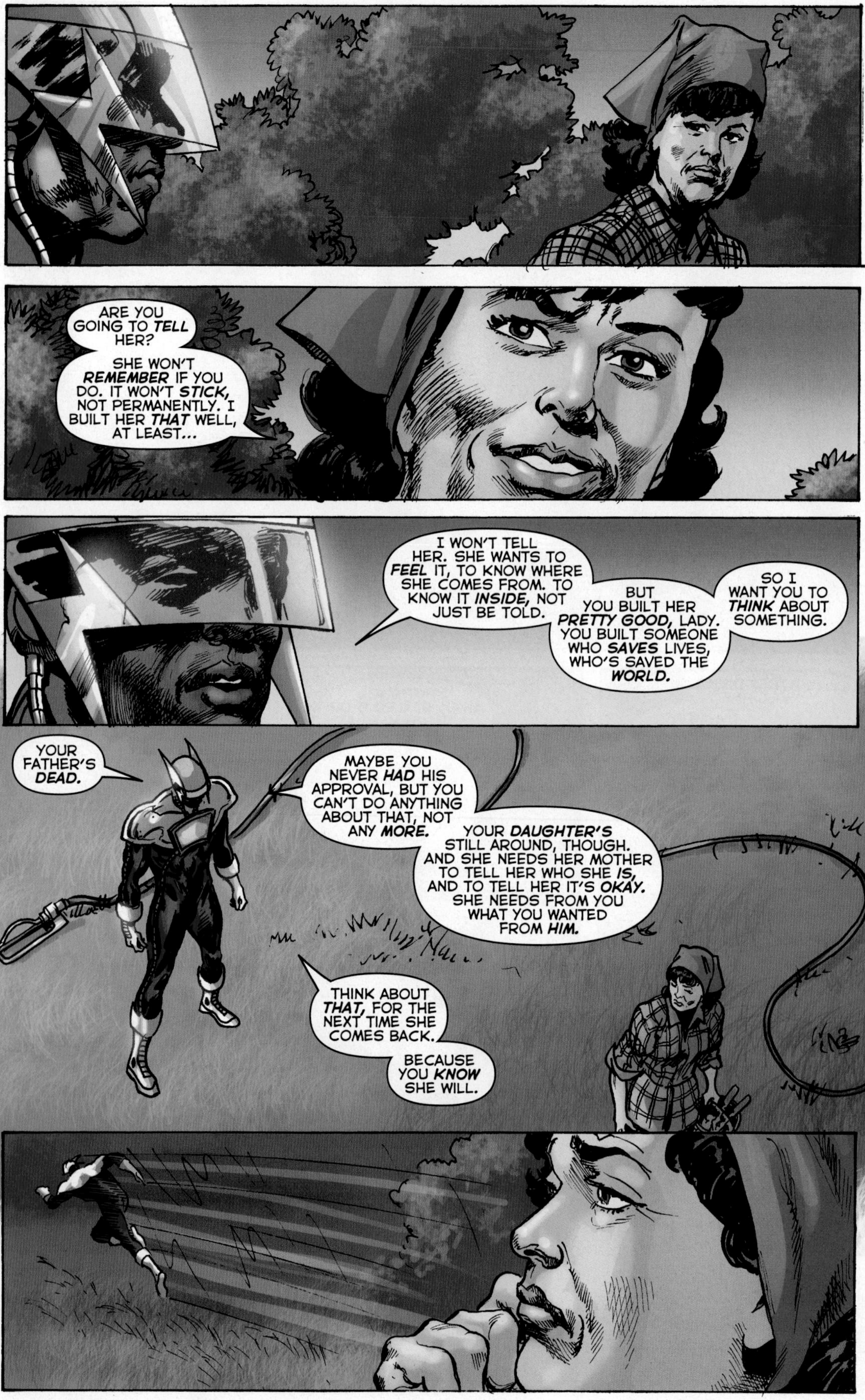
ARE YOU GOING TO TELL HER?
SHE WON'T REMEMBER IF YOU DO. IT WON'T STICK, NOT PERMANENTLY. I BUILT HER THAT WELL, AT LEAST...
I WON'T TELL HER. SHE WANTS TO FEEL IT, TO KNOW WHERE SHE COMES FROM. TO KNOW IT INSIDE, NOT JUST BE TOLD.
BUT YOU BUILT HER PRETTY GOOD, LADY. YOU BUILT SOMEONE WHO SAVES LIVES, WHO'S SAVED THE WORLD.
SO I WANT YOU TO THINK ABOUT SOMETHING.
YOUR FATHER'S DEAD.
MAYBE YOU NEVER HAD HIS APPROVAL, BUT YOU CAN'T DO ANYTHING ABOUT THAT, NOT ANY MORE.
YOUR DAUGHTER'S STILL AROUND, THOUGH. AND SHE NEEDS HER MOTHER TO TELL HER WHO SHE IS, AND TO TELL HER IT'S OKAY. SHE NEEDS FROM YOU WHAT YOU WANTED FROM HIM.
THINK ABOUT THAT, FOR THE NEXT TIME SHE COMES BACK.
BECAUSE YOU KNOW SHE WILL.

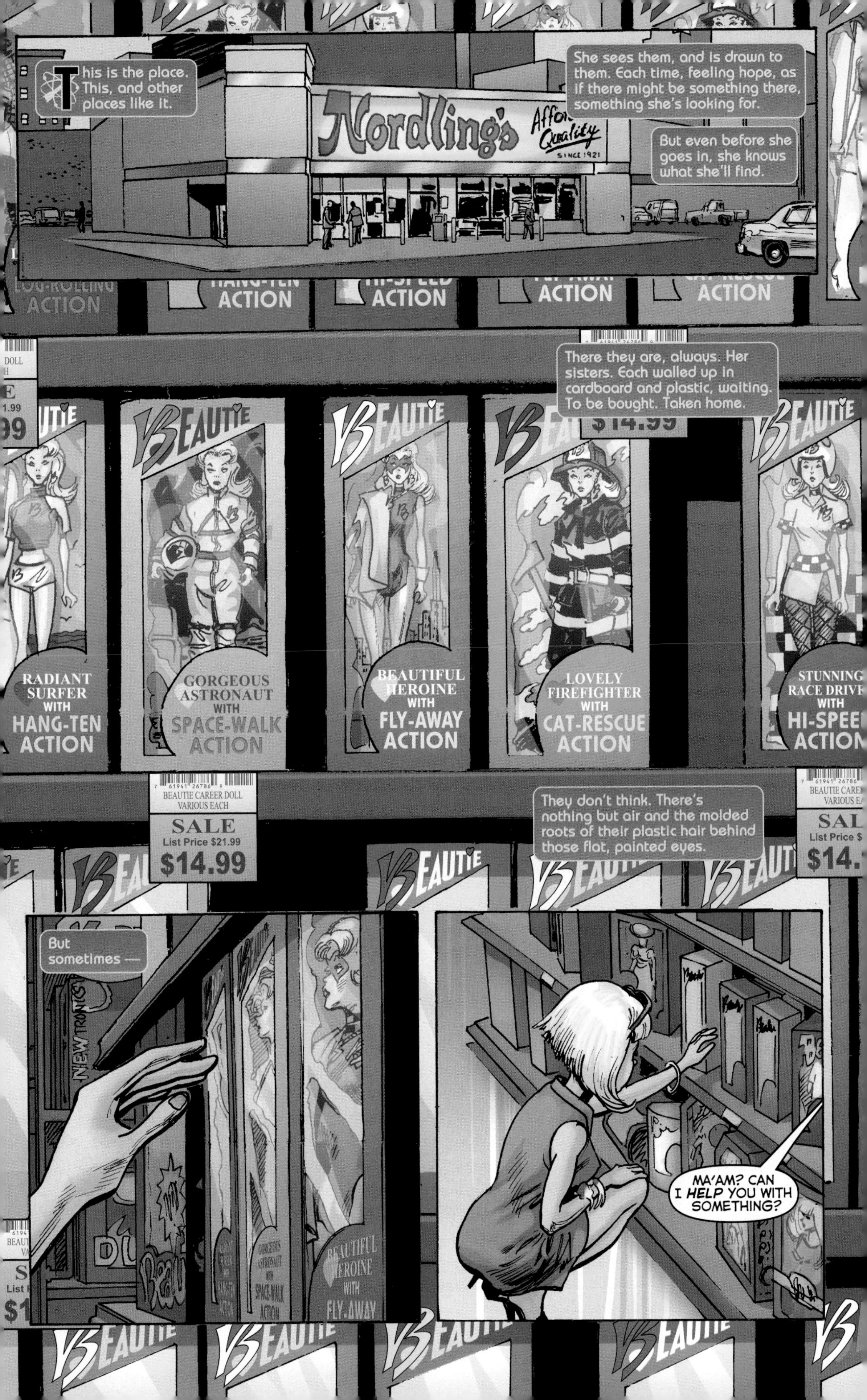

This is the place. This, and other places like it.
Nordling's
Affordable Quality
SINCE 1921
She sees them, and is drawn to them. Each time, feeling hope, as if there might be something there, something she's looking for.
But even before she goes in, she knows what she'll find.
There they are, always. Her sisters. Each walled up in cardboard and plastic, waiting. To be bought. Taken home.
BEAUTIE
RADIANT SURFER WITH HANG-TEN ACTION
GORGEOUS ASTRONAUT WITH SPACE-WALK ACTION
BEAUTIFUL HEROINE WITH FLY-AWAY ACTION
LOVELY FIREFIGHTER WITH CAT-RESCUE ACTION
STUNNING RACE DRIVE
BEAUTIE CAREER DOLL VARIOUS EACH
SALE
List Price $21.99
$14.99
They don't think. There's nothing but air and the molded roots of their plastic hair behind those flat, painted eyes.
But sometimes —
MA'AM? CAN I HELP YOU WITH SOMETHING?

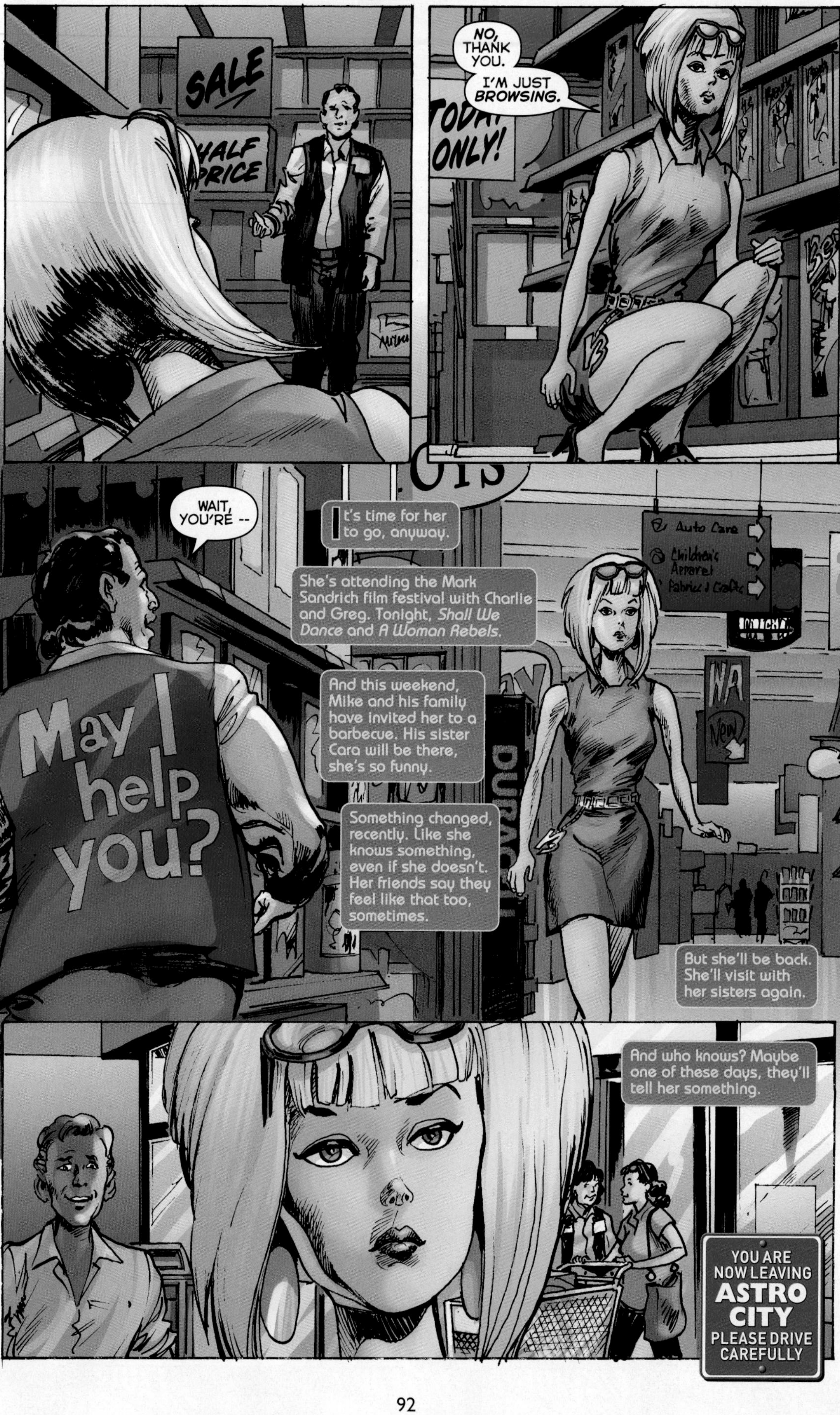

SALE
HALF PRICE
NO, THANK YOU.
I'M JUST BROWSING.
TODAY ONLY!
WAIT, YOU'RE --
It's time for her to go, anyway.
She's attending the Mark Sandrich film festival with Charlie and Greg. Tonight, Shall We Dance and A Woman Rebels.
And this weekend, Mike and his family have invited her to a barbecue. His sister Cara will be there, she's so funny.
Something changed, recently. Like she knows something, even if she doesn't. Her friends say they feel like that too, sometimes.
May I help you?
Auto Care
Children's Apparel
Fabrics & Crafts
But she'll be back. She'll visit with her sisters again.
And who knows? Maybe one of these days, they'll tell her something.
YOU ARE NOW LEAVING ASTRO CITY PLEASE DRIVE CAREFULLY

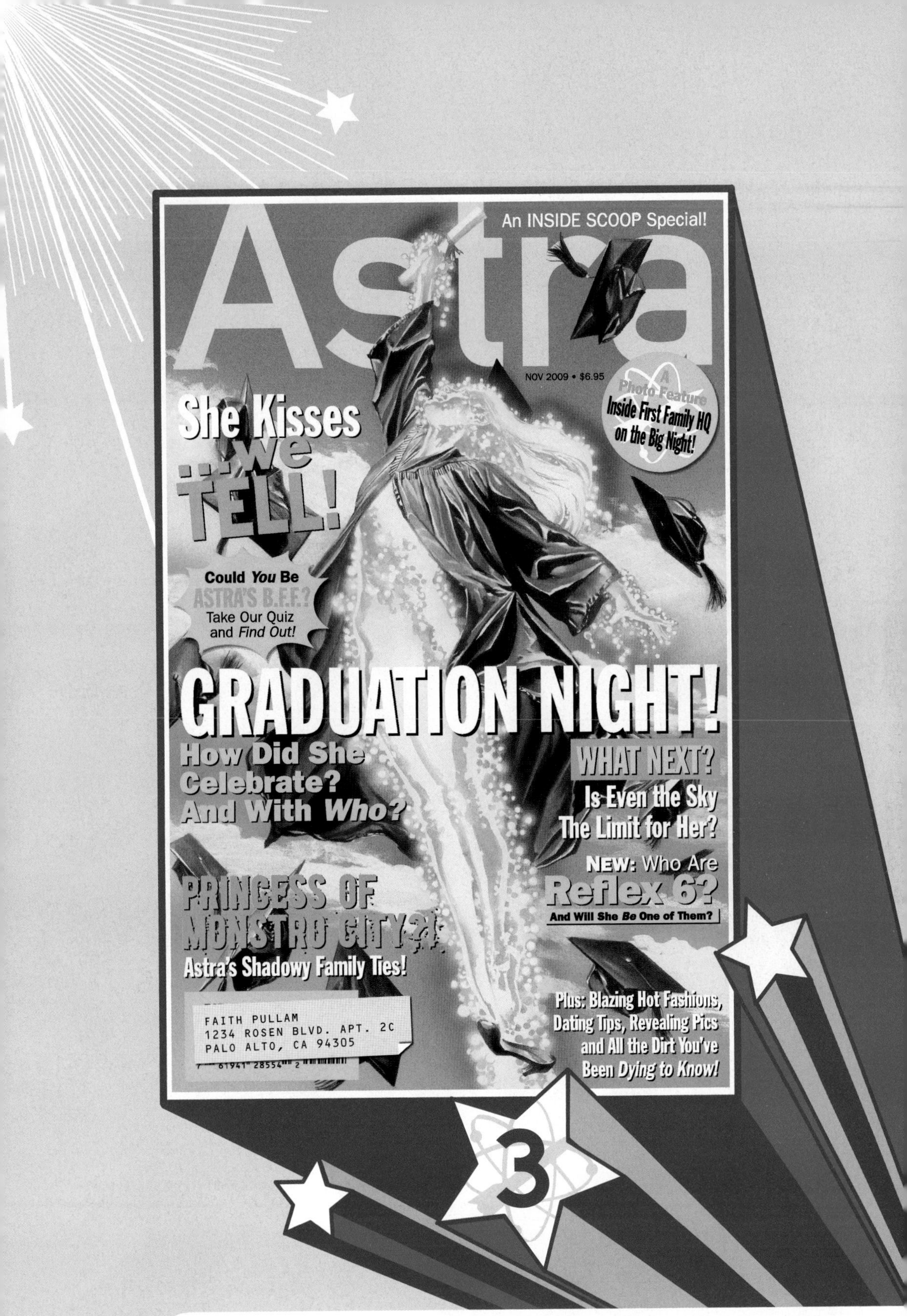
Astra
An INSIDE SCOOP Special!
NOV 2009 • $6.95
A Photo Feature
Inside First Family HQ on the Big Night!
She Kisses ...we TELL!
Could *You* Be ASTRA'S B.F.F.? Take Our Quiz and *Find Out!*
GRADUATION NIGHT!
How Did She Celebrate? And With *Who?*
WHAT NEXT? Is Even the Sky The Limit for Her?
NEW: Who Are Reflex 6?
And Will She *Be* One of Them?
PRINCESS OF MONSTRO CITY?!
Astra's Shadowy Family Ties!
FAITH PULLAM
1234 ROSEN BLVD. APT. 2C
PALO ALTO, CA 94305
Plus: Blazing Hot Fashions, Dating Tips, Revealing Pics and All the Dirt You've Been *Dying to Know!*

3

GRADUATION DAY

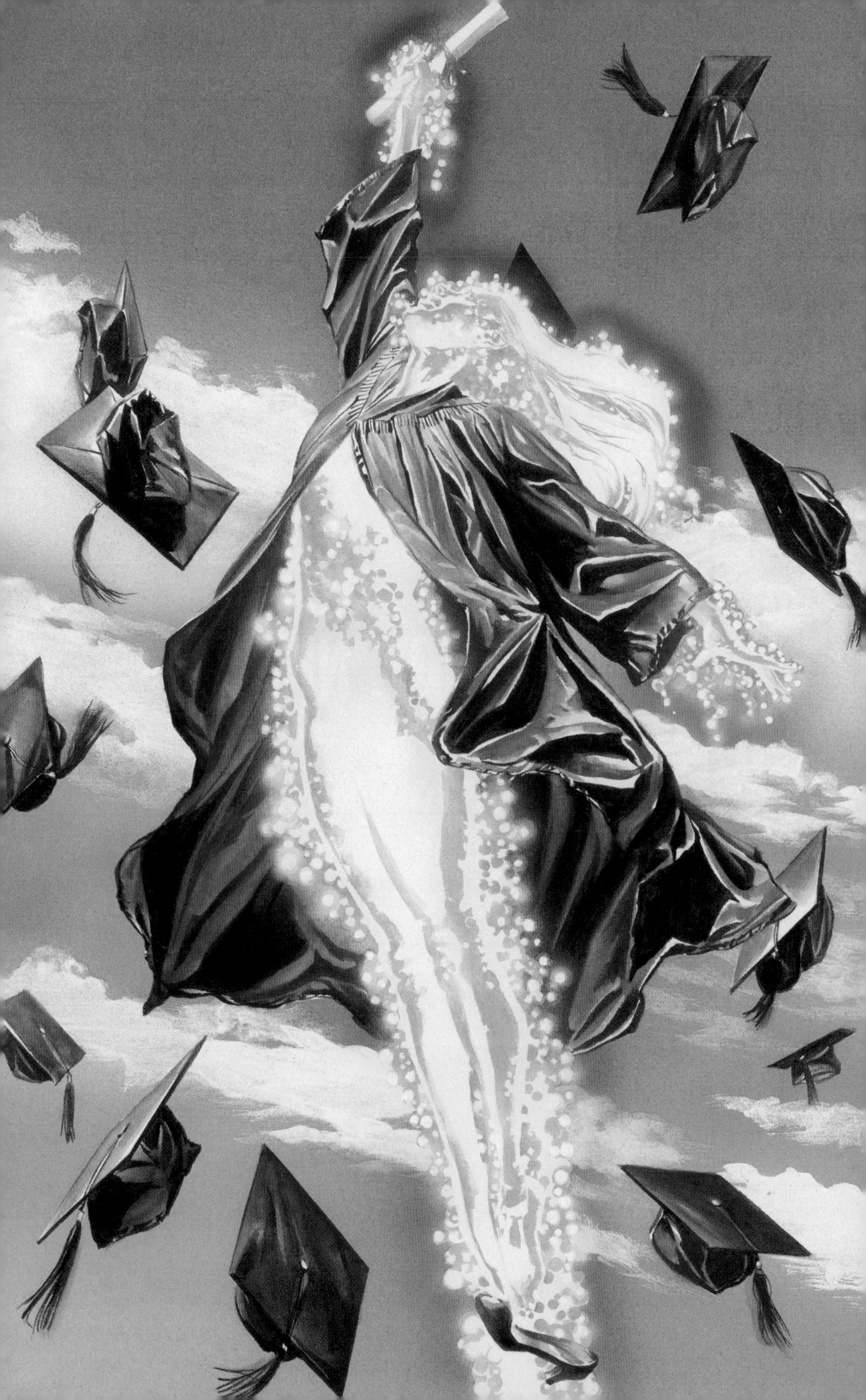

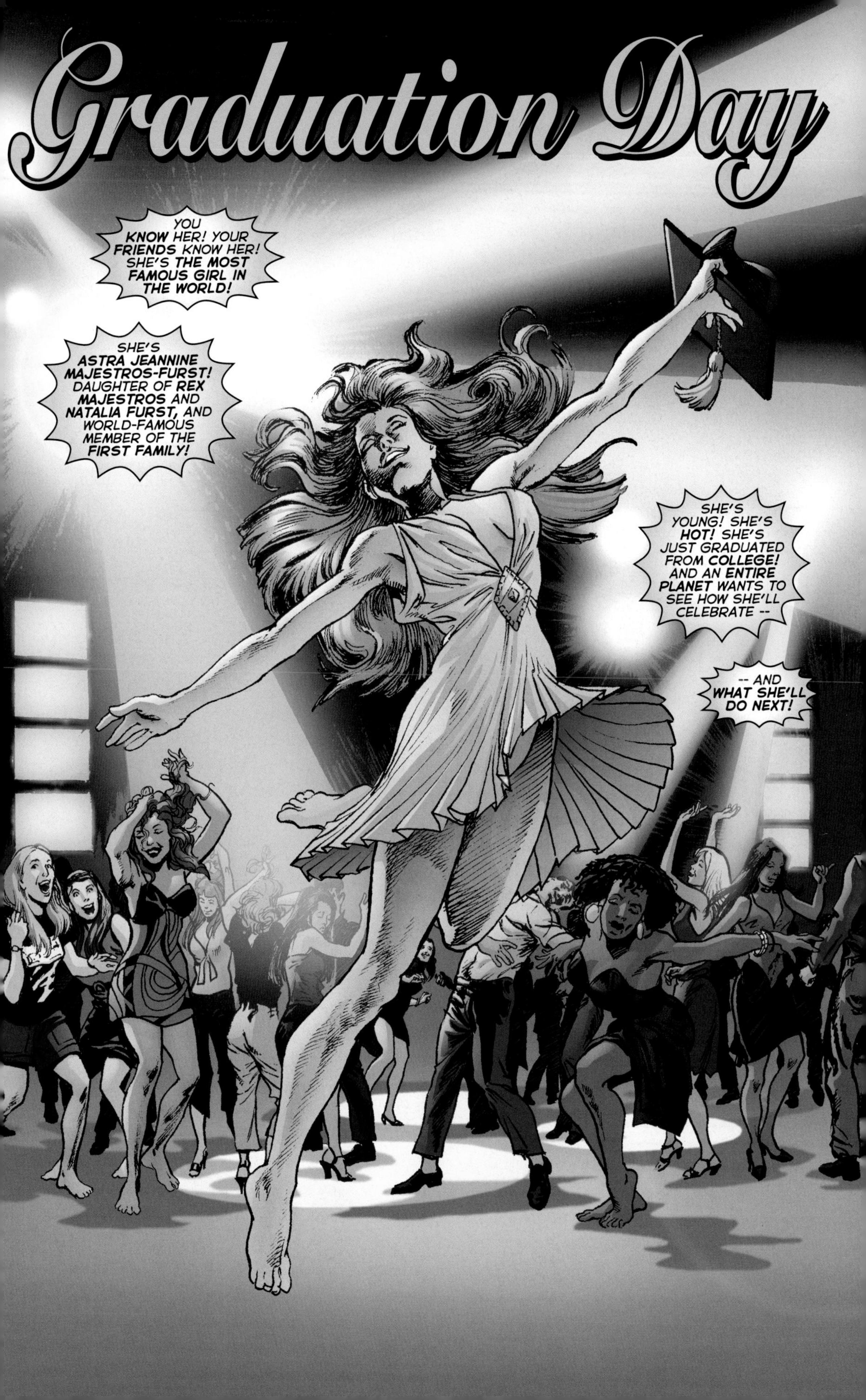
Graduation Day
YOU KNOW HER! YOUR FRIENDS KNOW HER! SHE'S THE MOST FAMOUS GIRL IN THE WORLD!
SHE'S ASTRA JEANNINE MAJESTROS-FURST! DAUGHTER OF REX MAJESTROS AND NATALIA FURST, AND WORLD-FAMOUS MEMBER OF THE FIRST FAMILY!
SHE'S YOUNG! SHE'S HOT! SHE'S JUST GRADUATED FROM COLLEGE! AND AN ENTIRE PLANET WANTS TO SEE HOW SHE'LL CELEBRATE --
-- AND WHAT SHE'LL DO NEXT!

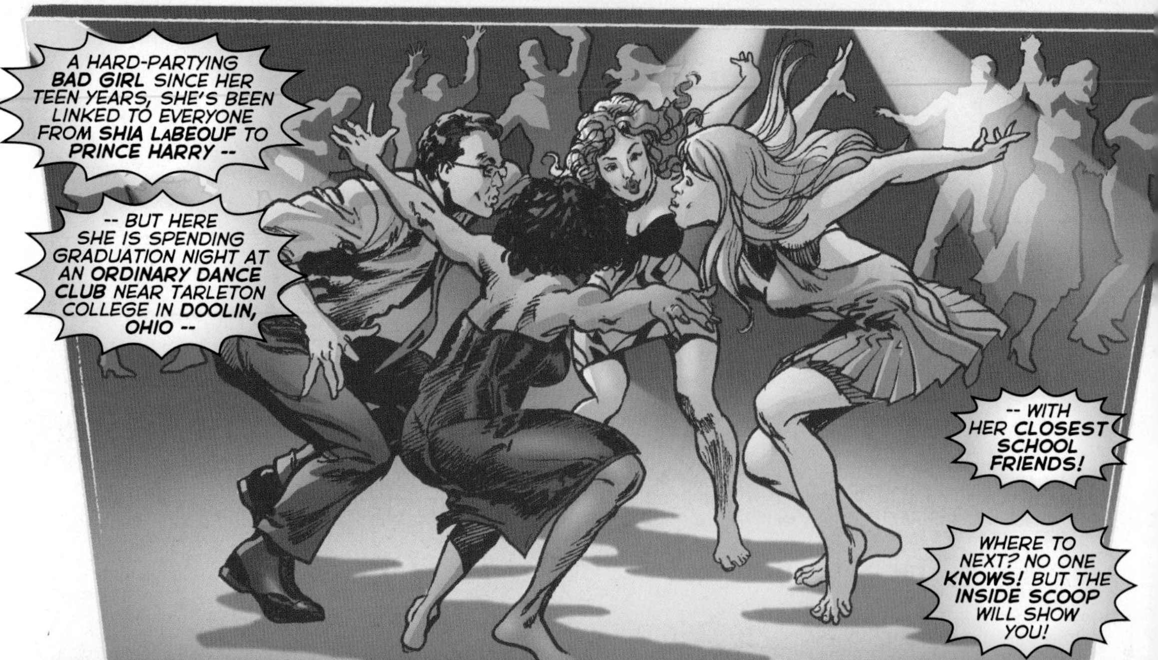
A HARD-PARTYING BAD GIRL SINCE HER TEEN YEARS, SHE'S BEEN LINKED TO EVERYONE FROM SHIA LaBEOUF TO PRINCE HARRY --
-- BUT HERE SHE IS SPENDING GRADUATION NIGHT AT AN ORDINARY DANCE CLUB NEAR TARLETON COLLEGE IN DOOLIN, OHIO --
-- WITH HER CLOSEST SCHOOL FRIENDS!
WHERE TO NEXT? NO ONE KNOWS! BUT THE INSIDE SCOOP WILL SHOW YOU!

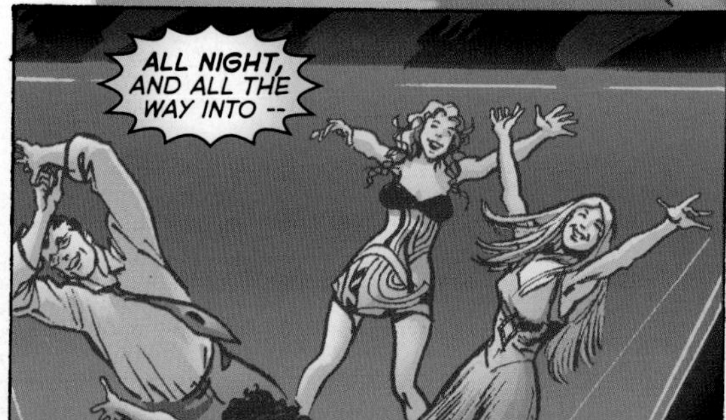
ALL NIGHT, AND ALL THE WAY INTO --
SEE?
THAT WAS JUST LIKE, A MINUTE AGO!

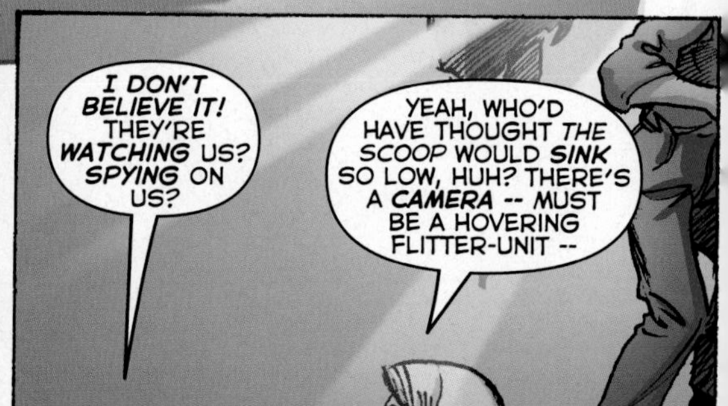
I DON'T BELIEVE IT! THEY'RE WATCHING US? SPYING ON US?
YEAH, WHO'D HAVE THOUGHT THE SCOOP WOULD SINK SO LOW, HUH? THERE'S A CAMERA -- MUST BE A HOVERING FLITTER-UNIT --
THERE! THERE IT IS!

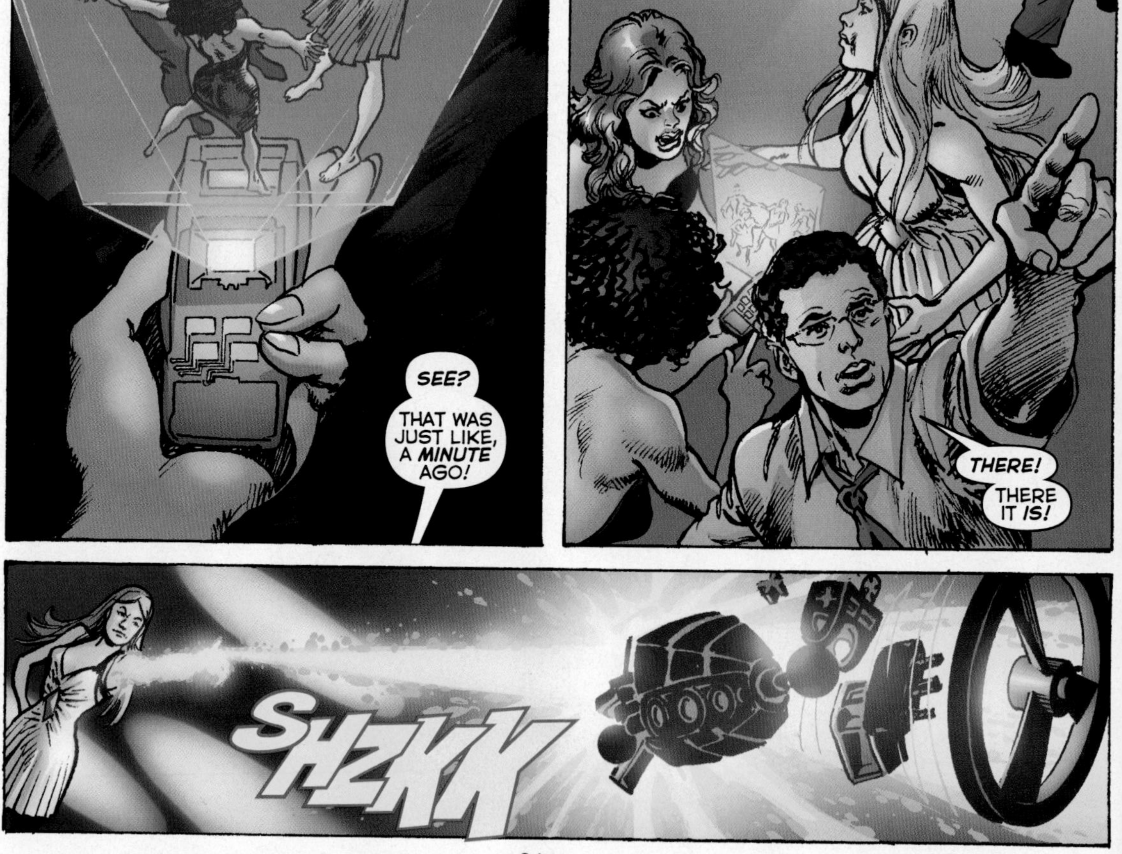
SHZKK

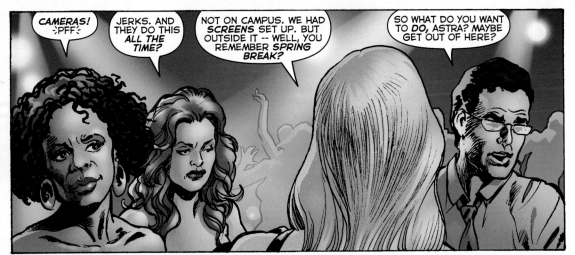

CAMERAS! :PFF:

JERKS. AND THEY DO THIS *ALL THE TIME?*

NOT ON CAMPUS. WE HAD *SCREENS* SET UP. BUT OUTSIDE IT -- WELL, YOU REMEMBER *SPRING BREAK?*

SO WHAT DO YOU WANT TO *DO,* ASTRA? MAYBE GET OUT OF HERE?

ARE YOU *KIDDING,* MATT? I'VE FACED DOWN *LORD VOLCANUS* -- THERE'S NO WAY I'M LETTING THE *INSIDE SCOOP* RUIN MY EVENING.

I'M A "HARD-PARTYING BAD GIRL" -- ISN'T *THAT* WHAT THEY SAY?

SO LET'S DANCE!

:HNEH:

GIRL KNOWS WHAT SHE *WANTS* -- !

OH, YEAH. GIRL KNOWS *PLENTY,* BOY...

"...YOU'D BE DOWNRIGHT *FLABBERGASTED,* WHAT SHE KNOWS...!"

Mythos

HEY --

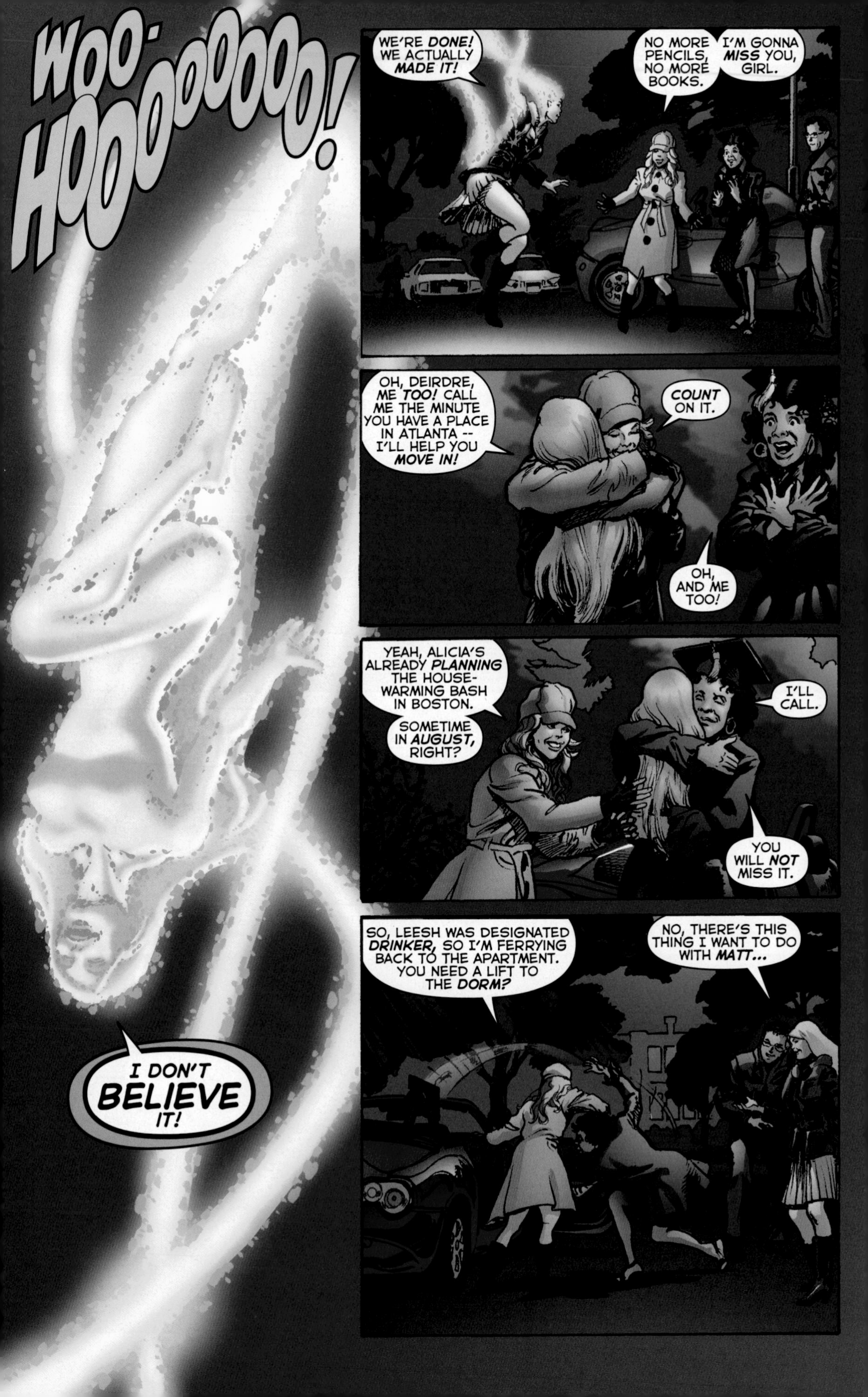
WOO-HOOOOOOOO!
WE'RE DONE! WE ACTUALLY MADE IT!
NO MORE PENCILS, NO MORE BOOKS.
I'M GONNA MISS YOU, GIRL.
OH, DEIRDRE, ME TOO! CALL ME THE MINUTE YOU HAVE A PLACE IN ATLANTA -- I'LL HELP YOU MOVE IN!
COUNT ON IT.
OH, AND ME TOO!
YEAH, ALICIA'S ALREADY PLANNING THE HOUSE-WARMING BASH IN BOSTON.
SOMETIME IN AUGUST, RIGHT?
I'LL CALL.
YOU WILL NOT MISS IT.
SO, LEESH WAS DESIGNATED DRINKER, SO I'M FERRYING BACK TO THE APARTMENT. YOU NEED A LIFT TO THE DORM?
NO, THERE'S THIS THING I WANT TO DO WITH MATT...
I DON'T BELIEVE IT!

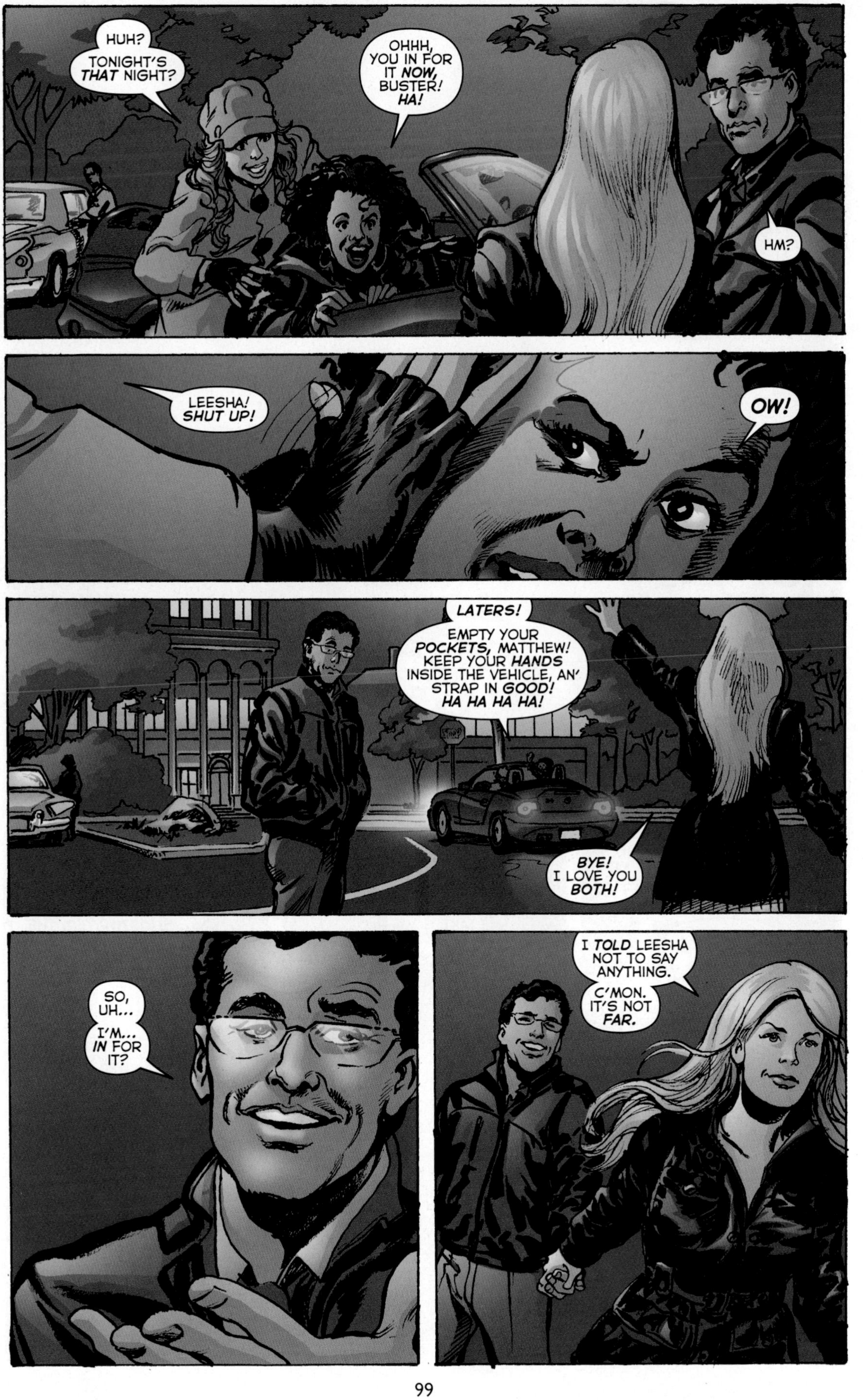
HUH? TONIGHT'S *THAT* NIGHT?
OHHH, YOU IN FOR IT *NOW,* BUSTER! *HA!*
HM?
LEESHA! *SHUT UP!*
OW!
LATERS!
EMPTY YOUR *POCKETS,* MATTHEW! KEEP YOUR *HANDS* INSIDE THE VEHICLE, AN' STRAP IN *GOOD!* *HA HA HA HA!*
BYE! I LOVE YOU *BOTH!*
SO, UH...
I'M... *IN* FOR IT?
I *TOLD* LEESHA NOT TO SAY ANYTHING.
C'MON. IT'S NOT *FAR.*

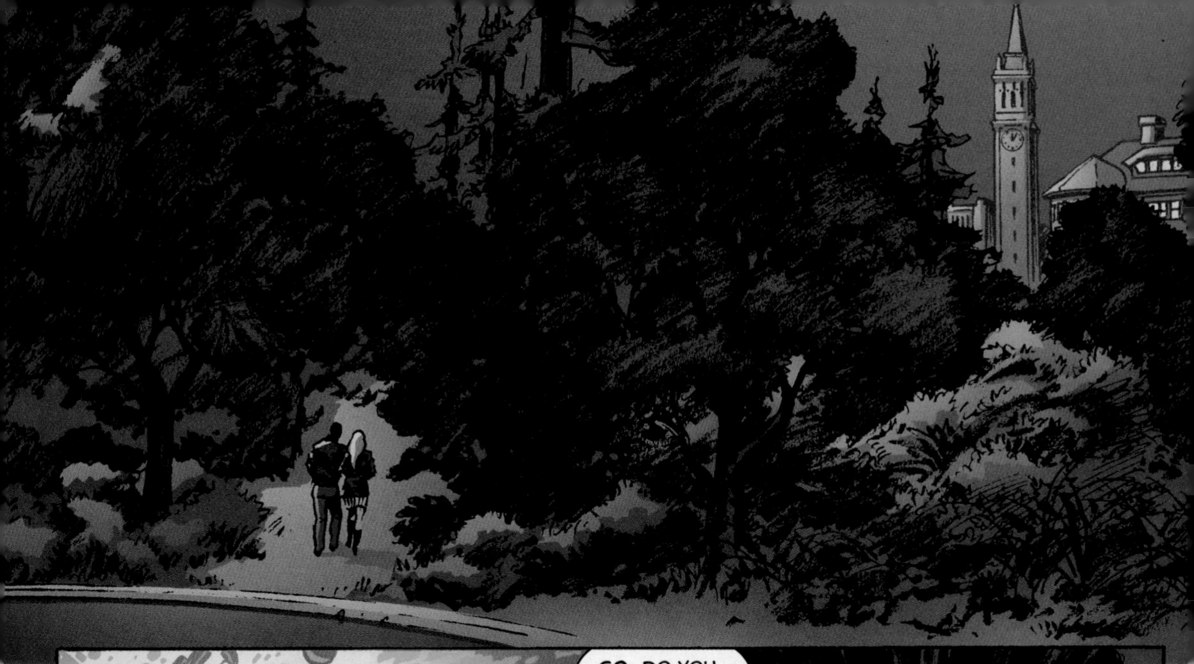

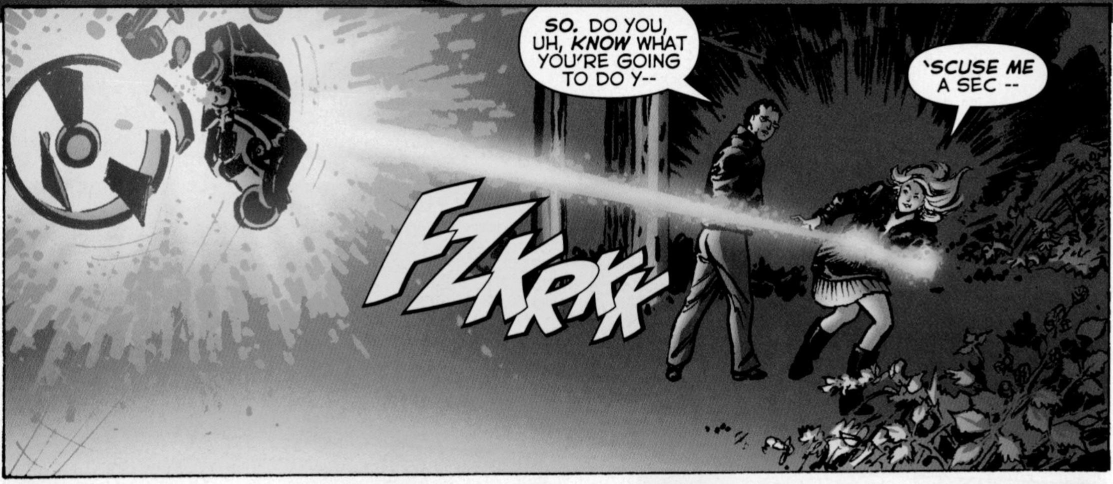

SO. DO YOU, UH, KNOW WHAT YOU'RE GOING TO DO Y--
'SCUSE ME A SEC --
FZKRKK

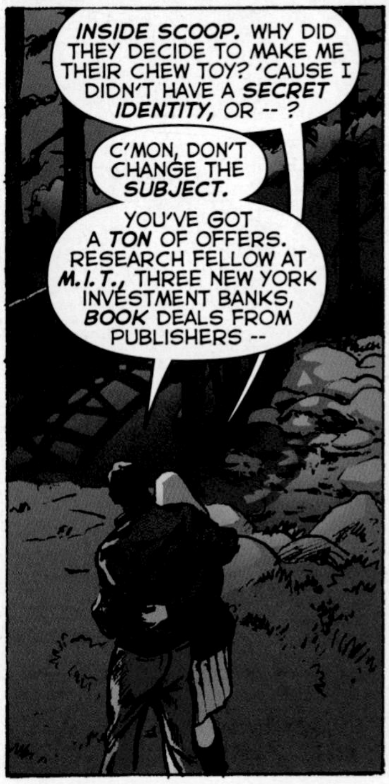

INSIDE SCOOP. WHY DID THEY DECIDE TO MAKE ME THEIR CHEW TOY? 'CAUSE I DIDN'T HAVE A SECRET IDENTITY, OR -- ?
C'MON, DON'T CHANGE THE SUBJECT.
YOU'VE GOT A TON OF OFFERS. RESEARCH FELLOW AT M.I.T., THREE NEW YORK INVESTMENT BANKS, BOOK DEALS FROM PUBLISHERS --

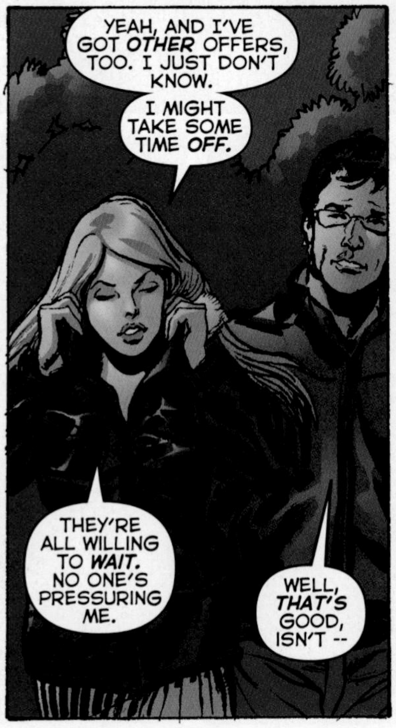

YEAH, AND I'VE GOT OTHER OFFERS, TOO. I JUST DON'T KNOW.
I MIGHT TAKE SOME TIME OFF.
THEY'RE ALL WILLING TO WAIT. NO ONE'S PRESSURING ME.
WELL, THAT'S GOOD, ISN'T --

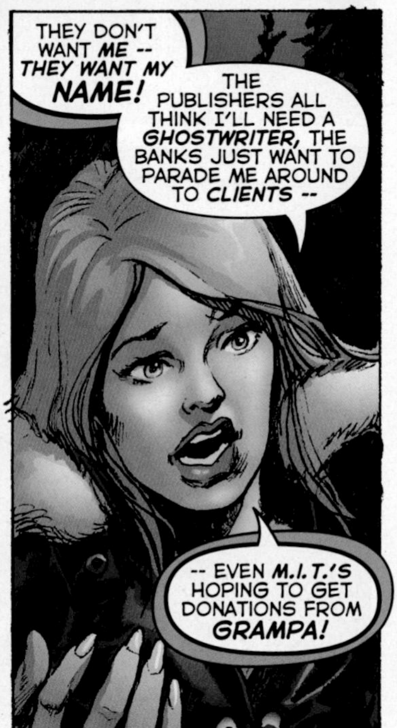

THEY DON'T WANT ME -- THEY WANT MY NAME!
THE PUBLISHERS ALL THINK I'LL NEED A GHOSTWRITER, THE BANKS JUST WANT TO PARADE ME AROUND TO CLIENTS --
-- EVEN M.I.T.'S HOPING TO GET DONATIONS FROM GRAMPA!

HEY.

HEY NOW.

WHATEVER YOU DO, ASTRA FURST, WHATEVER YOU *CHOOSE* --

-- YOU'RE GONNA BE *SENSATIONAL.* THAT'S ONE THING I KNOW FOR *SURE.*

YEAH, MAYBE.

BUT *"NORMAL"* SURE SOUNDS BETTER THAN *"SENSATIONAL,"* SOMETIMES.

TRUST ME, HONEY.

"NORMAL" ISN'T ALL IT'S *CRACKED UP* TO BE. AND YOU -- YOU'RE --

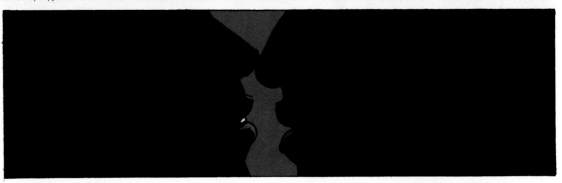

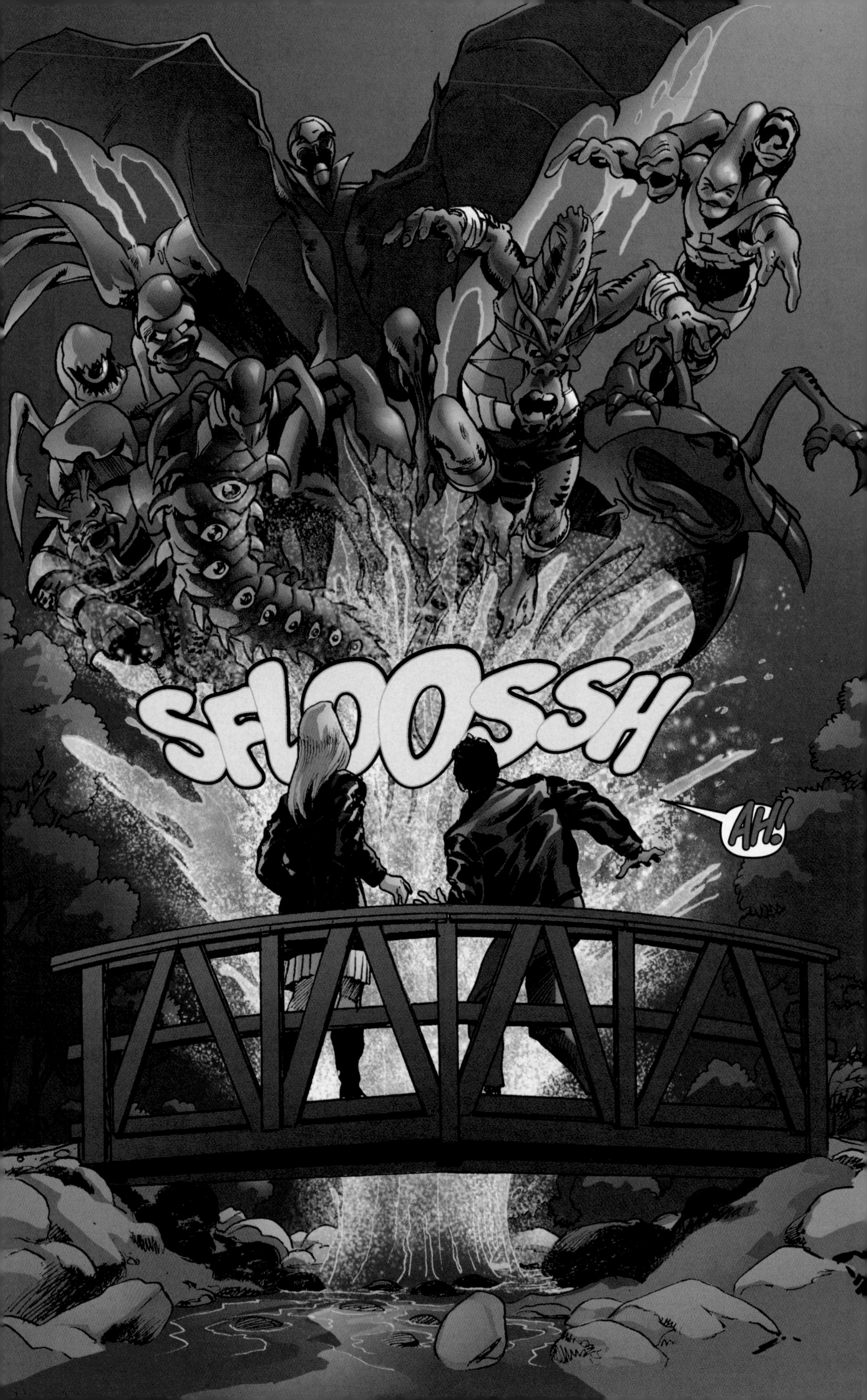
SFLOOSSH
AH!

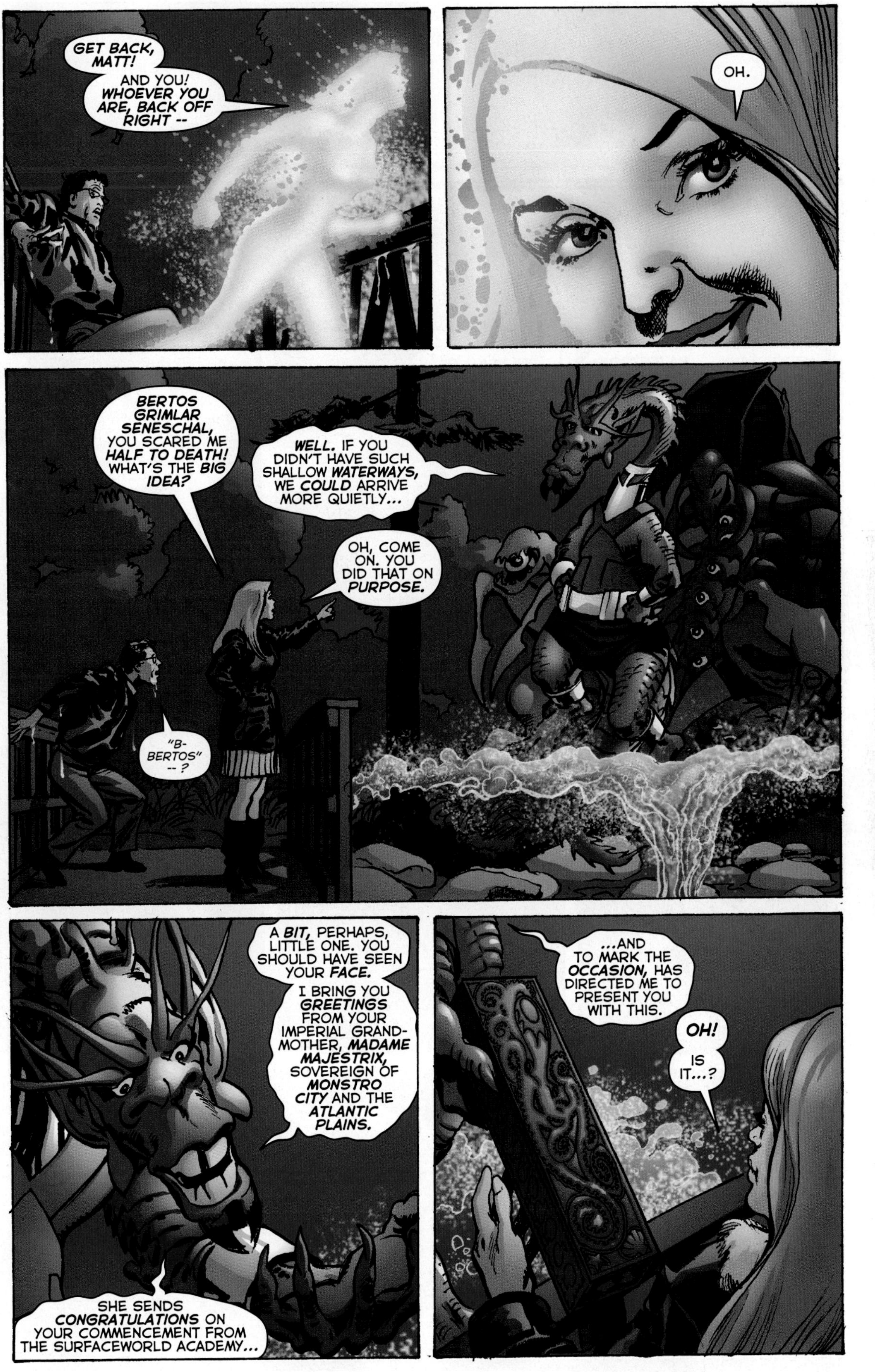
GET BACK, MATT!
AND YOU! WHOEVER YOU ARE, BACK OFF RIGHT --
OH.
BERTOS GRIMLAR SENESCHAL, YOU SCARED ME HALF TO DEATH! WHAT'S THE BIG IDEA?
WELL. IF YOU DIDN'T HAVE SUCH SHALLOW WATERWAYS, WE COULD ARRIVE MORE QUIETLY...
OH, COME ON. YOU DID THAT ON PURPOSE.
"B-BERTOS" -- ?
A BIT, PERHAPS, LITTLE ONE. YOU SHOULD HAVE SEEN YOUR FACE.
I BRING YOU GREETINGS FROM YOUR IMPERIAL GRAND-MOTHER, MADAME MAJESTRIX, SOVEREIGN OF MONSTRO CITY AND THE ATLANTIC PLAINS.
SHE SENDS CONGRATULATIONS ON YOUR COMMENCEMENT FROM THE SURFACEWORLD ACADEMY...
...AND TO MARK THE OCCASION, HAS DIRECTED ME TO PRESENT YOU WITH THIS.
OH!
IS IT...?

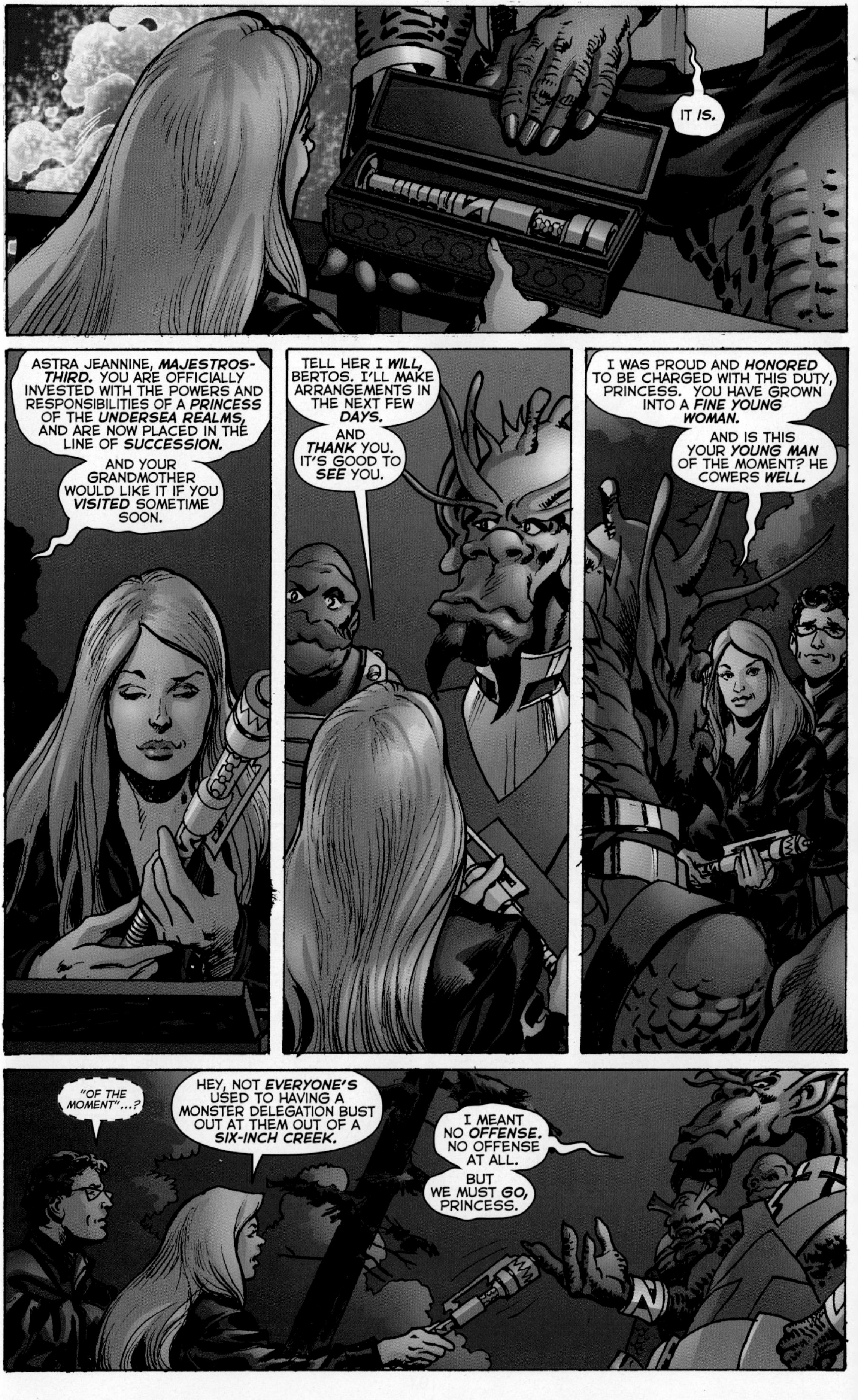
IT IS.
ASTRA JEANNINE, MAJESTROS-THIRD. YOU ARE OFFICIALLY INVESTED WITH THE POWERS AND RESPONSIBILITIES OF A PRINCESS OF THE UNDERSEA REALMS, AND ARE NOW PLACED IN THE LINE OF SUCCESSION.
AND YOUR GRANDMOTHER WOULD LIKE IT IF YOU VISITED SOMETIME SOON.
TELL HER I WILL, BERTOS. I'LL MAKE ARRANGEMENTS IN THE NEXT FEW DAYS.
AND THANK YOU. IT'S GOOD TO SEE YOU.
I WAS PROUD AND HONORED TO BE CHARGED WITH THIS DUTY, PRINCESS. YOU HAVE GROWN INTO A FINE YOUNG WOMAN.
AND IS THIS YOUR YOUNG MAN OF THE MOMENT? HE COWERS WELL.
"OF THE MOMENT"...?
HEY, NOT EVERYONE'S USED TO HAVING A MONSTER DELEGATION BUST OUT AT THEM OUT OF A SIX-INCH CREEK.
I MEANT NO OFFENSE. NO OFFENSE AT ALL.
BUT WE MUST GO, PRINCESS.

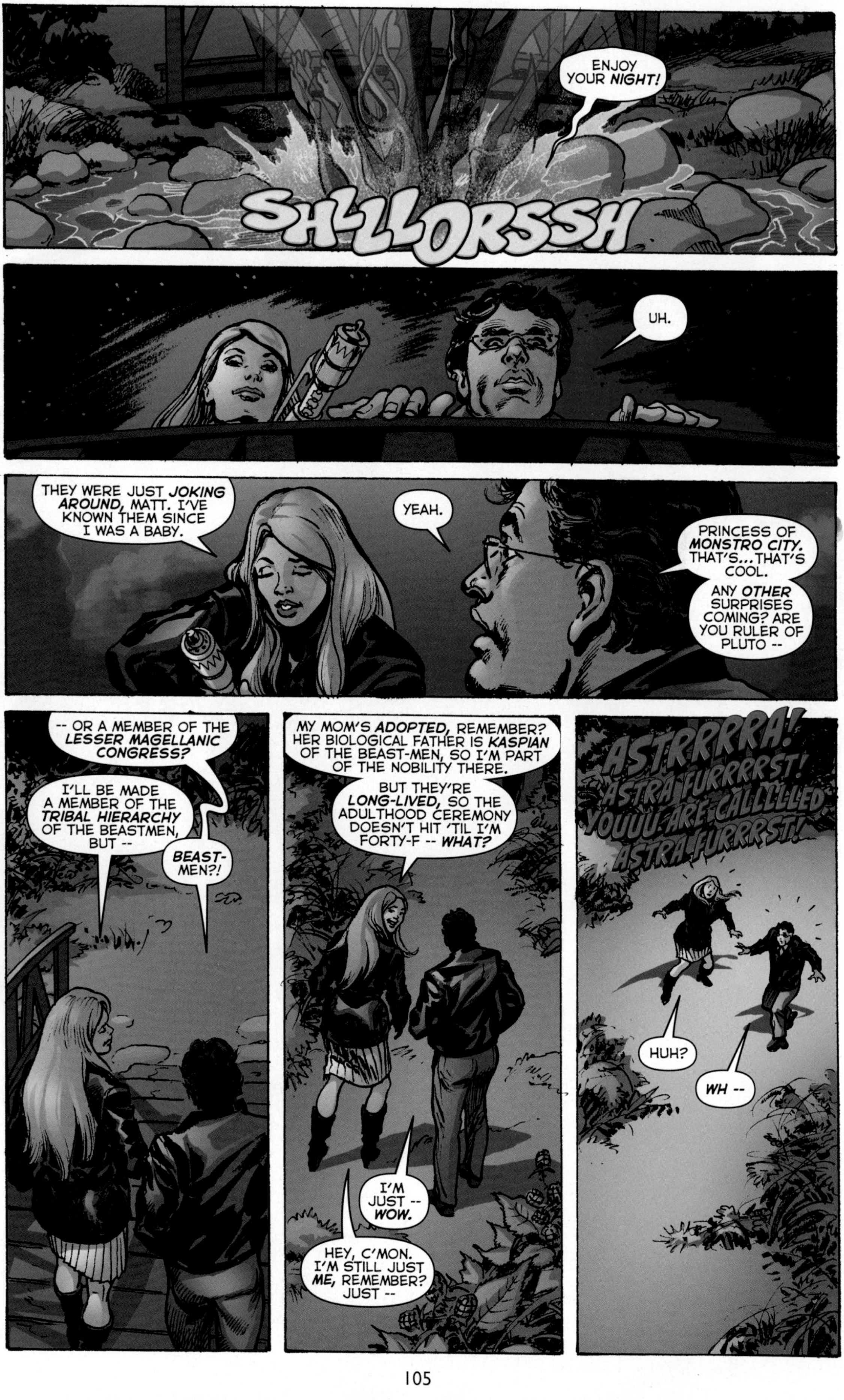

ENJOY YOUR NIGHT!
SHLLORSSH
UH.
THEY WERE JUST JOKING AROUND, MATT. I'VE KNOWN THEM SINCE I WAS A BABY.
YEAH.
PRINCESS OF MONSTRO CITY. THAT'S...THAT'S COOL.
ANY OTHER SURPRISES COMING? ARE YOU RULER OF PLUTO --
-- OR A MEMBER OF THE LESSER MAGELLANIC CONGRESS?
I'LL BE MADE A MEMBER OF THE TRIBAL HIERARCHY OF THE BEASTMEN, BUT --
BEAST-MEN?!
MY MOM'S ADOPTED, REMEMBER? HER BIOLOGICAL FATHER IS KASPIAN OF THE BEAST-MEN, SO I'M PART OF THE NOBILITY THERE.
BUT THEY'RE LONG-LIVED, SO THE ADULTHOOD CEREMONY DOESN'T HIT 'TIL I'M FORTY-F -- WHAT?
I'M JUST -- WOW.
HEY, C'MON. I'M STILL JUST ME, REMEMBER? JUST --
ASTRRRRRA! ASTRA FURRRRST! YOUUU ARE CALLLLLED ASTRA FURRRST!
HUH?
WH --

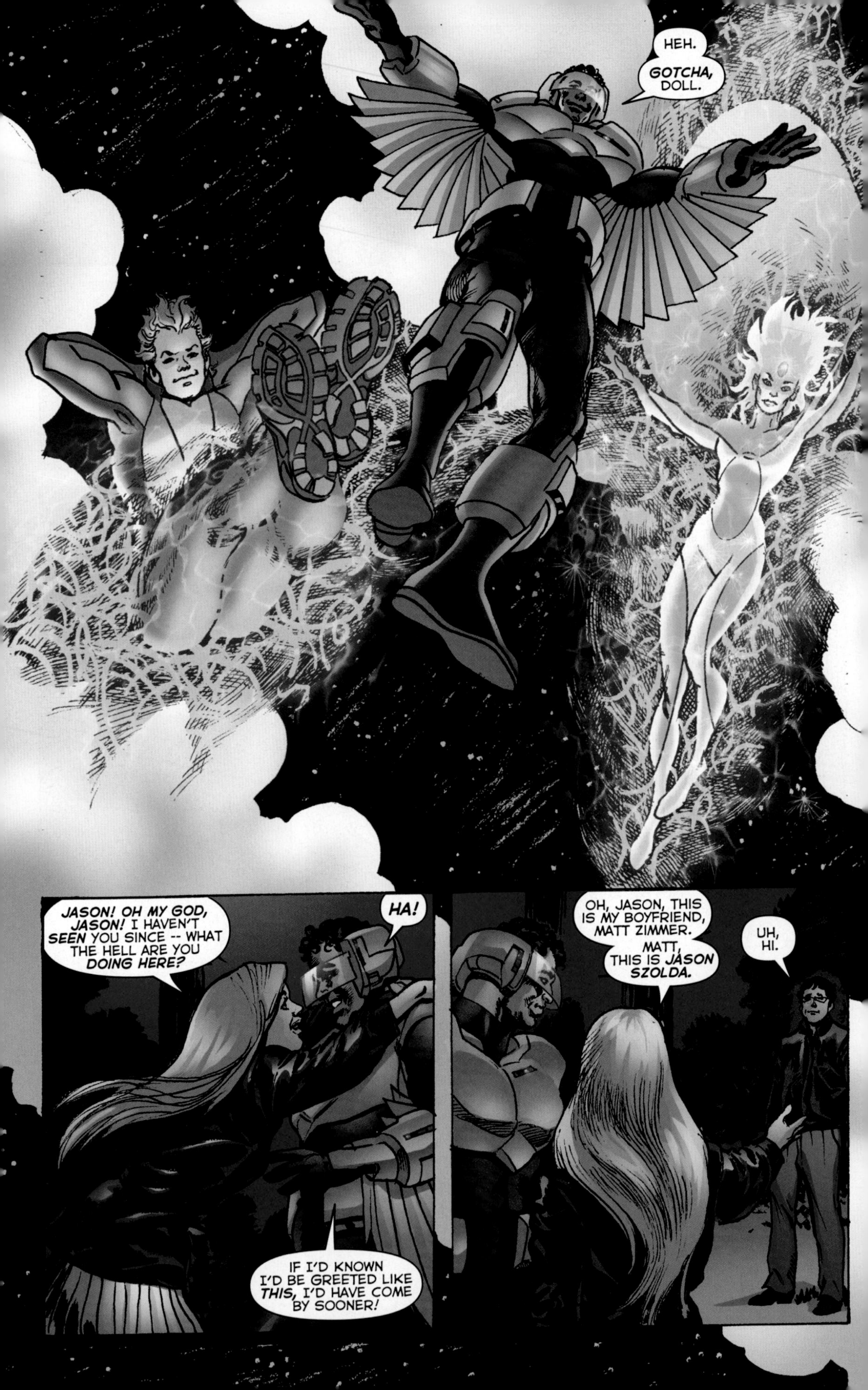
HEH.
GOTCHA, DOLL.
JASON! OH MY GOD, JASON! I HAVEN'T SEEN YOU SINCE -- WHAT THE HELL ARE YOU DOING HERE?
HA!
IF I'D KNOWN I'D BE GREETED LIKE THIS, I'D HAVE COME BY SOONER!
OH, JASON, THIS IS MY BOYFRIEND, MATT ZIMMER.
MATT, THIS IS JASON SZOLDA.
UH, HI.

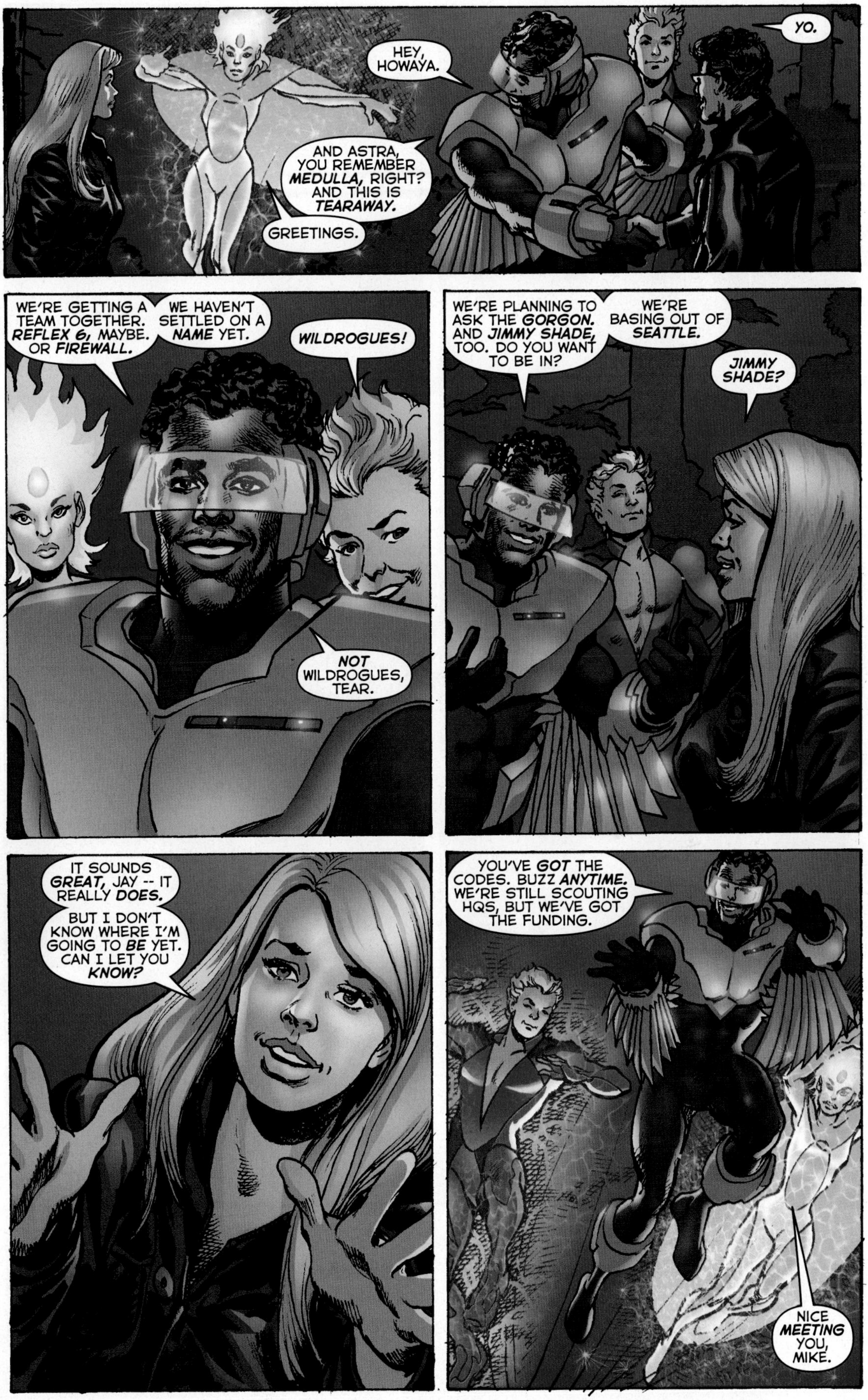
YO.
HEY, HOWAYA.
AND ASTRA, YOU REMEMBER MEDULLA, RIGHT? AND THIS IS TEARAWAY.
GREETINGS.
WE'RE GETTING A TEAM TOGETHER. REFLEX 6, MAYBE. OR FIREWALL.
WE HAVEN'T SETTLED ON A NAME YET.
WILDROGUES!
NOT WILDROGUES, TEAR.
WE'RE PLANNING TO ASK THE GORGON. AND JIMMY SHADE, TOO. DO YOU WANT TO BE IN?
WE'RE BASING OUT OF SEATTLE.
JIMMY SHADE?
IT SOUNDS GREAT, JAY -- IT REALLY DOES.
BUT I DON'T KNOW WHERE I'M GOING TO BE YET. CAN I LET YOU KNOW?
YOU'VE GOT THE CODES. BUZZ ANYTIME. WE'RE STILL SCOUTING HQS, BUT WE'VE GOT THE FUNDING.
NICE MEETING YOU, MIKE.

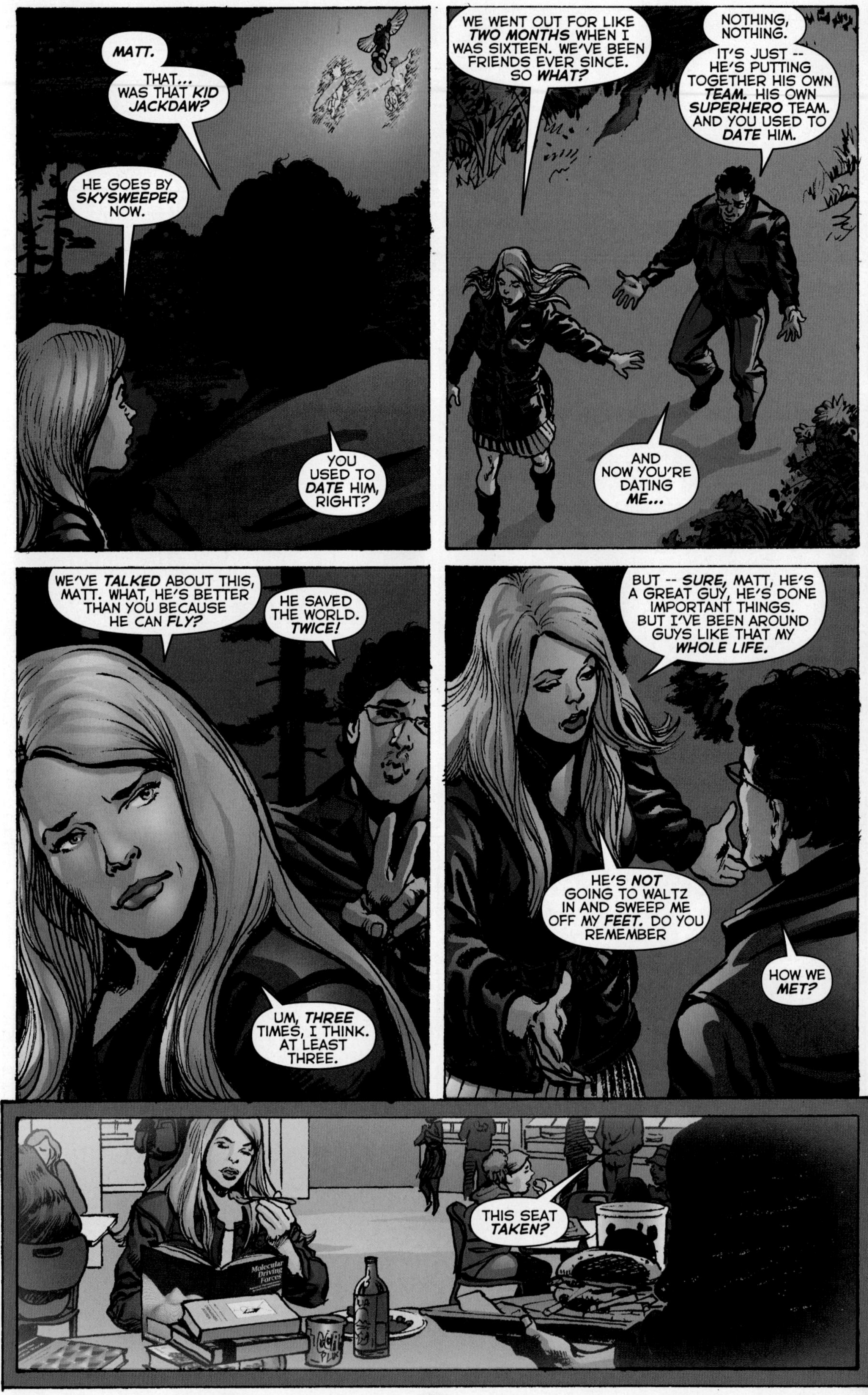

MATT.
THAT... WAS THAT KID JACKDAW?
HE GOES BY SKYSWEEPER NOW.
YOU USED TO DATE HIM, RIGHT?
WE WENT OUT FOR LIKE TWO MONTHS WHEN I WAS SIXTEEN. WE'VE BEEN FRIENDS EVER SINCE. SO WHAT?
NOTHING, NOTHING.
IT'S JUST -- HE'S PUTTING TOGETHER HIS OWN TEAM. HIS OWN SUPERHERO TEAM. AND YOU USED TO DATE HIM.
AND NOW YOU'RE DATING ME...
WE'VE TALKED ABOUT THIS, MATT. WHAT, HE'S BETTER THAN YOU BECAUSE HE CAN FLY?
HE SAVED THE WORLD. TWICE!
UM, THREE TIMES, I THINK. AT LEAST THREE.
BUT -- SURE, MATT, HE'S A GREAT GUY, HE'S DONE IMPORTANT THINGS. BUT I'VE BEEN AROUND GUYS LIKE THAT MY WHOLE LIFE.
HE'S NOT GOING TO WALTZ IN AND SWEEP ME OFF MY FEET. DO YOU REMEMBER
HOW WE MET?
THIS SEAT TAKEN?

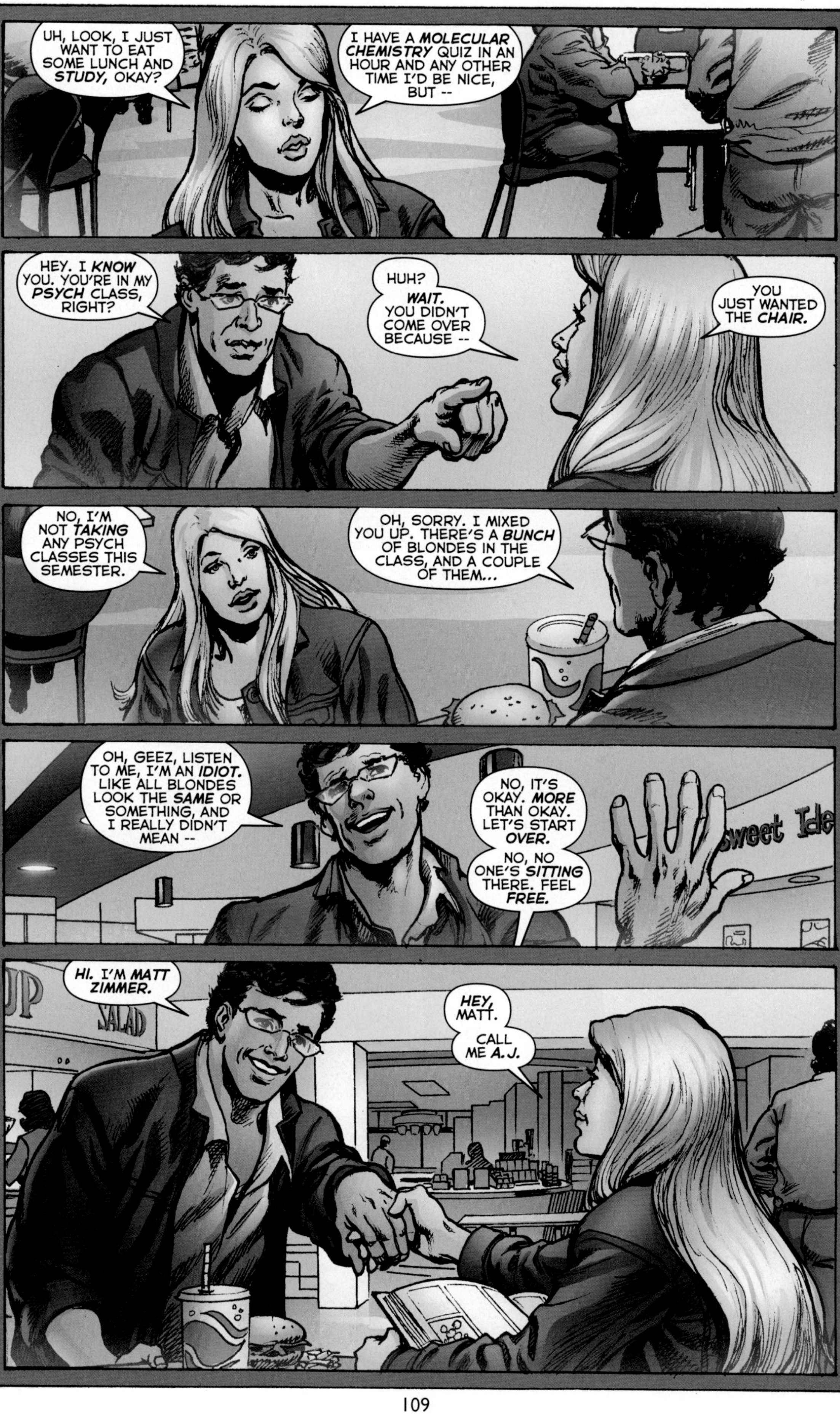
UH, LOOK, I JUST WANT TO EAT SOME LUNCH AND STUDY, OKAY?
I HAVE A MOLECULAR CHEMISTRY QUIZ IN AN HOUR AND ANY OTHER TIME I'D BE NICE, BUT --
HEY. I KNOW YOU. YOU'RE IN MY PSYCH CLASS, RIGHT?
HUH? WAIT. YOU DIDN'T COME OVER BECAUSE --
YOU JUST WANTED THE CHAIR.
NO, I'M NOT TAKING ANY PSYCH CLASSES THIS SEMESTER.
OH, SORRY. I MIXED YOU UP. THERE'S A BUNCH OF BLONDES IN THE CLASS, AND A COUPLE OF THEM...
OH, GEEZ, LISTEN TO ME, I'M AN IDIOT. LIKE ALL BLONDES LOOK THE SAME OR SOMETHING, AND I REALLY DIDN'T MEAN --
NO, IT'S OKAY. MORE THAN OKAY. LET'S START OVER.
NO, NO ONE'S SITTING THERE. FEEL FREE.
Sweet Ide
HI. I'M MATT ZIMMER.
HEY, MATT.
CALL ME A.J.
SALAD

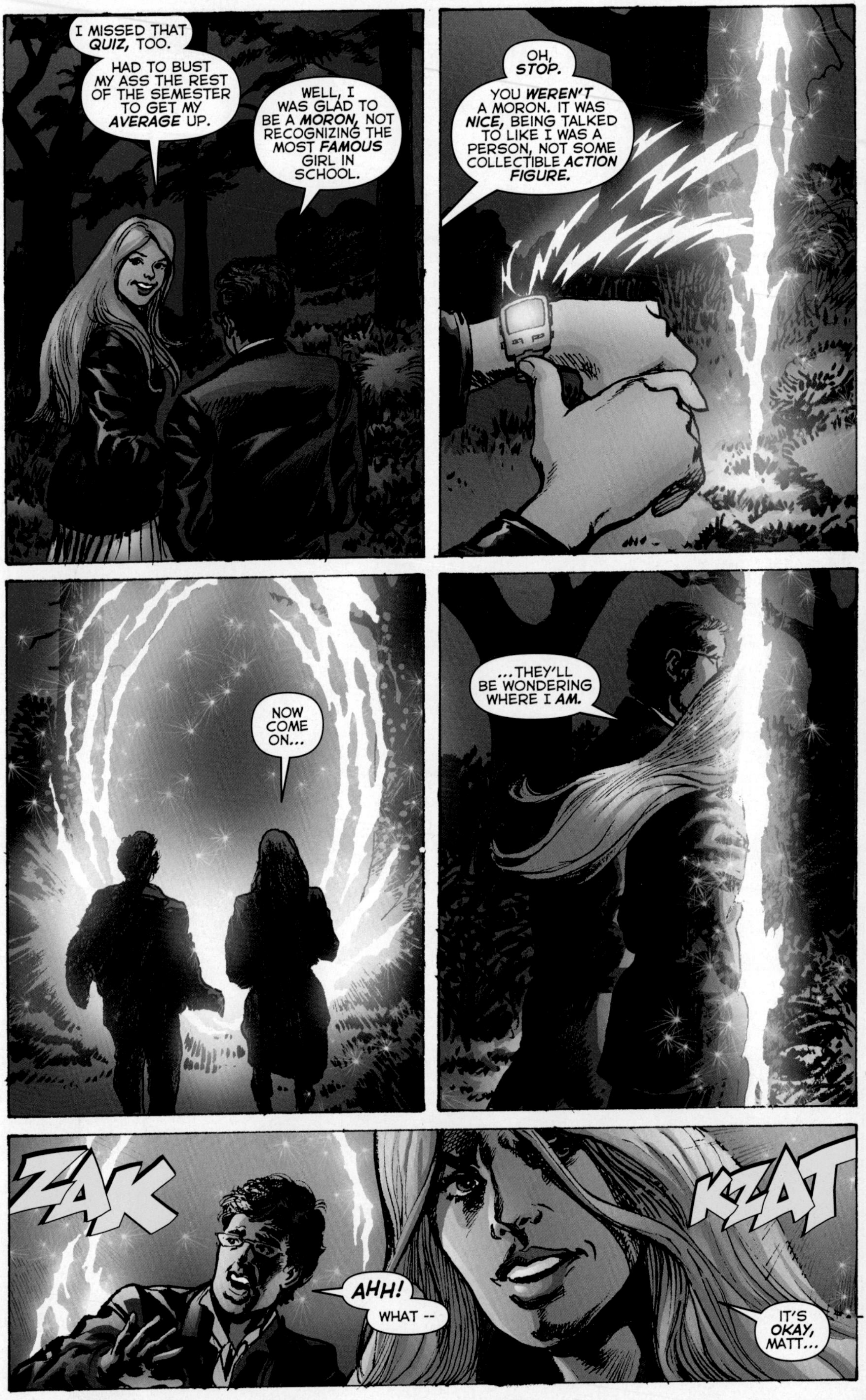
I MISSED THAT QUIZ, TOO.
HAD TO BUST MY ASS THE REST OF THE SEMESTER TO GET MY AVERAGE UP.
WELL, I WAS GLAD TO BE A MORON, NOT RECOGNIZING THE MOST FAMOUS GIRL IN SCHOOL.
OH, STOP.
YOU WEREN'T A MORON. IT WAS NICE, BEING TALKED TO LIKE I WAS A PERSON, NOT SOME COLLECTIBLE ACTION FIGURE.
NOW COME ON...
...THEY'LL BE WONDERING WHERE I AM.
ZAK
KZAT
AHH!
WHAT --
IT'S OKAY, MATT...

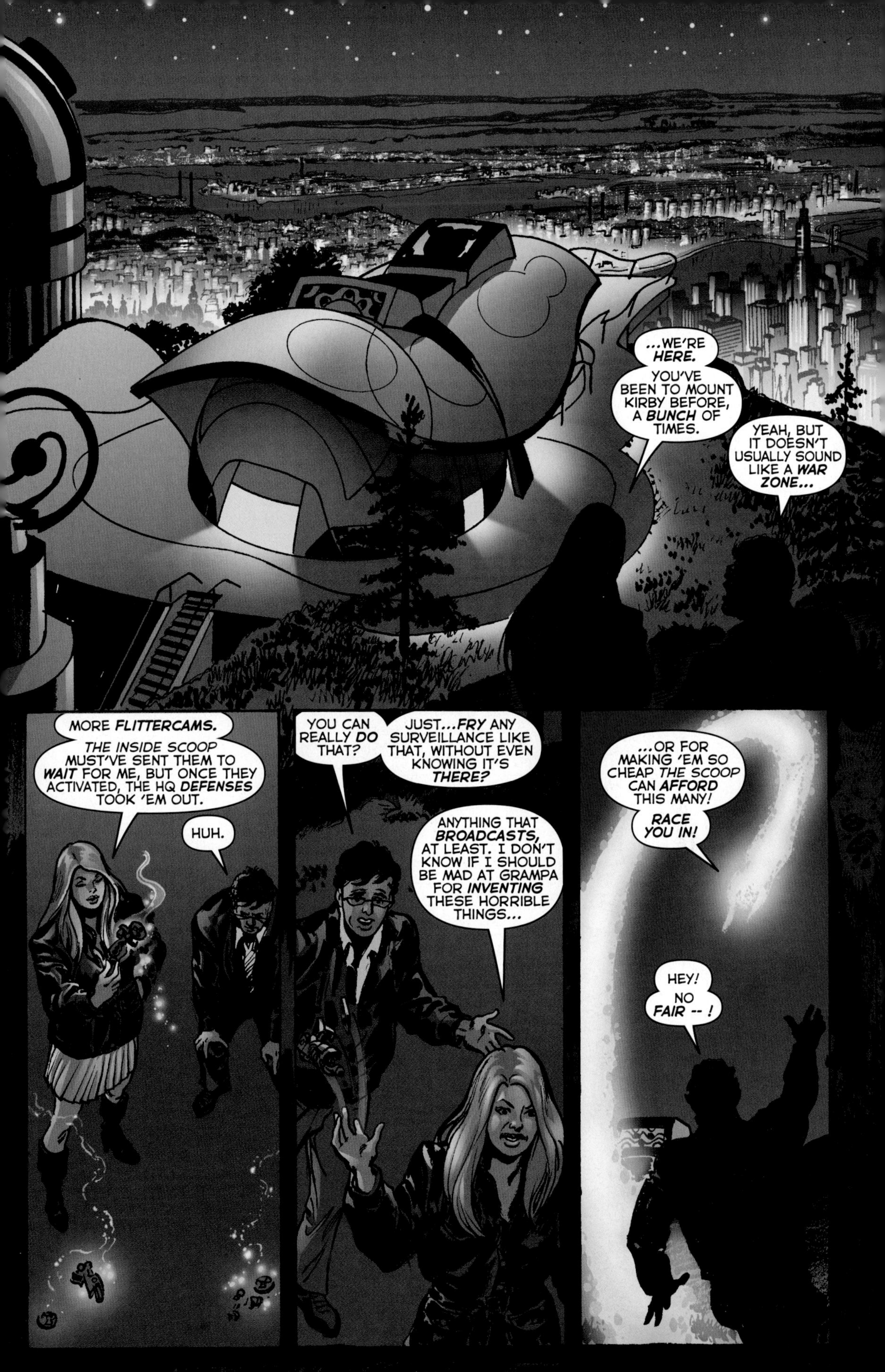
...WE'RE HERE.
YOU'VE BEEN TO MOUNT KIRBY BEFORE, A BUNCH OF TIMES.
YEAH, BUT IT DOESN'T USUALLY SOUND LIKE A WAR ZONE...
MORE FLITTERCAMS.
THE INSIDE SCOOP MUST'VE SENT THEM TO WAIT FOR ME, BUT ONCE THEY ACTIVATED, THE HQ DEFENSES TOOK 'EM OUT.
HUH.
YOU CAN REALLY DO THAT?
JUST...FRY ANY SURVEILLANCE LIKE THAT, WITHOUT EVEN KNOWING IT'S THERE?
ANYTHING THAT BROADCASTS, AT LEAST. I DON'T KNOW IF I SHOULD BE MAD AT GRAMPA FOR INVENTING THESE HORRIBLE THINGS...
...OR FOR MAKING 'EM SO CHEAP THE SCOOP CAN AFFORD THIS MANY!
RACE YOU IN!
HEY! NO FAIR -- !

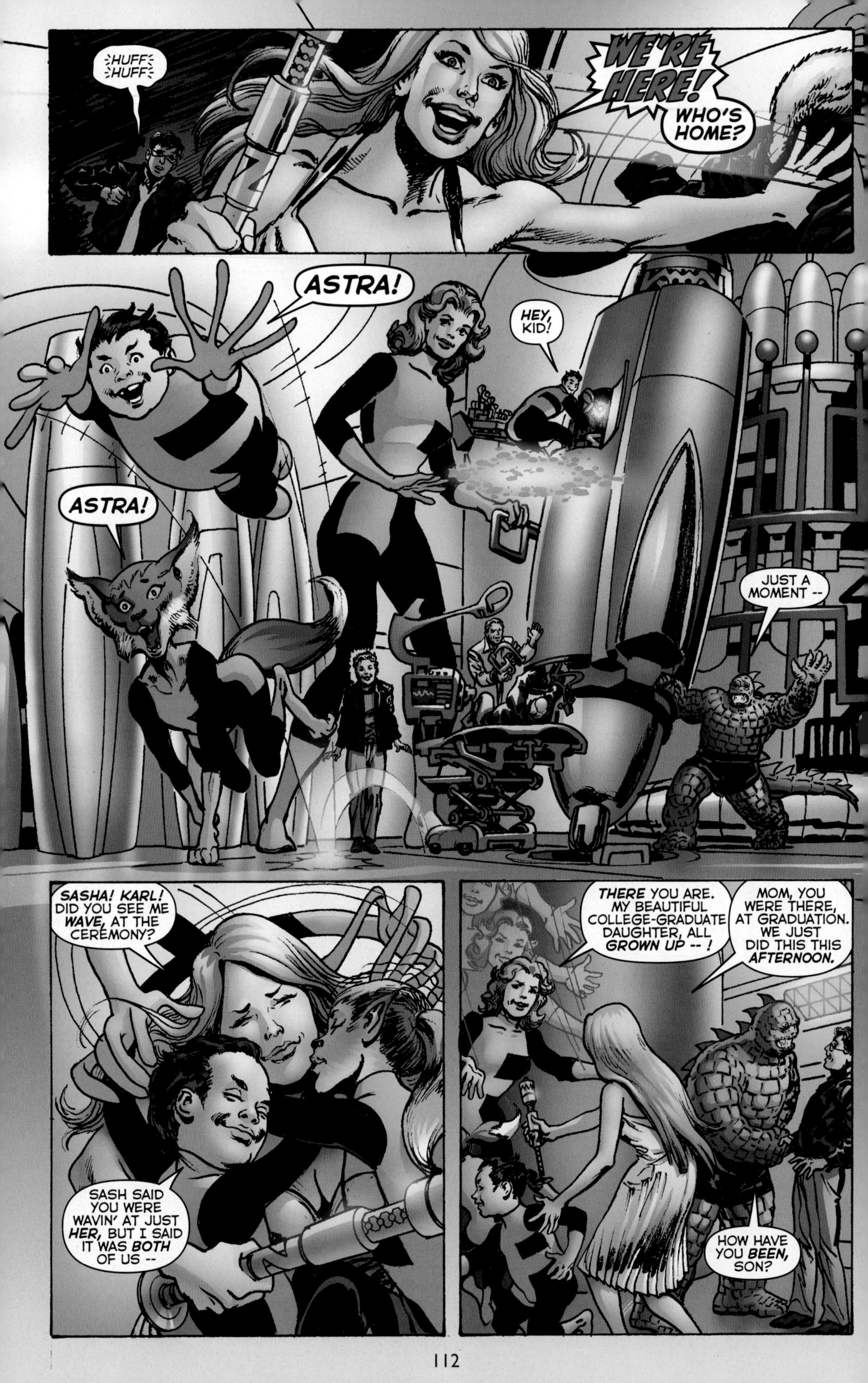
HUFF HUFF
WE'RE HERE!
WHO'S HOME?
ASTRA!
HEY, KID!
ASTRA!
JUST A MOMENT --
SASHA! KARL! DID YOU SEE ME WAVE, AT THE CEREMONY?
SASH SAID YOU WERE WAVIN' AT JUST HER, BUT I SAID IT WAS BOTH OF US --
THERE YOU ARE. MY BEAUTIFUL COLLEGE-GRADUATE DAUGHTER, ALL GROWN UP -- !
MOM, YOU WERE THERE, AT GRADUATION. WE JUST DID THIS THIS AFTERNOON.
HOW HAVE YOU BEEN, SON?

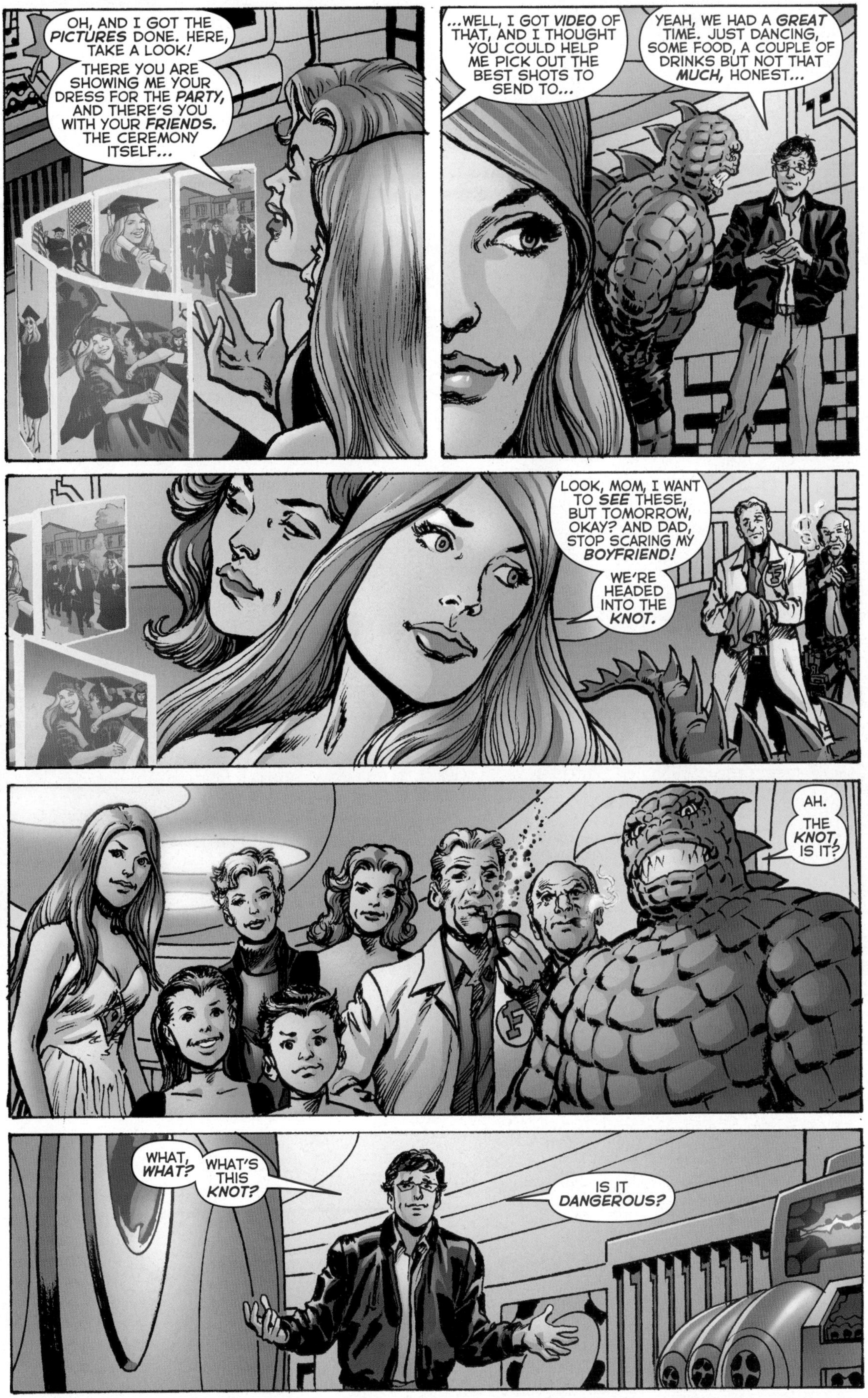
OH, AND I GOT THE PICTURES DONE. HERE, TAKE A LOOK!
THERE YOU ARE SHOWING ME YOUR DRESS FOR THE PARTY, AND THERE'S YOU WITH YOUR FRIENDS. THE CEREMONY ITSELF...
...WELL, I GOT VIDEO OF THAT, AND I THOUGHT YOU COULD HELP ME PICK OUT THE BEST SHOTS TO SEND TO...
YEAH, WE HAD A GREAT TIME. JUST DANCING, SOME FOOD, A COUPLE OF DRINKS BUT NOT THAT MUCH, HONEST...
LOOK, MOM, I WANT TO SEE THESE, BUT TOMORROW, OKAY? AND DAD, STOP SCARING MY BOYFRIEND!
WE'RE HEADED INTO THE KNOT.
AH. THE KNOT, IS IT?
WHAT, WHAT?
WHAT'S THIS KNOT?
IS IT DANGEROUS?

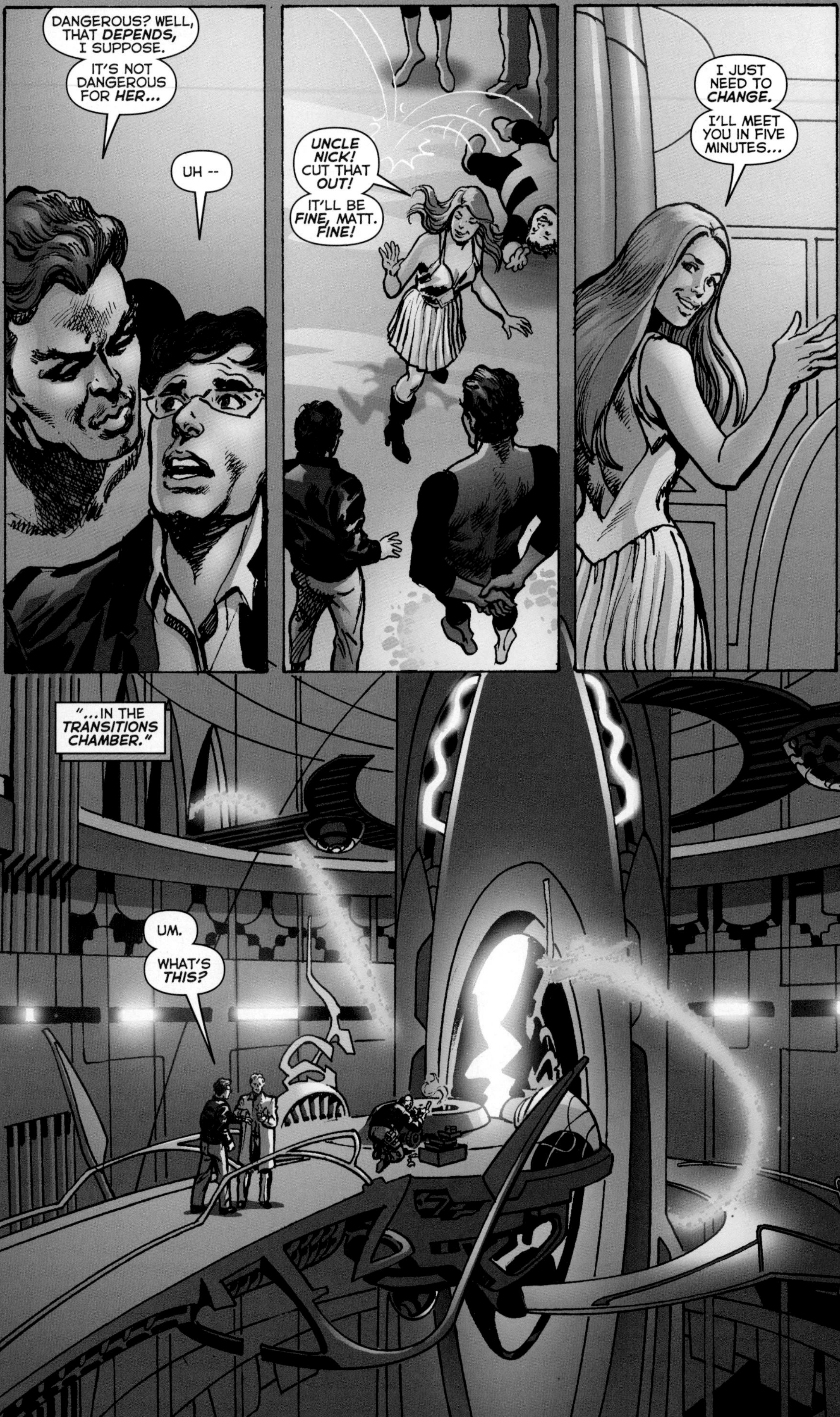
DANGEROUS? WELL, THAT DEPENDS, I SUPPOSE.
IT'S NOT DANGEROUS FOR HER...
UH --
UNCLE NICK! CUT THAT OUT!
IT'LL BE FINE, MATT. FINE!
I JUST NEED TO CHANGE.
I'LL MEET YOU IN FIVE MINUTES...
"...IN THE TRANSITIONS CHAMBER."
UM.
WHAT'S THIS?

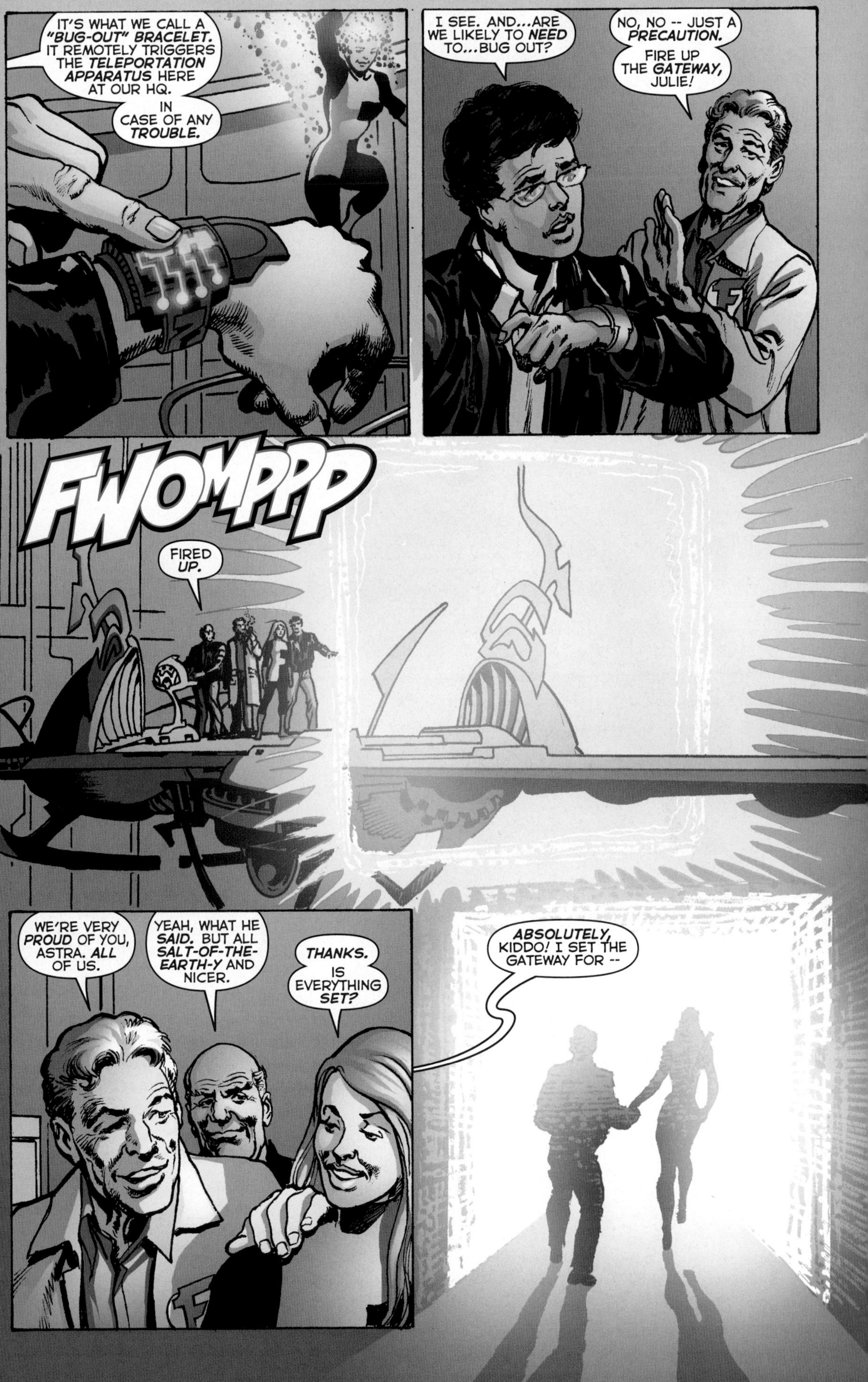
IT'S WHAT WE CALL A "BUG-OUT" BRACELET. IT REMOTELY TRIGGERS THE TELEPORTATION APPARATUS HERE AT OUR HQ.
IN CASE OF ANY TROUBLE.
I SEE. AND...ARE WE LIKELY TO NEED TO...BUG OUT?
NO, NO -- JUST A PRECAUTION.
FIRE UP THE GATEWAY, JULIE!
FWOMPPP
FIRED UP.
WE'RE VERY PROUD OF YOU, ASTRA. ALL OF US.
YEAH, WHAT HE SAID. BUT ALL SALT-OF-THE-EARTH-Y AND NICER.
THANKS.
IS EVERYTHING SET?
ABSOLUTELY, KIDDO! I SET THE GATEWAY FOR --

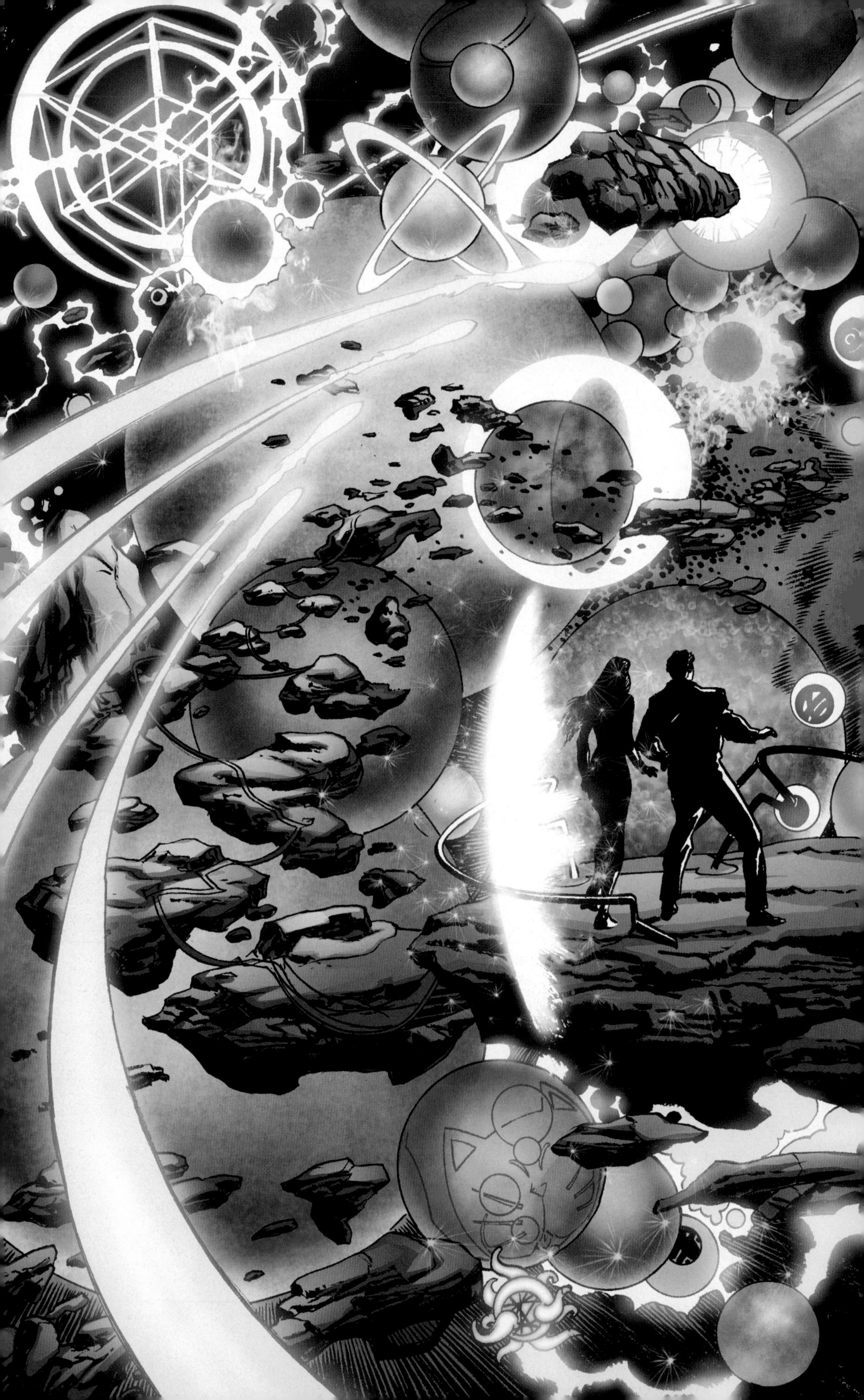

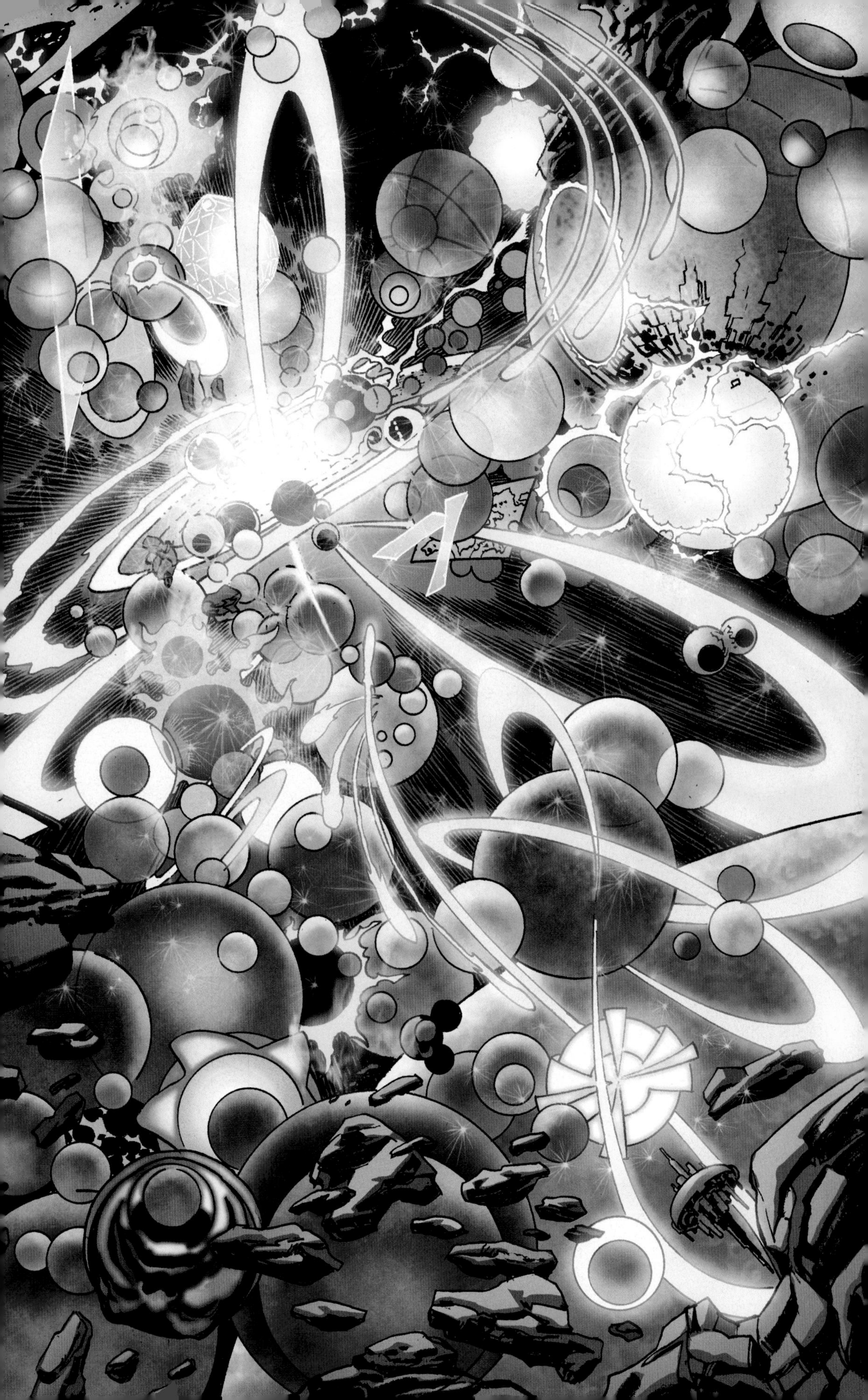

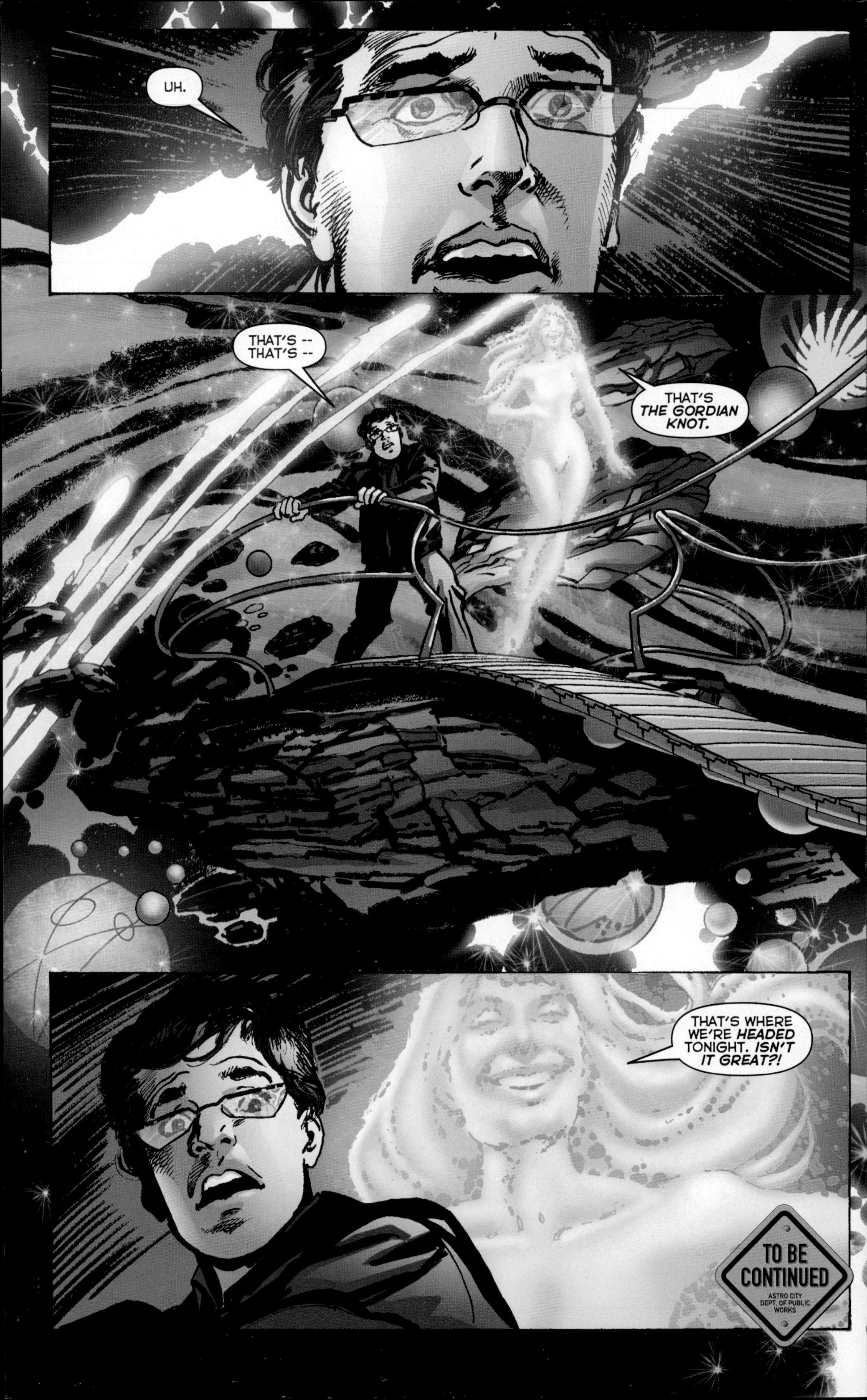
UH.
THAT'S -- THAT'S --
THAT'S THE GORDIAN KNOT.
THAT'S WHERE WE'RE HEADED TONIGHT. ISN'T IT GREAT?!
TO BE CONTINUED
ASTRO CITY DEPT. OF PUBLIC WORKS

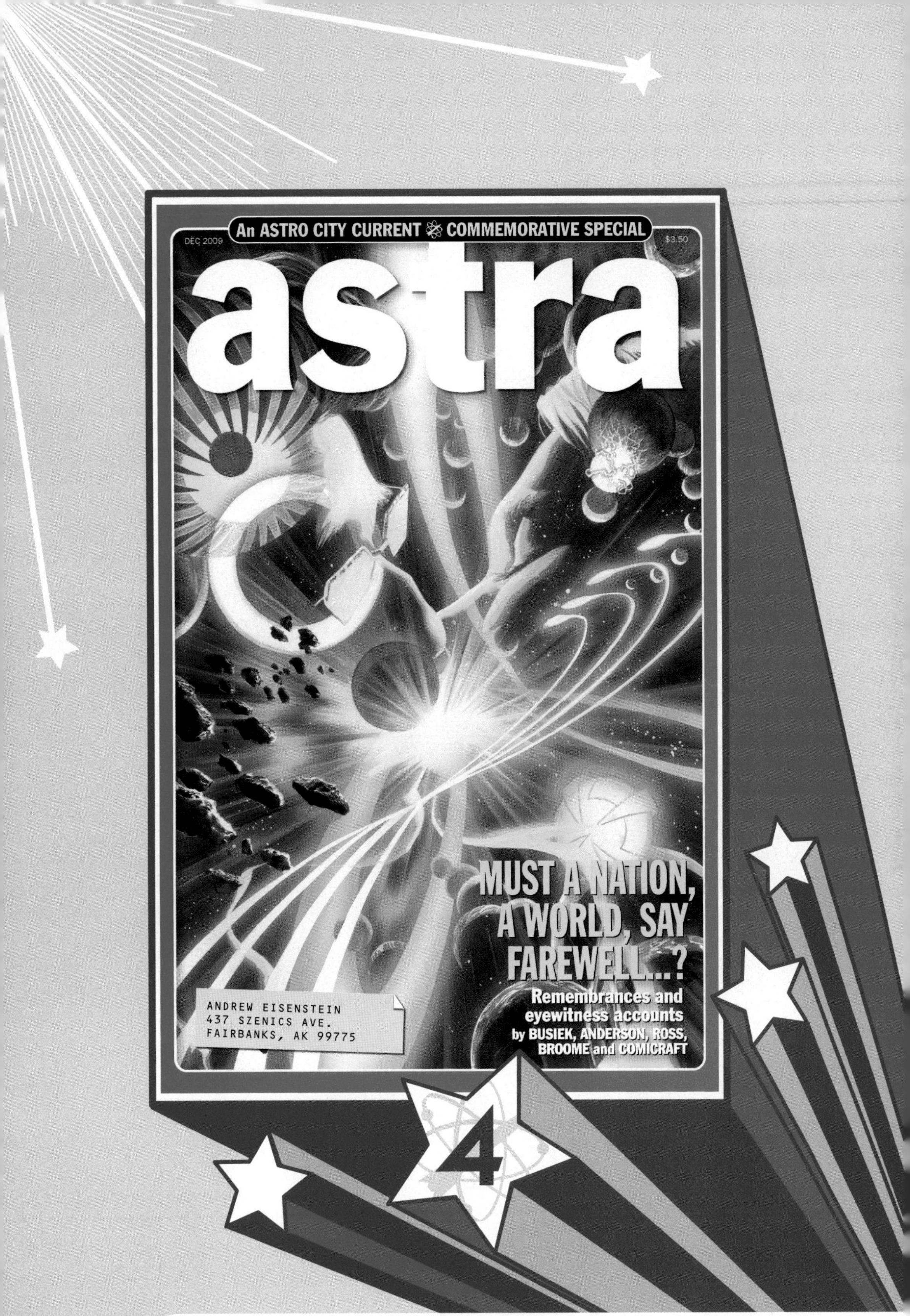
An ASTRO CITY CURRENT COMMEMORATIVE SPECIAL
DEC 2009
$3.50
astra
MUST A NATION, A WORLD, SAY FAREWELL...?
Remembrances and eyewitness accounts
by BUSIEK, ANDERSON, ROSS, BROOME and COMICRAFT
ANDREW EISENSTEIN
437 SZENICS AVE.
FAIRBANKS, AK 99775
4

THE GORDIAN KNOT

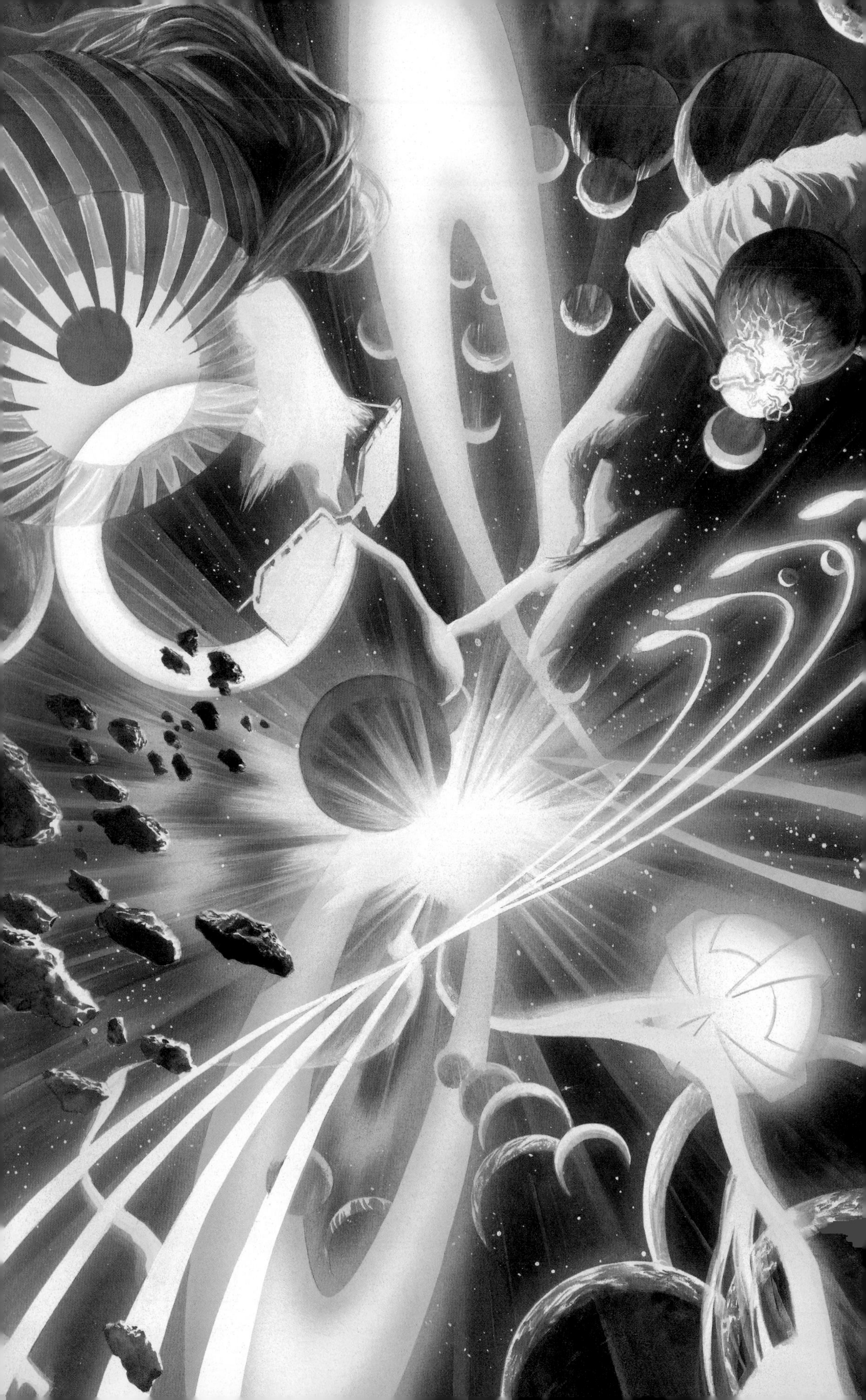

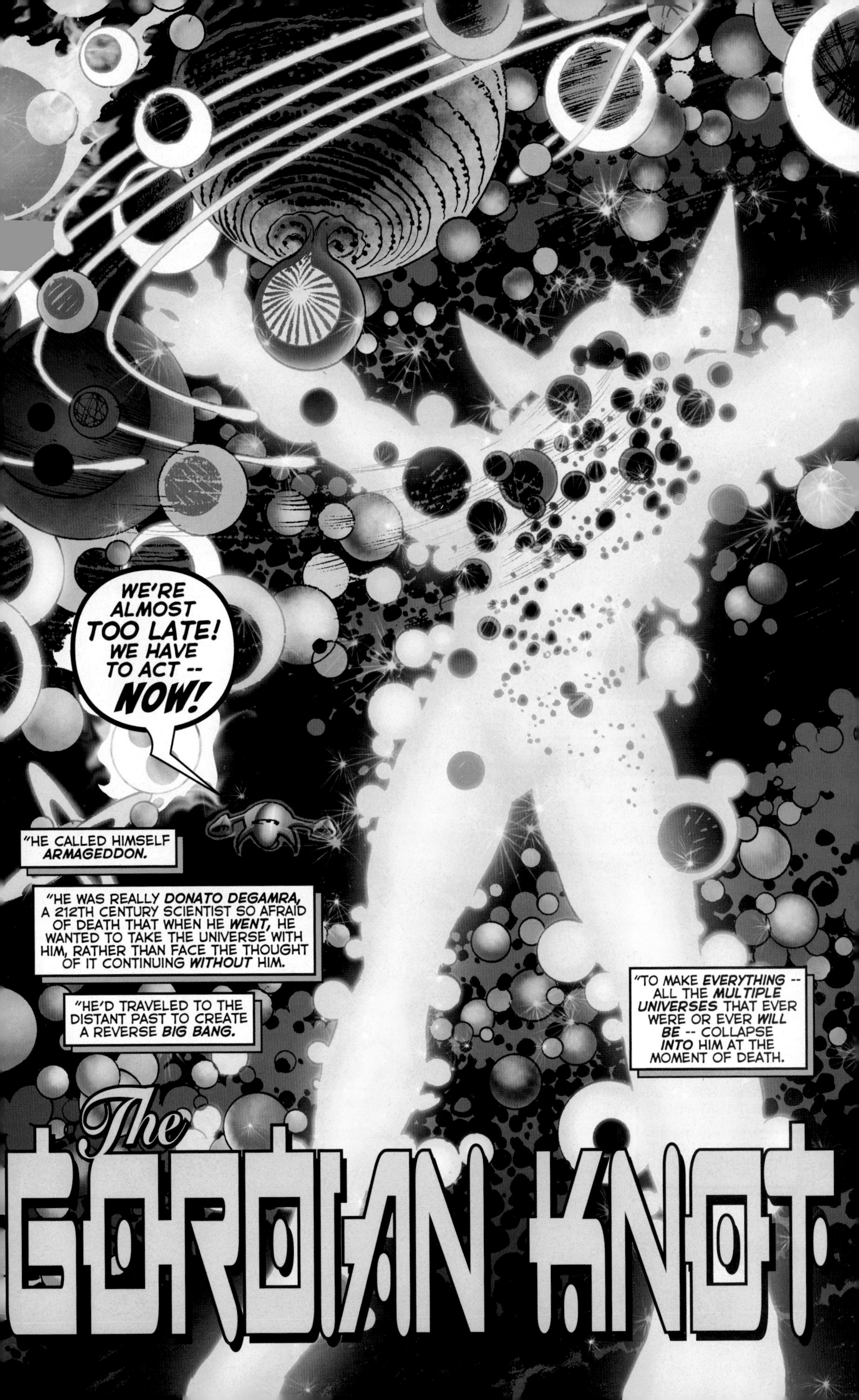
WE'RE ALMOST TOO LATE! WE HAVE TO ACT -- NOW!
"HE CALLED HIMSELF ARMAGEDDON.
"HE WAS REALLY DONATO DEGAMRA, A 212TH CENTURY SCIENTIST SO AFRAID OF DEATH THAT WHEN HE WENT, HE WANTED TO TAKE THE UNIVERSE WITH HIM, RATHER THAN FACE THE THOUGHT OF IT CONTINUING WITHOUT HIM.
"HE'D TRAVELED TO THE DISTANT PAST TO CREATE A REVERSE BIG BANG.
"TO MAKE EVERYTHING -- ALL THE MULTIPLE UNIVERSES THAT EVER WERE OR EVER WILL BE -- COLLAPSE INTO HIM AT THE MOMENT OF DEATH.
The GORDIAN KNOT

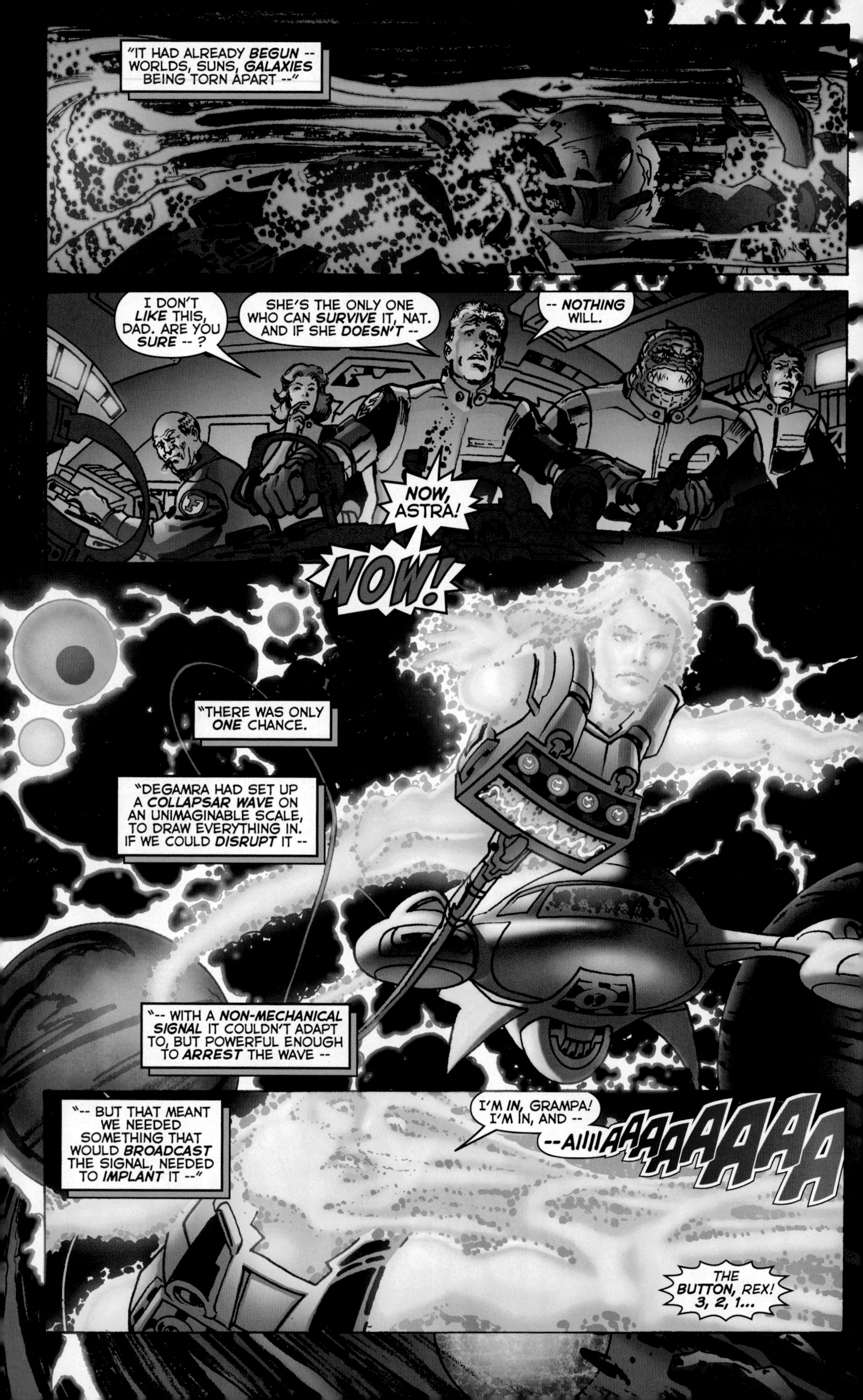
"IT HAD ALREADY BEGUN -- WORLDS, SUNS, GALAXIES BEING TORN APART --"
I DON'T LIKE THIS, DAD. ARE YOU SURE -- ?
SHE'S THE ONLY ONE WHO CAN SURVIVE IT, NAT. AND IF SHE DOESN'T --
-- NOTHING WILL.
NOW, ASTRA!
NOW!
"THERE WAS ONLY ONE CHANCE.
"DEGAMRA HAD SET UP A COLLAPSAR WAVE ON AN UNIMAGINABLE SCALE, TO DRAW EVERYTHING IN. IF WE COULD DISRUPT IT --
"-- WITH A NON-MECHANICAL SIGNAL IT COULDN'T ADAPT TO, BUT POWERFUL ENOUGH TO ARREST THE WAVE --
"-- BUT THAT MEANT WE NEEDED SOMETHING THAT WOULD BROADCAST THE SIGNAL, NEEDED TO IMPLANT IT --"
I'M IN, GRAMPA! I'M IN, AND --
--AIIIIAAAAAAAAAA
THE BUTTON, REX! 3, 2, 1...

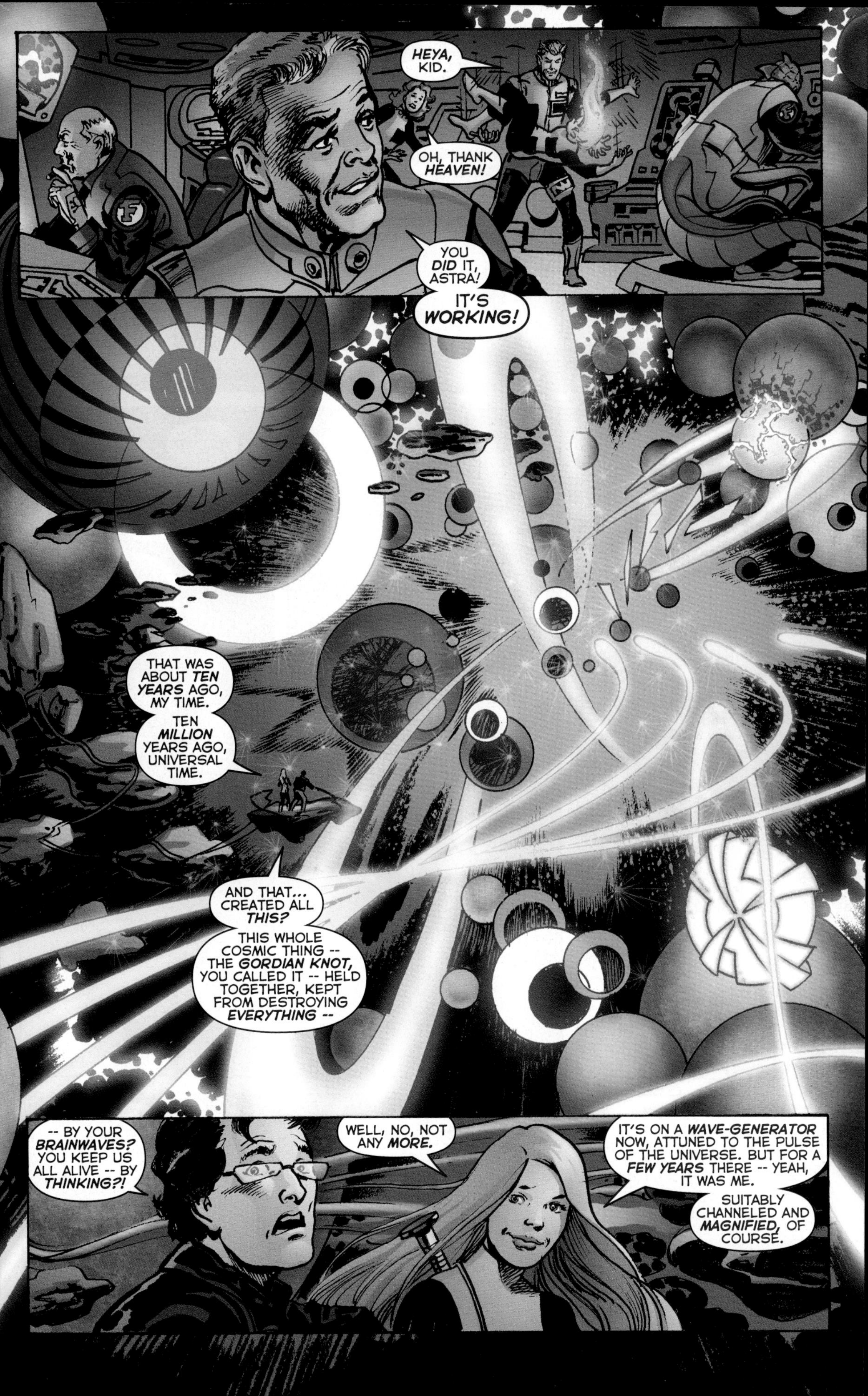
HEYA, KID.
OH, THANK HEAVEN!
YOU DID IT, ASTRA!
IT'S WORKING!
THAT WAS ABOUT TEN YEARS AGO, MY TIME.
TEN MILLION YEARS AGO, UNIVERSAL TIME.
AND THAT... CREATED ALL THIS?
THIS WHOLE COSMIC THING -- THE GORDIAN KNOT, YOU CALLED IT -- HELD TOGETHER, KEPT FROM DESTROYING EVERYTHING --
-- BY YOUR BRAINWAVES? YOU KEEP US ALL ALIVE -- BY THINKING?!
WELL, NO, NOT ANY MORE.
IT'S ON A WAVE-GENERATOR NOW, ATTUNED TO THE PULSE OF THE UNIVERSE. BUT FOR A FEW YEARS THERE -- YEAH, IT WAS ME.
SUITABLY CHANNELED AND MAGNIFIED, OF COURSE.

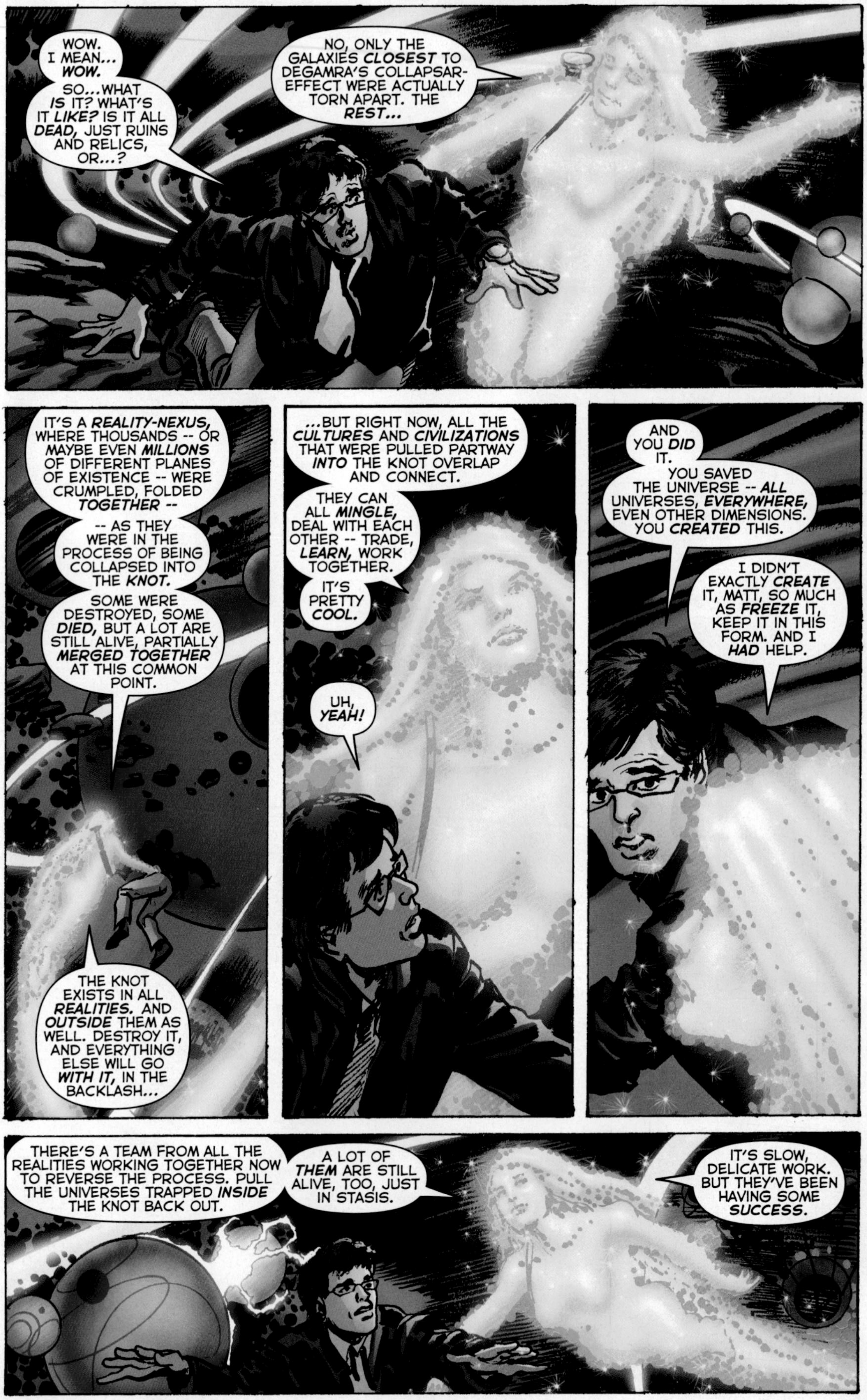

WOW. I MEAN... WOW.
SO...WHAT IS IT? WHAT'S IT LIKE? IS IT ALL DEAD, JUST RUINS AND RELICS, OR...?
NO, ONLY THE GALAXIES CLOSEST TO DEGAMRA'S COLLAPSAR-EFFECT WERE ACTUALLY TORN APART. THE REST...
IT'S A REALITY-NEXUS, WHERE THOUSANDS -- OR MAYBE EVEN MILLIONS OF DIFFERENT PLANES OF EXISTENCE -- WERE CRUMPLED, FOLDED TOGETHER --
-- AS THEY WERE IN THE PROCESS OF BEING COLLAPSED INTO THE KNOT.
SOME WERE DESTROYED, SOME DIED, BUT A LOT ARE STILL ALIVE, PARTIALLY MERGED TOGETHER AT THIS COMMON POINT.
THE KNOT EXISTS IN ALL REALITIES. AND OUTSIDE THEM AS WELL. DESTROY IT, AND EVERYTHING ELSE WILL GO WITH IT, IN THE BACKLASH...
...BUT RIGHT NOW, ALL THE CULTURES AND CIVILIZATIONS THAT WERE PULLED PARTWAY INTO THE KNOT OVERLAP AND CONNECT.
THEY CAN ALL MINGLE, DEAL WITH EACH OTHER -- TRADE, LEARN, WORK TOGETHER.
IT'S PRETTY COOL.
UH, YEAH!
AND YOU DID IT.
YOU SAVED THE UNIVERSE -- ALL UNIVERSES, EVERYWHERE, EVEN OTHER DIMENSIONS. YOU CREATED THIS.
I DIDN'T EXACTLY CREATE IT, MATT, SO MUCH AS FREEZE IT, KEEP IT IN THIS FORM. AND I HAD HELP.
THERE'S A TEAM FROM ALL THE REALITIES WORKING TOGETHER NOW TO REVERSE THE PROCESS. PULL THE UNIVERSES TRAPPED INSIDE THE KNOT BACK OUT.
A LOT OF THEM ARE STILL ALIVE, TOO, JUST IN STASIS.
IT'S SLOW, DELICATE WORK. BUT THEY'VE BEEN HAVING SOME SUCCESS.

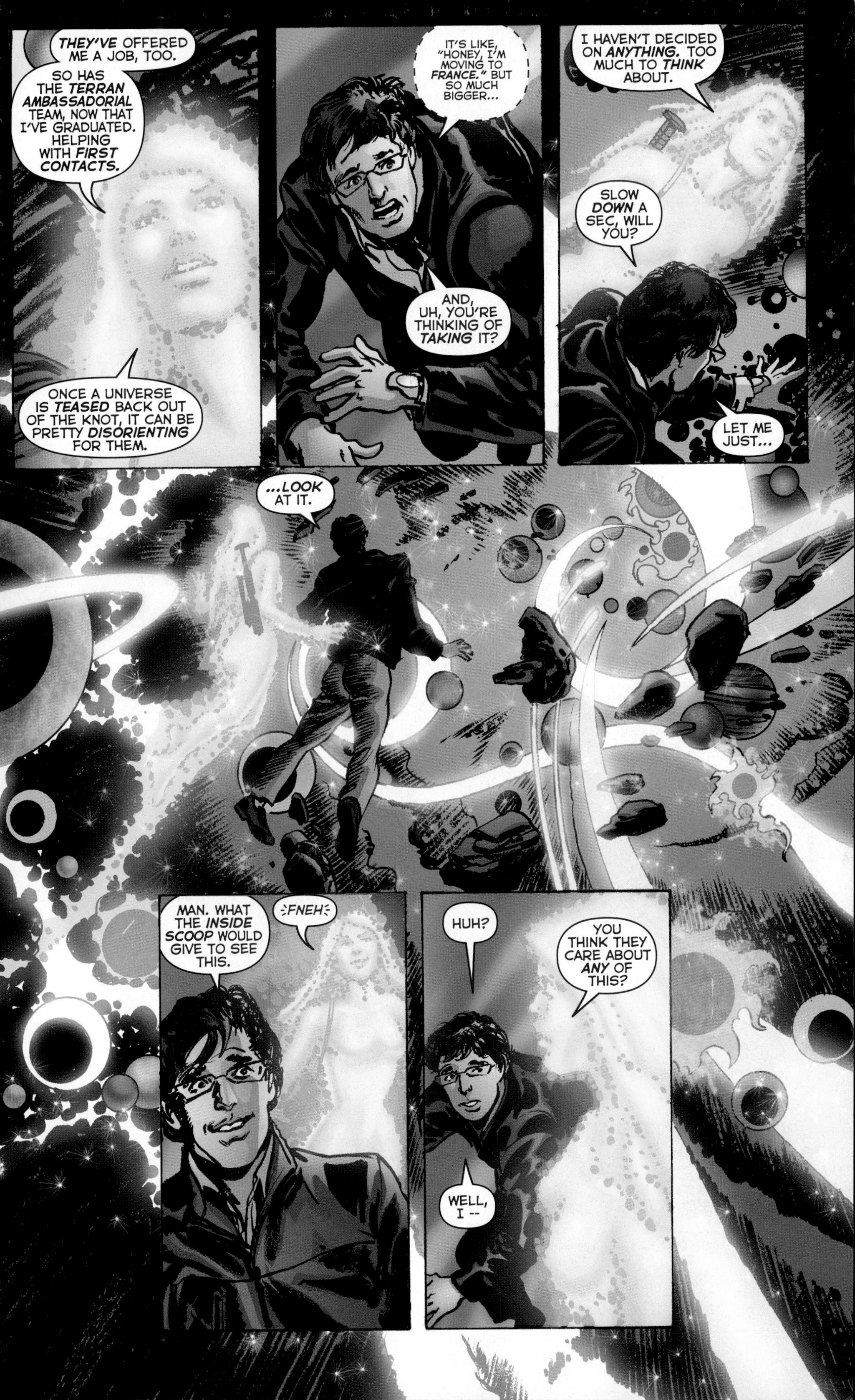
THEY'VE OFFERED ME A JOB, TOO.
SO HAS THE TERRAN AMBASSADORIAL TEAM, NOW THAT I'VE GRADUATED. HELPING WITH FIRST CONTACTS.
ONCE A UNIVERSE IS TEASED BACK OUT OF THE KNOT, IT CAN BE PRETTY DISORIENTING FOR THEM.
IT'S LIKE, "HONEY, I'M MOVING TO FRANCE." BUT SO MUCH BIGGER...
AND, UH, YOU'RE THINKING OF TAKING IT?
I HAVEN'T DECIDED ON ANYTHING. TOO MUCH TO THINK ABOUT.
SLOW DOWN A SEC, WILL YOU?
LET ME JUST...
...LOOK AT IT.
MAN. WHAT THE INSIDE SCOOP WOULD GIVE TO SEE THIS.
FNEH
HUH?
YOU THINK THEY CARE ABOUT ANY OF THIS?
WELL, I --

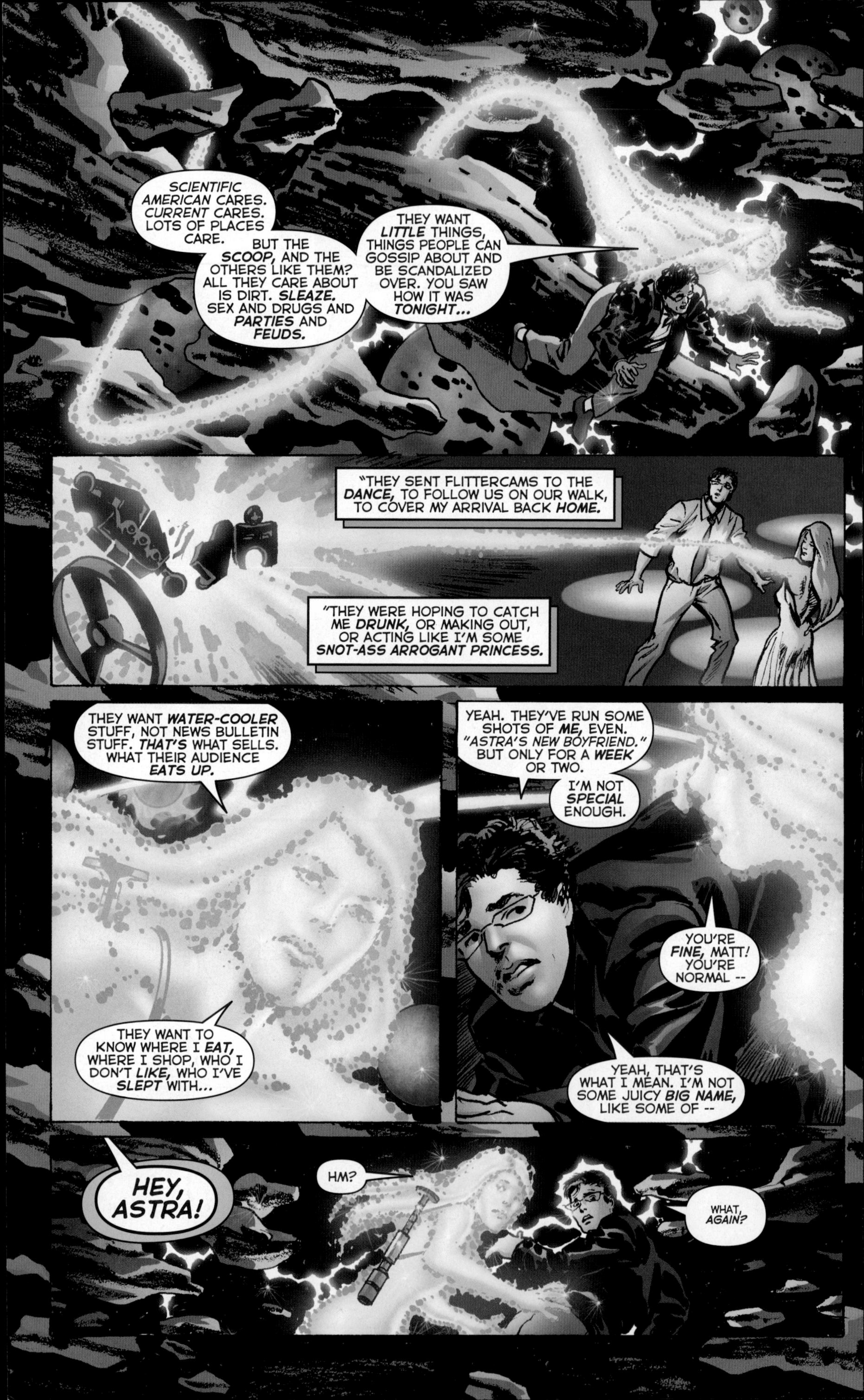

SCIENTIFIC AMERICAN CARES. CURRENT CARES. LOTS OF PLACES CARE.
BUT THE SCOOP, AND THE OTHERS LIKE THEM? ALL THEY CARE ABOUT IS DIRT. SLEAZE. SEX AND DRUGS AND PARTIES AND FEUDS.
THEY WANT LITTLE THINGS, THINGS PEOPLE CAN GOSSIP ABOUT AND BE SCANDALIZED OVER. YOU SAW HOW IT WAS TONIGHT...
"THEY SENT FLITTERCAMS TO THE DANCE, TO FOLLOW US ON OUR WALK, TO COVER MY ARRIVAL BACK HOME.
"THEY WERE HOPING TO CATCH ME DRUNK, OR MAKING OUT, OR ACTING LIKE I'M SOME SNOT-ASS ARROGANT PRINCESS.
THEY WANT WATER-COOLER STUFF, NOT NEWS BULLETIN STUFF. THAT'S WHAT SELLS. WHAT THEIR AUDIENCE EATS UP.
THEY WANT TO KNOW WHERE I EAT, WHERE I SHOP, WHO I DON'T LIKE, WHO I'VE SLEPT WITH...
YEAH. THEY'VE RUN SOME SHOTS OF ME, EVEN. "ASTRA'S NEW BOYFRIEND." BUT ONLY FOR A WEEK OR TWO.
I'M NOT SPECIAL ENOUGH.
YOU'RE FINE, MATT! YOU'RE NORMAL --
YEAH, THAT'S WHAT I MEAN. I'M NOT SOME JUICY BIG NAME, LIKE SOME OF --
HEY, ASTRA!
HM?
WHAT, AGAIN?

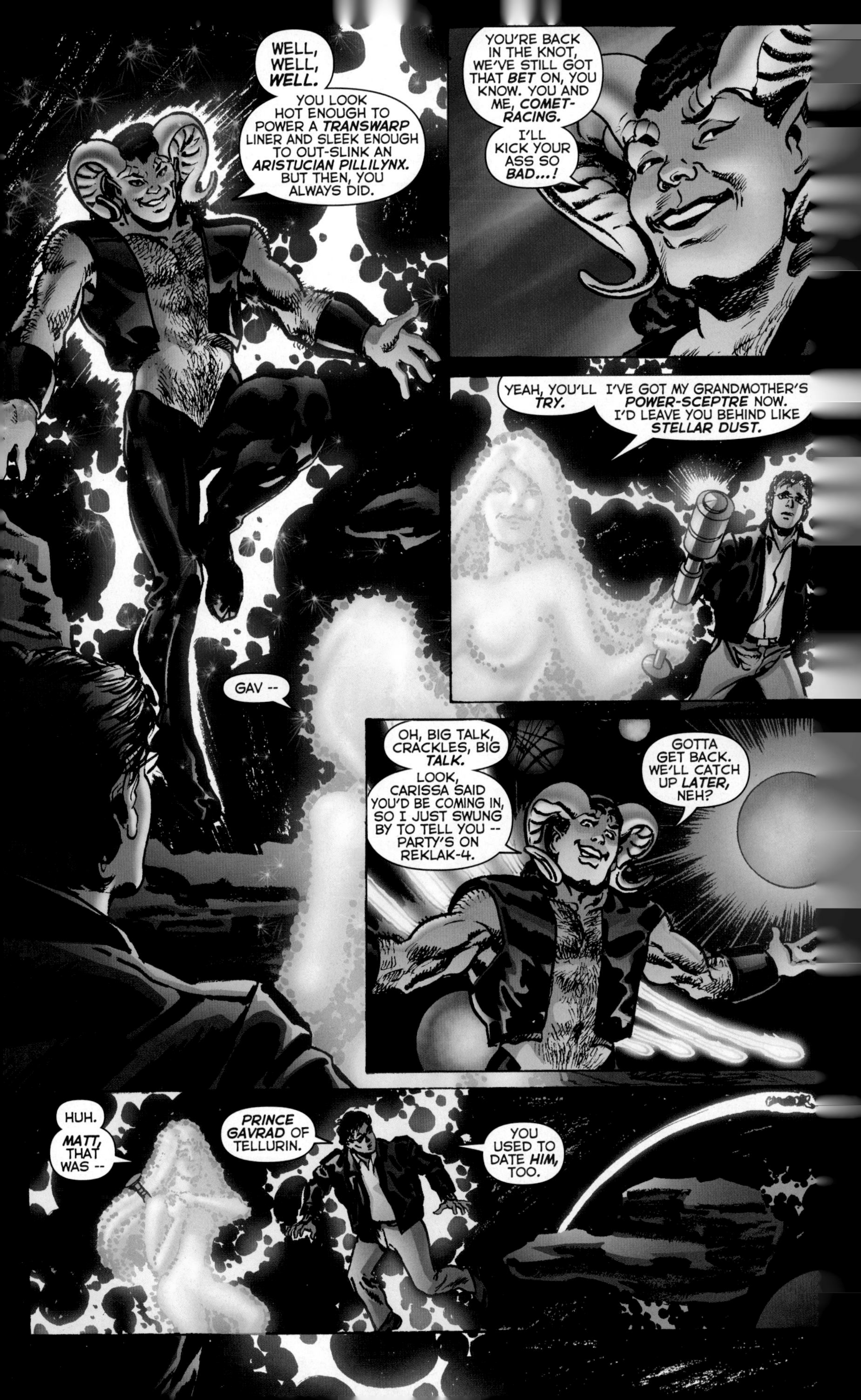
WELL, WELL, WELL.
YOU LOOK HOT ENOUGH TO POWER A TRANSWARP LINER AND SLEEK ENOUGH TO OUT-SLINK AN ARISTUCIAN PILLILYNX. BUT THEN, YOU ALWAYS DID.
YOU'RE BACK IN THE KNOT, WE'VE STILL GOT THAT BET ON, YOU KNOW. YOU AND ME, COMET-RACING.
I'LL KICK YOUR ASS SO BAD...!
YEAH, YOU'LL TRY.
I'VE GOT MY GRANDMOTHER'S POWER-SCEPTRE NOW. I'D LEAVE YOU BEHIND LIKE STELLAR DUST.
GAV --
OH, BIG TALK, CRACKLES, BIG TALK.
LOOK, CARISSA SAID YOU'D BE COMING IN, SO I JUST SWUNG BY TO TELL YOU -- PARTY'S ON REKLAK-4.
GOTTA GET BACK. WE'LL CATCH UP LATER, NEH?
HUH. MATT, THAT WAS --
PRINCE GAVRAD OF TELLURIN.
YOU USED TO DATE HIM, TOO.

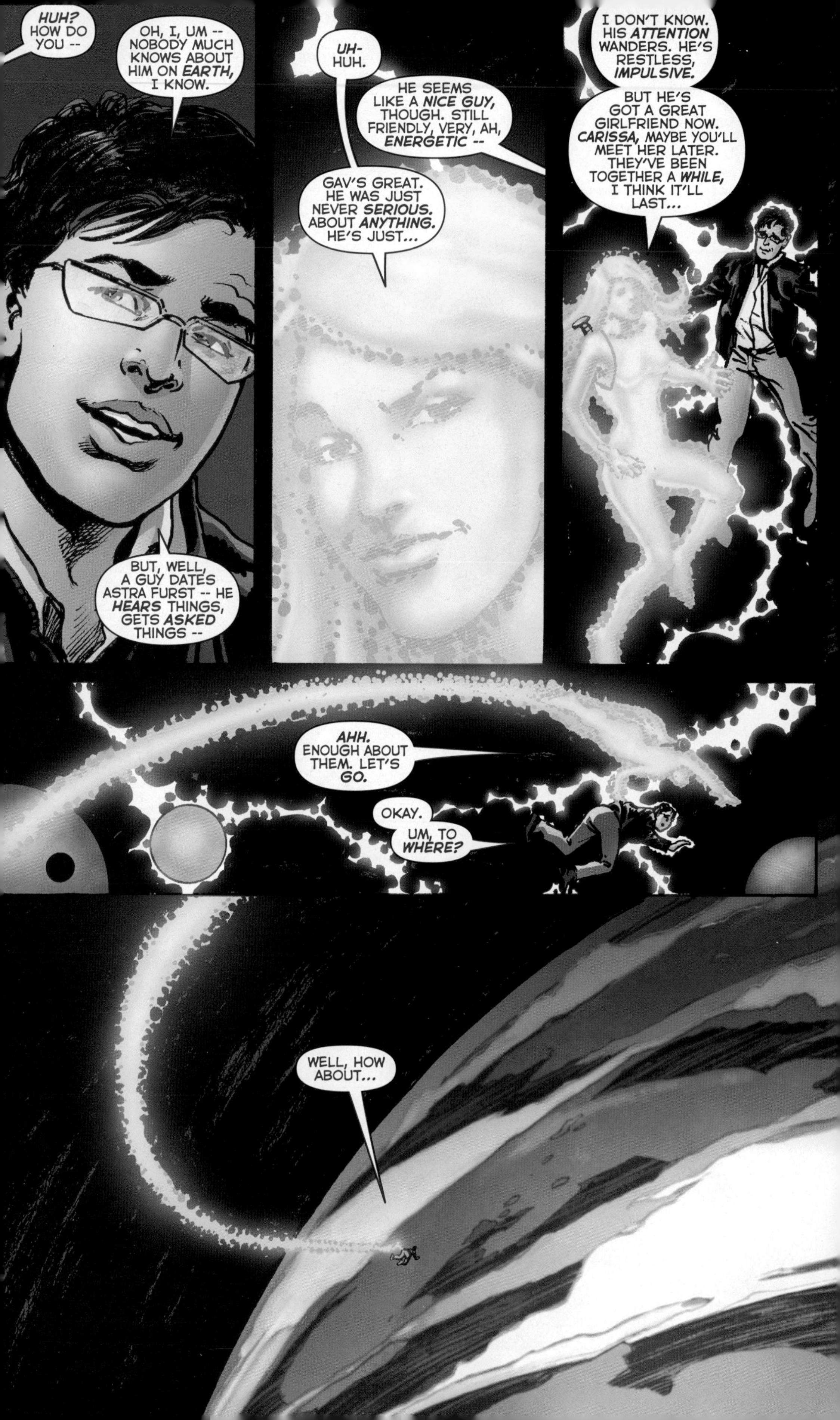
HUH? HOW DO YOU --
OH, I, UM -- NOBODY MUCH KNOWS ABOUT HIM ON EARTH, I KNOW.
BUT, WELL, A GUY DATES ASTRA FURST -- HE HEARS THINGS, GETS ASKED THINGS --
UH-HUH.
HE SEEMS LIKE A NICE GUY, THOUGH. STILL FRIENDLY, VERY, AH, ENERGETIC --
GAV'S GREAT. HE WAS JUST NEVER SERIOUS. ABOUT ANYTHING. HE'S JUST...
I DON'T KNOW. HIS ATTENTION WANDERS. HE'S RESTLESS, IMPULSIVE.
BUT HE'S GOT A GREAT GIRLFRIEND NOW. CARISSA, MAYBE YOU'LL MEET HER LATER. THEY'VE BEEN TOGETHER A WHILE, I THINK IT'LL LAST...
AHH. ENOUGH ABOUT THEM. LET'S GO.
OKAY.
UM, TO WHERE?
WELL, HOW ABOUT...

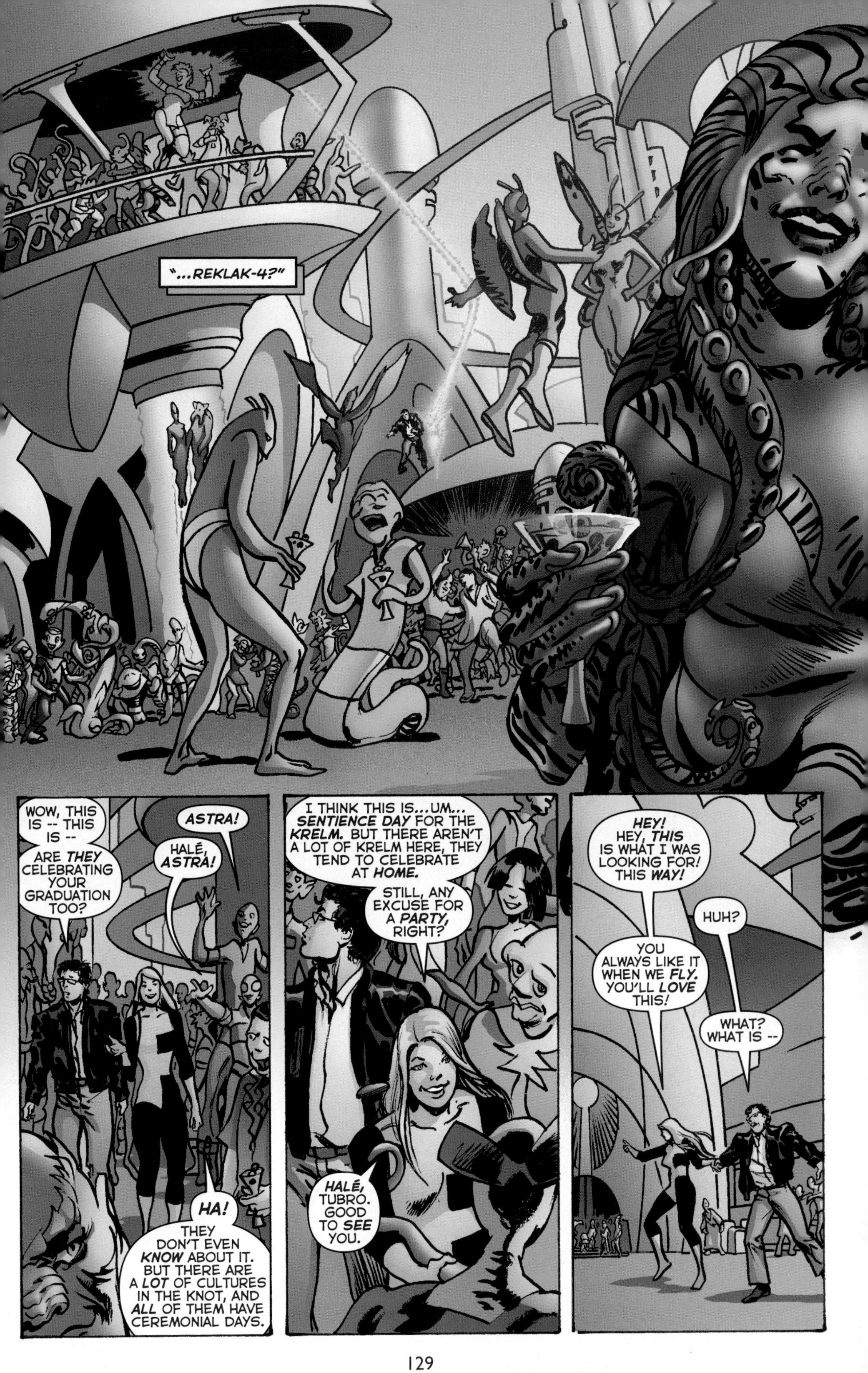

"...REKLAK-4?"
WOW, THIS IS -- THIS IS --
ARE THEY CELEBRATING YOUR GRADUATION TOO?
ASTRA!
HALÉ, ASTRA!
HA!
THEY DON'T EVEN KNOW ABOUT IT. BUT THERE ARE A LOT OF CULTURES IN THE KNOT, AND ALL OF THEM HAVE CEREMONIAL DAYS.
I THINK THIS IS...UM... SENTIENCE DAY FOR THE KRELM. BUT THERE AREN'T A LOT OF KRELM HERE, THEY TEND TO CELEBRATE AT HOME.
STILL, ANY EXCUSE FOR A PARTY, RIGHT?
HALÉ, TUBRO. GOOD TO SEE YOU.
HEY! HEY, THIS IS WHAT I WAS LOOKING FOR! THIS WAY!
HUH?
YOU ALWAYS LIKE IT WHEN WE FLY. YOU'LL LOVE THIS!
WHAT? WHAT IS --

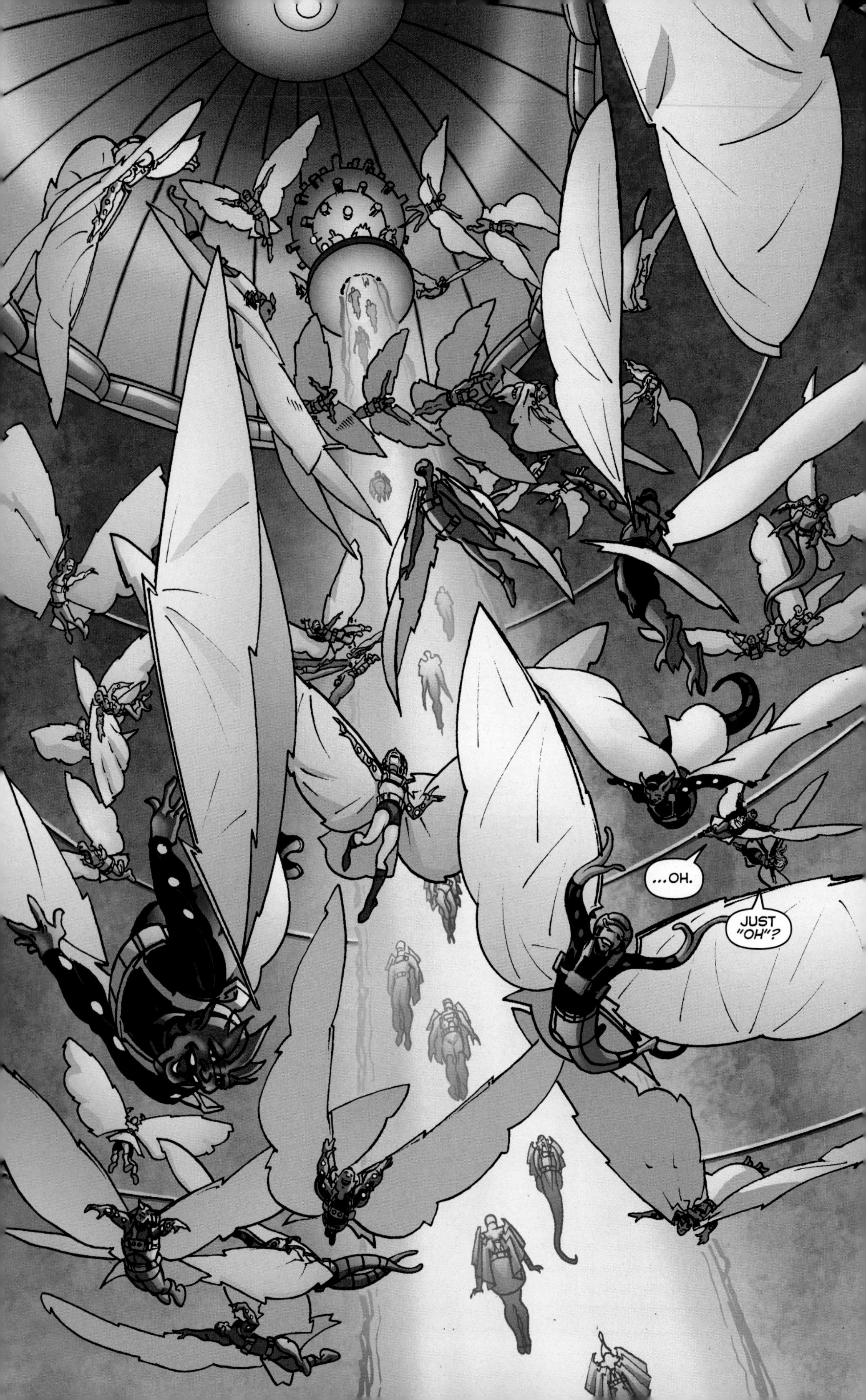
...OH.
JUST "OH"?

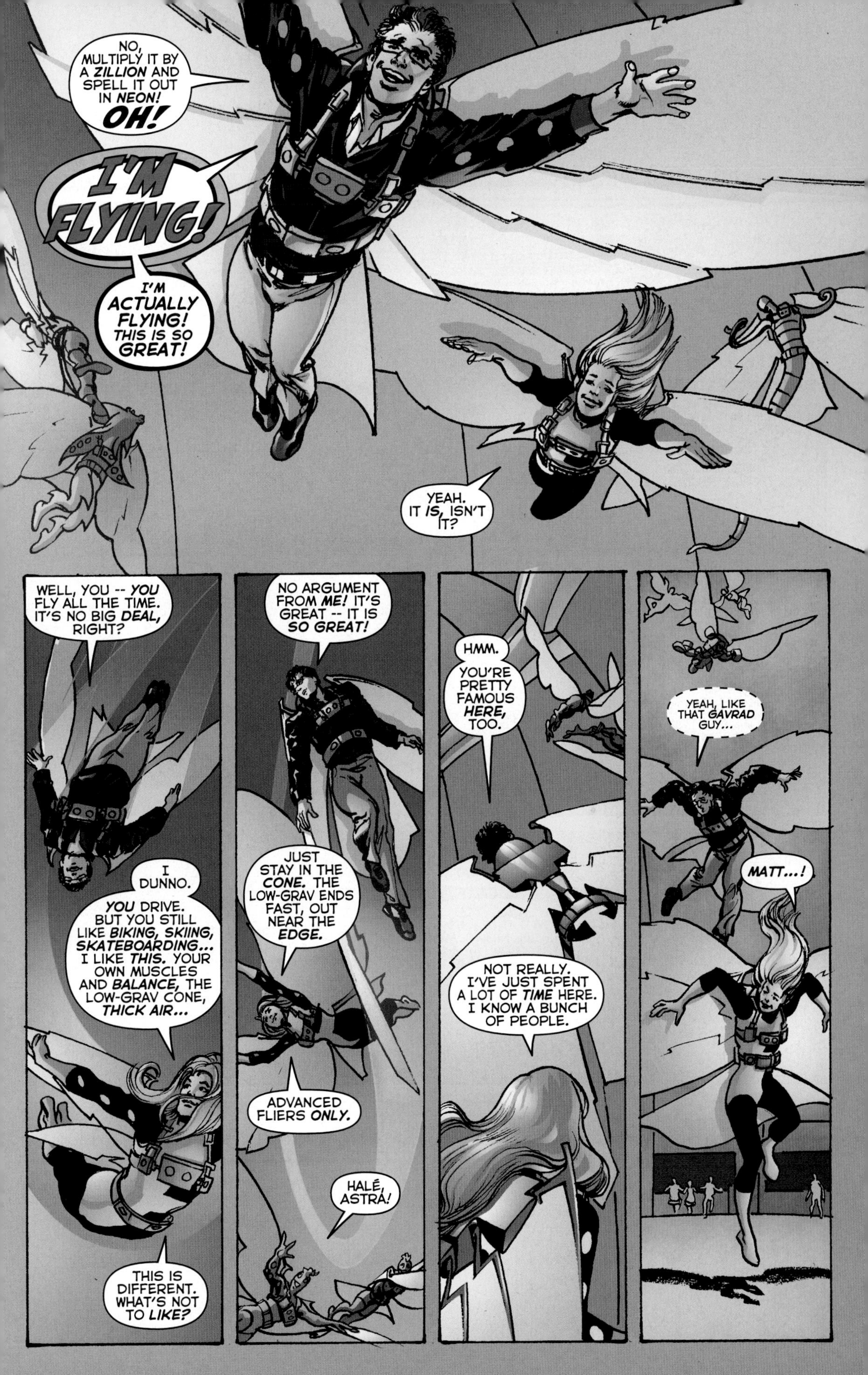
NO, MULTIPLY IT BY A ZILLION AND SPELL IT OUT IN NEON! OH!
I'M FLYING!
I'M ACTUALLY FLYING! THIS IS SO GREAT!
YEAH. IT IS, ISN'T IT?
WELL, YOU -- YOU FLY ALL THE TIME. IT'S NO BIG DEAL, RIGHT?
I DUNNO.
YOU DRIVE. BUT YOU STILL LIKE BIKING, SKIING, SKATEBOARDING... I LIKE THIS. YOUR OWN MUSCLES AND BALANCE, THE LOW-GRAV CONE, THICK AIR...
THIS IS DIFFERENT. WHAT'S NOT TO LIKE?
NO ARGUMENT FROM ME! IT'S GREAT -- IT IS SO GREAT!
JUST STAY IN THE CONE. THE LOW-GRAV ENDS FAST, OUT NEAR THE EDGE.
ADVANCED FLIERS ONLY.
HALÉ, ASTRÁ!
HMM.
YOU'RE PRETTY FAMOUS HERE, TOO.
NOT REALLY. I'VE JUST SPENT A LOT OF TIME HERE. I KNOW A BUNCH OF PEOPLE.
YEAH, LIKE THAT GAVRAD GUY...
MATT...!

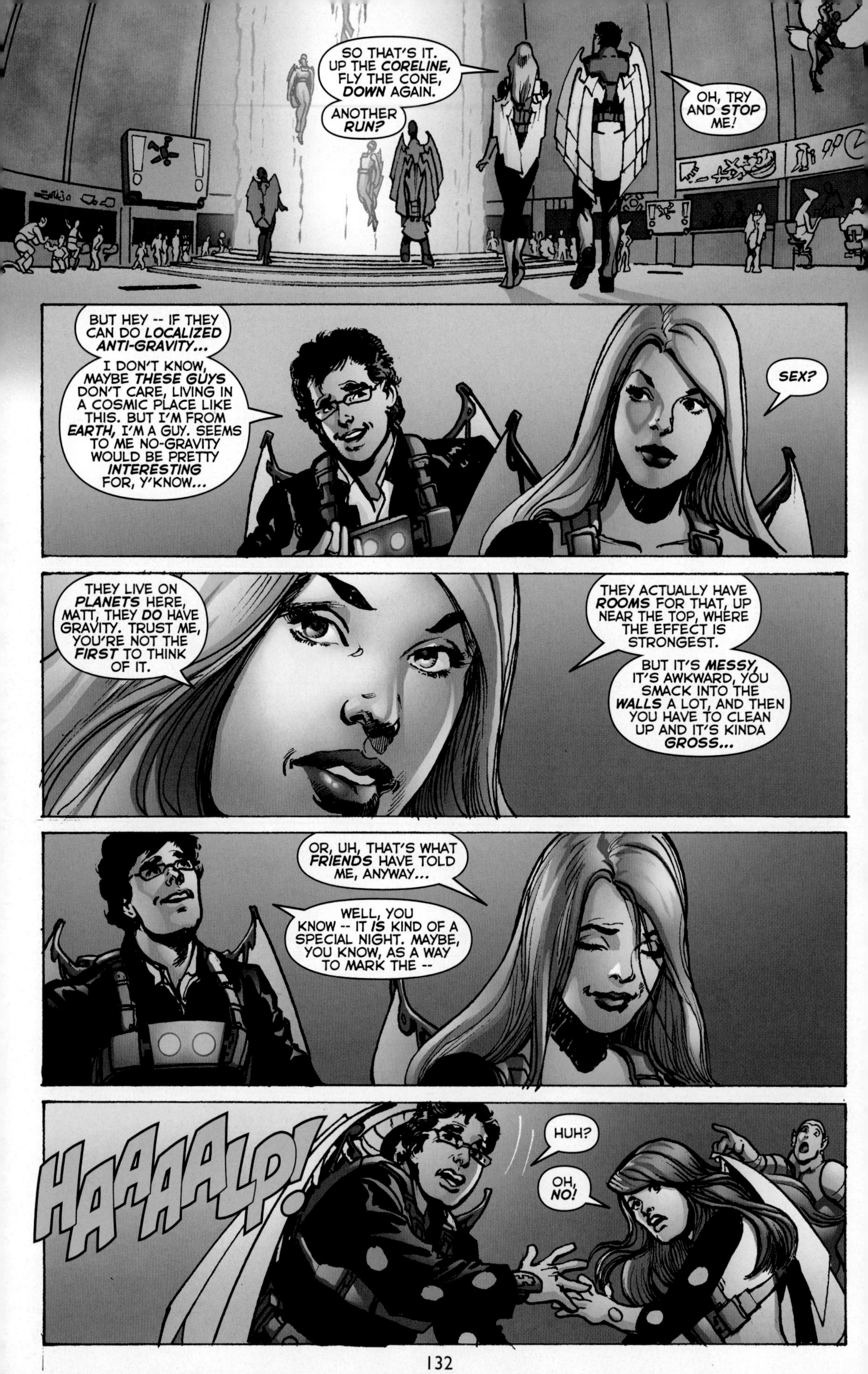
SO THAT'S IT. UP THE CORELINE, FLY THE CONE, DOWN AGAIN.
ANOTHER RUN?
OH, TRY AND STOP ME!
BUT HEY -- IF THEY CAN DO LOCALIZED ANTI-GRAVITY...
I DON'T KNOW, MAYBE THESE GUYS DON'T CARE, LIVING IN A COSMIC PLACE LIKE THIS. BUT I'M FROM EARTH, I'M A GUY. SEEMS TO ME NO-GRAVITY WOULD BE PRETTY INTERESTING FOR, Y'KNOW...
SEX?
THEY LIVE ON PLANETS HERE, MATT, THEY DO HAVE GRAVITY. TRUST ME, YOU'RE NOT THE FIRST TO THINK OF IT.
THEY ACTUALLY HAVE ROOMS FOR THAT, UP NEAR THE TOP, WHERE THE EFFECT IS STRONGEST.
BUT IT'S MESSY, IT'S AWKWARD, YOU SMACK INTO THE WALLS A LOT, AND THEN YOU HAVE TO CLEAN UP AND IT'S KINDA GROSS...
OR, UH, THAT'S WHAT FRIENDS HAVE TOLD ME, ANYWAY...
WELL, YOU KNOW -- IT IS KIND OF A SPECIAL NIGHT. MAYBE, YOU KNOW, AS A WAY TO MARK THE --
HAAAALP!
HUH?
OH, NO!

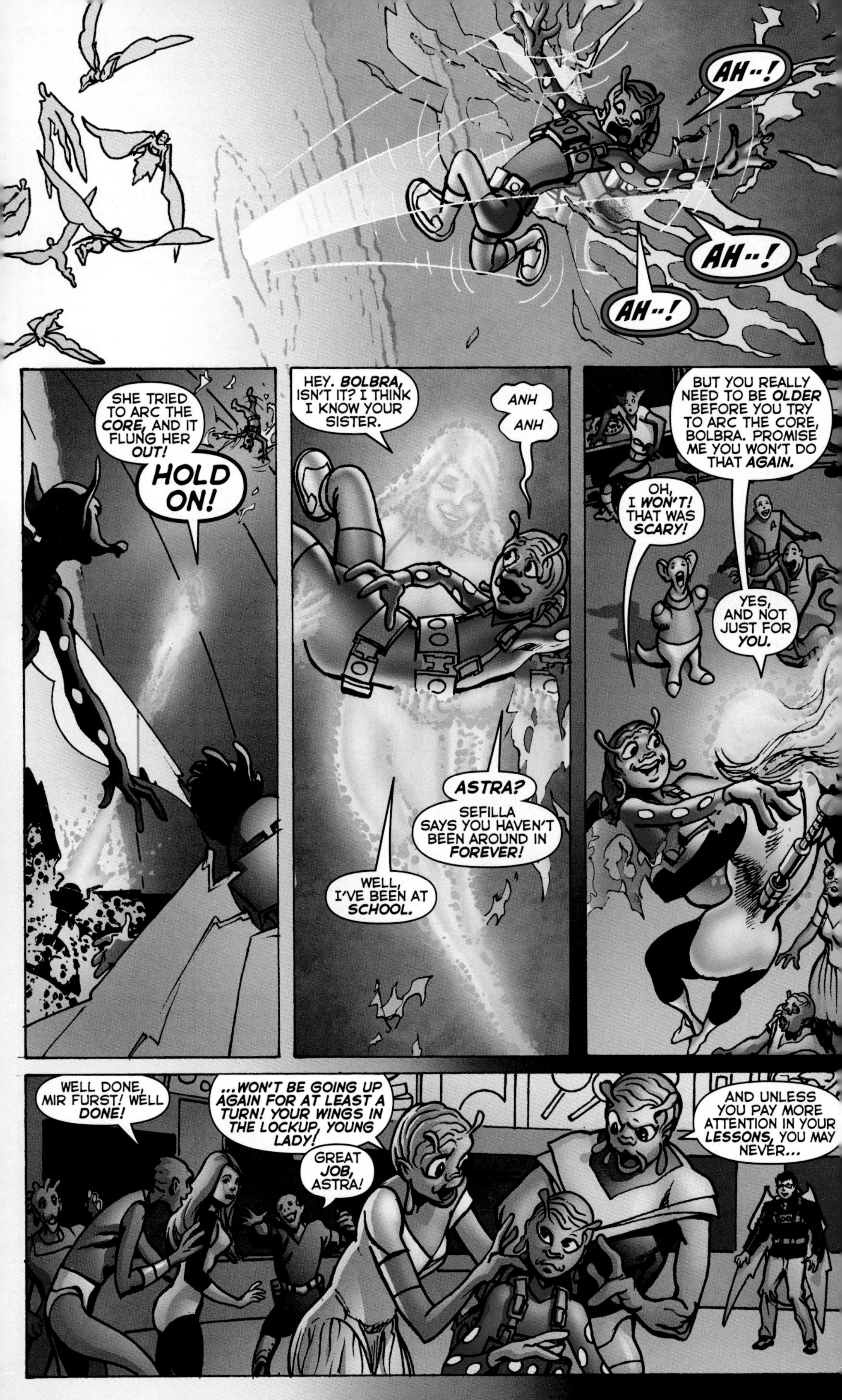
AH..!
AH..!
AH..!
SHE TRIED TO ARC THE CORE, AND IT FLUNG HER OUT!
HOLD ON!
HEY. BOLBRA, ISN'T IT? I THINK I KNOW YOUR SISTER.
ANH
ANH
ASTRA?
SEFILLA SAYS YOU HAVEN'T BEEN AROUND IN FOREVER!
WELL, I'VE BEEN AT SCHOOL.
BUT YOU REALLY NEED TO BE OLDER BEFORE YOU TRY TO ARC THE CORE, BOLBRA. PROMISE ME YOU WON'T DO THAT AGAIN.
OH, I WON'T! THAT WAS SCARY!
YES, AND NOT JUST FOR YOU.
WELL DONE, MIR FURST! WELL DONE!
...WON'T BE GOING UP AGAIN FOR AT LEAST A TURN! YOUR WINGS IN THE LOCKUP, YOUNG LADY!
GREAT JOB, ASTRA!
AND UNLESS YOU PAY MORE ATTENTION IN YOUR LESSONS, YOU MAY NEVER...

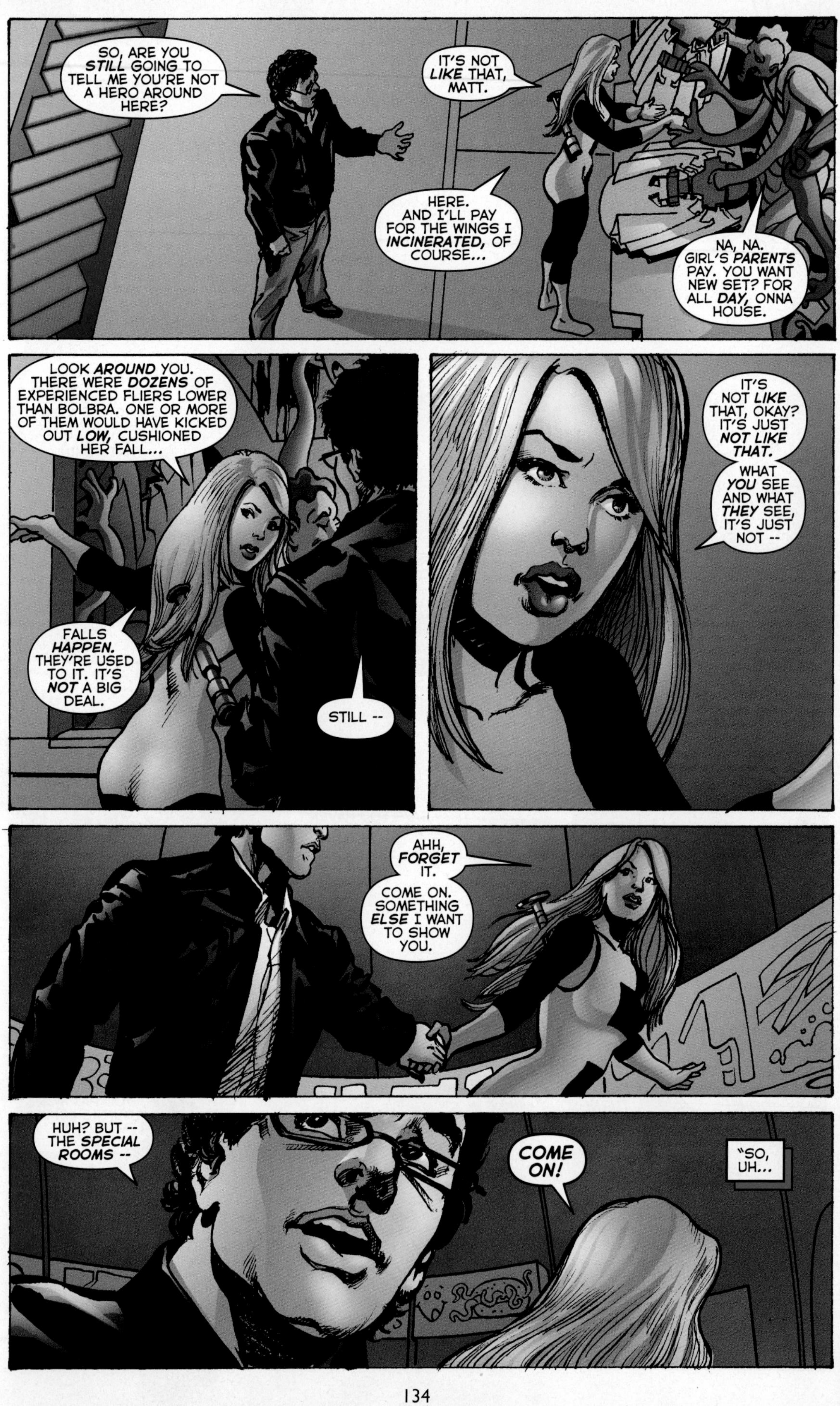
SO, ARE YOU STILL GOING TO TELL ME YOU'RE NOT A HERO AROUND HERE?
IT'S NOT LIKE THAT, MATT.
HERE. AND I'LL PAY FOR THE WINGS I INCINERATED, OF COURSE...
NA, NA. GIRL'S PARENTS PAY. YOU WANT NEW SET? FOR ALL DAY, ONNA HOUSE.
LOOK AROUND YOU. THERE WERE DOZENS OF EXPERIENCED FLIERS LOWER THAN BOLBRA. ONE OR MORE OF THEM WOULD HAVE KICKED OUT LOW, CUSHIONED HER FALL...
FALLS HAPPEN. THEY'RE USED TO IT. IT'S NOT A BIG DEAL.
STILL --
IT'S NOT LIKE THAT, OKAY? IT'S JUST NOT LIKE THAT.
WHAT YOU SEE AND WHAT THEY SEE, IT'S JUST NOT --
AHH, FORGET IT.
COME ON. SOMETHING ELSE I WANT TO SHOW YOU.
HUH? BUT -- THE SPECIAL ROOMS --
COME ON!
"SO, UH...

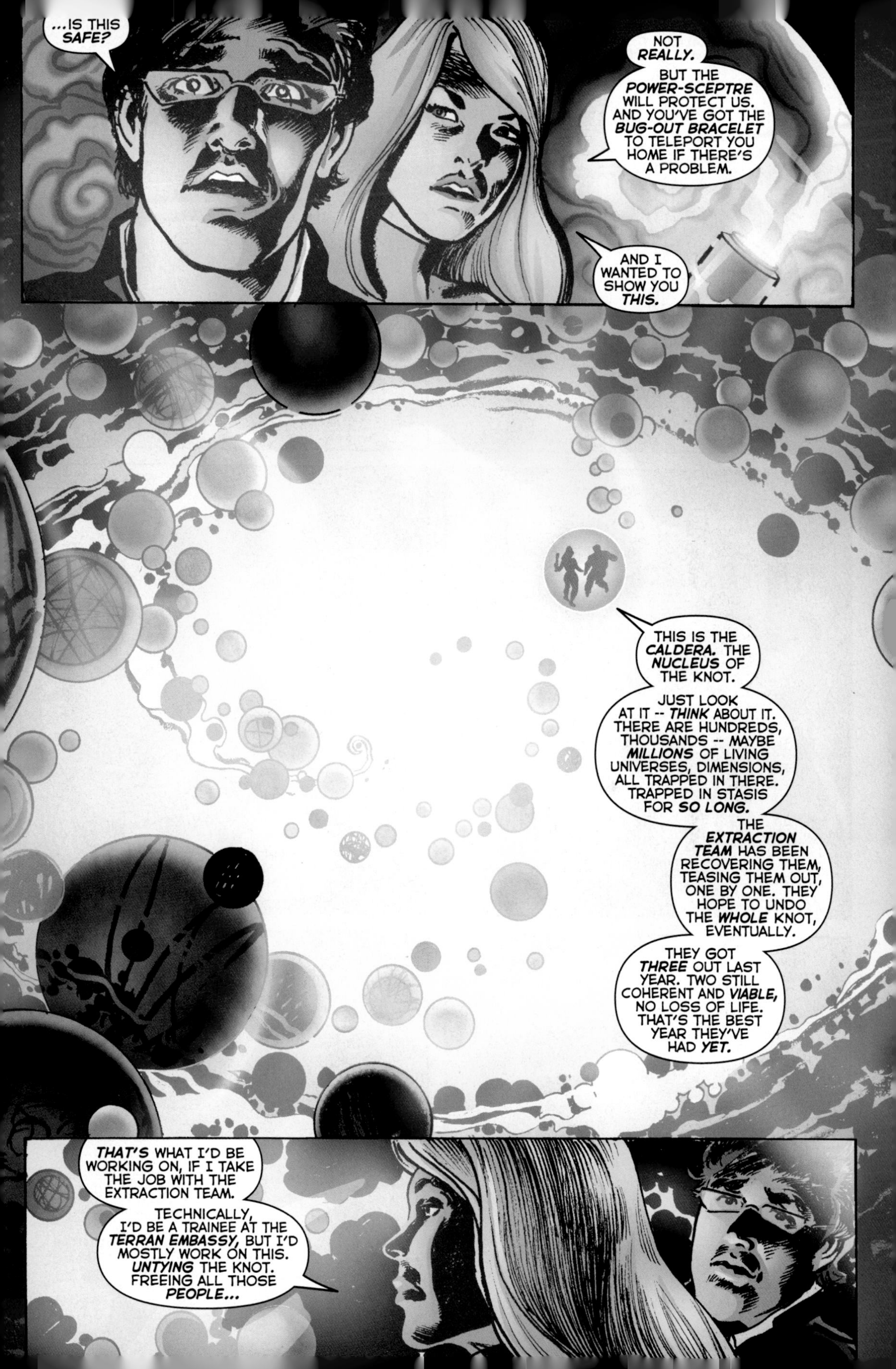

...IS THIS SAFE?
NOT REALLY.
BUT THE POWER-SCEPTRE WILL PROTECT US. AND YOU'VE GOT THE BUG-OUT BRACELET TO TELEPORT YOU HOME IF THERE'S A PROBLEM.
AND I WANTED TO SHOW YOU THIS.
THIS IS THE CALDERA. THE NUCLEUS OF THE KNOT.
JUST LOOK AT IT -- THINK ABOUT IT. THERE ARE HUNDREDS, THOUSANDS -- MAYBE MILLIONS OF LIVING UNIVERSES, DIMENSIONS, ALL TRAPPED IN THERE. TRAPPED IN STASIS FOR SO LONG.
THE EXTRACTION TEAM HAS BEEN RECOVERING THEM, TEASING THEM OUT, ONE BY ONE. THEY HOPE TO UNDO THE WHOLE KNOT, EVENTUALLY.
THEY GOT THREE OUT LAST YEAR. TWO STILL COHERENT AND VIABLE, NO LOSS OF LIFE. THAT'S THE BEST YEAR THEY'VE HAD YET.
THAT'S WHAT I'D BE WORKING ON, IF I TAKE THE JOB WITH THE EXTRACTION TEAM.
TECHNICALLY, I'D BE A TRAINEE AT THE TERRAN EMBASSY, BUT I'D MOSTLY WORK ON THIS. UNTYING THE KNOT. FREEING ALL THOSE PEOPLE...

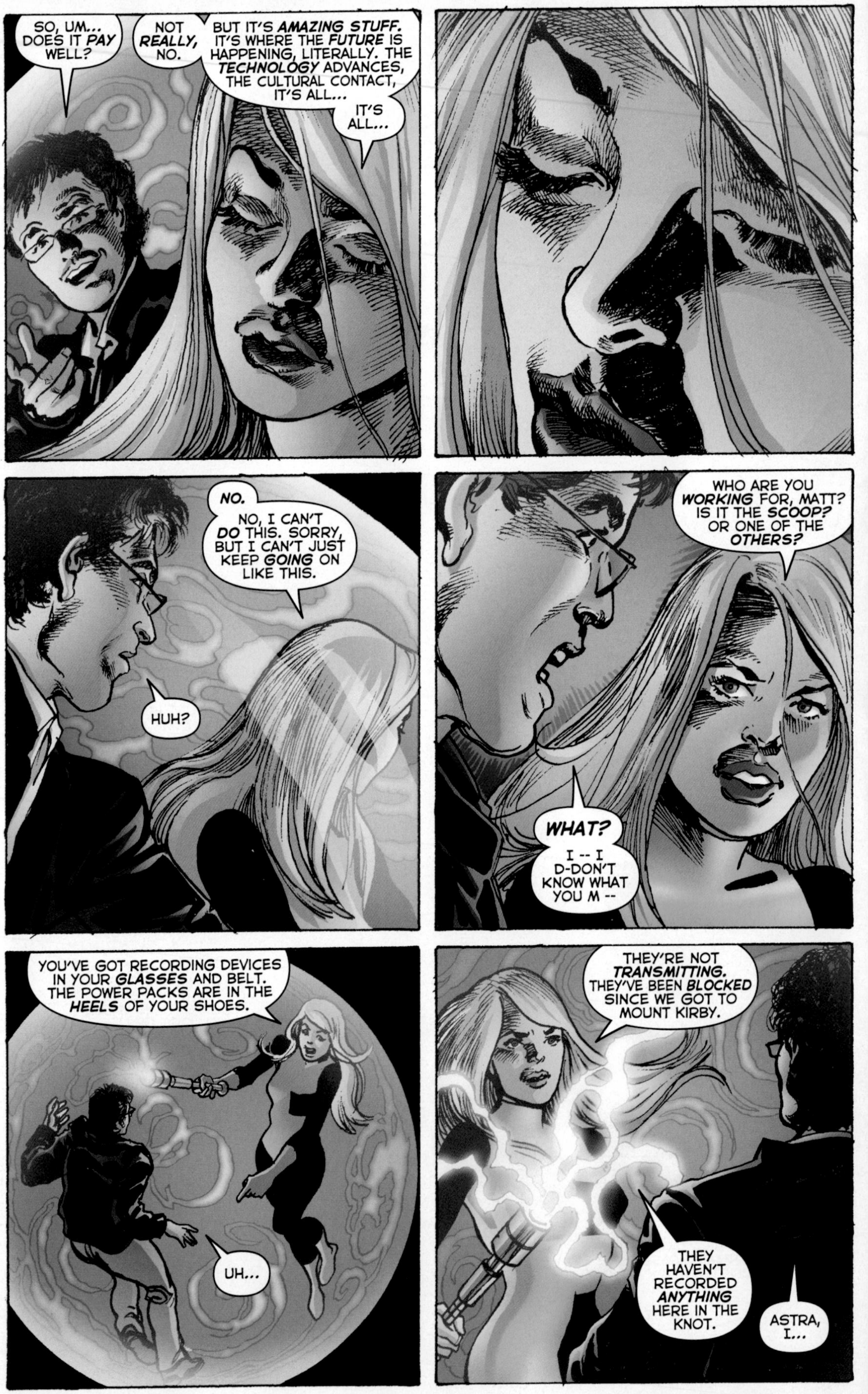
SO, UM... DOES IT PAY WELL?
NOT REALLY, NO.
BUT IT'S AMAZING STUFF. IT'S WHERE THE FUTURE IS HAPPENING, LITERALLY. THE TECHNOLOGY ADVANCES, THE CULTURAL CONTACT, IT'S ALL...
IT'S ALL...
NO.
NO, I CAN'T DO THIS. SORRY, BUT I CAN'T JUST KEEP GOING ON LIKE THIS.
HUH?
WHO ARE YOU WORKING FOR, MATT? IS IT THE SCOOP? OR ONE OF THE OTHERS?
WHAT?
I -- I D-DON'T KNOW WHAT YOU M --
YOU'VE GOT RECORDING DEVICES IN YOUR GLASSES AND BELT. THE POWER PACKS ARE IN THE HEELS OF YOUR SHOES.
UH...
THEY'RE NOT TRANSMITTING. THEY'VE BEEN BLOCKED SINCE WE GOT TO MOUNT KIRBY.
THEY HAVEN'T RECORDED ANYTHING HERE IN THE KNOT.
ASTRA, I...

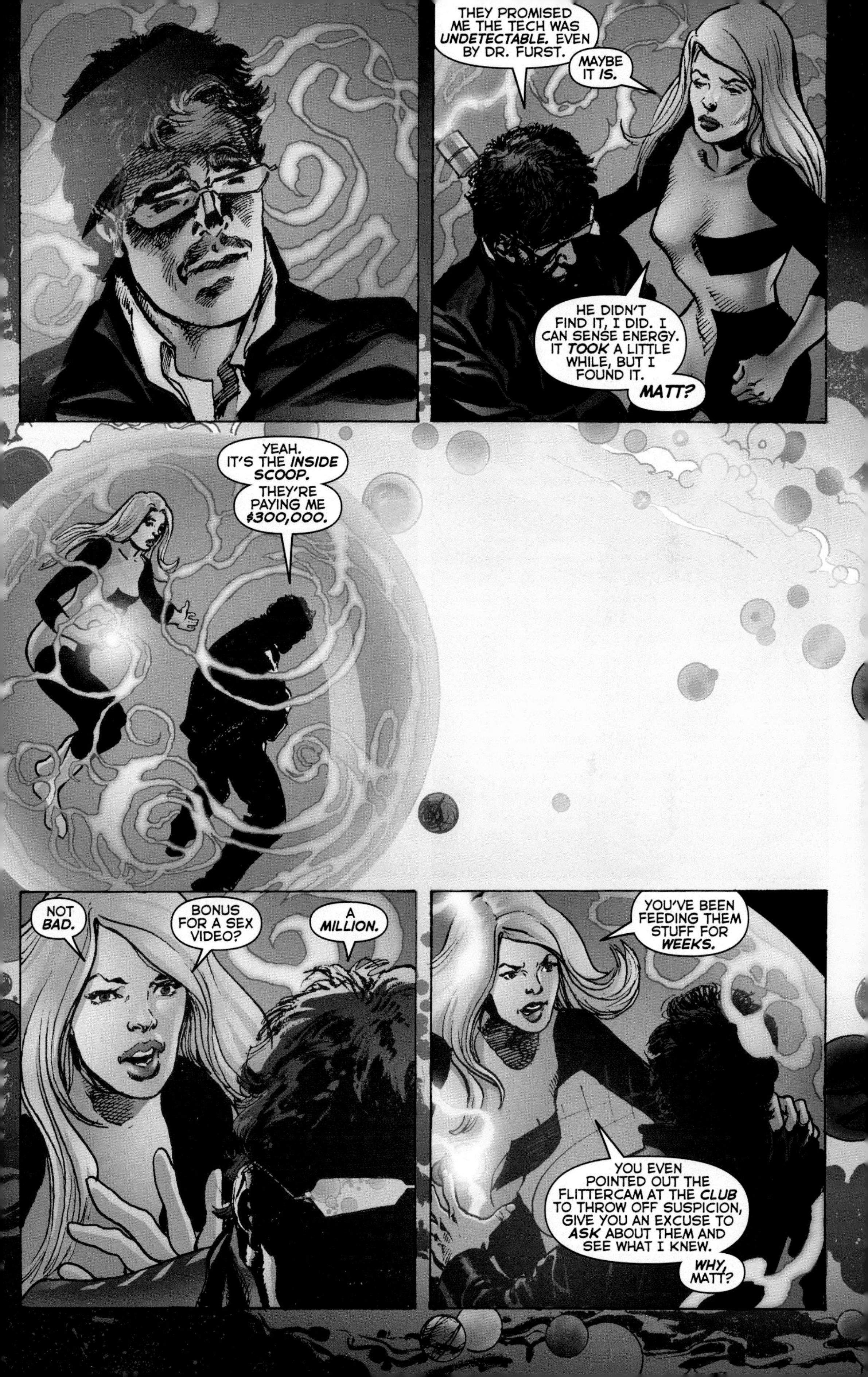
THEY PROMISED ME THE TECH WAS UNDETECTABLE. EVEN BY DR. FURST.
MAYBE IT IS.
HE DIDN'T FIND IT, I DID. I CAN SENSE ENERGY. IT TOOK A LITTLE WHILE, BUT I FOUND IT.
MATT?
YEAH. IT'S THE INSIDE SCOOP.
THEY'RE PAYING ME $300,000.
NOT BAD.
BONUS FOR A SEX VIDEO?
A MILLION.
YOU'VE BEEN FEEDING THEM STUFF FOR WEEKS.
YOU EVEN POINTED OUT THE FLITTERCAM AT THE CLUB TO THROW OFF SUSPICION, GIVE YOU AN EXCUSE TO ASK ABOUT THEM AND SEE WHAT I KNEW.
WHY, MATT?

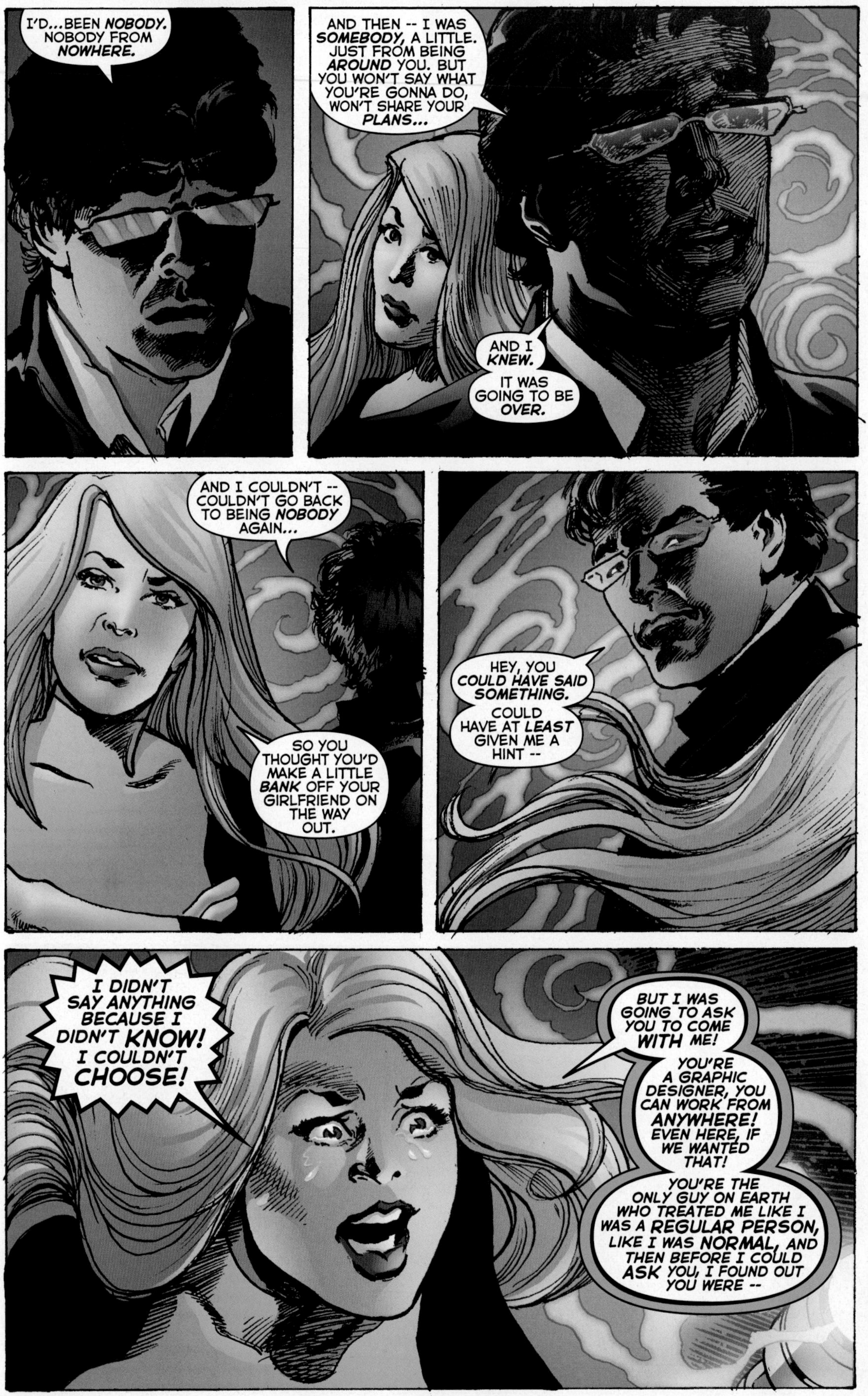
I'D...BEEN NOBODY. NOBODY FROM NOWHERE.
AND THEN -- I WAS SOMEBODY, A LITTLE. JUST FROM BEING AROUND YOU. BUT YOU WON'T SAY WHAT YOU'RE GONNA DO, WON'T SHARE YOUR PLANS...
AND I KNEW.
IT WAS GOING TO BE OVER.
AND I COULDN'T -- COULDN'T GO BACK TO BEING NOBODY AGAIN...
SO YOU THOUGHT YOU'D MAKE A LITTLE BANK OFF YOUR GIRLFRIEND ON THE WAY OUT.
HEY, YOU COULD HAVE SAID SOMETHING.
COULD HAVE AT LEAST GIVEN ME A HINT --
I DIDN'T SAY ANYTHING BECAUSE I DIDN'T KNOW! I COULDN'T CHOOSE!
BUT I WAS GOING TO ASK YOU TO COME WITH ME!
YOU'RE A GRAPHIC DESIGNER, YOU CAN WORK FROM ANYWHERE! EVEN HERE, IF WE WANTED THAT!
YOU'RE THE ONLY GUY ON EARTH WHO TREATED ME LIKE I WAS A REGULAR PERSON, LIKE I WAS NORMAL, AND THEN BEFORE I COULD ASK YOU, I FOUND OUT YOU WERE --

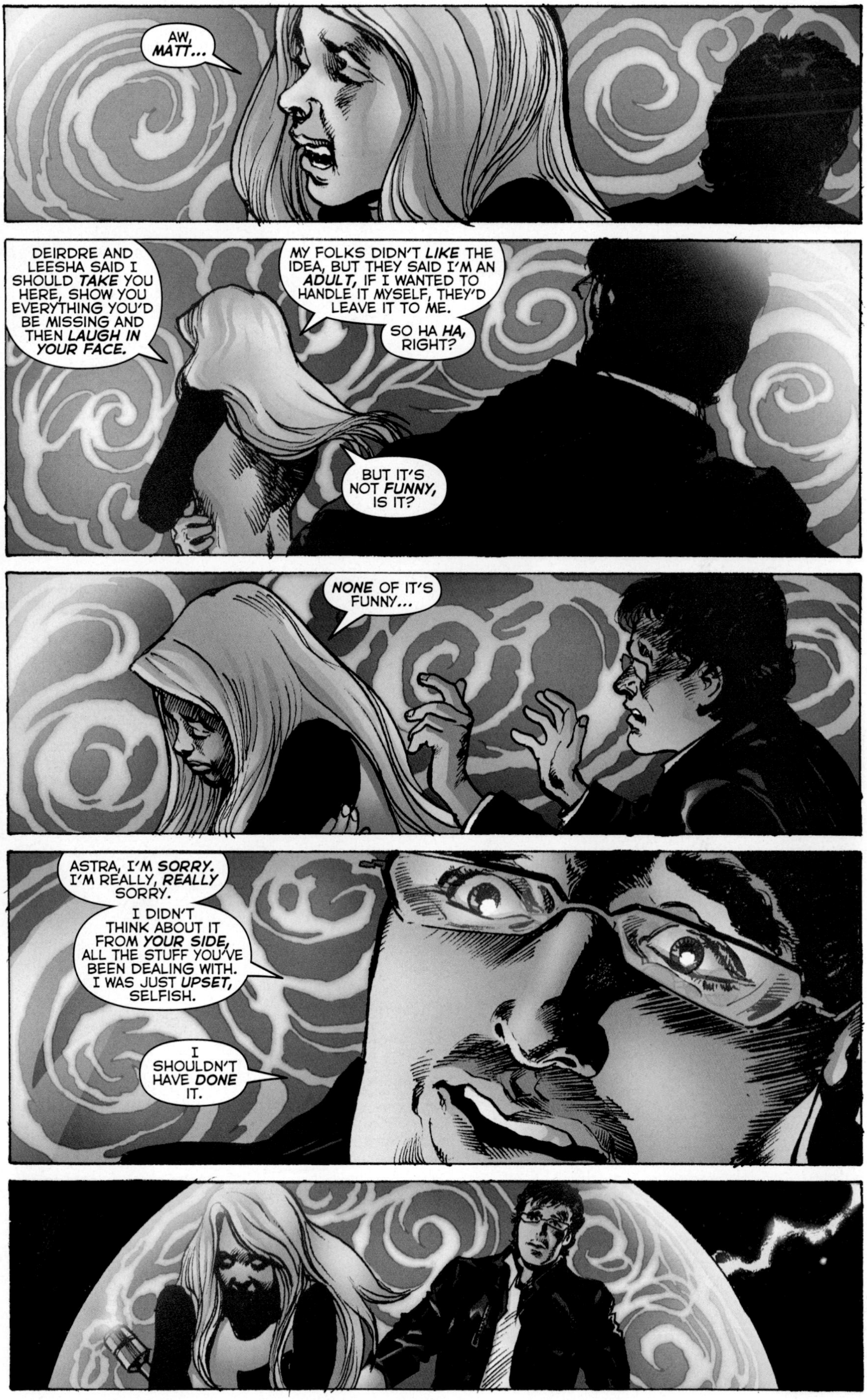
AW, MATT...
DEIRDRE AND LEESHA SAID I SHOULD TAKE YOU HERE, SHOW YOU EVERYTHING YOU'D BE MISSING AND THEN LAUGH IN YOUR FACE.
MY FOLKS DIDN'T LIKE THE IDEA, BUT THEY SAID I'M AN ADULT, IF I WANTED TO HANDLE IT MYSELF, THEY'D LEAVE IT TO ME.
SO HA HA, RIGHT?
BUT IT'S NOT FUNNY, IS IT?
NONE OF IT'S FUNNY...
ASTRA, I'M SORRY. I'M REALLY, REALLY SORRY.
I DIDN'T THINK ABOUT IT FROM YOUR SIDE, ALL THE STUFF YOU'VE BEEN DEALING WITH. I WAS JUST UPSET, SELFISH.
I SHOULDN'T HAVE DONE IT.

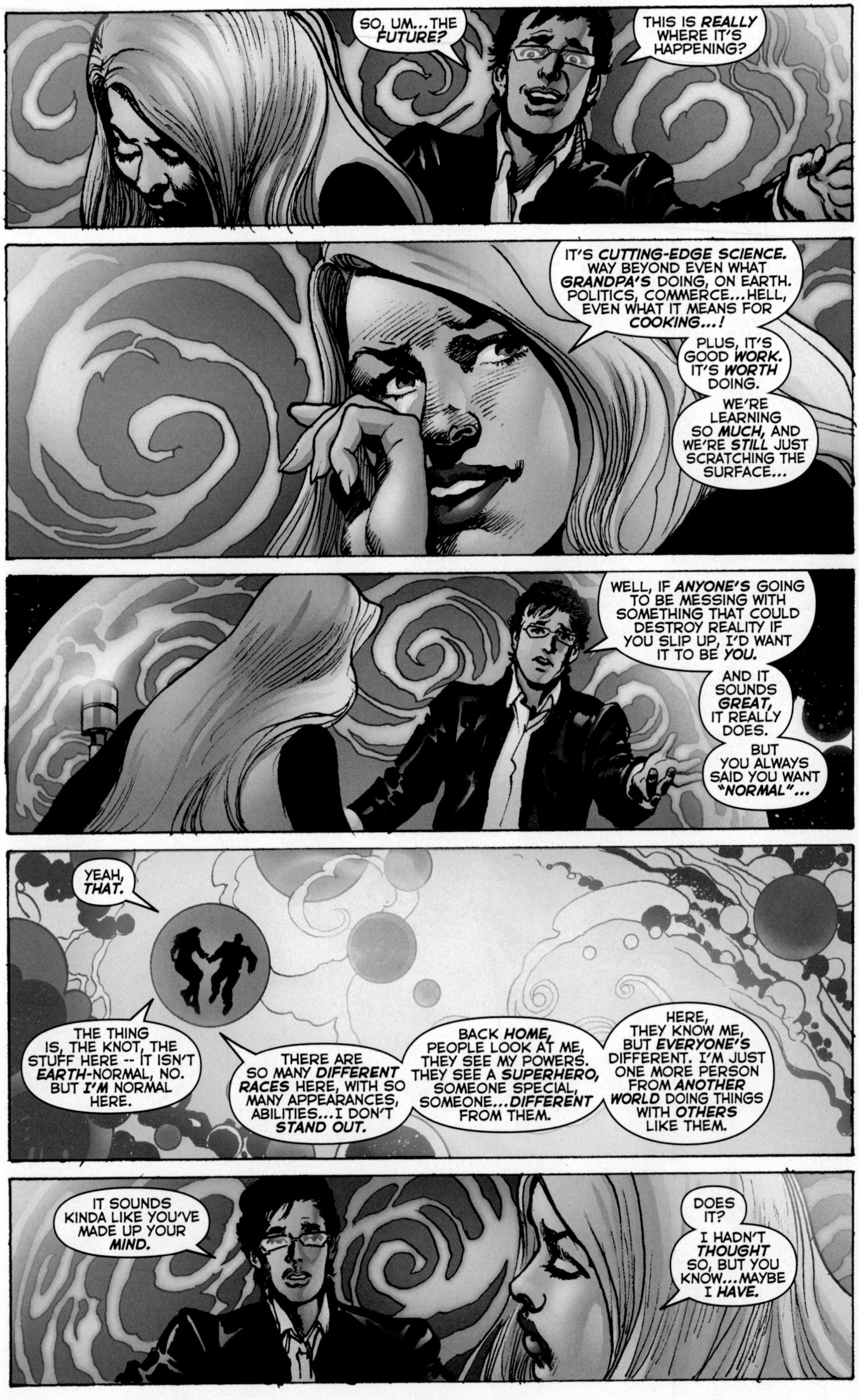
SO, UM...THE FUTURE?
THIS IS REALLY WHERE IT'S HAPPENING?
IT'S CUTTING-EDGE SCIENCE. WAY BEYOND EVEN WHAT GRANDPA'S DOING, ON EARTH. POLITICS, COMMERCE...HELL, EVEN WHAT IT MEANS FOR COOKING...!
PLUS, IT'S GOOD WORK. IT'S WORTH DOING.
WE'RE LEARNING SO MUCH, AND WE'RE STILL JUST SCRATCHING THE SURFACE...
WELL, IF ANYONE'S GOING TO BE MESSING WITH SOMETHING THAT COULD DESTROY REALITY IF YOU SLIP UP, I'D WANT IT TO BE YOU.
AND IT SOUNDS GREAT, IT REALLY DOES.
BUT YOU ALWAYS SAID YOU WANT "NORMAL"...
YEAH, THAT.
THE THING IS, THE KNOT, THE STUFF HERE -- IT ISN'T EARTH-NORMAL, NO. BUT I'M NORMAL HERE.
THERE ARE SO MANY DIFFERENT RACES HERE, WITH SO MANY APPEARANCES, ABILITIES...I DON'T STAND OUT.
BACK HOME, PEOPLE LOOK AT ME, THEY SEE MY POWERS. THEY SEE A SUPERHERO, SOMEONE SPECIAL, SOMEONE...DIFFERENT FROM THEM.
HERE, THEY KNOW ME, BUT EVERYONE'S DIFFERENT. I'M JUST ONE MORE PERSON FROM ANOTHER WORLD DOING THINGS WITH OTHERS LIKE THEM.
IT SOUNDS KINDA LIKE YOU'VE MADE UP YOUR MIND.
DOES IT?
I HADN'T THOUGHT SO, BUT YOU KNOW...MAYBE I HAVE.

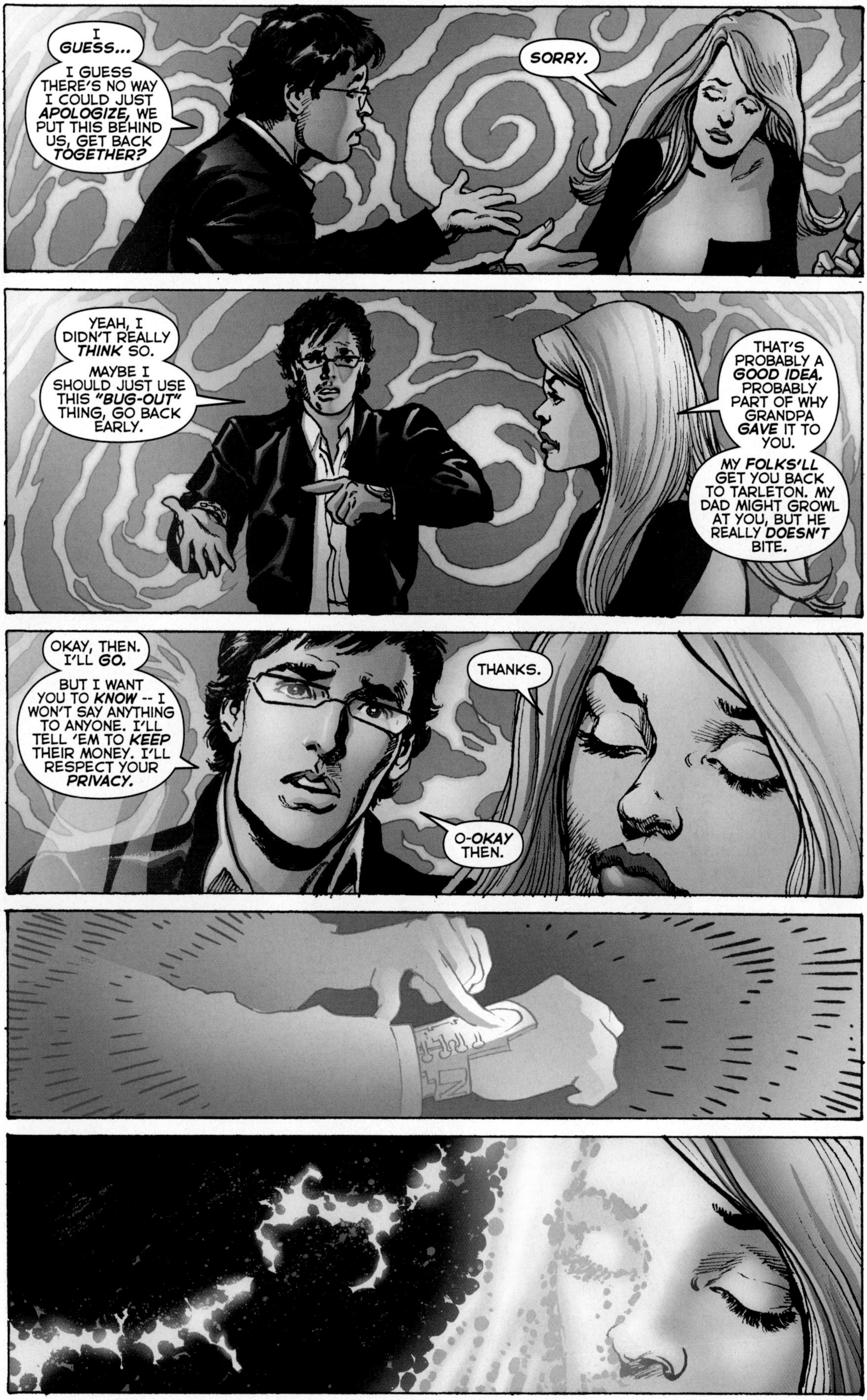
I GUESS...
I GUESS THERE'S NO WAY I COULD JUST APOLOGIZE, WE PUT THIS BEHIND US, GET BACK TOGETHER?
SORRY.
YEAH, I DIDN'T REALLY THINK SO.
MAYBE I SHOULD JUST USE THIS "BUG-OUT" THING, GO BACK EARLY.
THAT'S PROBABLY A GOOD IDEA. PROBABLY PART OF WHY GRANDPA GAVE IT TO YOU.
MY FOLKS'LL GET YOU BACK TO TARLETON. MY DAD MIGHT GROWL AT YOU, BUT HE REALLY DOESN'T BITE.
OKAY, THEN. I'LL GO.
BUT I WANT YOU TO KNOW -- I WON'T SAY ANYTHING TO ANYONE. I'LL TELL 'EM TO KEEP THEIR MONEY. I'LL RESPECT YOUR PRIVACY.
THANKS.
O-OKAY THEN.

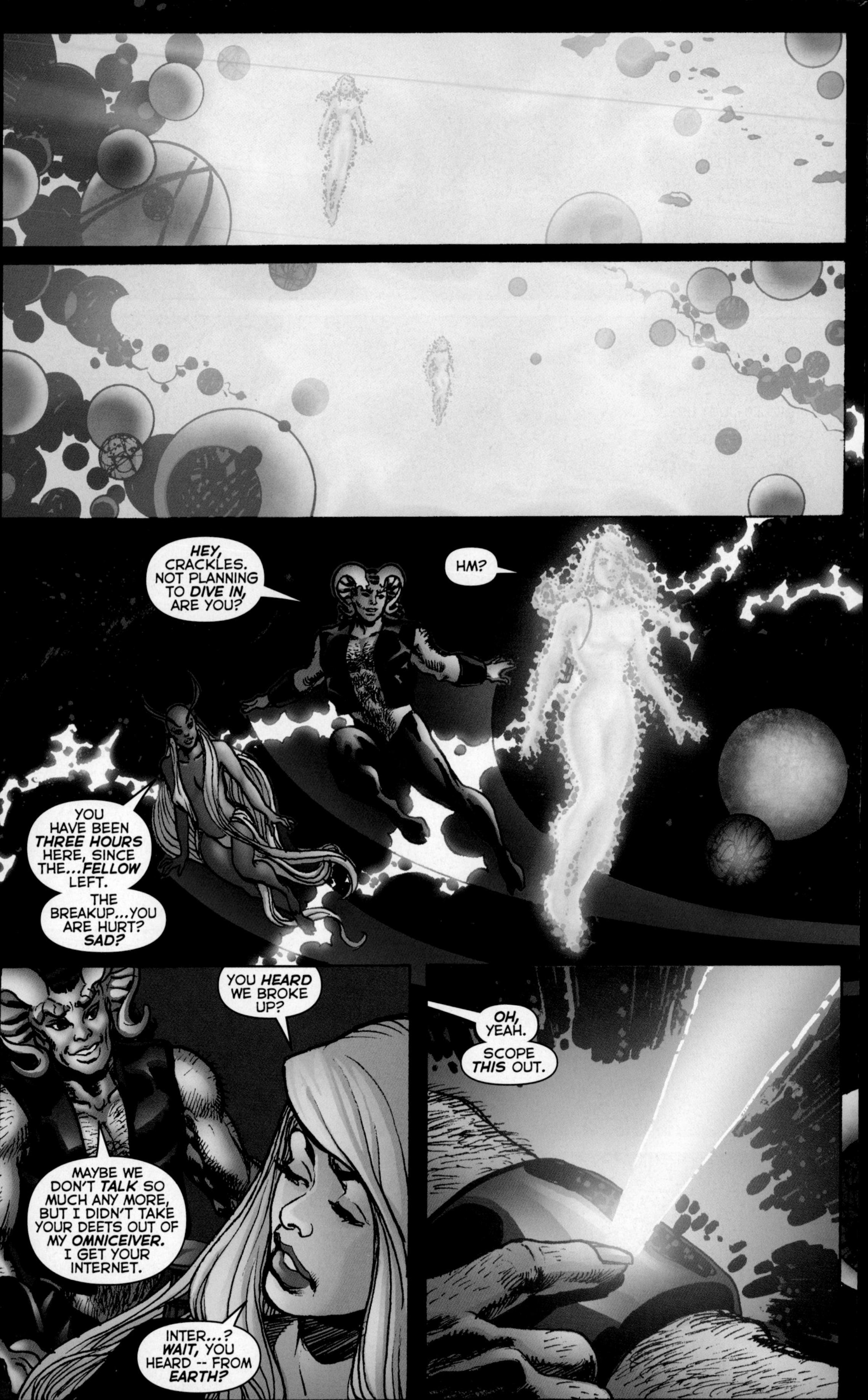
HEY, CRACKLES. NOT PLANNING TO DIVE IN, ARE YOU?
HM?
YOU HAVE BEEN THREE HOURS HERE, SINCE THE...FELLOW LEFT.
THE BREAKUP...YOU ARE HURT? SAD?
YOU HEARD WE BROKE UP?
MAYBE WE DON'T TALK SO MUCH ANY MORE, BUT I DIDN'T TAKE YOUR DEETS OUT OF MY OMNICEIVER. I GET YOUR INTERNET.
INTER...? WAIT, YOU HEARD -- FROM EARTH?
OH, YEAH.
SCOPE THIS OUT.

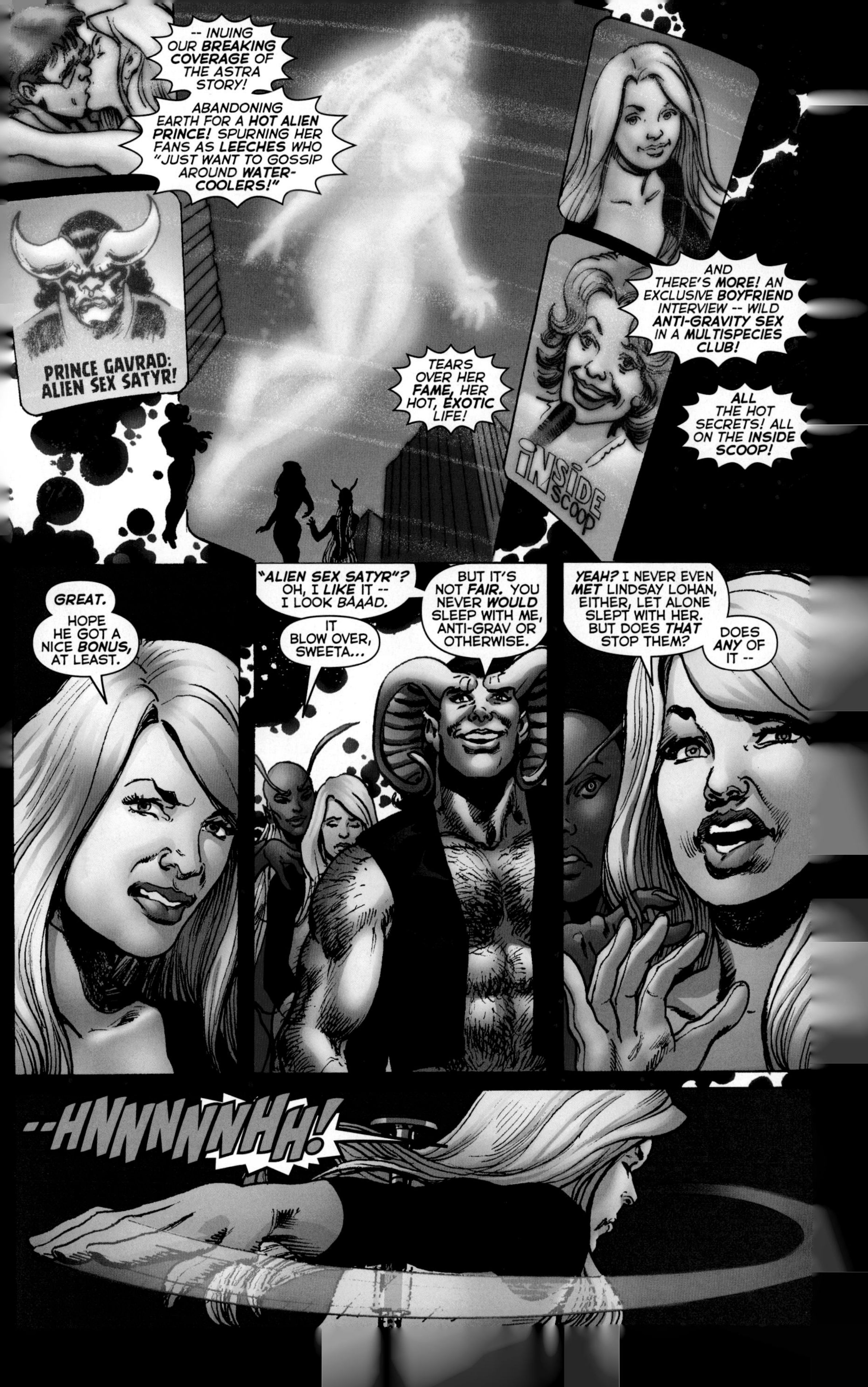
-- INUING OUR BREAKING COVERAGE OF THE ASTRA STORY!
ABANDONING EARTH FOR A HOT ALIEN PRINCE! SPURNING HER FANS AS LEECHES WHO "JUST WANT TO GOSSIP AROUND WATER-COOLERS!"
PRINCE GAVRAD: ALIEN SEX SATYR!
TEARS OVER HER FAME, HER HOT, EXOTIC LIFE!
AND THERE'S MORE! AN EXCLUSIVE BOYFRIEND INTERVIEW -- WILD ANTI-GRAVITY SEX IN A MULTISPECIES CLUB!
ALL THE HOT SECRETS! ALL ON THE INSIDE SCOOP!
INSIDE SCOOP
GREAT.
HOPE HE GOT A NICE BONUS, AT LEAST.
"ALIEN SEX SATYR"? OH, I LIKE IT -- I LOOK BAAAD.
IT BLOW OVER, SWEETA...
BUT IT'S NOT FAIR. YOU NEVER WOULD SLEEP WITH ME, ANTI-GRAV OR OTHERWISE.
YEAH? I NEVER EVEN MET LINDSAY LOHAN, EITHER, LET ALONE SLEPT WITH HER. BUT DOES THAT STOP THEM?
DOES ANY OF IT --
--HNNNNNHA!

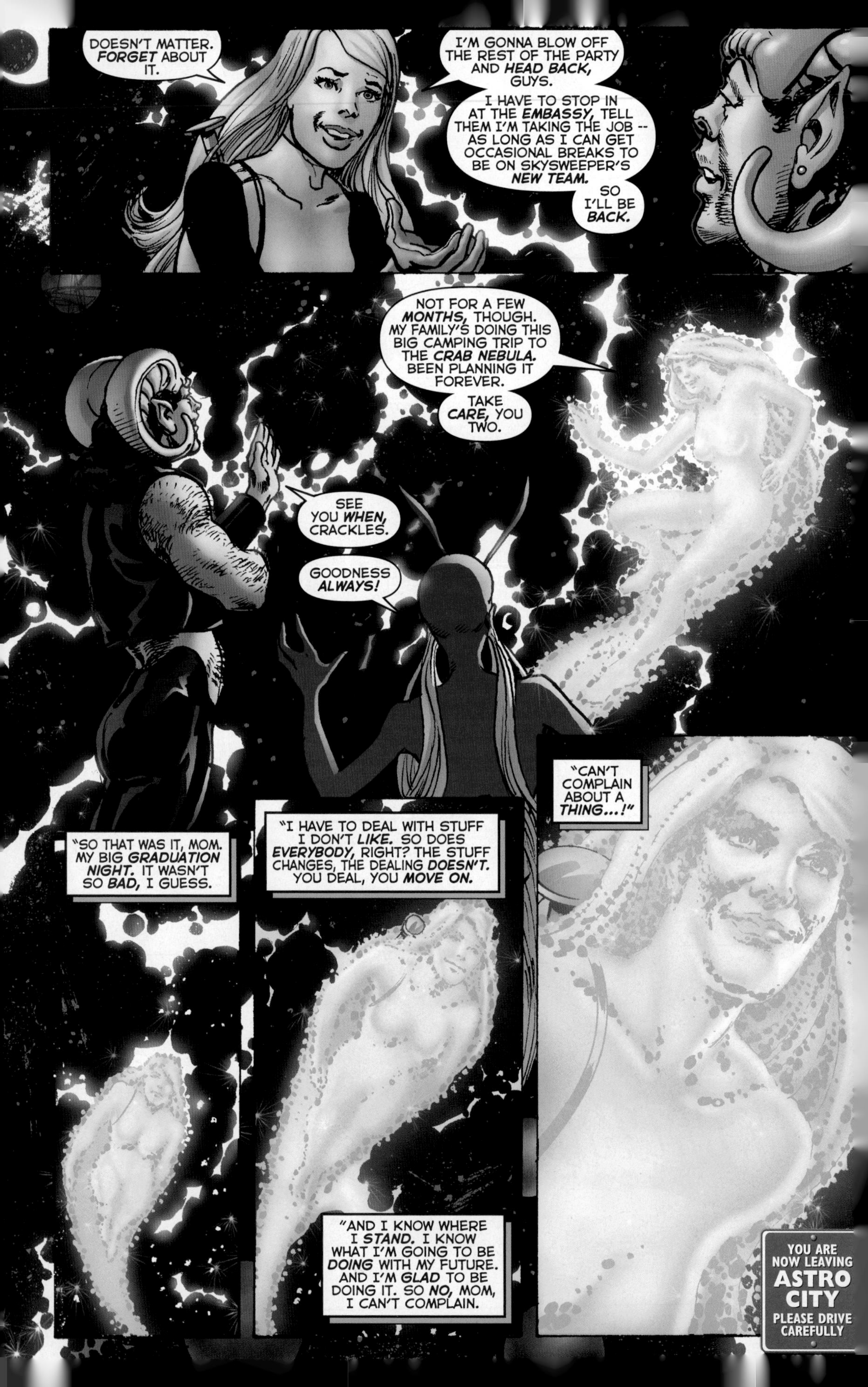
DOESN'T MATTER. FORGET ABOUT IT.
I'M GONNA BLOW OFF THE REST OF THE PARTY AND HEAD BACK, GUYS.
I HAVE TO STOP IN AT THE EMBASSY, TELL THEM I'M TAKING THE JOB -- AS LONG AS I CAN GET OCCASIONAL BREAKS TO BE ON SKYSWEEPER'S NEW TEAM.
SO I'LL BE BACK.
NOT FOR A FEW MONTHS, THOUGH. MY FAMILY'S DOING THIS BIG CAMPING TRIP TO THE CRAB NEBULA. BEEN PLANNING IT FOREVER.
TAKE CARE, YOU TWO.
SEE YOU WHEN, CRACKLES.
GOODNESS ALWAYS!
"SO THAT WAS IT, MOM. MY BIG GRADUATION NIGHT. IT WASN'T SO BAD, I GUESS.
"I HAVE TO DEAL WITH STUFF I DON'T LIKE. SO DOES EVERYBODY, RIGHT? THE STUFF CHANGES, THE DEALING DOESN'T. YOU DEAL, YOU MOVE ON.
"AND I KNOW WHERE I STAND. I KNOW WHAT I'M GOING TO BE DOING WITH MY FUTURE. AND I'M GLAD TO BE DOING IT. SO NO, MOM, I CAN'T COMPLAIN.
"CAN'T COMPLAIN ABOUT A THING...!"
YOU ARE NOW LEAVING ASTRO CITY PLEASE DRIVE CAREFULLY

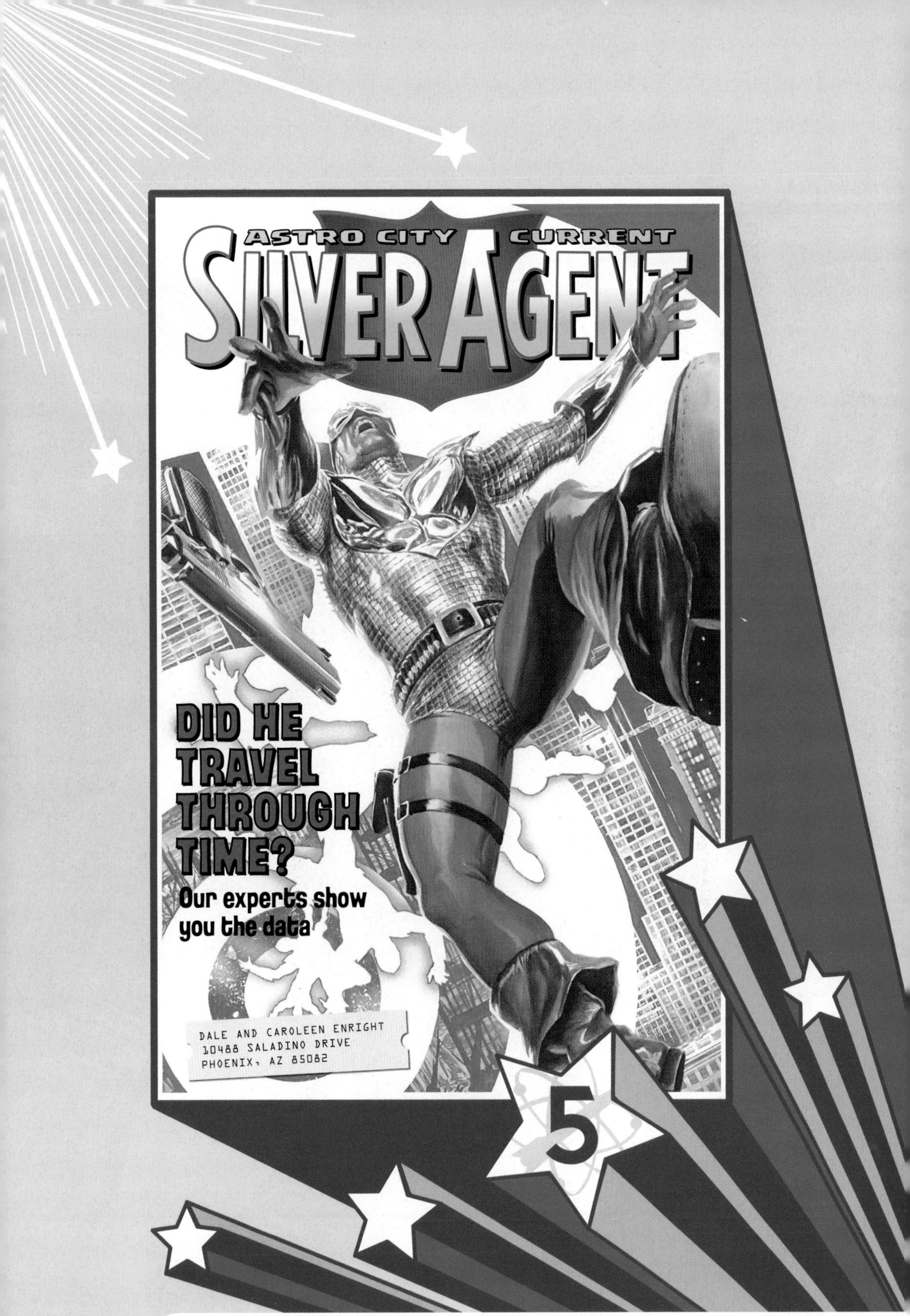
ASTRO CITY CURRENT
SILVER AGENT
DID HE TRAVEL THROUGH TIME?
Our experts show you the data
DALE AND CAROLEEN ENRIGHT
10488 SALADINO DRIVE
PHOENIX, AZ 85082
5

TO SERVE AND PROTECT

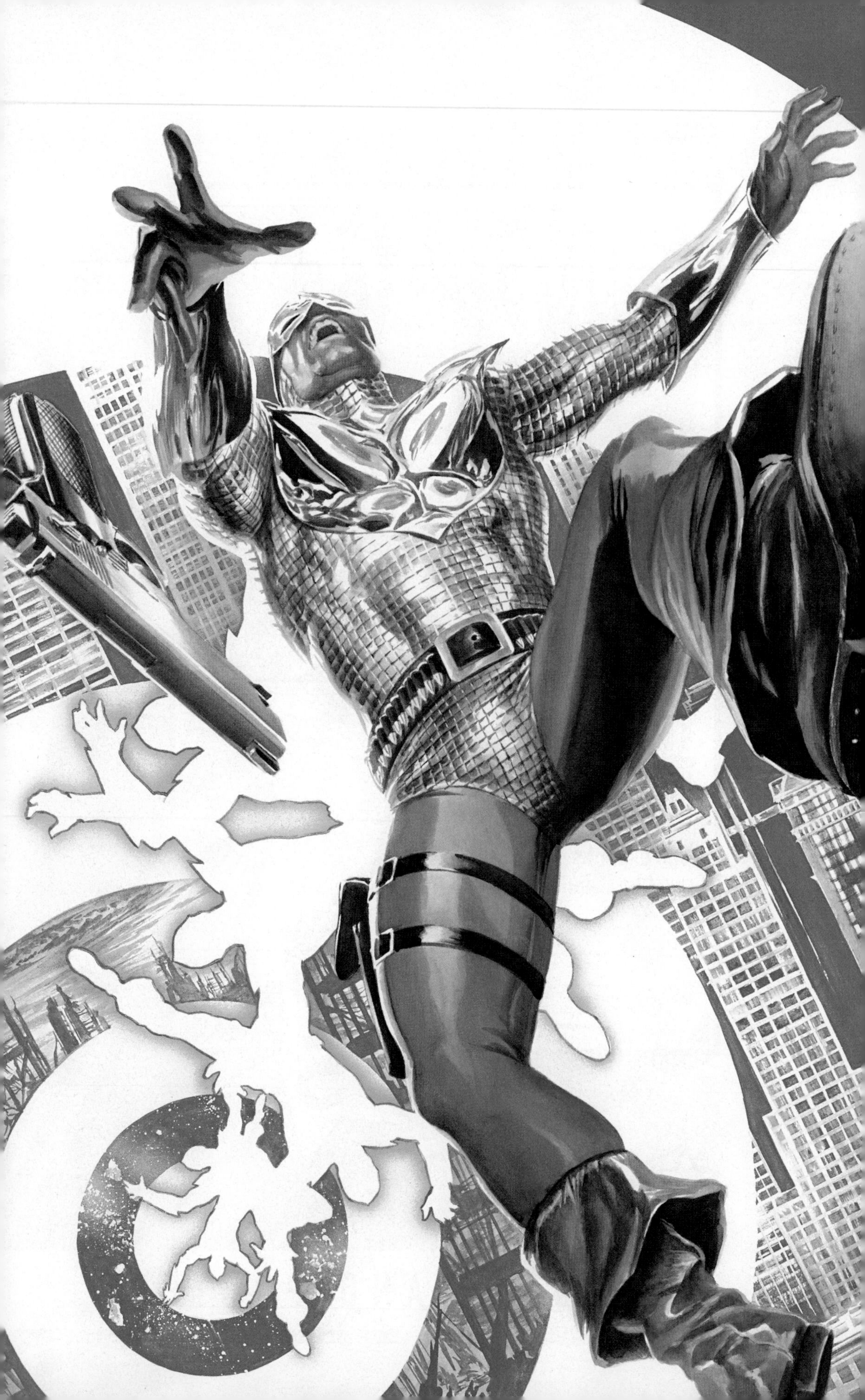

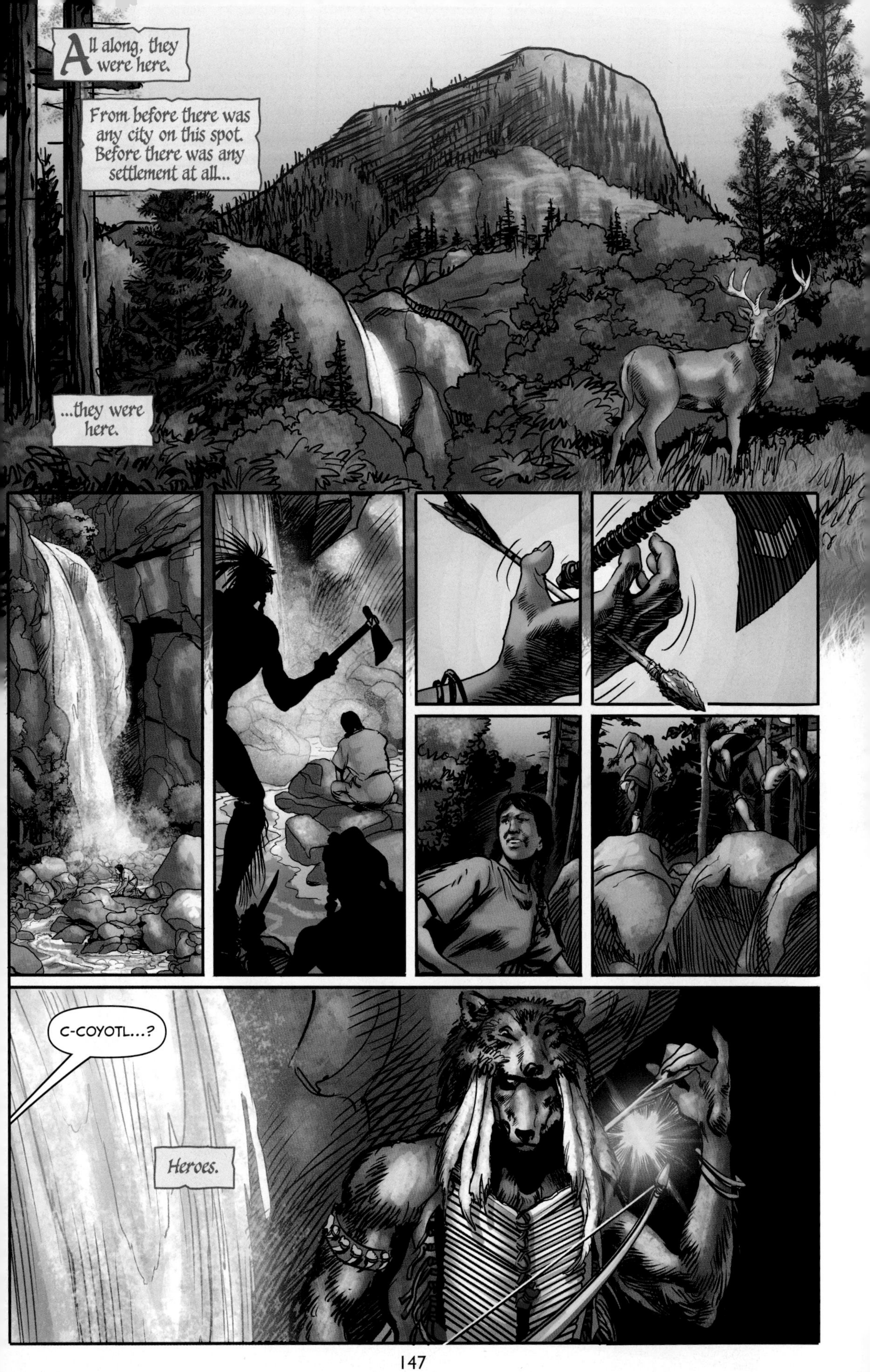
All along, they were here.
From before there was any city on this spot. Before there was any settlement at all...
...they were here.
C-COYOTL...?
Heroes.

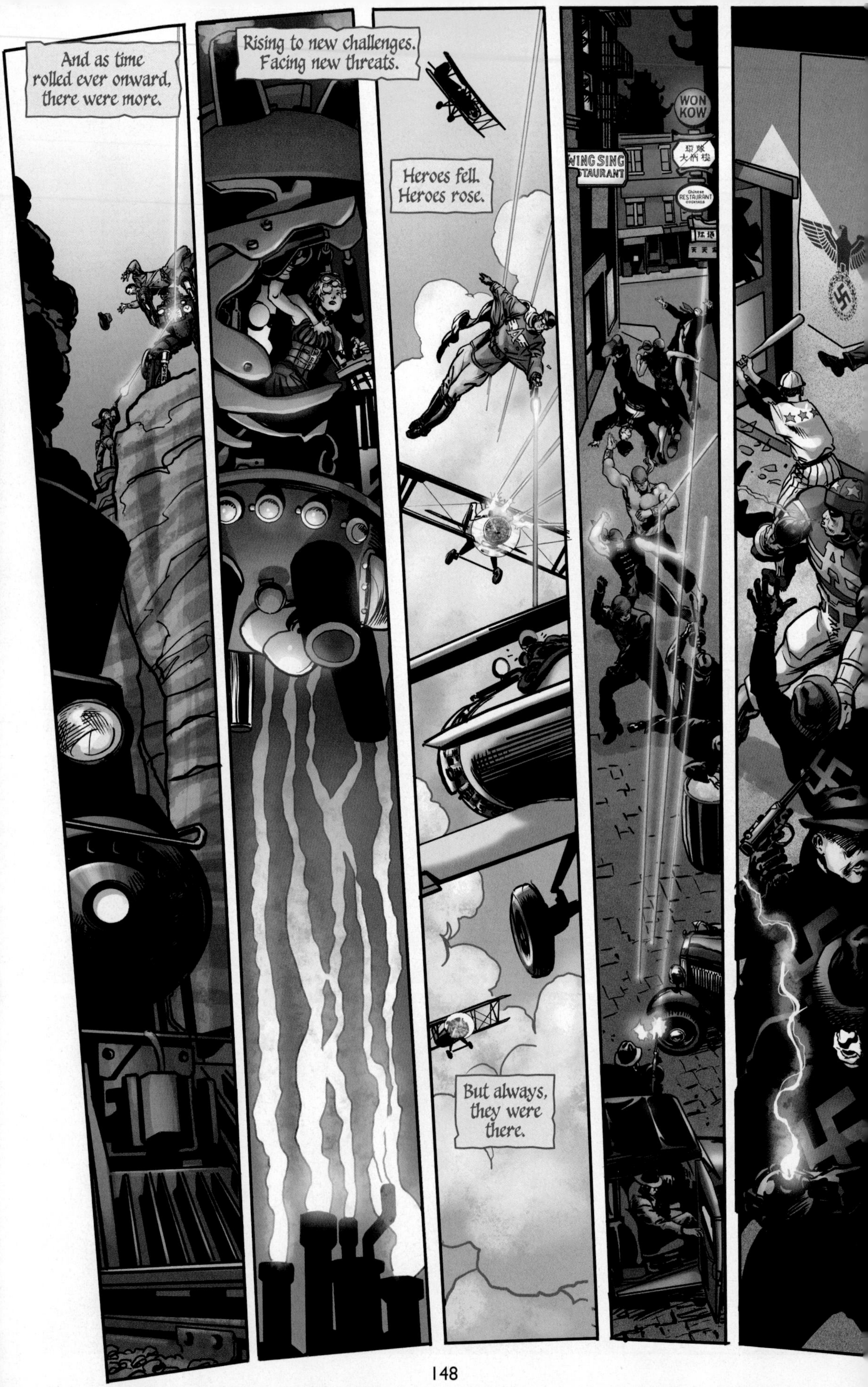
And as time rolled ever onward, there were more.
Rising to new challenges. Facing new threats.
Heroes fell. Heroes rose.
But always, they were there.
WON KOW
WING SING
STAURANT
Chinese RESTAURANT

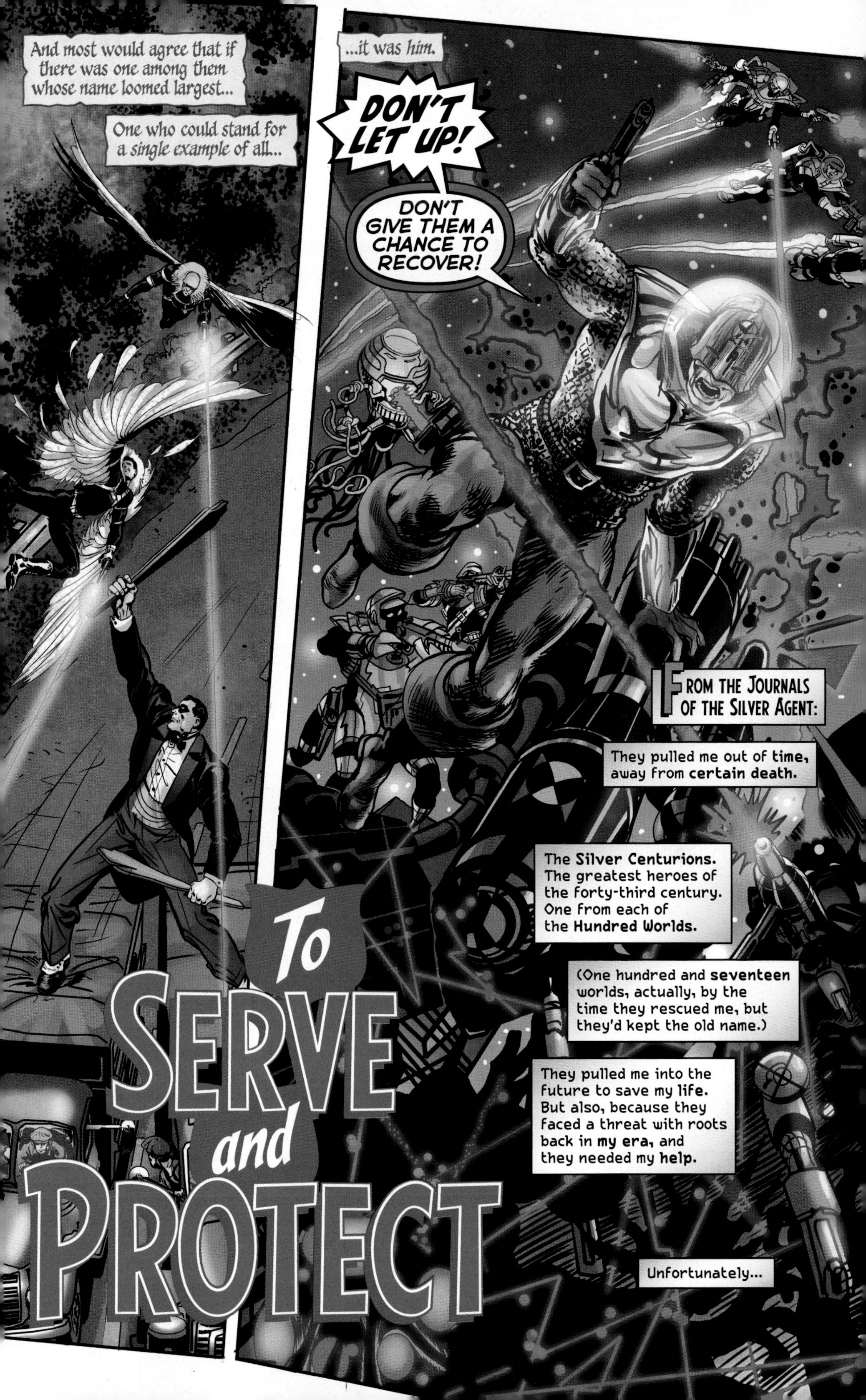
And most would agree that if there was one among them whose name loomed largest...
One who could stand for a single example of all...
...it was him.
DON'T LET UP!
DON'T GIVE THEM A CHANCE TO RECOVER!
To Serve and Protect
FROM THE JOURNALS OF THE SILVER AGENT:
They pulled me out of time, away from certain death.
The Silver Centurions. The greatest heroes of the forty-third century. One from each of the Hundred Worlds.
(One hundred and seventeen worlds, actually, by the time they rescued me, but they'd kept the old name.)
They pulled me into the future to save my life. But also, because they faced a threat with roots back in my era, and they needed my help.
Unfortunately...

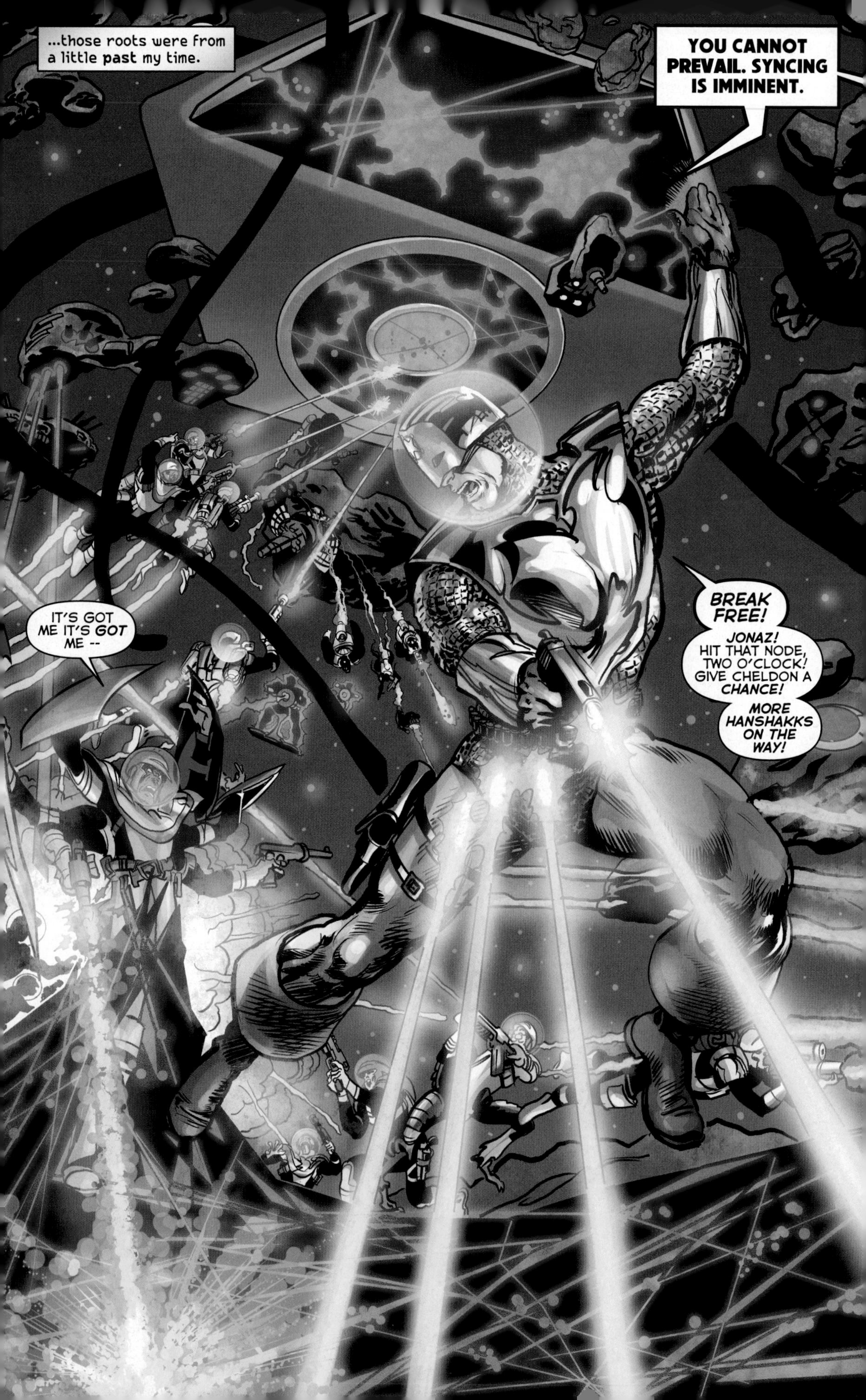
...those roots were from a little past my time.
YOU CANNOT PREVAIL. SYNCING IS IMMINENT.
IT'S GOT ME IT'S GOT ME --
BREAK FREE!
JONAZ! HIT THAT NODE, TWO O'CLOCK! GIVE CHELDON A CHANCE!
MORE HANSHAKKS ON THE WAY!

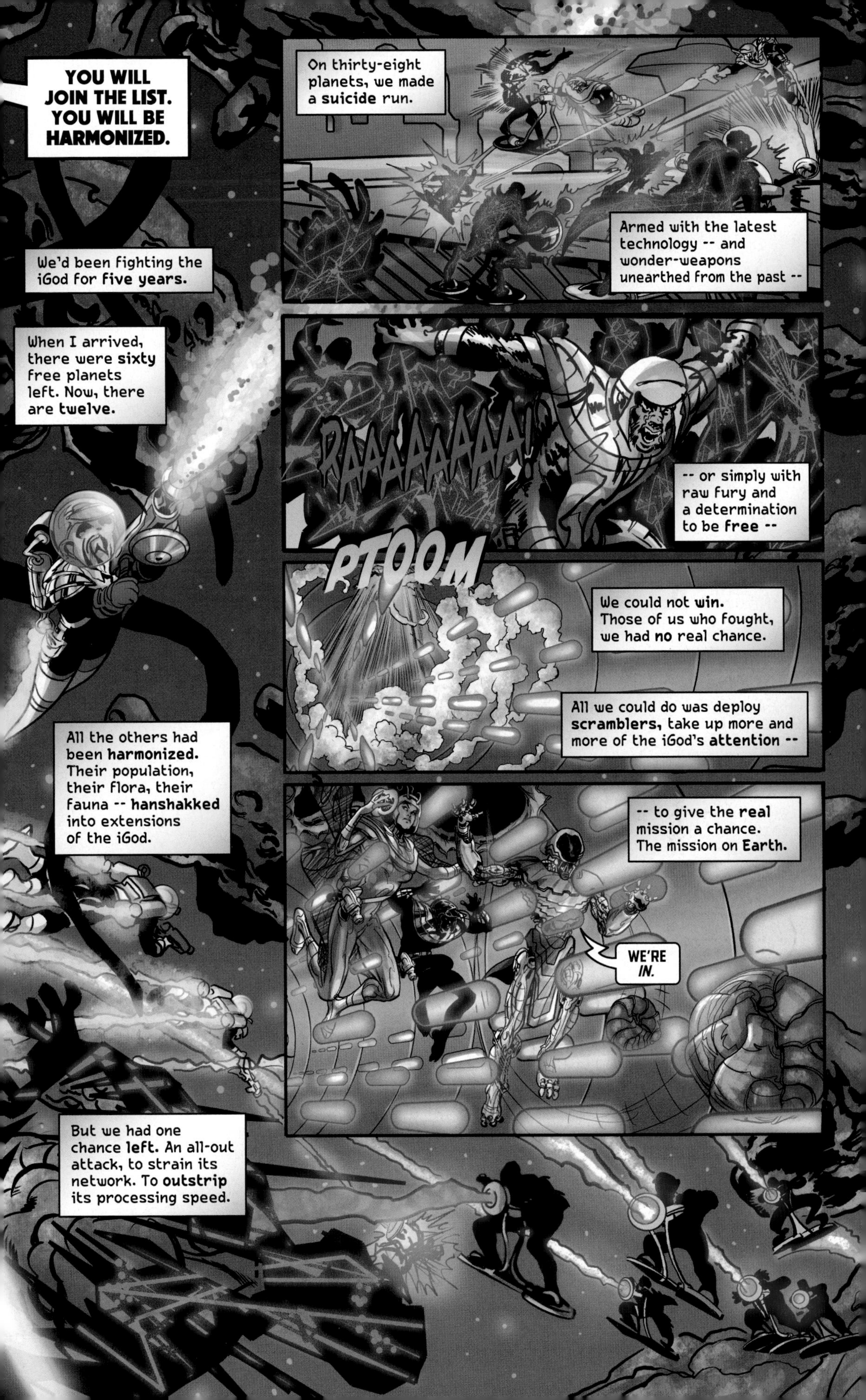
YOU WILL JOIN THE LIST. YOU WILL BE HARMONIZED.
We'd been fighting the iGod for five years.
When I arrived, there were sixty free planets left. Now, there are twelve.
On thirty-eight planets, we made a suicide run.
Armed with the latest technology -- and wonder-weapons unearthed from the past --
RAAAAAAAA!
-- or simply with raw fury and a determination to be free --
PTOOM
We could not win. Those of us who fought, we had no real chance.
All we could do was deploy scramblers, take up more and more of the iGod's attention --
All the others had been harmonized. Their population, their flora, their fauna -- hanshakked into extensions of the iGod.
-- to give the real mission a chance. The mission on Earth.
WE'RE IN.
But we had one chance left. An all-out attack, to strain its network. To outstrip its processing speed.

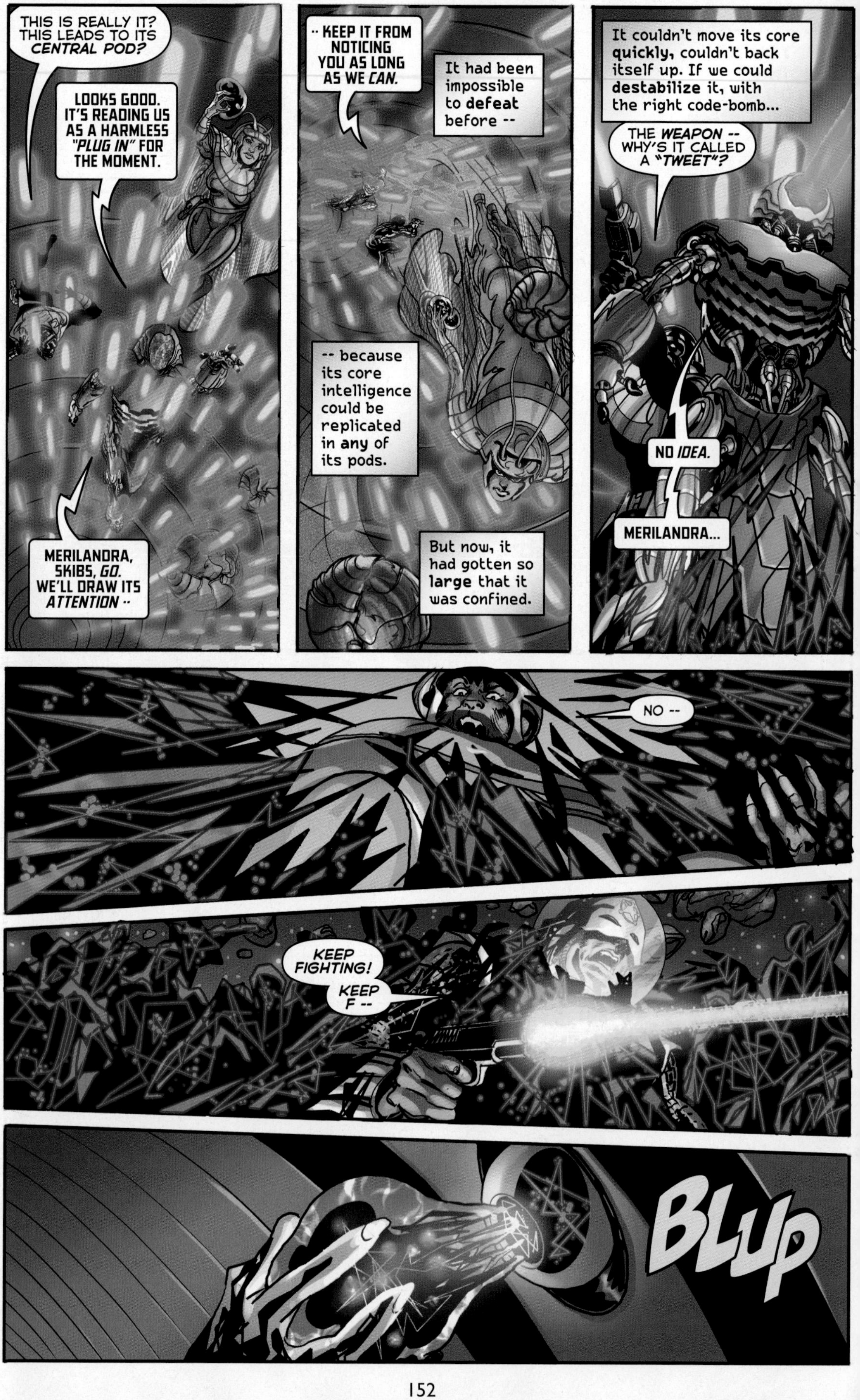
THIS IS REALLY IT? THIS LEADS TO ITS CENTRAL POD?
LOOKS GOOD. IT'S READING US AS A HARMLESS "PLUG IN" FOR THE MOMENT.
MERILANDRA, SKIBS, GO. WE'LL DRAW ITS ATTENTION --
-- KEEP IT FROM NOTICING YOU AS LONG AS WE CAN.
It had been impossible to defeat before --
-- because its core intelligence could be replicated in any of its pods.
But now, it had gotten so large that it was confined.
It couldn't move its core quickly, couldn't back itself up. If we could destabilize it, with the right code-bomb...
THE WEAPON -- WHY'S IT CALLED A "TWEET"?
NO IDEA.
MERILANDRA...
NO --
KEEP FIGHTING! KEEP F --
BLUP

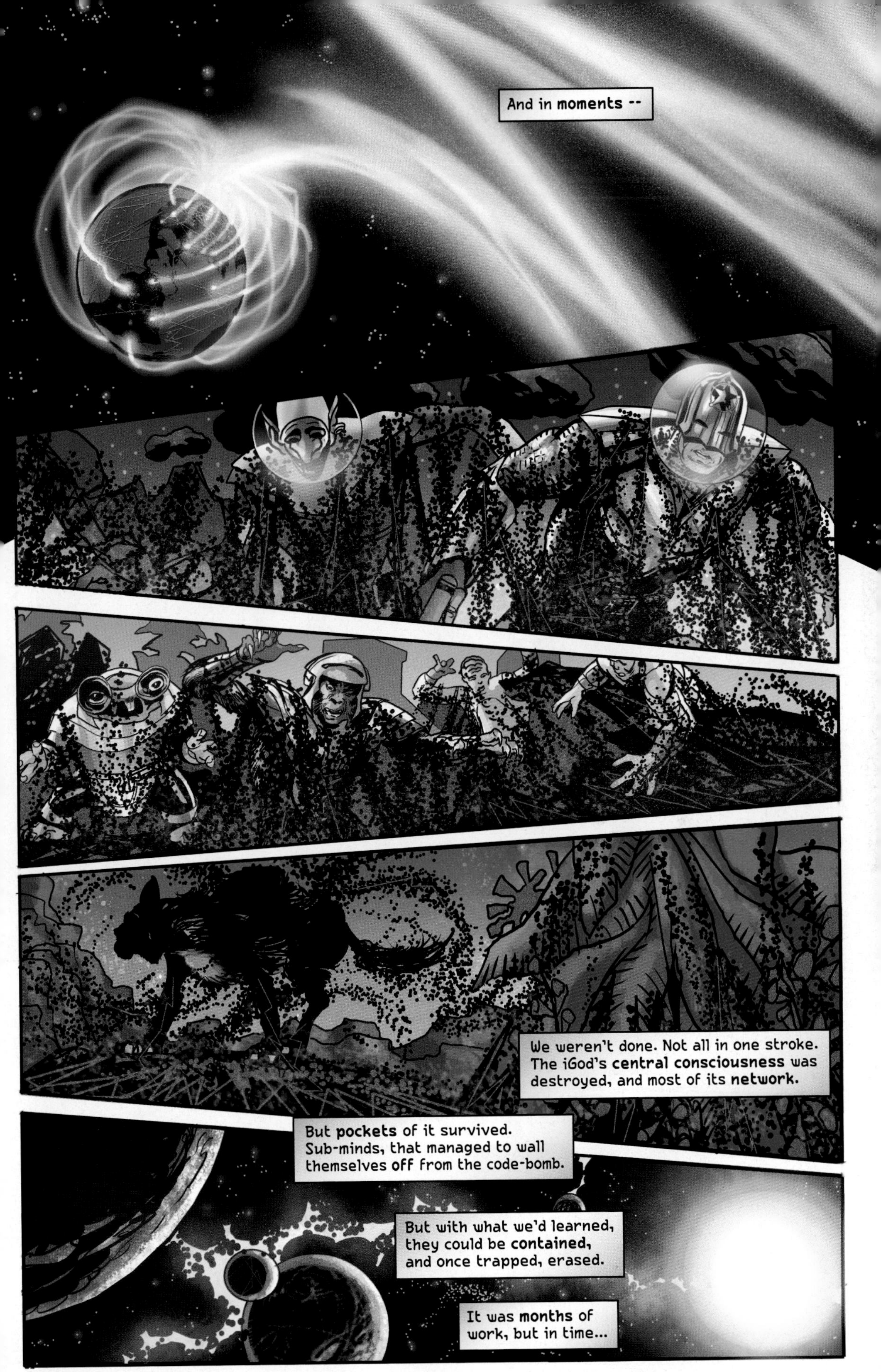
And in **moments** --
We weren't done. Not all in one stroke. The iGod's **central consciousness** was destroyed, and most of its **network**.
But **pockets** of it survived. Sub-minds, that managed to wall themselves **off** from the code-bomb.
But with what we'd learned, they could be **contained**, and once trapped, erased.
It was **months** of work, but in time...

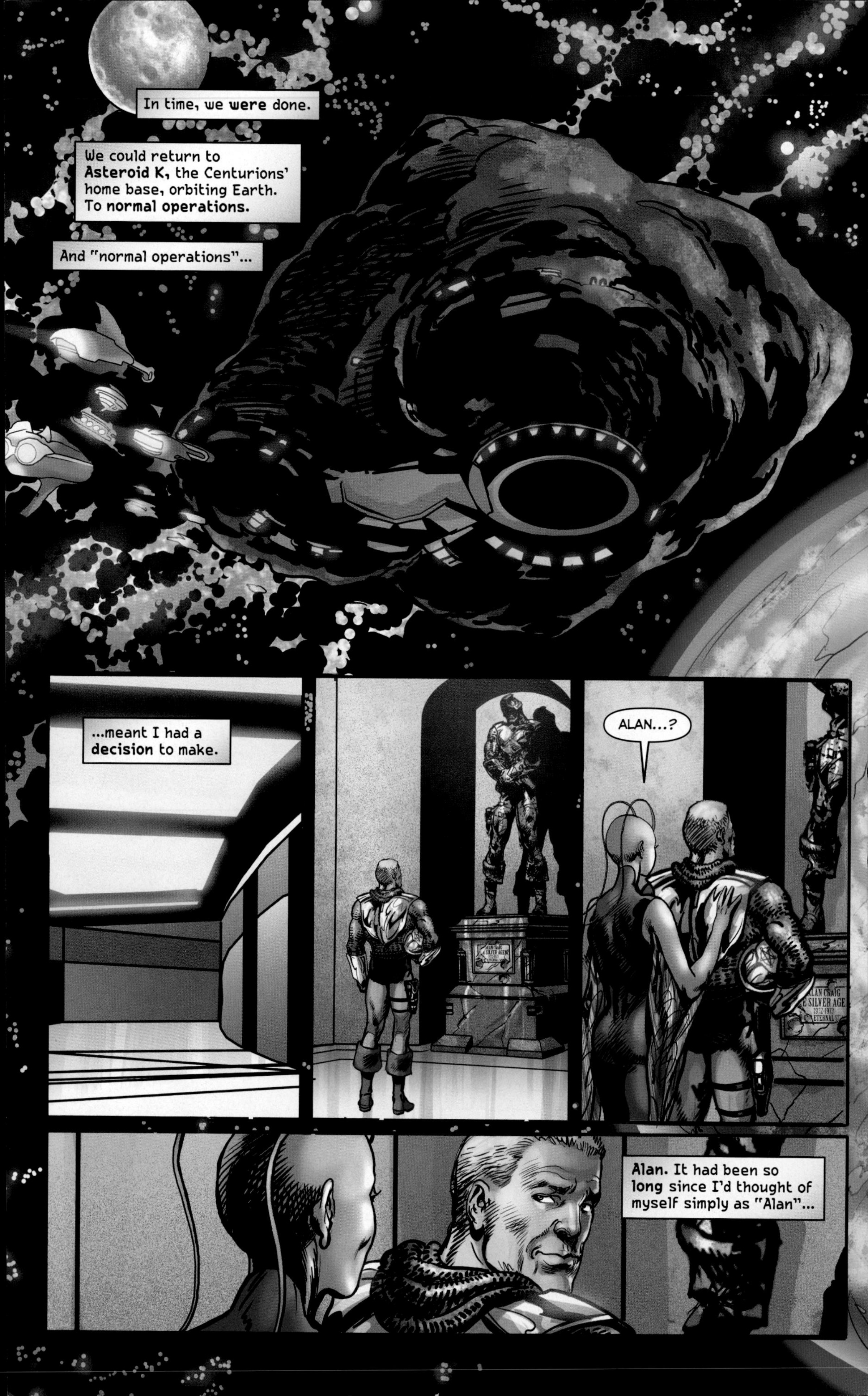
In time, we were done.
We could return to Asteroid K, the Centurions' home base, orbiting Earth. To normal operations.
And "normal operations"...
...meant I had a decision to make.
ALAN...?
Alan. It had been so long since I'd thought of myself simply as "Alan"...

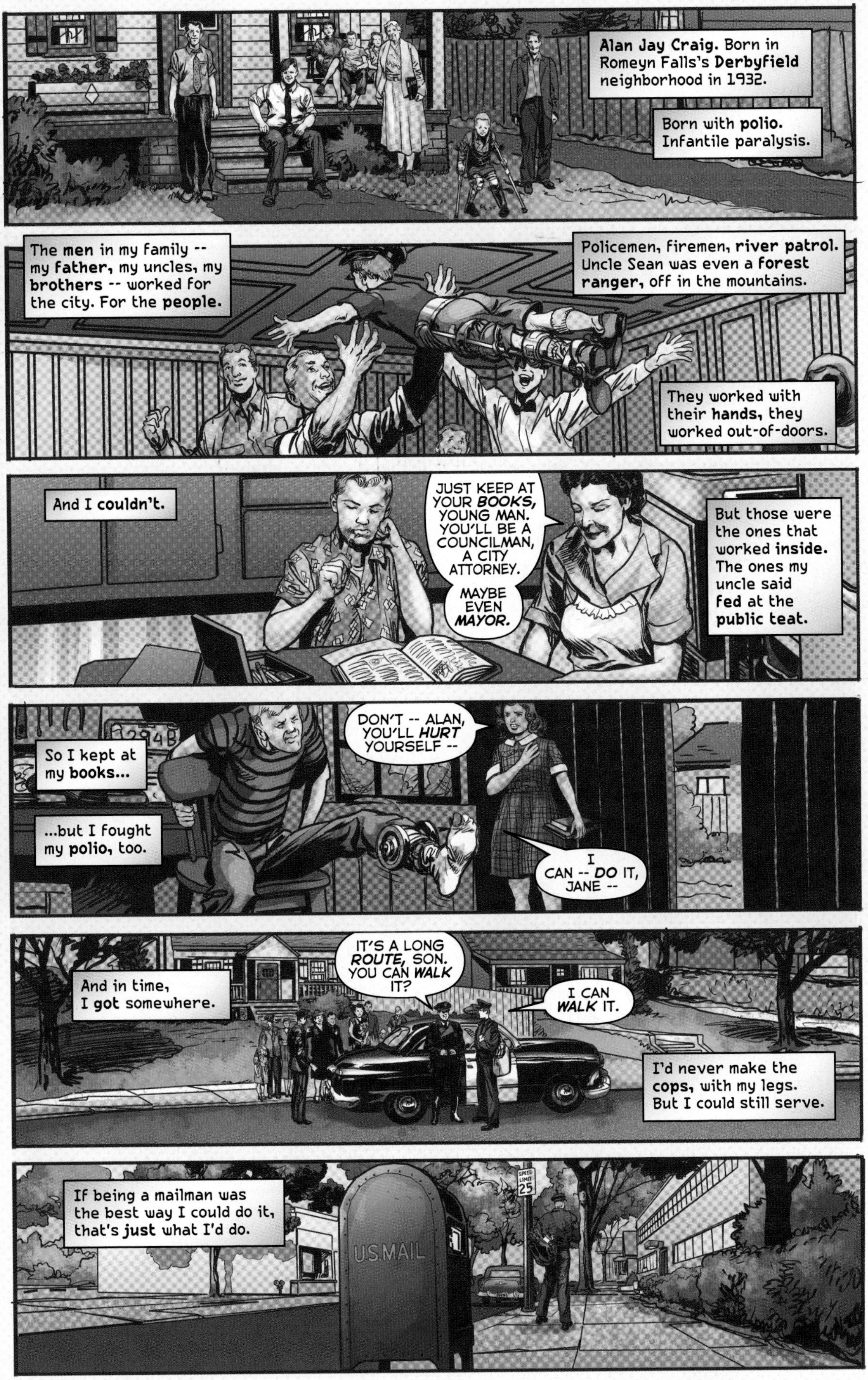
Alan Jay Craig. Born in Romeyn Falls's Derbyfield neighborhood in 1932.
Born with polio. Infantile paralysis.
The men in my family -- my father, my uncles, my brothers -- worked for the city. For the people.
Policemen, firemen, river patrol. Uncle Sean was even a forest ranger, off in the mountains.
They worked with their hands, they worked out-of-doors.
And I couldn't.
JUST KEEP AT YOUR BOOKS, YOUNG MAN. YOU'LL BE A COUNCILMAN, A CITY ATTORNEY.
MAYBE EVEN MAYOR.
But those were the ones that worked inside. The ones my uncle said fed at the public teat.
So I kept at my books...
...but I fought my polio, too.
DON'T -- ALAN, YOU'LL HURT YOURSELF --
I CAN -- DO IT, JANE --
And in time, I got somewhere.
IT'S A LONG ROUTE, SON. YOU CAN WALK IT?
I CAN WALK IT.
I'd never make the cops, with my legs. But I could still serve.
If being a mailman was the best way I could do it, that's just what I'd do.
U.S. MAIL
SPEED LIMIT 25

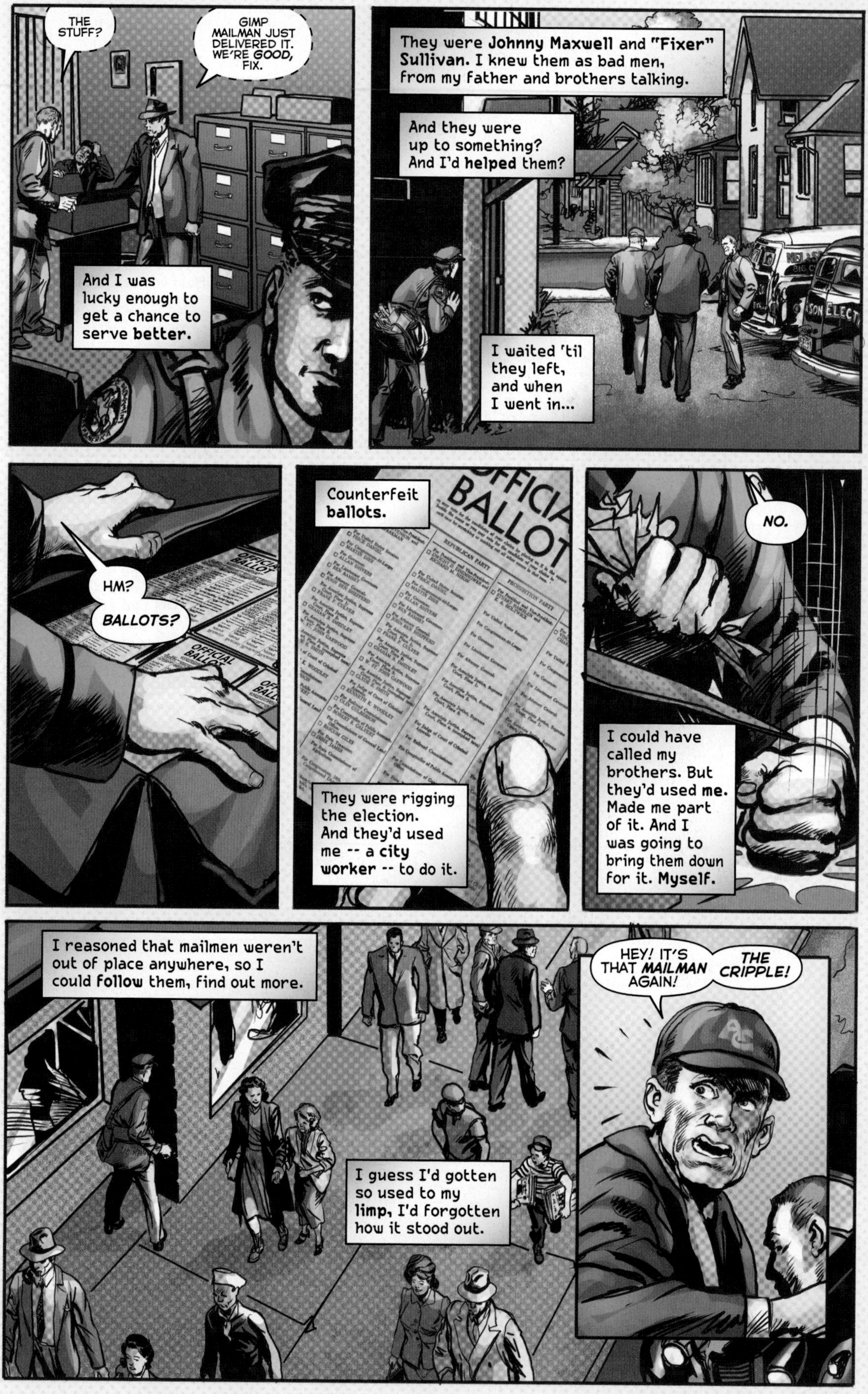
THE STUFF?
GIMP MAILMAN JUST DELIVERED IT. WE'RE GOOD, FIX.
And I was lucky enough to get a chance to serve better.
They were Johnny Maxwell and "Fixer" Sullivan. I knew them as bad men, from my father and brothers talking.
And they were up to something? And I'd helped them?
I waited 'til they left, and when I went in...
HM?
BALLOTS?
OFFICIAL BALLOT
Counterfeit ballots.
OFFICIAL BALLOT
They were rigging the election. And they'd used me -- a city worker -- to do it.
NO.
I could have called my brothers. But they'd used me. Made me part of it. And I was going to bring them down for it. Myself.
I reasoned that mailmen weren't out of place anywhere, so I could follow them, find out more.
I guess I'd gotten so used to my limp, I'd forgotten how it stood out.
HEY! IT'S THAT MAILMAN AGAIN!
THE CRIPPLE!

BAM BTAM

There was no hope I could lose them on **city streets**, not with my leg.

But we were near **Romeyn Park** when they spotted me, not far from the base of the falls...

...so I ducked into the **hills**.

THERE! UP AHEAD!

I'd played in those **trees** and **gullies** all my life. But even so...

...I'd never seen that **cave** before.

HM?

It had been there a **long time**, though. There were Indian arrowheads...

HEY --

And a **souvenir**. One of those where you put a coin in a machine and **flatten** it, remold it.

It was from 1900, the **Century Fair**. Older men in the neighborhood kept them in their **pockets**, or displayed them on mantels.

IN THERE -- !

ROMEYN FALLS CELEBRA...
THE TWENTIETH...

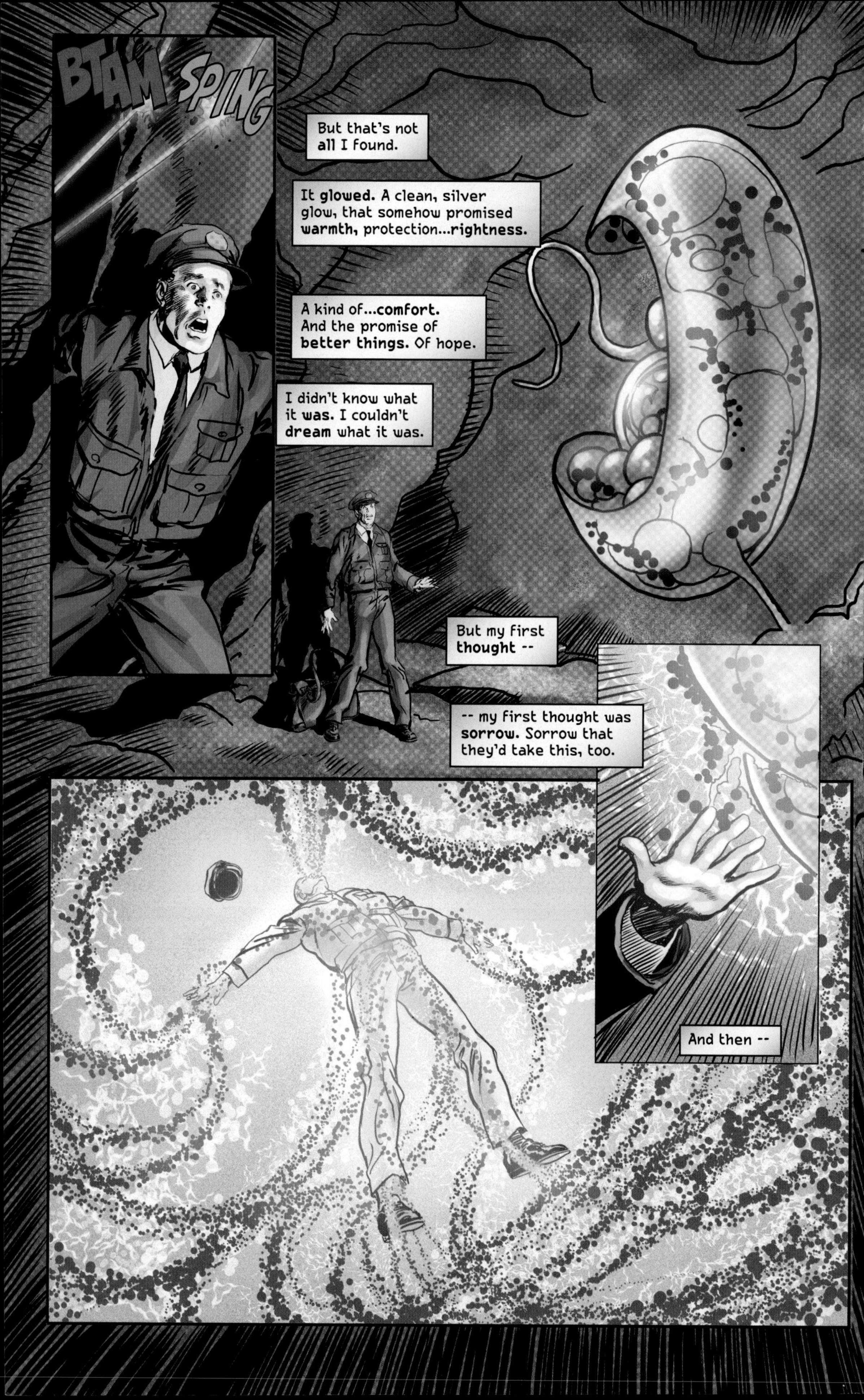
BTAM
SPING
But that's not all I found.
It glowed. A clean, silver glow, that somehow promised warmth, protection...rightness.
A kind of...comfort. And the promise of better things. Of hope.
I didn't know what it was. I couldn't dream what it was.
But my first thought --
-- my first thought was sorrow. Sorrow that they'd take this, too.
And then --

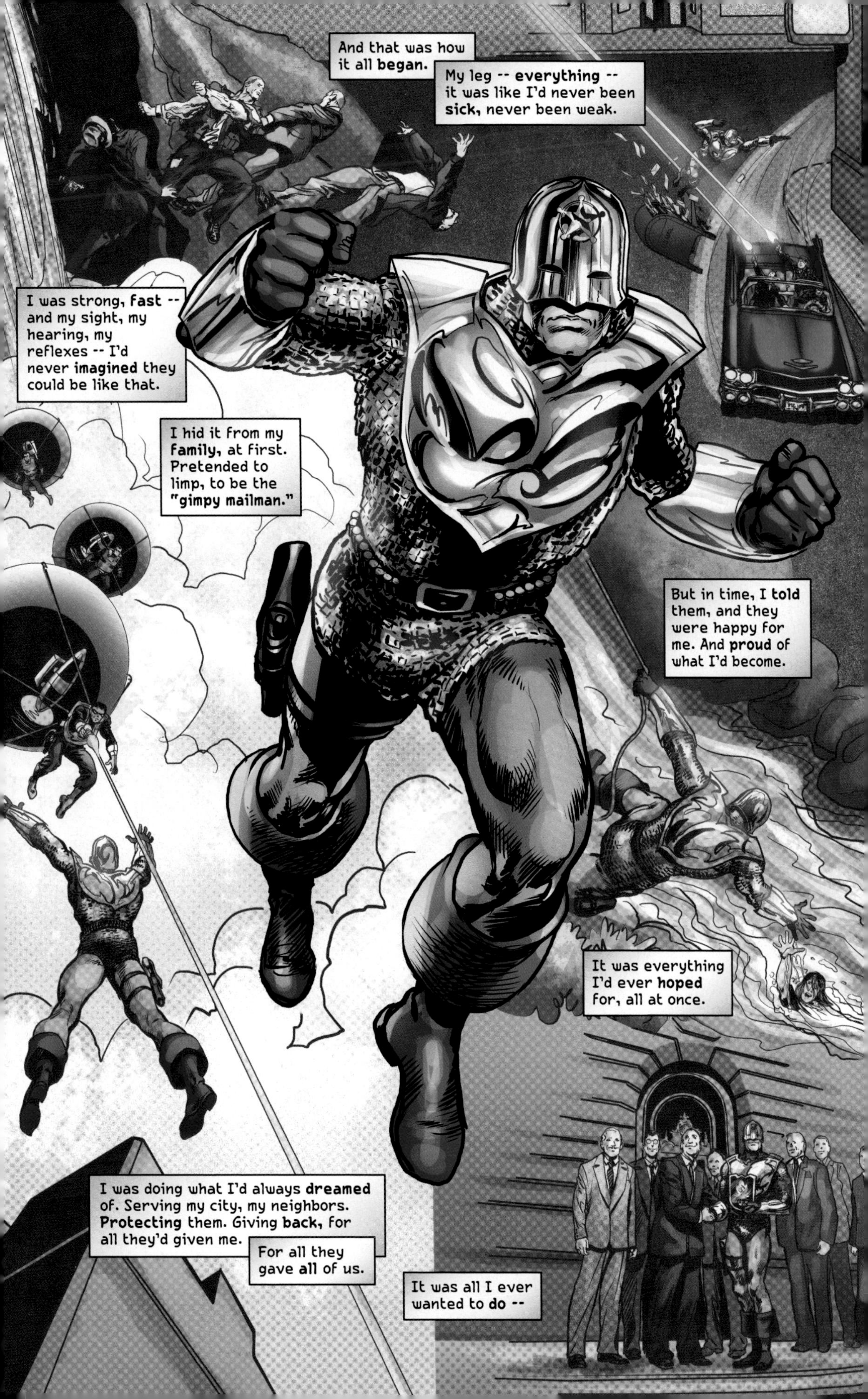

And that was how it all began.
My leg -- everything -- it was like I'd never been sick, never been weak.
I was strong, fast -- and my sight, my hearing, my reflexes -- I'd never imagined they could be like that.
I hid it from my family, at first. Pretended to limp, to be the "gimpy mailman."
But in time, I told them, and they were happy for me. And proud of what I'd become.
It was everything I'd ever hoped for, all at once.
I was doing what I'd always dreamed of. Serving my city, my neighbors. Protecting them. Giving back, for all they'd given me.
For all they gave all of us.
It was all I ever wanted to do --

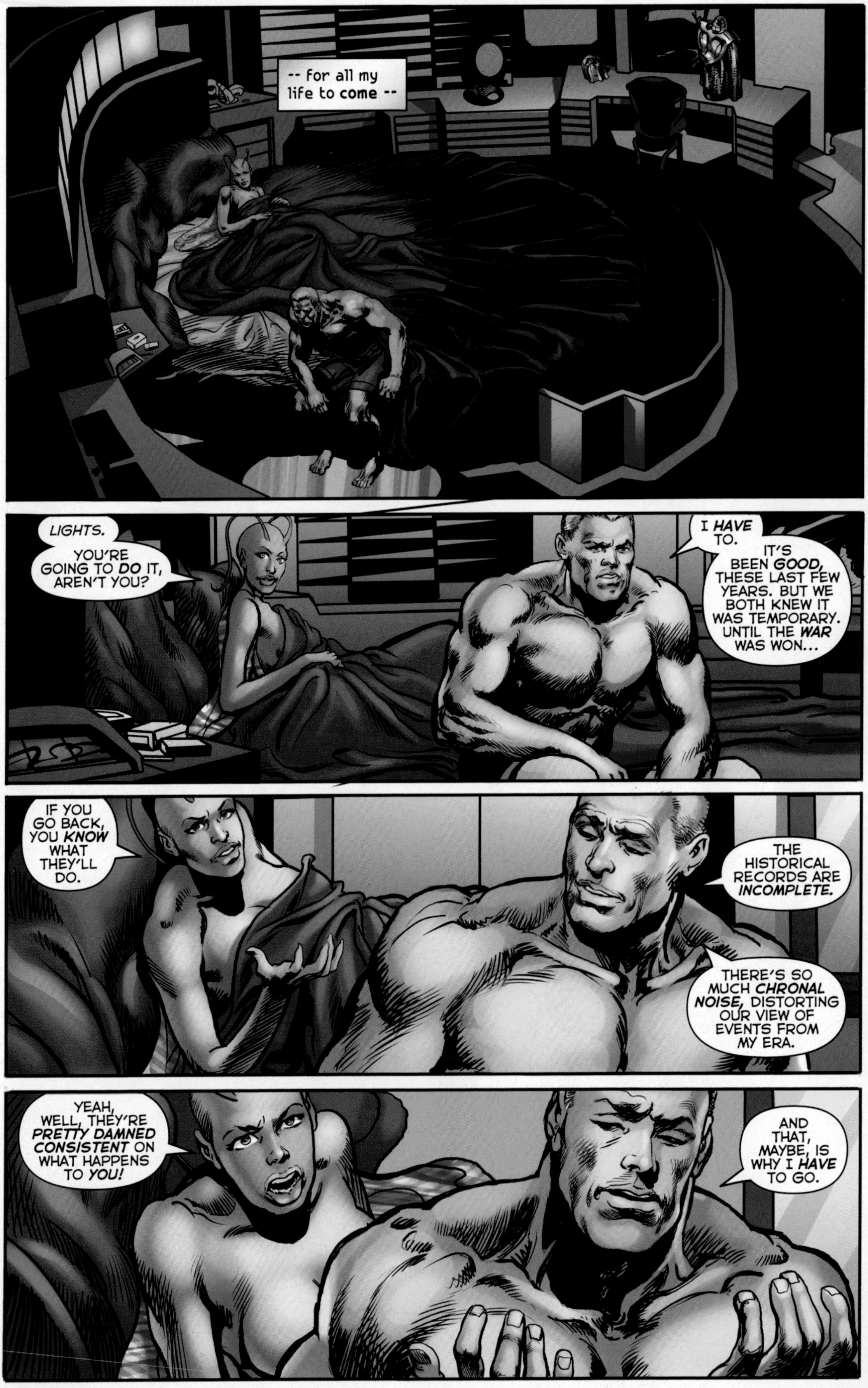
-- for all my life to come --
LIGHTS.
YOU'RE GOING TO DO IT, AREN'T YOU?
I HAVE TO.
IT'S BEEN GOOD, THESE LAST FEW YEARS. BUT WE BOTH KNEW IT WAS TEMPORARY. UNTIL THE WAR WAS WON...
IF YOU GO BACK, YOU KNOW WHAT THEY'LL DO.
THE HISTORICAL RECORDS ARE INCOMPLETE.
THERE'S SO MUCH CHRONAL NOISE, DISTORTING OUR VIEW OF EVENTS FROM MY ERA.
YEAH, WELL, THEY'RE PRETTY DAMNED CONSISTENT ON WHAT HAPPENS TO YOU!
AND THAT, MAYBE, IS WHY I HAVE TO GO.

THEY *LEARNED*, ALAN. THEY LEARNED THEY WERE WRONG. THEY WOULDN'T HAVE *DONE* IT IF THEY KNEW.

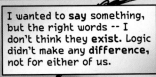

YOU COULD BRING BACK EVIDENCE --

I wanted to *say* something, but the right words -- I don't think they *exist*. Logic didn't make any *difference*, not for either of us.

I *still* felt like a heel.

LIGHTS.

I've left *too* many women. Hurt them by going.

And it doesn't help to know that from *time immemorial*, men and women *have* to leave, sometimes, for a greater cause...

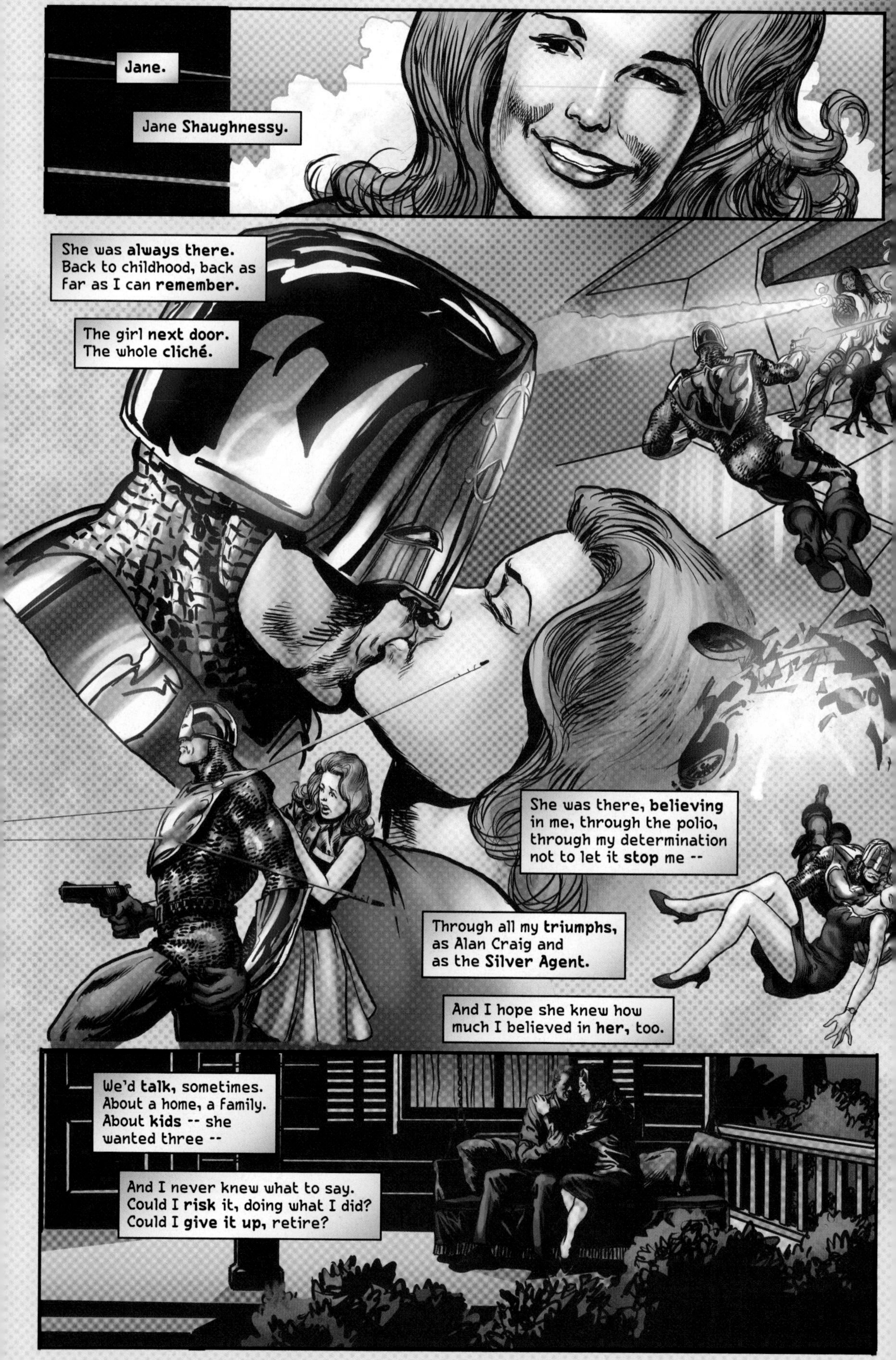
Jane.
Jane Shaughnessy.
She was always there. Back to childhood, back as far as I can remember.
The girl next door. The whole cliché.
She was there, believing in me, through the polio, through my determination not to let it stop me --
Through all my triumphs, as Alan Craig and as the Silver Agent.
And I hope she knew how much I believed in her, too.
We'd talk, sometimes. About a home, a family. About kids -- she wanted three --
And I never knew what to say. Could I risk it, doing what I did? Could I give it up, retire?

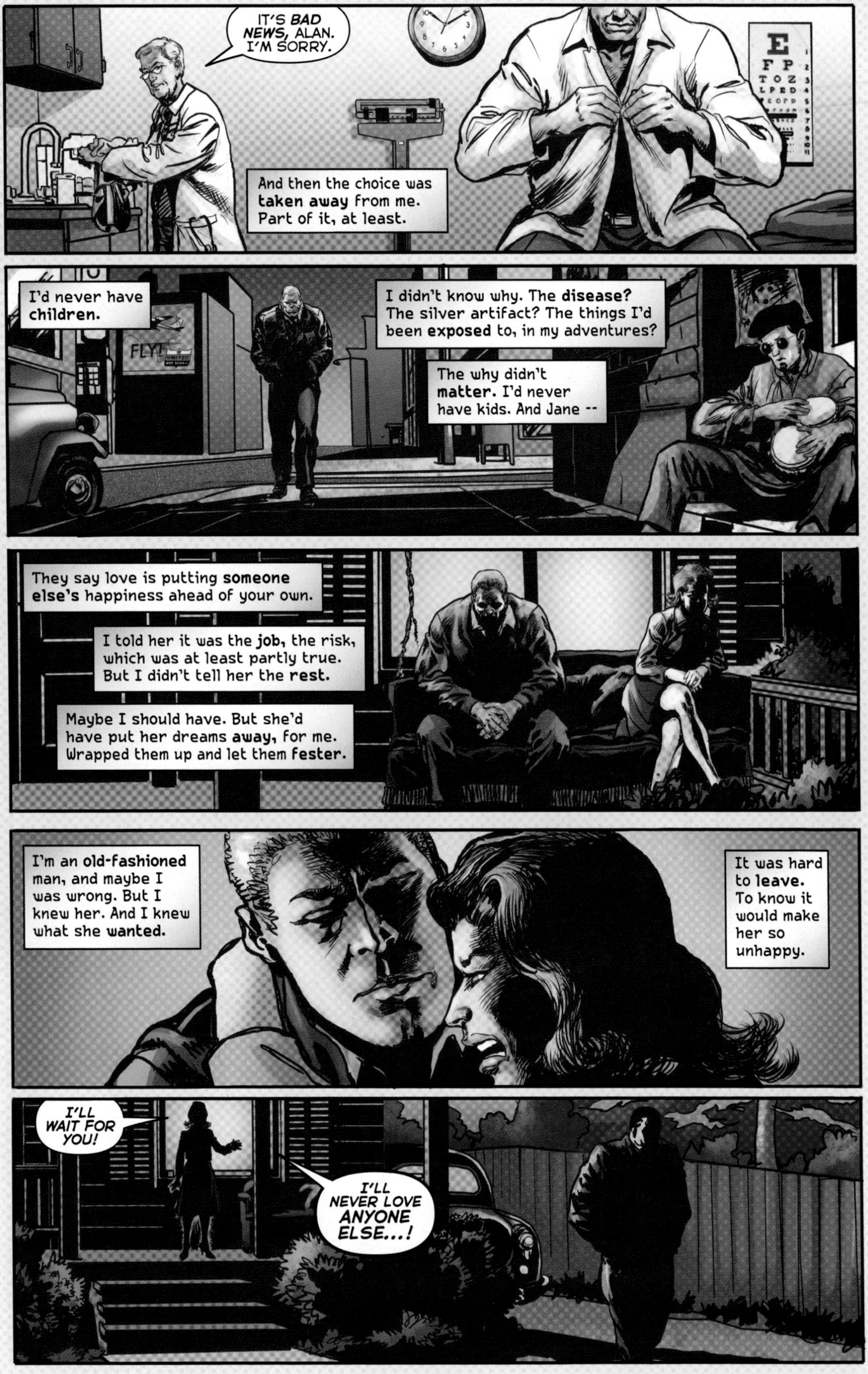
IT'S BAD NEWS, ALAN. I'M SORRY.
And then the choice was taken away from me. Part of it, at least.
I'd never have children.
I didn't know why. The disease? The silver artifact? The things I'd been exposed to, in my adventures?
The why didn't matter. I'd never have kids. And Jane --
They say love is putting someone else's happiness ahead of your own.
I told her it was the job, the risk, which was at least partly true. But I didn't tell her the rest.
Maybe I should have. But she'd have put her dreams away, for me. Wrapped them up and let them fester.
I'm an old-fashioned man, and maybe I was wrong. But I knew her. And I knew what she wanted.
It was hard to leave. To know it would make her so unhappy.
I'LL WAIT FOR YOU!
I'LL NEVER LOVE ANYONE ELSE...!

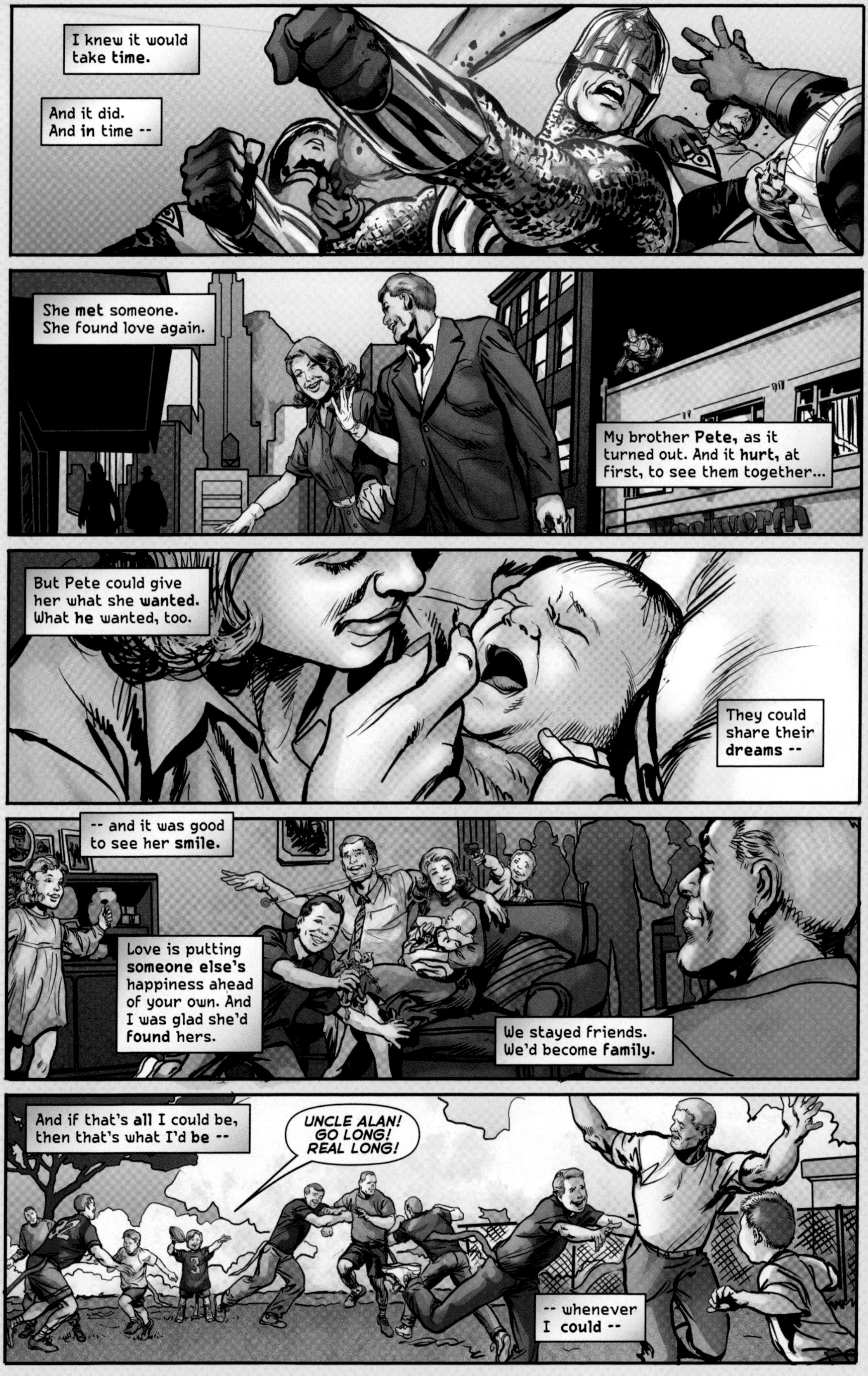
I knew it would take time.
And it did. And in time --
She met someone. She found love again.
My brother Pete, as it turned out. And it hurt, at first, to see them together...
But Pete could give her what she wanted. What he wanted, too.
They could share their dreams --
-- and it was good to see her smile.
Love is putting someone else's happiness ahead of your own. And I was glad she'd found hers.
We stayed friends. We'd become family.
And if that's all I could be, then that's what I'd be --
UNCLE ALAN! GO LONG! REAL LONG!
-- whenever I could --

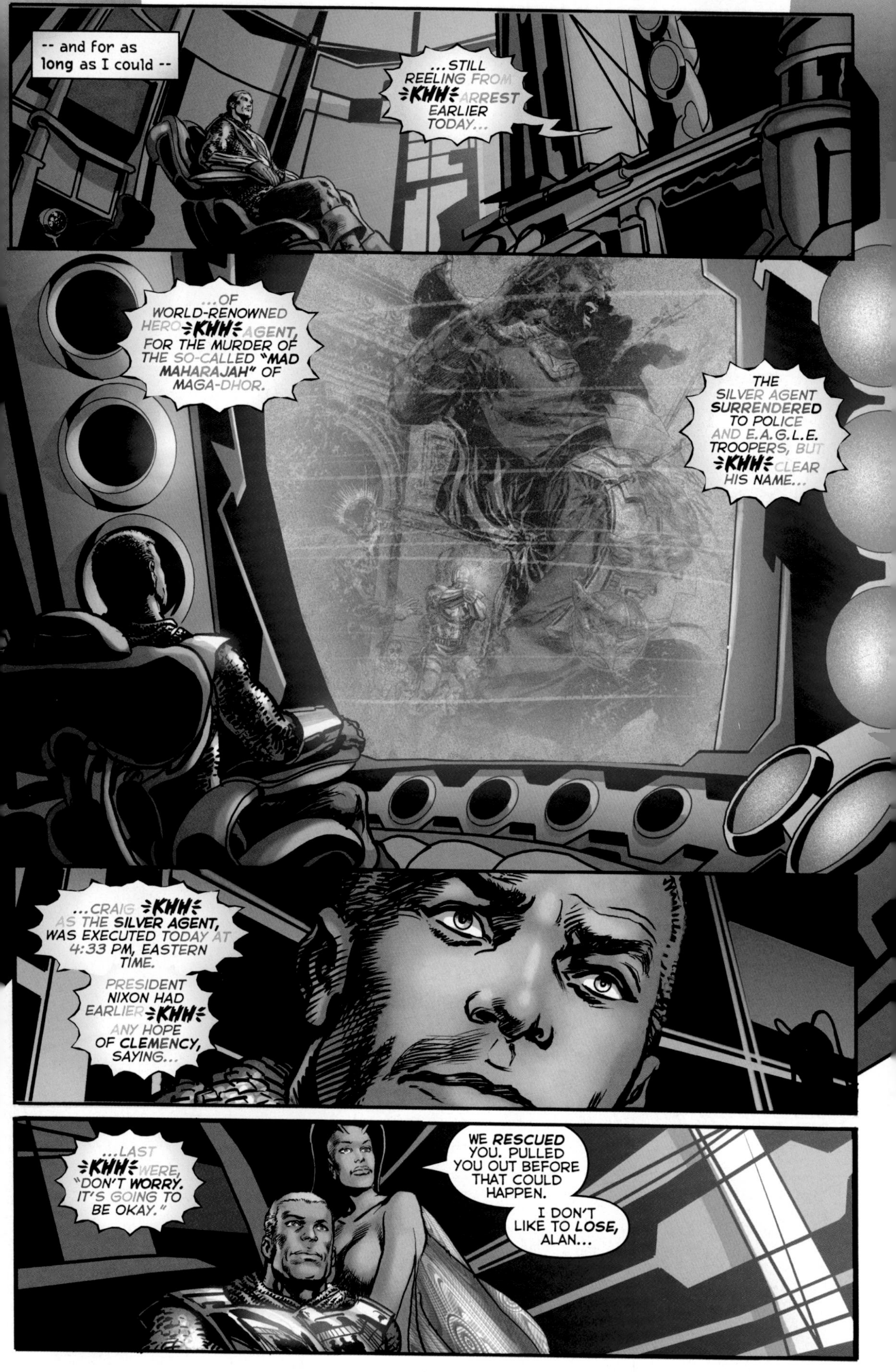

-- and for as long as I could --
...STILL REELING FROM KHH ARREST EARLIER TODAY...
...OF WORLD-RENOWNED HERO KHH AGENT, FOR THE MURDER OF THE SO-CALLED "MAD MAHARAJAH" OF MAGA-DHOR.
THE SILVER AGENT SURRENDERED TO POLICE AND E.A.G.L.E. TROOPERS, BUT KHH CLEAR HIS NAME...
...CRAIG KHH AS THE SILVER AGENT, WAS EXECUTED TODAY AT 4:33 PM, EASTERN TIME.
PRESIDENT NIXON HAD EARLIER KHH ANY HOPE OF CLEMENCY, SAYING...
...LAST KHH WERE, "DON'T WORRY. IT'S GOING TO BE OKAY."
WE RESCUED YOU. PULLED YOU OUT BEFORE THAT COULD HAPPEN.
I DON'T LIKE TO LOSE, ALAN...

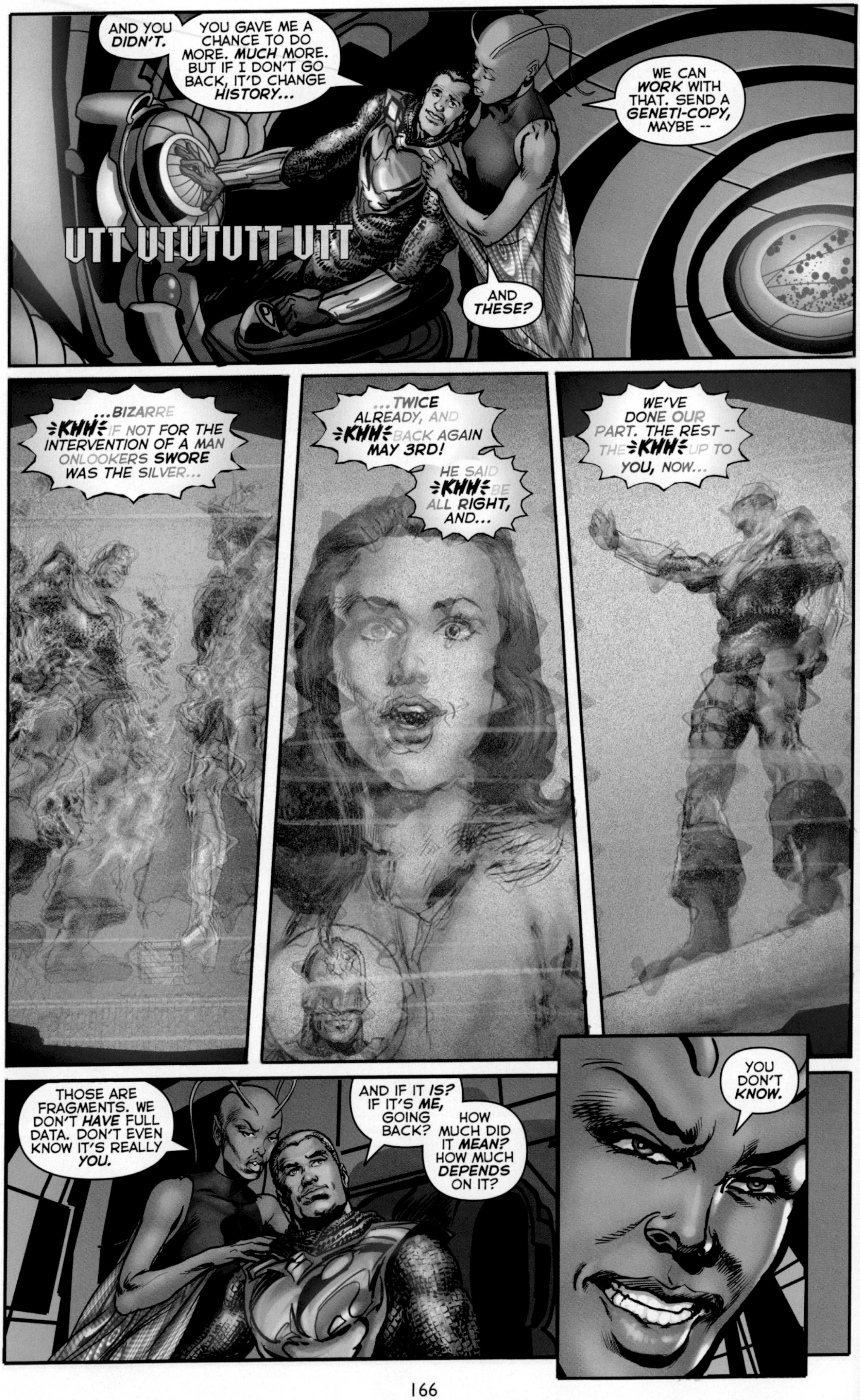
AND YOU DIDN'T.
YOU GAVE ME A CHANCE TO DO MORE. MUCH MORE. BUT IF I DON'T GO BACK, IT'D CHANGE HISTORY...
WE CAN WORK WITH THAT. SEND A GENETI-COPY, MAYBE --
UTT UTUTUTT UTT
AND THESE?
...BIZARRE KHH IF NOT FOR THE INTERVENTION OF A MAN ONLOOKERS SWORE WAS THE SILVER...
...TWICE ALREADY, AND KHH BACK AGAIN MAY 3RD!
HE SAID KHH BE ALL RIGHT, AND...
WE'VE DONE OUR PART. THE REST -- THE KHH UP TO YOU, NOW...
THOSE ARE FRAGMENTS. WE DON'T HAVE FULL DATA. DON'T EVEN KNOW IT'S REALLY YOU.
AND IF IT IS? IF IT'S ME, GOING BACK?
HOW MUCH DID IT MEAN? HOW MUCH DEPENDS ON IT?
YOU DON'T KNOW.

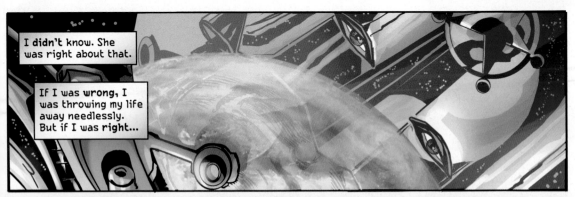

I didn't know. She was right about that.

If I was **wrong**, I was throwing my life away needlessly. But if I was **right**...

It's so **beautiful**.

It's **worth** fighting for. Worth **dying** for. All of it.

And I **found** something...

...something that tells me why Centurion HQ is called "Asteroid K."

ROMEYN FALLS CELEBRATES
THE TWENTIETH CENTURY

Something that makes up my **mind**.

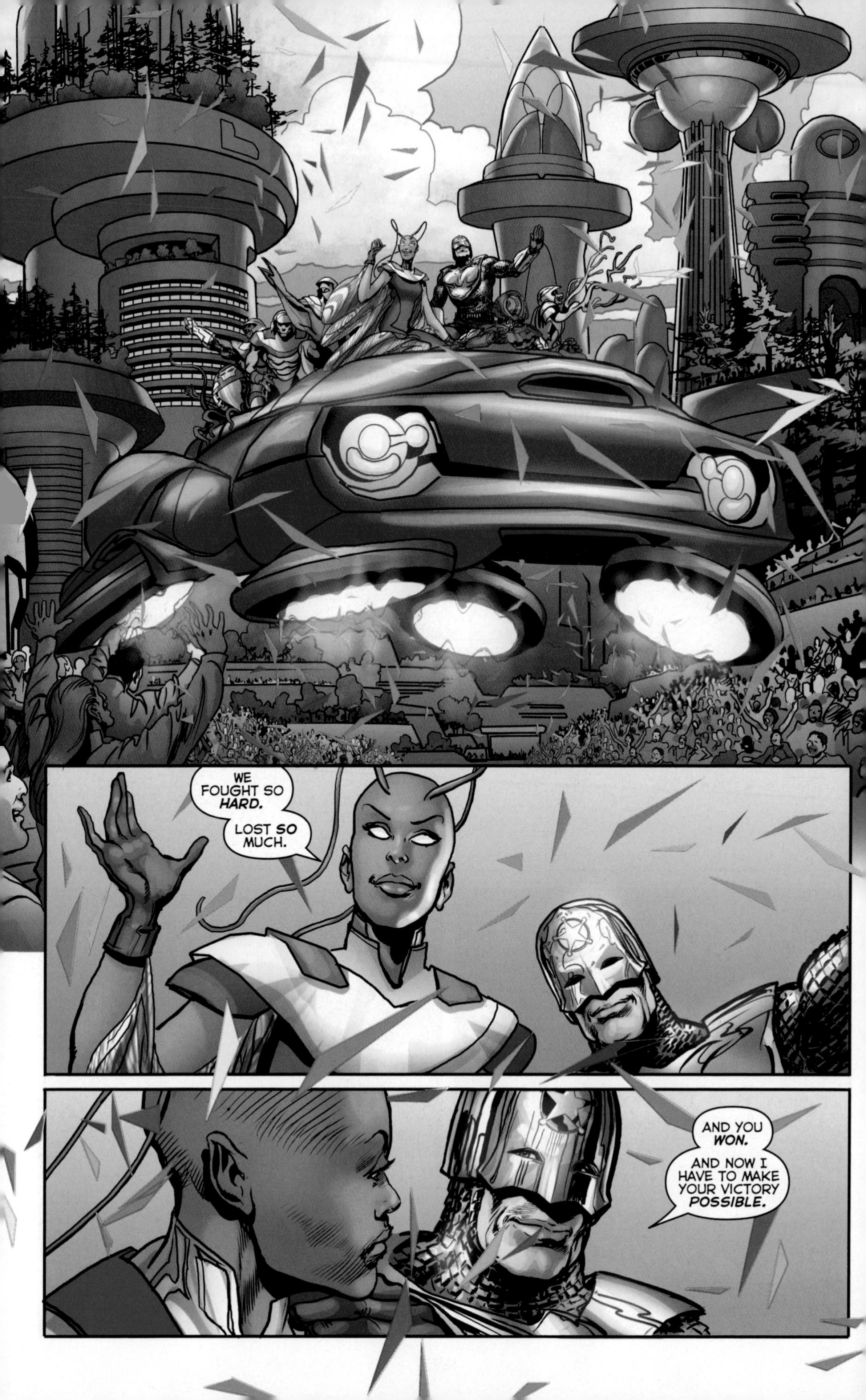
WE FOUGHT SO *HARD.*
LOST *SO* MUCH.
AND YOU *WON.*
AND NOW I HAVE TO MAKE YOUR VICTORY *POSSIBLE.*

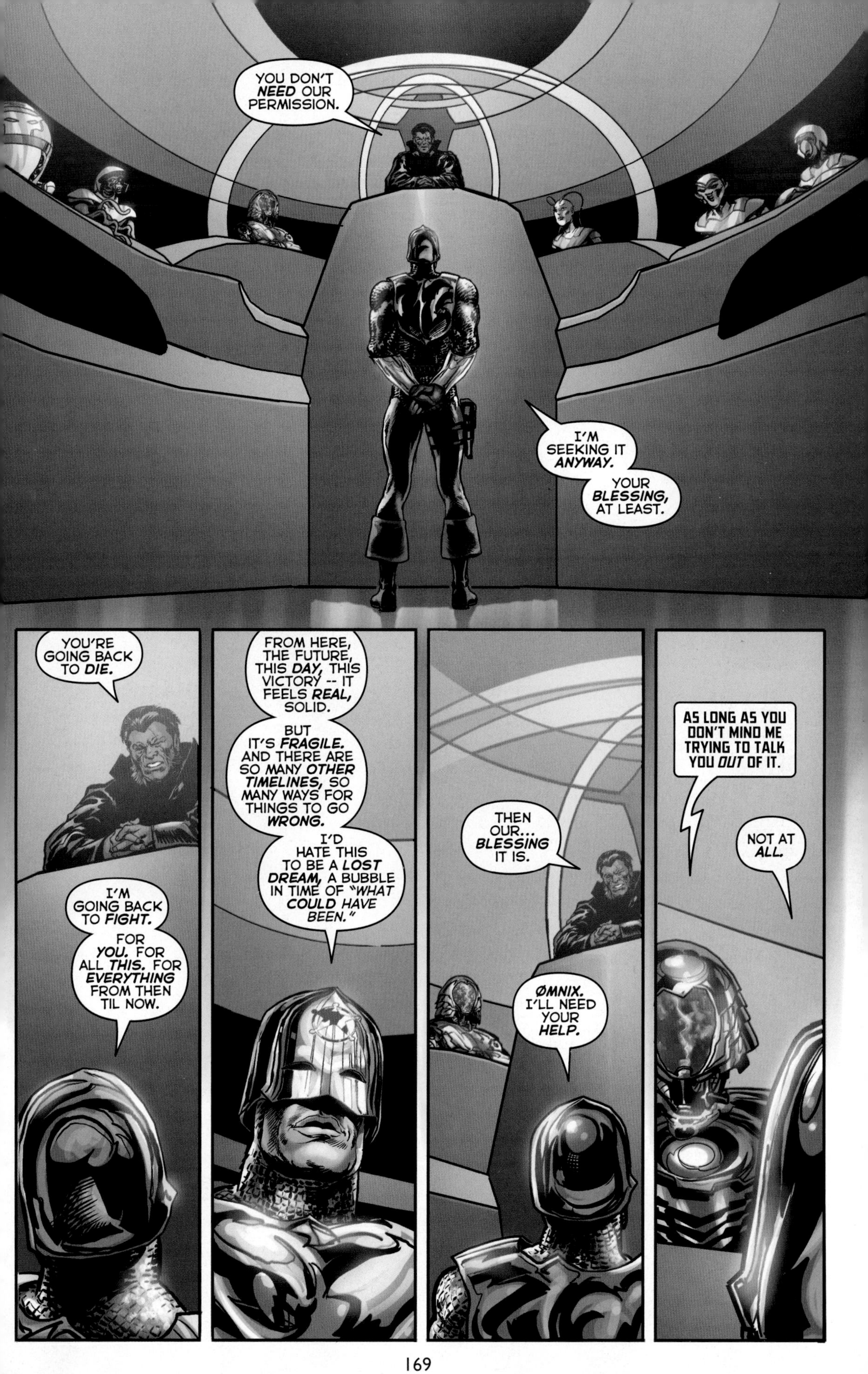
YOU DON'T *NEED* OUR PERMISSION.
I'M SEEKING IT *ANYWAY.*
YOUR *BLESSING,* AT LEAST.
YOU'RE GOING BACK TO *DIE.*
I'M GOING BACK TO *FIGHT.*
FOR *YOU.* FOR ALL *THIS.* FOR *EVERYTHING* FROM THEN TIL NOW.
FROM HERE, THE FUTURE, THIS *DAY,* THIS VICTORY -- IT FEELS *REAL,* SOLID.
BUT IT'S *FRAGILE.* AND THERE ARE SO MANY *OTHER TIMELINES,* SO MANY WAYS FOR THINGS TO GO *WRONG.*
I'D HATE THIS TO BE A *LOST DREAM,* A BUBBLE IN TIME OF *"WHAT COULD HAVE BEEN."*
THEN OUR... *BLESSING* IT IS.
ØMNIX. I'LL NEED YOUR *HELP.*
AS LONG AS YOU DON'T MIND ME TRYING TO TALK YOU *OUT* OF IT.
NOT AT *ALL.*

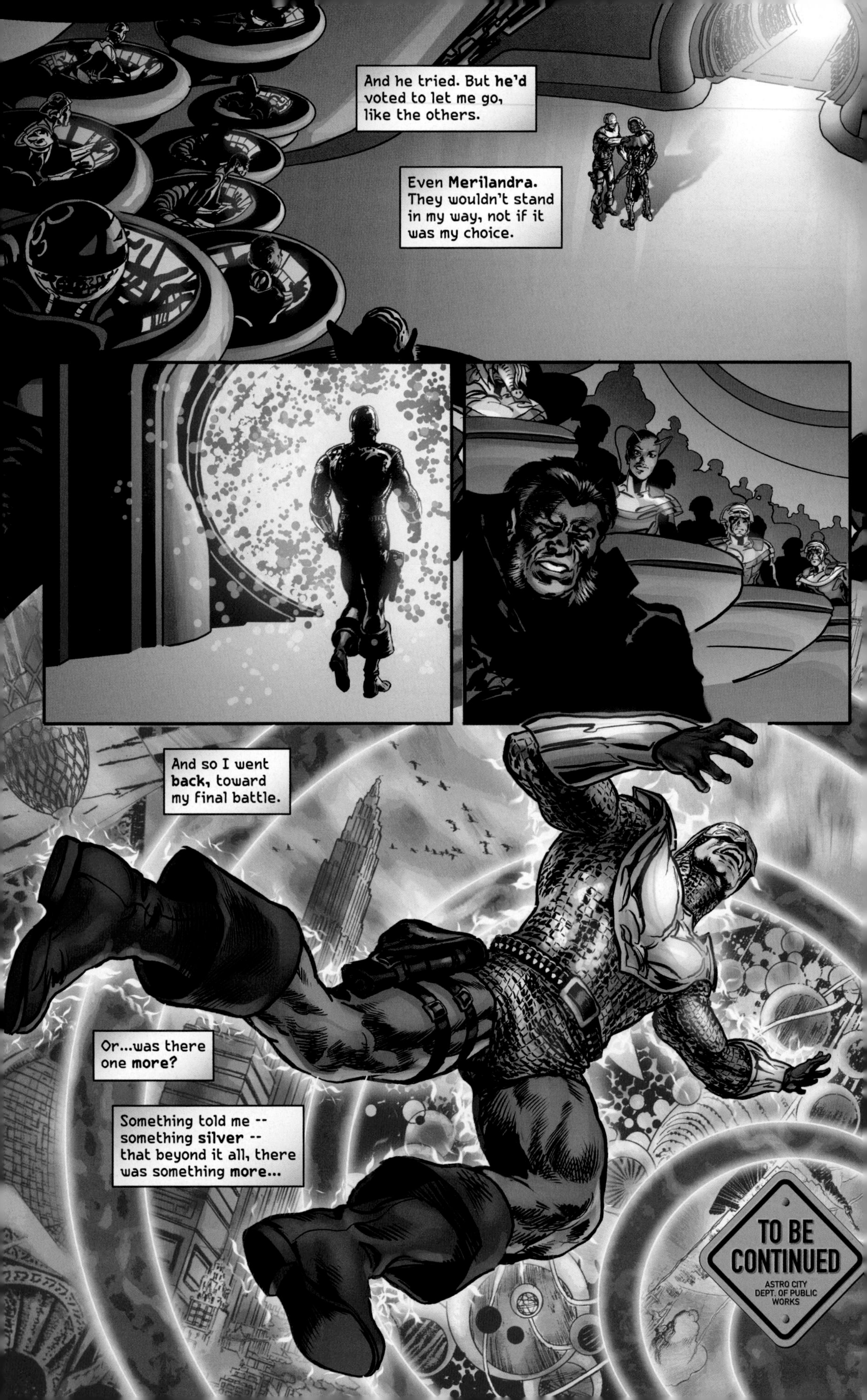
And he tried. But he'd voted to let me go, like the others.
Even Merilandra. They wouldn't stand in my way, not if it was my choice.
And so I went back, toward my final battle.
Or...was there one more?
Something told me -- something silver -- that beyond it all, there was something more...
TO BE CONTINUED
ASTRO CITY DEPT. OF PUBLIC WORKS

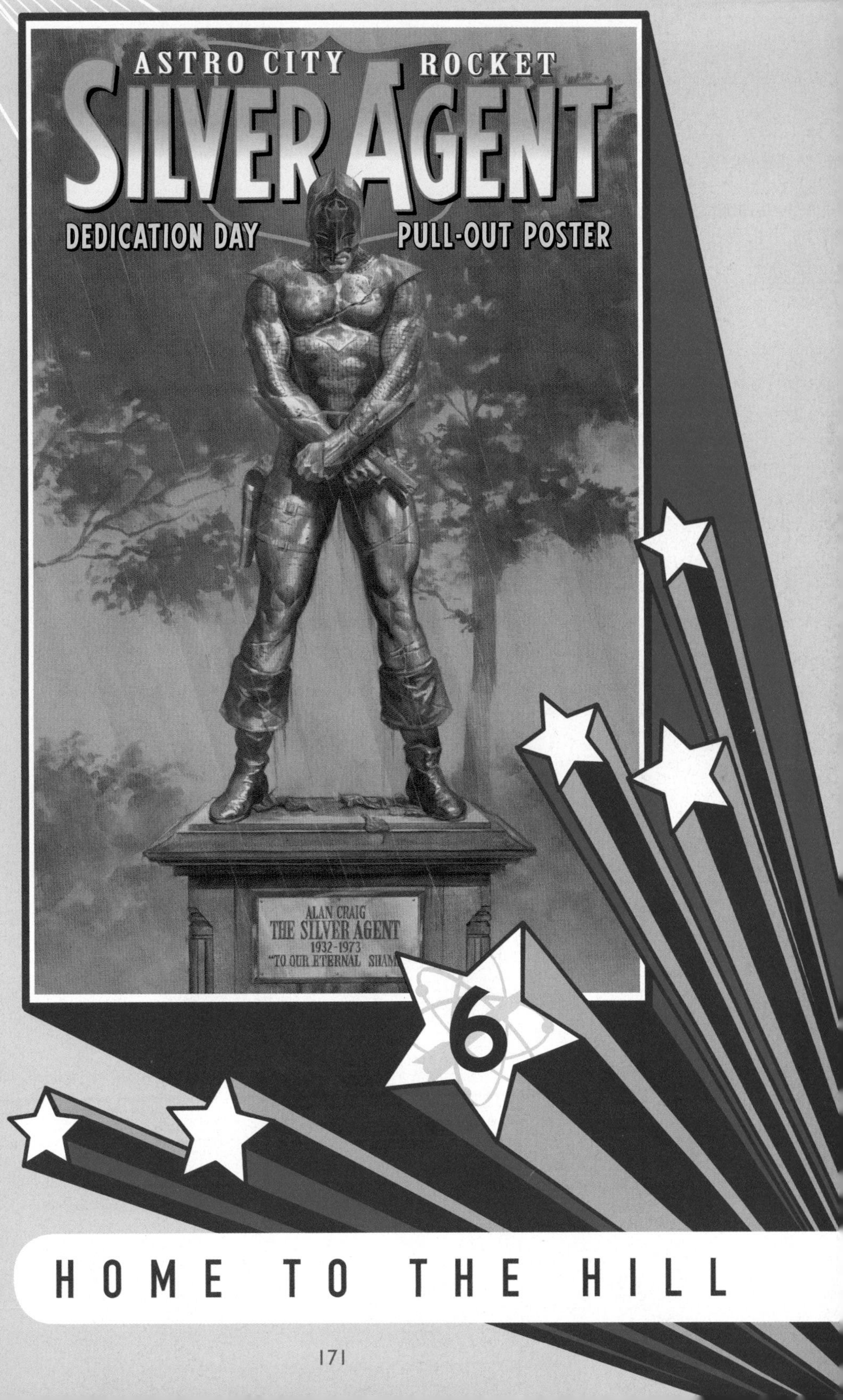
ASTRO CITY ROCKET
SILVER AGENT
DEDICATION DAY
PULL-OUT POSTER
ALAN CRAIG
THE SILVER AGENT
1932-1973
"TO OUR ETERNAL SHAM

6

HOME TO THE HILL

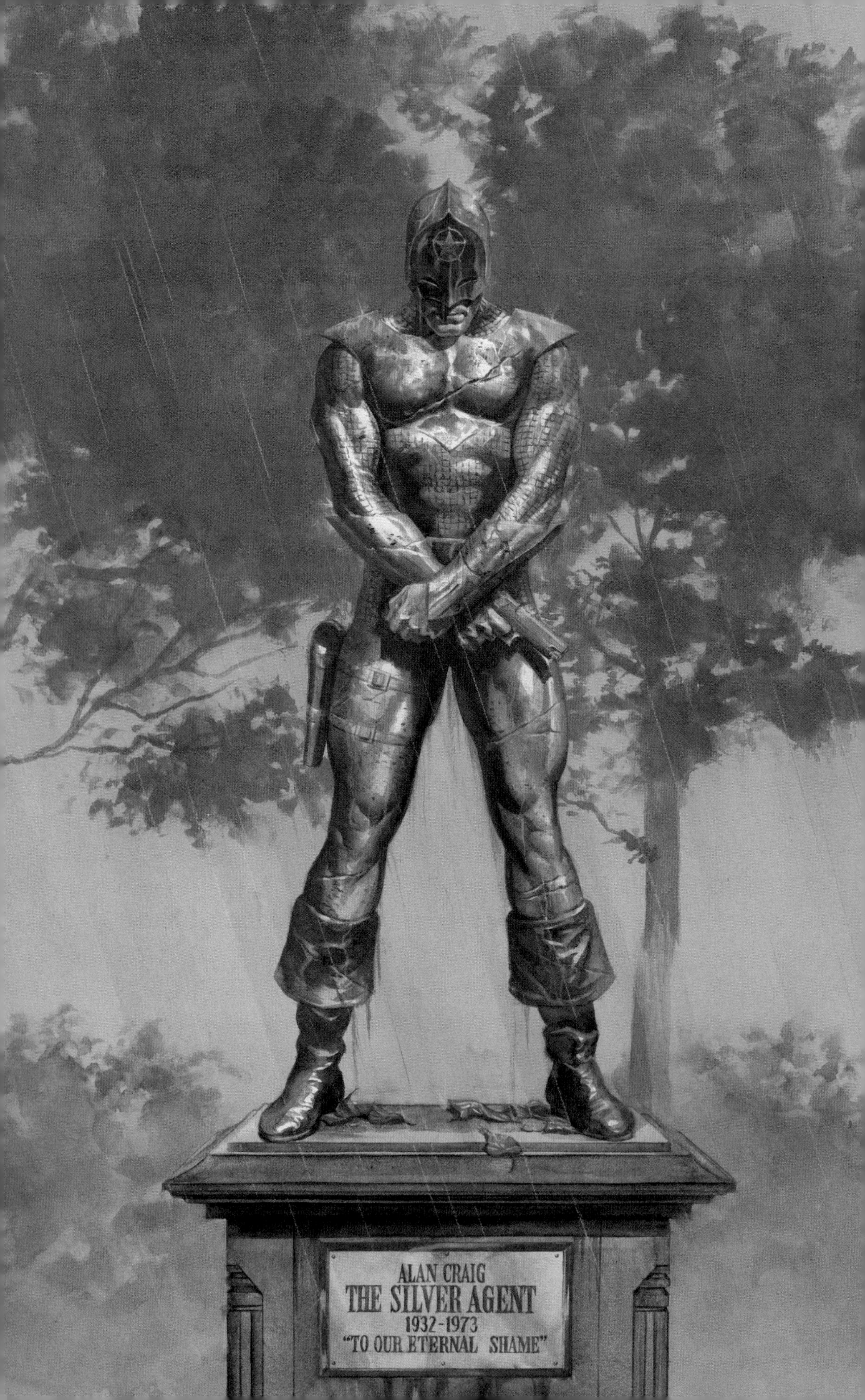
ALAN CRAIG
THE SILVER AGENT
1932-1973
"TO OUR ETERNAL SHAME"

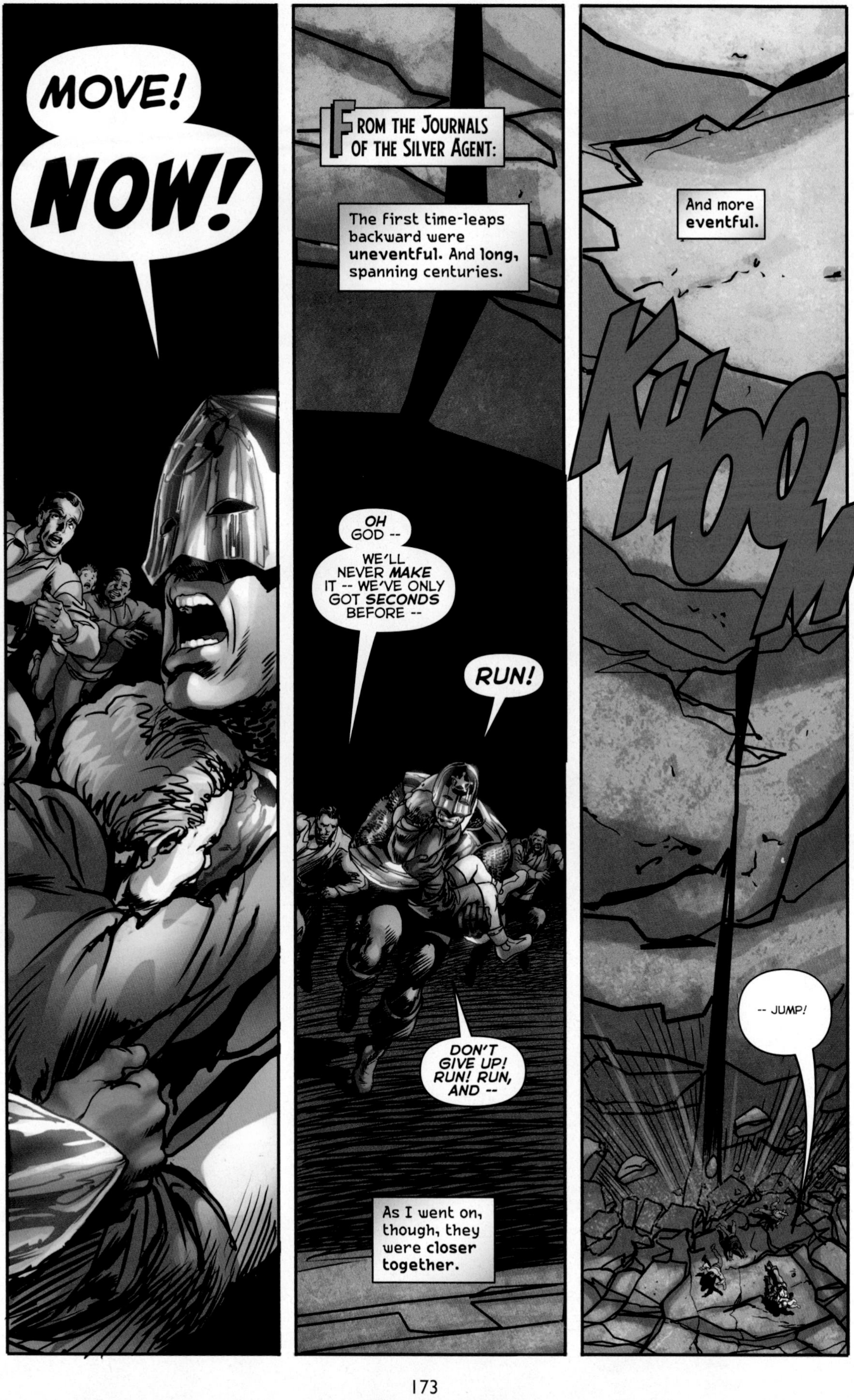
MOVE!
NOW!
FROM THE JOURNALS OF THE SILVER AGENT:
The first time-leaps backward were uneventful. And long, spanning centuries.
OH GOD --
WE'LL NEVER MAKE IT -- WE'VE ONLY GOT SECONDS BEFORE --
RUN!
DON'T GIVE UP! RUN! RUN, AND --
As I went on, though, they were closer together.
And more eventful.
KHOOM
-- JUMP!

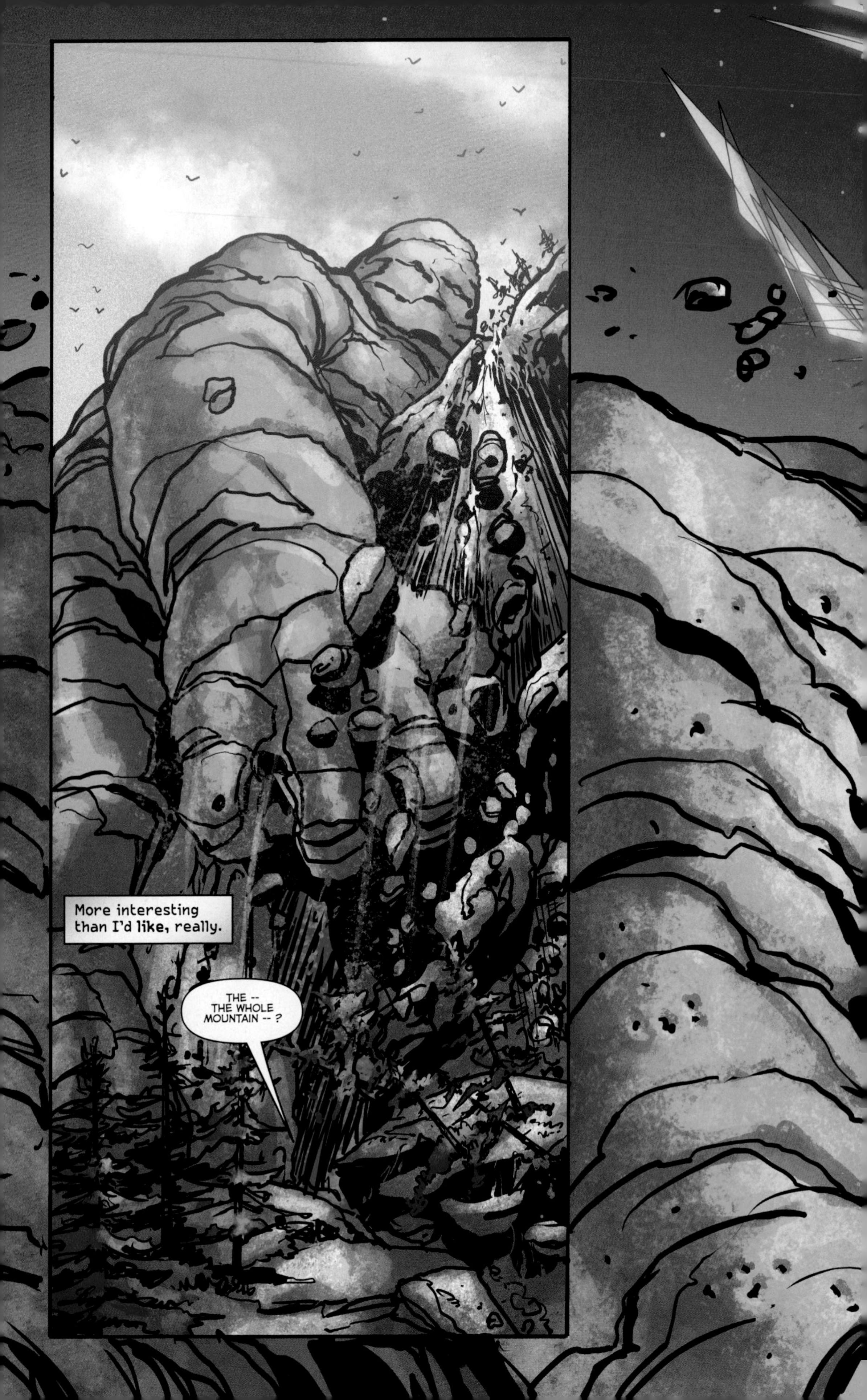
More interesting than I'd like, really.
THE -- THE WHOLE MOUNTAIN -- ?

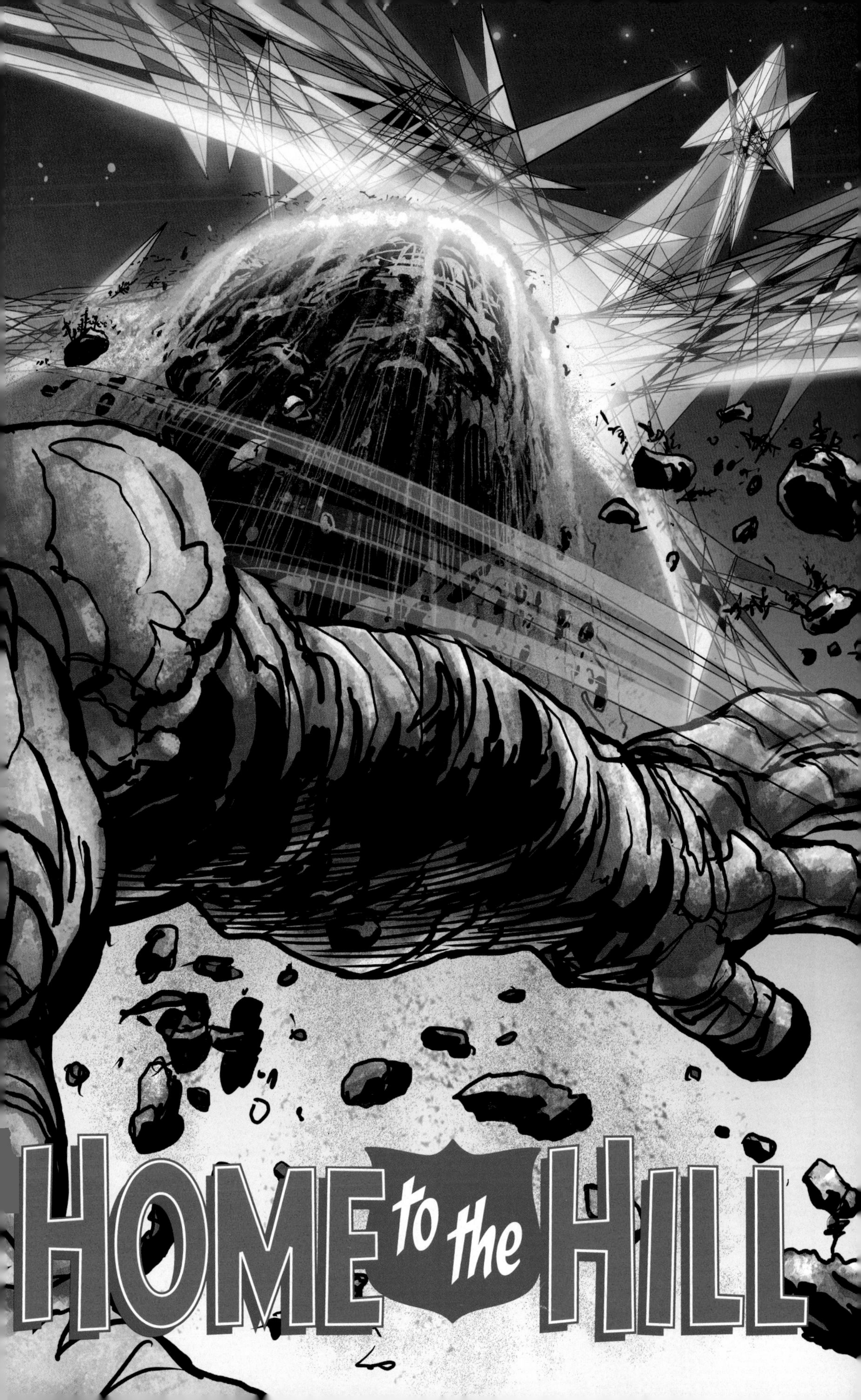
HOME to the HILL

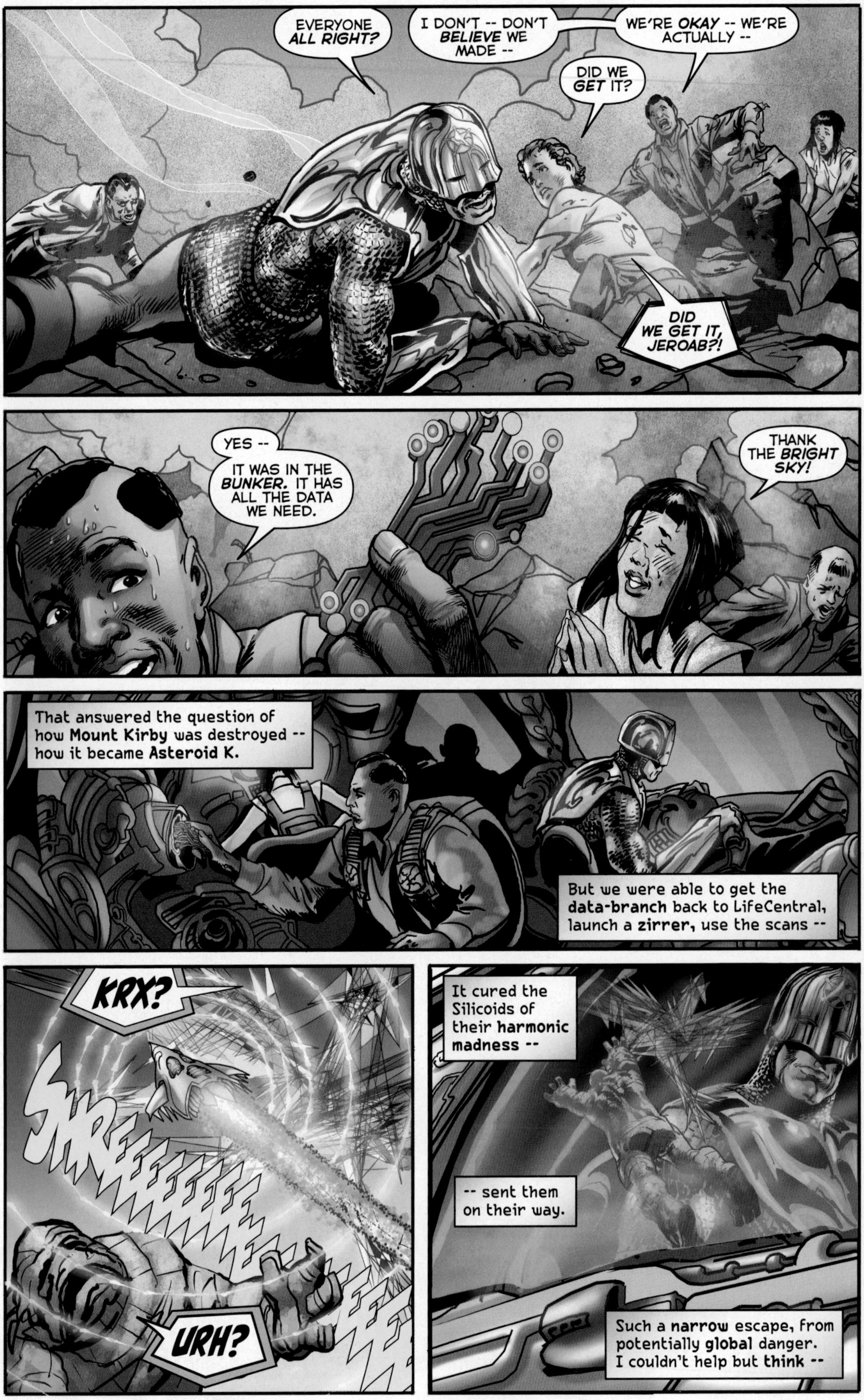
EVERYONE ALL RIGHT?
I DON'T -- DON'T BELIEVE WE MADE --
WE'RE OKAY -- WE'RE ACTUALLY --
DID WE GET IT?
DID WE GET IT, JEROAB?!
YES --
IT WAS IN THE BUNKER. IT HAS ALL THE DATA WE NEED.
THANK THE BRIGHT SKY!
That answered the question of how Mount Kirby was destroyed -- how it became Asteroid K.
But we were able to get the data-branch back to LifeCentral, launch a zirrer, use the scans --
KRX?
SHREEEEEEEEEEEEEE
URH?
It cured the Silicoids of their harmonic madness --
-- sent them on their way.
Such a narrow escape, from potentially global danger. I couldn't help but think --

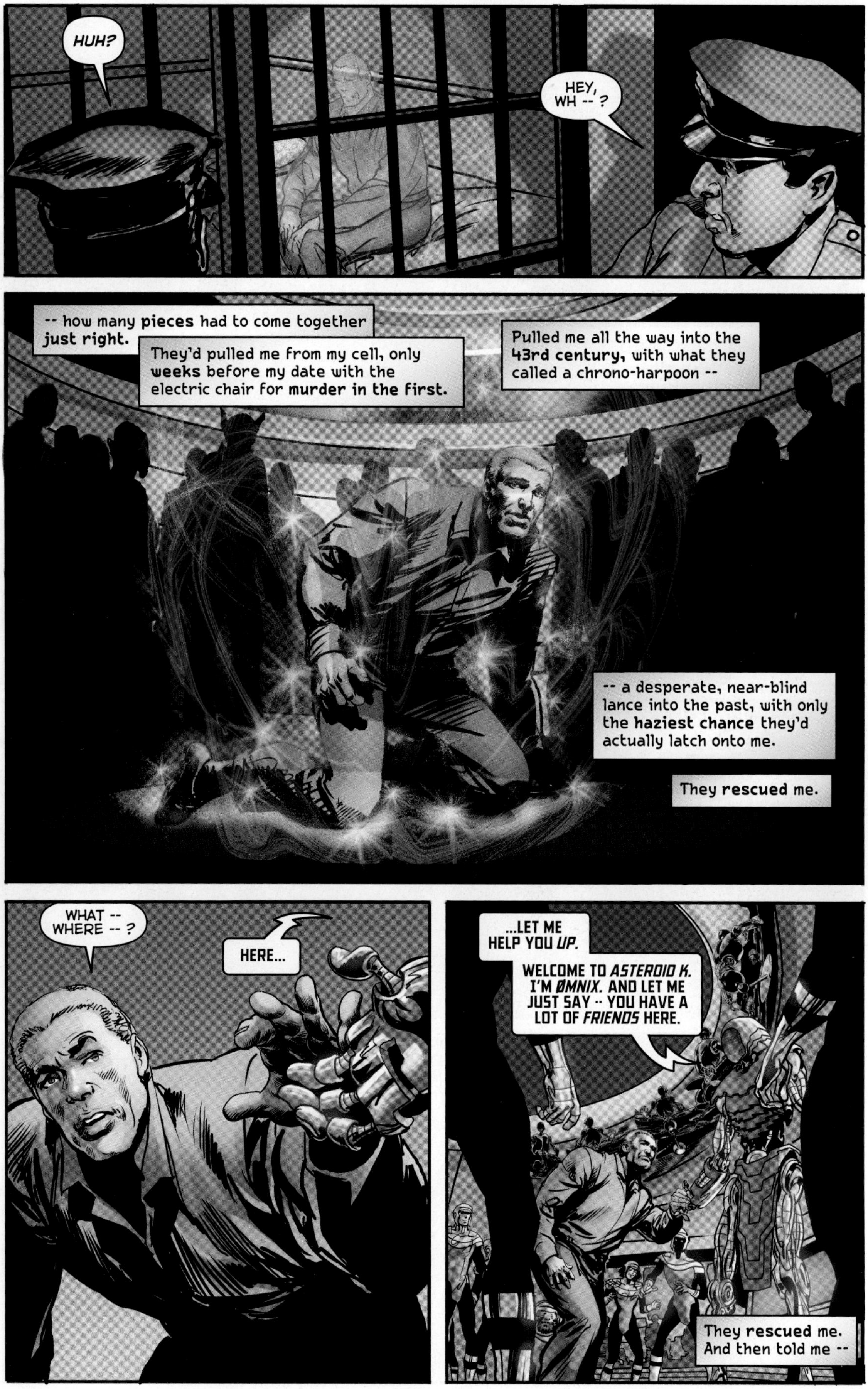
HUH?
HEY, WH -- ?
-- how many pieces had to come together just right.
They'd pulled me from my cell, only weeks before my date with the electric chair for murder in the first.
Pulled me all the way into the 43rd century, with what they called a chrono-harpoon --
-- a desperate, near-blind lance into the past, with only the haziest chance they'd actually latch onto me.
They rescued me.
WHAT -- WHERE -- ?
HERE...
...LET ME HELP YOU UP.
WELCOME TO ASTEROID K. I'M ØMNIX. AND LET ME JUST SAY -- YOU HAVE A LOT OF FRIENDS HERE.
They rescued me. And then told me --

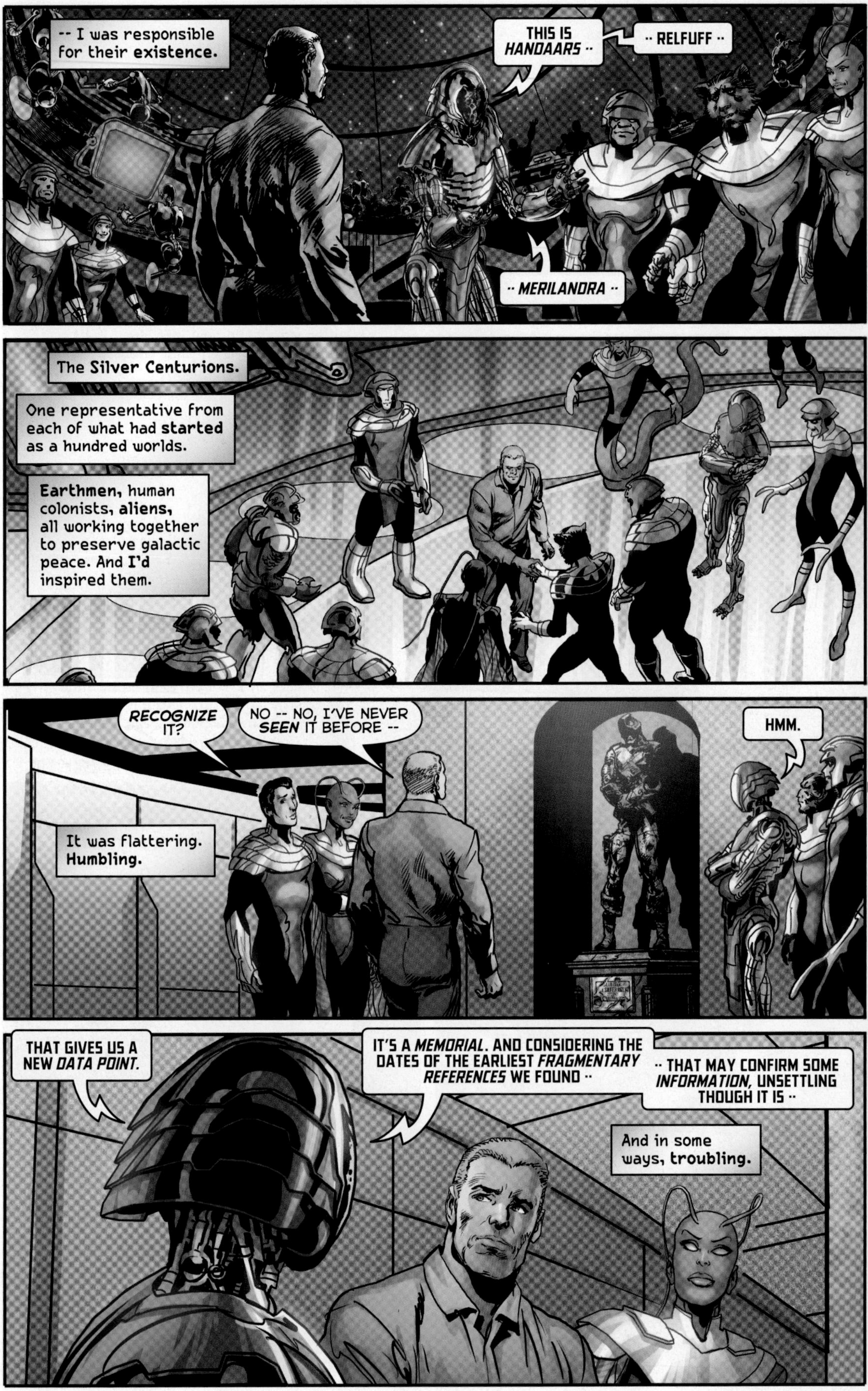

-- I was responsible for their existence.
THIS IS HANDAARS --
-- RELFUFF --
-- MERILANDRA --
The Silver Centurions.
One representative from each of what had started as a hundred worlds.
Earthmen, human colonists, aliens, all working together to preserve galactic peace. And I'd inspired them.
RECOGNIZE IT?
NO -- NO, I'VE NEVER SEEN IT BEFORE --
HMM.
It was flattering. Humbling.
THAT GIVES US A NEW DATA POINT.
IT'S A MEMORIAL. AND CONSIDERING THE DATES OF THE EARLIEST FRAGMENTARY REFERENCES WE FOUND --
-- THAT MAY CONFIRM SOME INFORMATION, UNSETTLING THOUGH IT IS --
And in some ways, troubling.

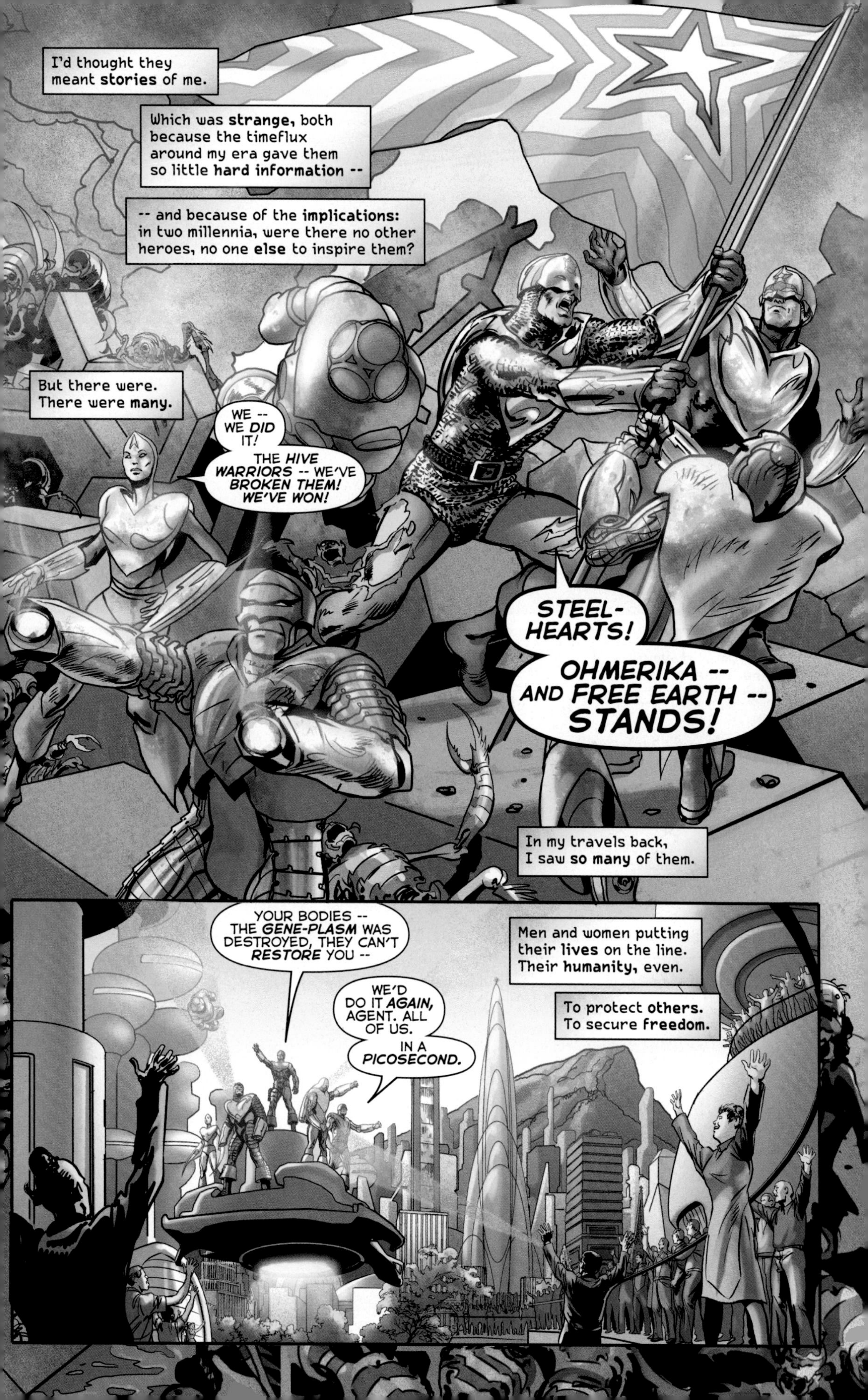
I'd thought they meant **stories** of me.
Which was **strange,** both because the timeflux around my era gave them so little **hard information** --
-- and because of the **implications:** in two millennia, were there no other heroes, no one **else** to inspire them?
But there were. There were **many.**
WE -- WE *DID* IT!
THE *HIVE WARRIORS* -- WE'VE *BROKEN THEM! WE'VE WON!*
STEEL-HEARTS!
OHMERIKA -- AND FREE EARTH -- STANDS!
In my travels back, I saw **so many** of them.
YOUR BODIES -- THE *GENE-PLASM* WAS DESTROYED, THEY CAN'T *RESTORE* YOU --
WE'D DO IT *AGAIN,* AGENT. ALL OF US.
IN A *PICOSECOND.*
Men and women putting their **lives** on the line. Their **humanity,** even.
To protect **others.** To secure **freedom.**

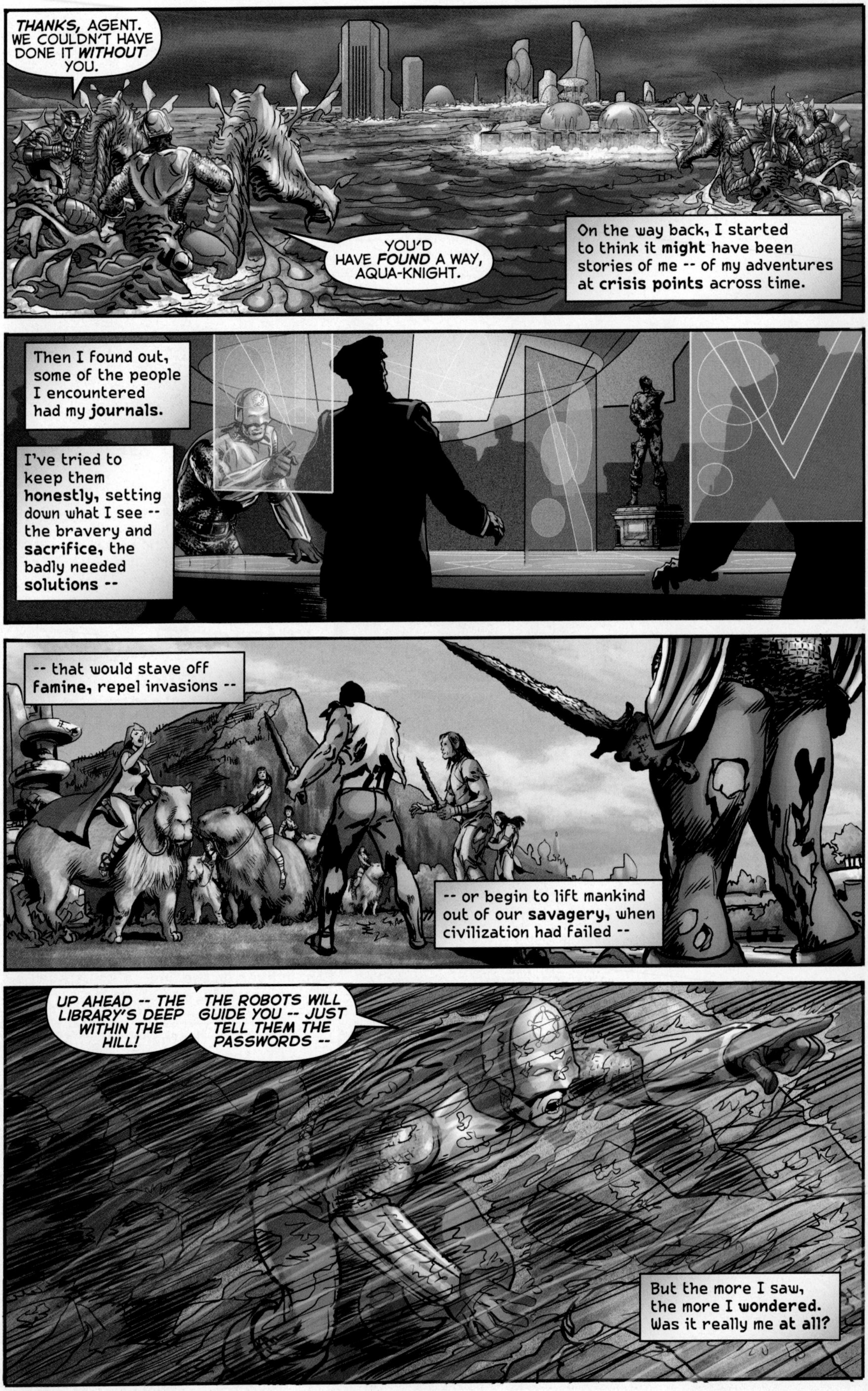
THANKS, AGENT. WE COULDN'T HAVE DONE IT WITHOUT YOU.
YOU'D HAVE FOUND A WAY, AQUA-KNIGHT.
On the way back, I started to think it might have been stories of me -- of my adventures at crisis points across time.
Then I found out, some of the people I encountered had my journals.
I've tried to keep them honestly, setting down what I see -- the bravery and sacrifice, the badly needed solutions --
-- that would stave off famine, repel invasions --
-- or begin to lift mankind out of our savagery, when civilization had failed --
UP AHEAD -- THE LIBRARY'S DEEP WITHIN THE HILL!
THE ROBOTS WILL GUIDE YOU -- JUST TELL THEM THE PASSWORDS --
But the more I saw, the more I wondered. Was it really me at all?

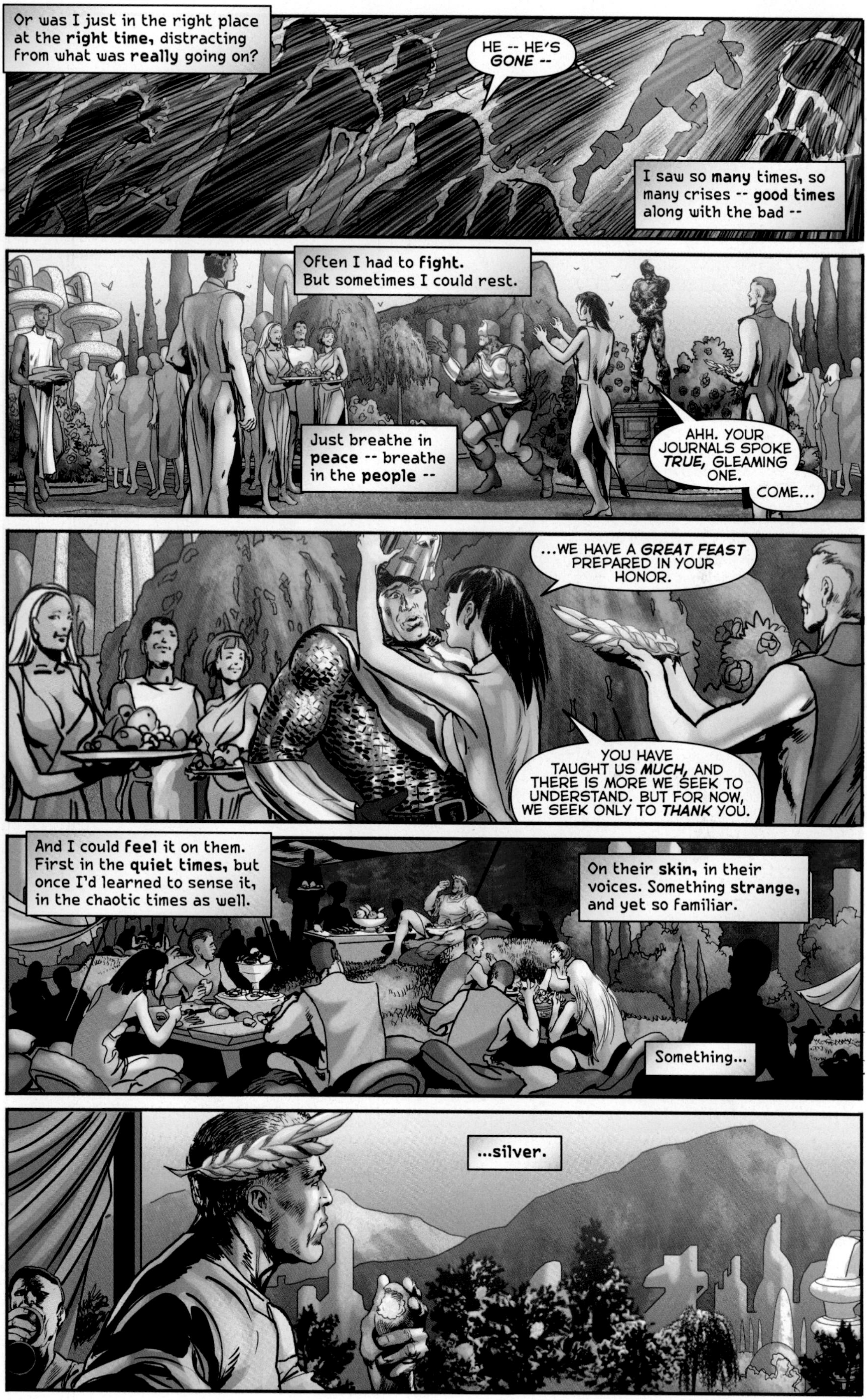
Or was I just in the right place at the right time, distracting from what was really going on?
HE -- HE'S GONE --
I saw so many times, so many crises -- good times along with the bad --
Often I had to fight. But sometimes I could rest.
Just breathe in peace -- breathe in the people --
AHH. YOUR JOURNALS SPOKE TRUE, GLEAMING ONE.
COME...
...WE HAVE A GREAT FEAST PREPARED IN YOUR HONOR.
YOU HAVE TAUGHT US MUCH, AND THERE IS MORE WE SEEK TO UNDERSTAND. BUT FOR NOW, WE SEEK ONLY TO THANK YOU.
And I could feel it on them. First in the quiet times, but once I'd learned to sense it, in the chaotic times as well.
On their skin, in their voices. Something strange, and yet so familiar.
Something...
...silver.

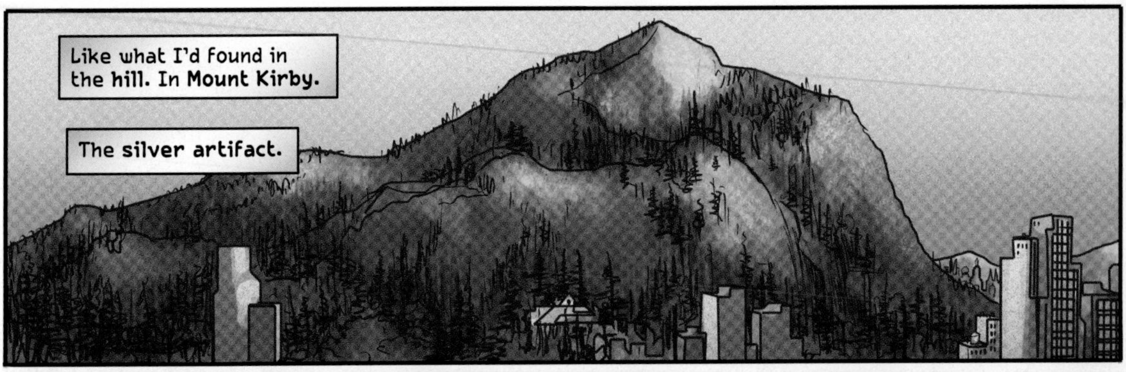
Like what I'd found in the hill. In Mount Kirby.
The silver artifact.

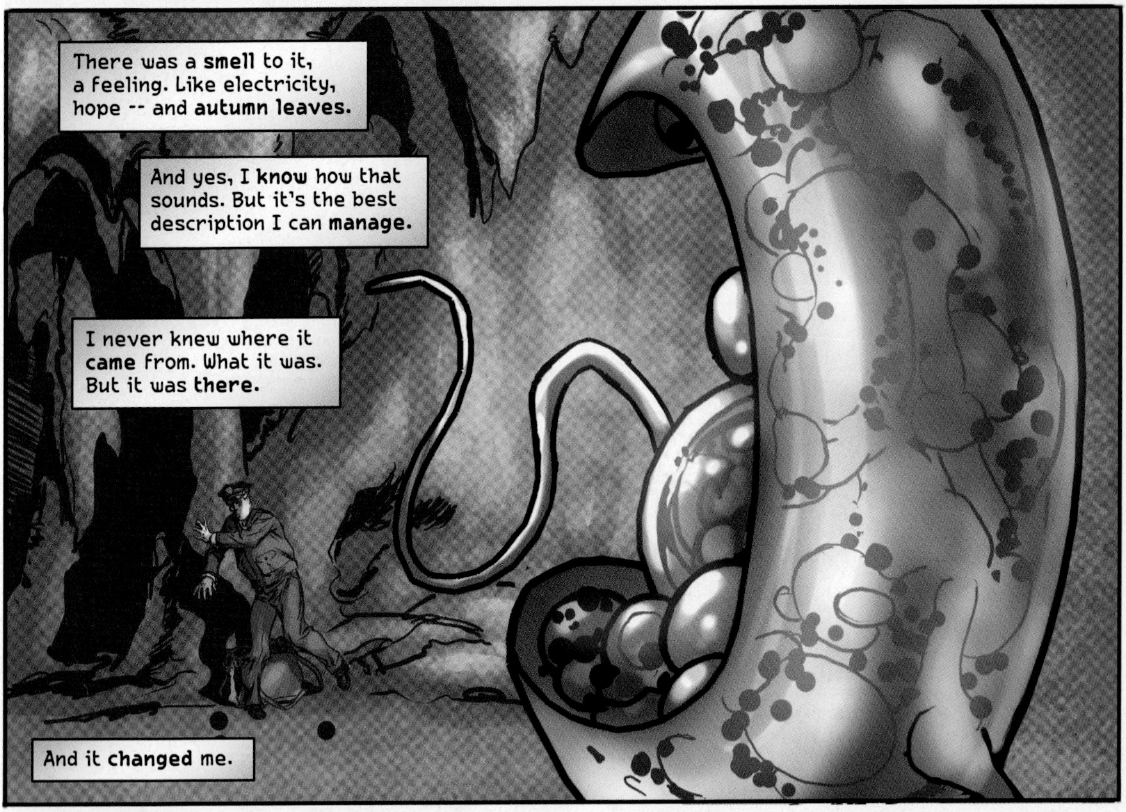
There was a smell to it, a feeling. Like electricity, hope -- and autumn leaves.
And yes, I know how that sounds. But it's the best description I can manage.
I never knew where it came from. What it was. But it was there.
And it changed me.

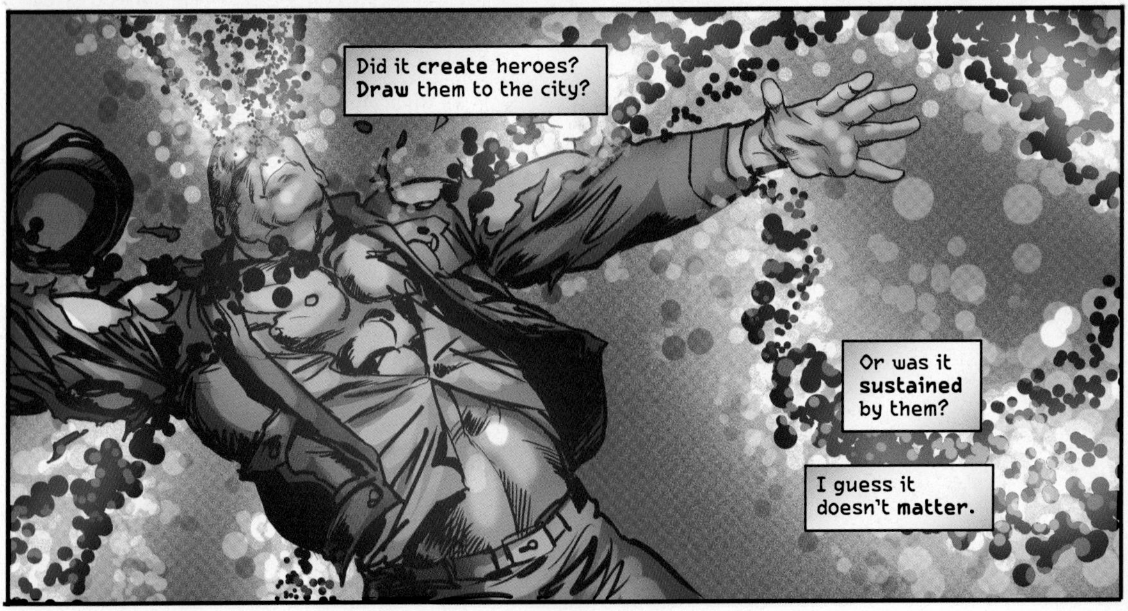
Did it create heroes? Draw them to the city?
Or was it sustained by them?
I guess it doesn't matter.

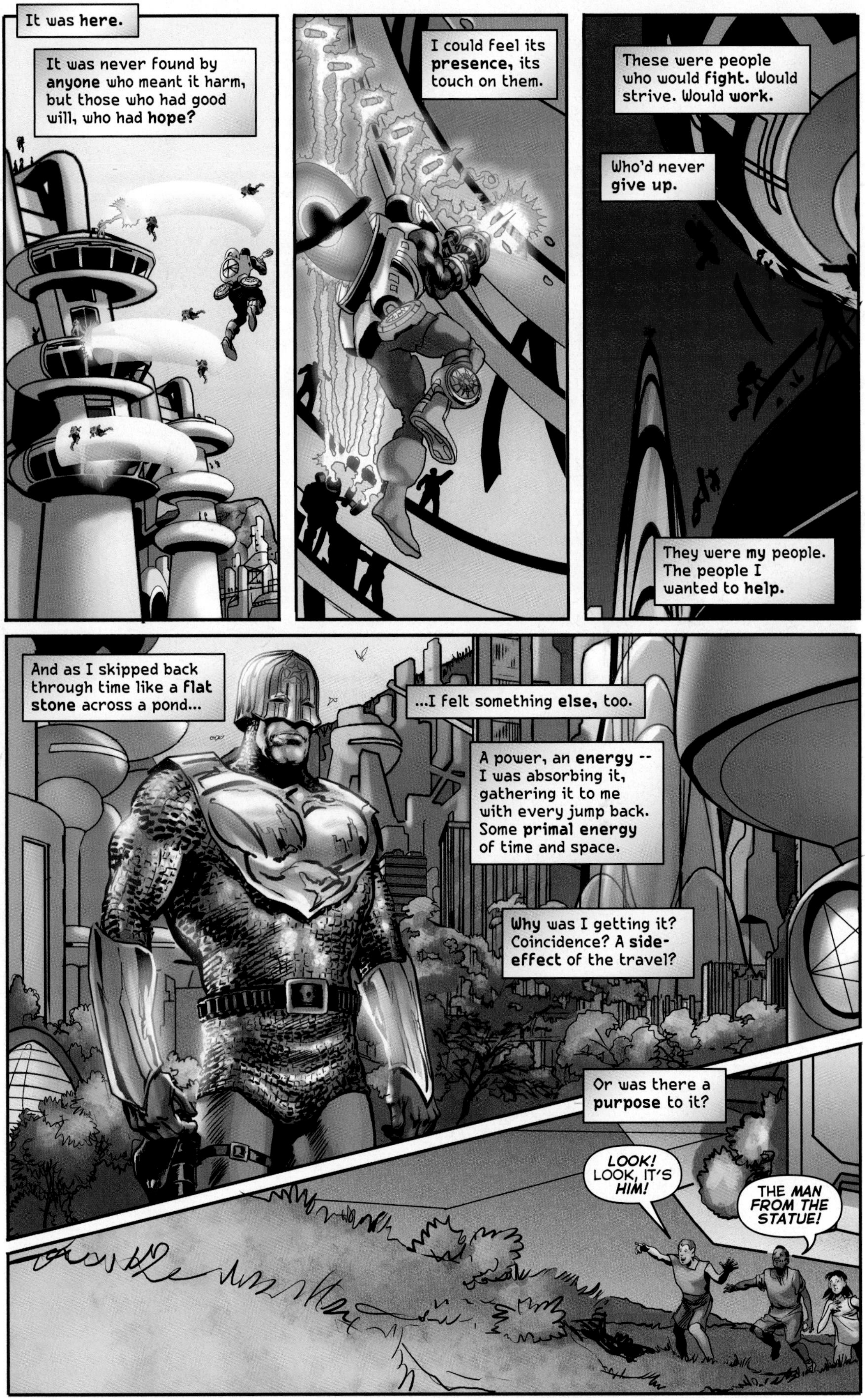
It was here.
It was never found by anyone who meant it harm, but those who had good will, who had hope?
I could feel its presence, its touch on them.
These were people who would fight. Would strive. Would work.
Who'd never give up.
They were my people. The people I wanted to help.
And as I skipped back through time like a flat stone across a pond...
...I felt something else, too.
A power, an energy -- I was absorbing it, gathering it to me with every jump back. Some primal energy of time and space.
Why was I getting it? Coincidence? A side-effect of the travel?
Or was there a purpose to it?
LOOK! LOOK, IT'S HIM!
THE MAN FROM THE STATUE!

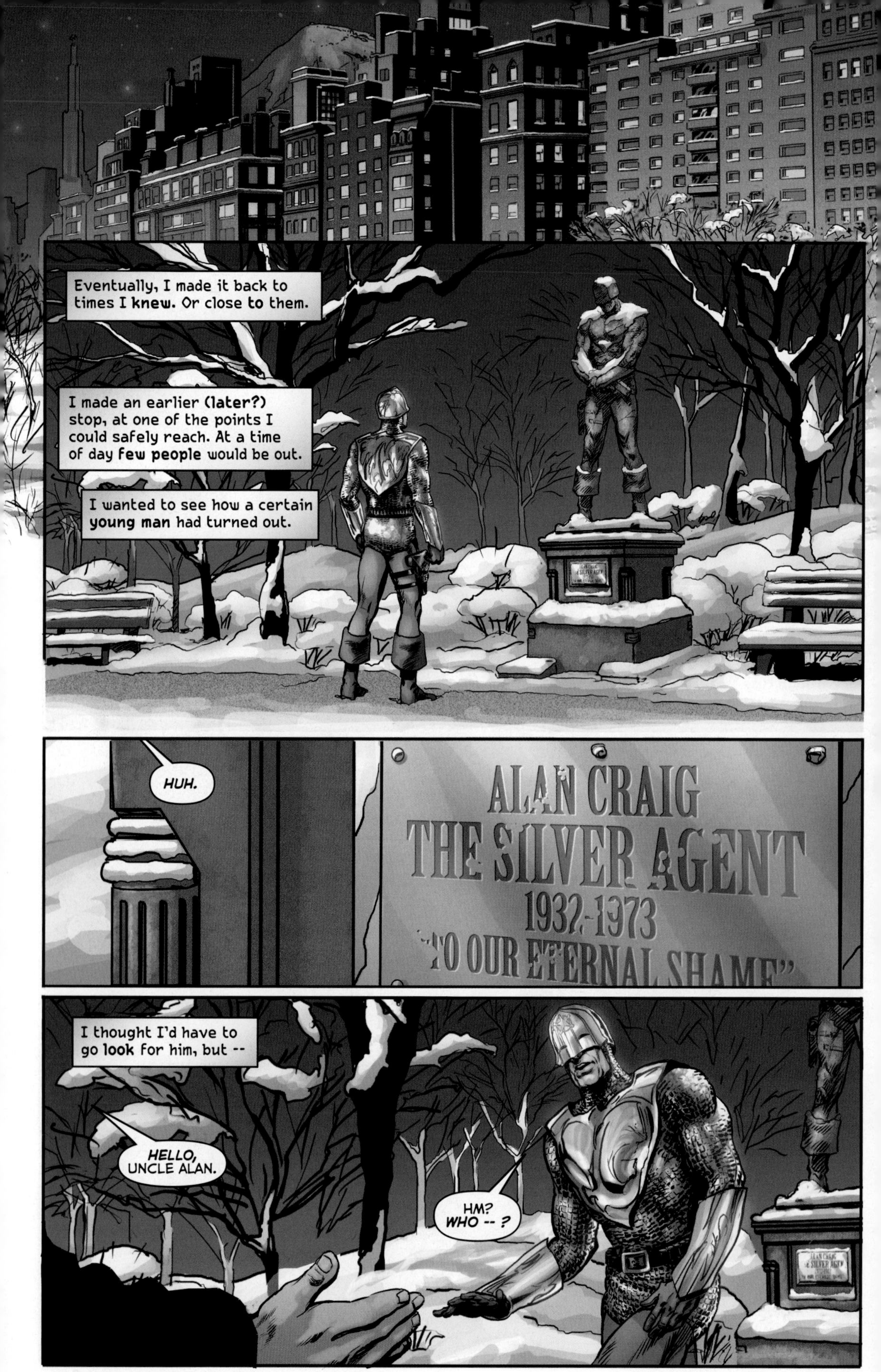

Eventually, I made it back to times I knew. Or close to them.
I made an earlier (later?) stop, at one of the points I could safely reach. At a time of day few people would be out.
I wanted to see how a certain young man had turned out.
HUH.
ALAN CRAIG
THE SILVER AGENT
1932-1973
"TO OUR ETERNAL SHAME"
I thought I'd have to go look for him, but --
HELLO, UNCLE ALAN.
HM? WHO -- ?

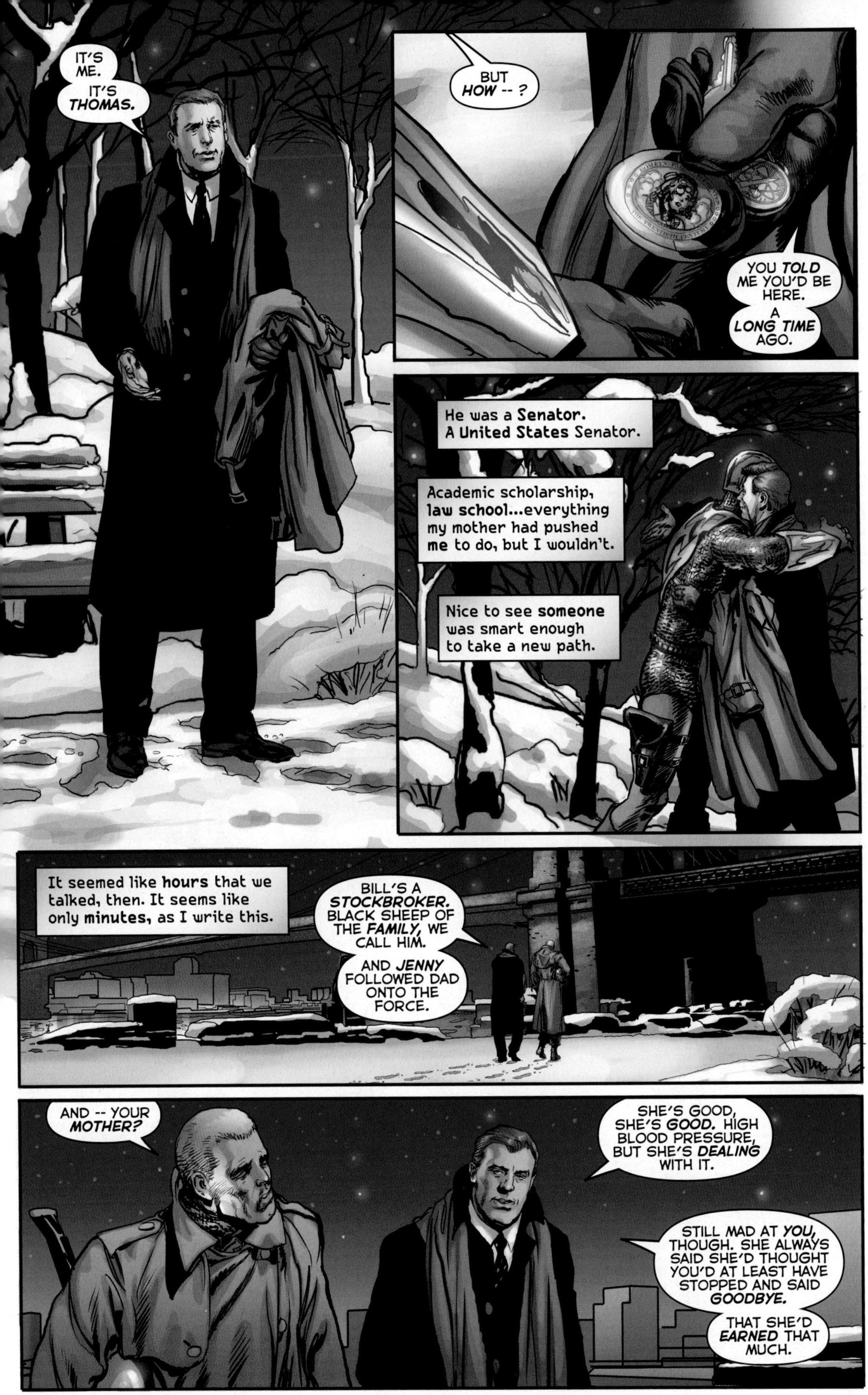
IT'S ME. IT'S THOMAS.
BUT HOW -- ?
YOU TOLD ME YOU'D BE HERE. A LONG TIME AGO.
He was a Senator. A United States Senator.
Academic scholarship, law school...everything my mother had pushed me to do, but I wouldn't.
Nice to see someone was smart enough to take a new path.
It seemed like hours that we talked, then. It seems like only minutes, as I write this.
BILL'S A STOCKBROKER. BLACK SHEEP OF THE FAMILY, WE CALL HIM.
AND JENNY FOLLOWED DAD ONTO THE FORCE.
AND -- YOUR MOTHER?
SHE'S GOOD, SHE'S GOOD. HIGH BLOOD PRESSURE, BUT SHE'S DEALING WITH IT.
STILL MAD AT YOU, THOUGH. SHE ALWAYS SAID SHE'D THOUGHT YOU'D AT LEAST HAVE STOPPED AND SAID GOODBYE.
THAT SHE'D EARNED THAT MUCH.

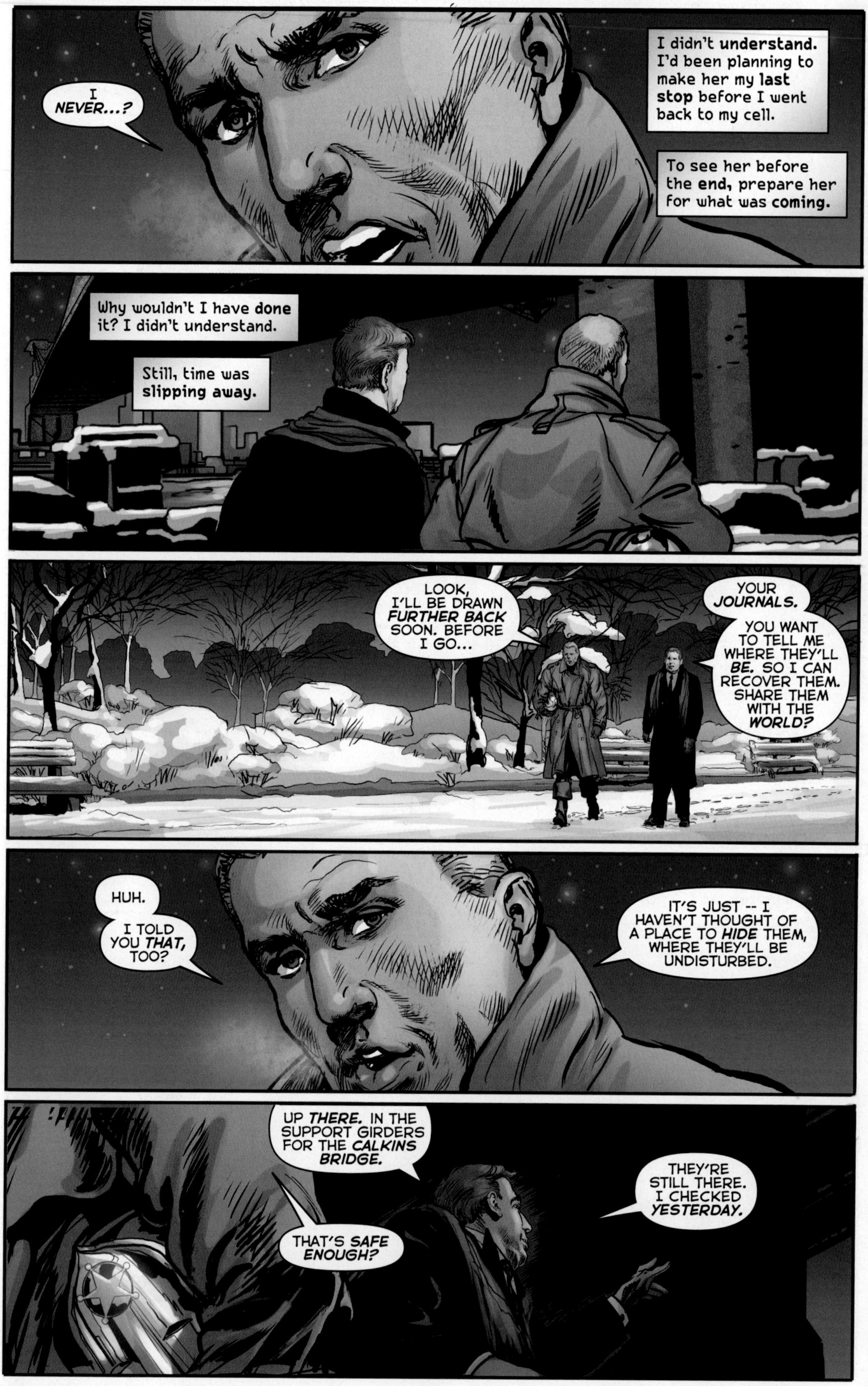
I NEVER...?
I didn't understand. I'd been planning to make her my last stop before I went back to my cell.
To see her before the end, prepare her for what was coming.
Why wouldn't I have done it? I didn't understand.
Still, time was slipping away.
LOOK, I'LL BE DRAWN FURTHER BACK SOON. BEFORE I GO...
YOUR JOURNALS.
YOU WANT TO TELL ME WHERE THEY'LL BE. SO I CAN RECOVER THEM. SHARE THEM WITH THE WORLD?
HUH.
I TOLD YOU THAT, TOO?
IT'S JUST -- I HAVEN'T THOUGHT OF A PLACE TO HIDE THEM, WHERE THEY'LL BE UNDISTURBED.
UP THERE. IN THE SUPPORT GIRDERS FOR THE CALKINS BRIDGE.
THAT'S SAFE ENOUGH?
THEY'RE STILL THERE. I CHECKED YESTERDAY.

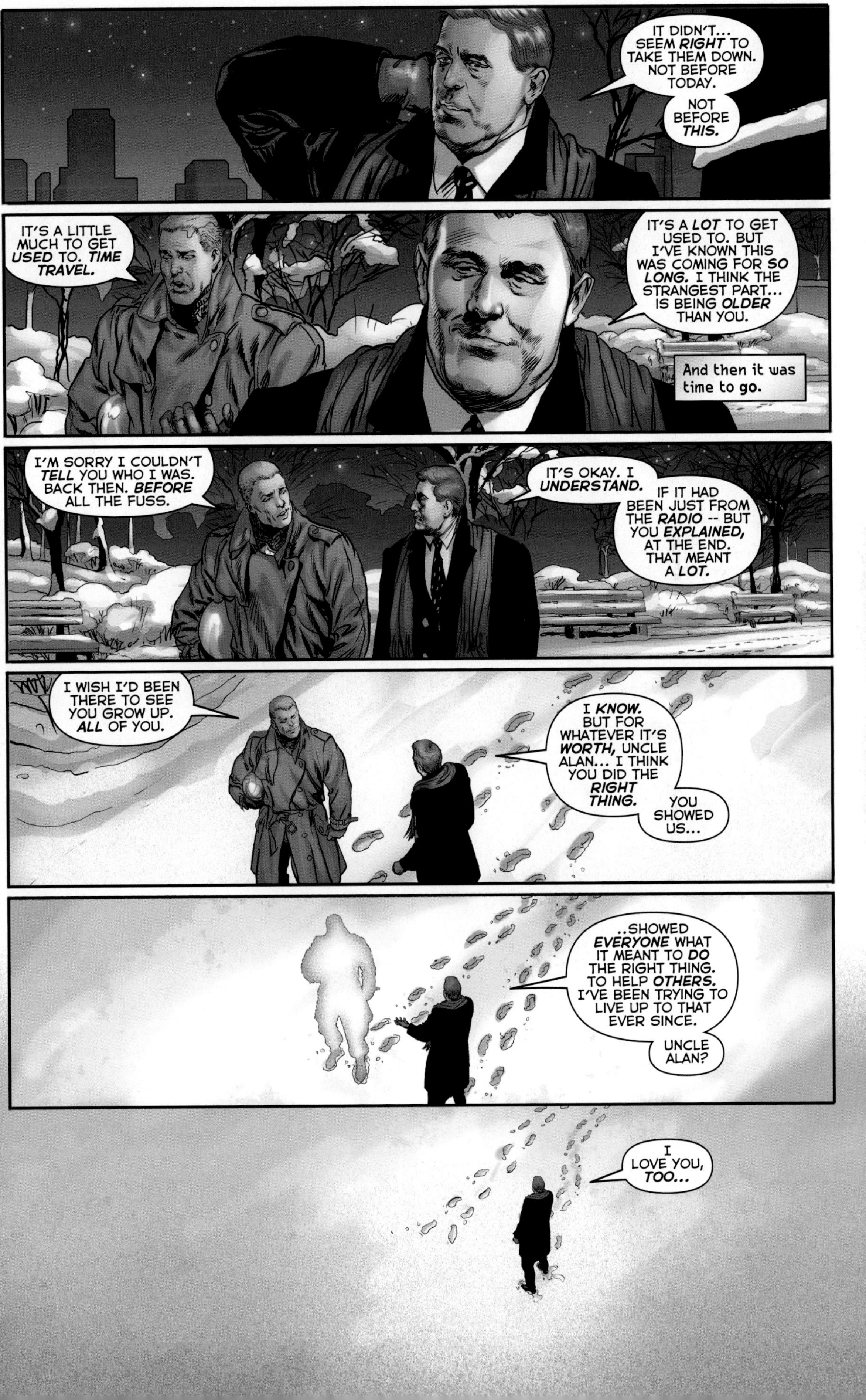

IT DIDN'T... SEEM RIGHT TO TAKE THEM DOWN. NOT BEFORE TODAY.
NOT BEFORE THIS.
IT'S A LITTLE MUCH TO GET USED TO. TIME TRAVEL.
IT'S A LOT TO GET USED TO. BUT I'VE KNOWN THIS WAS COMING FOR SO LONG. I THINK THE STRANGEST PART... IS BEING OLDER THAN YOU.
And then it was time to go.
I'M SORRY I COULDN'T TELL YOU WHO I WAS. BACK THEN. BEFORE ALL THE FUSS.
IT'S OKAY. I UNDERSTAND.
IF IT HAD BEEN JUST FROM THE RADIO -- BUT YOU EXPLAINED, AT THE END. THAT MEANT A LOT.
I WISH I'D BEEN THERE TO SEE YOU GROW UP. ALL OF YOU.
I KNOW. BUT FOR WHATEVER IT'S WORTH, UNCLE ALAN... I THINK YOU DID THE RIGHT THING.
YOU SHOWED US...
..SHOWED EVERYONE WHAT IT MEANT TO DO THE RIGHT THING. TO HELP OTHERS. I'VE BEEN TRYING TO LIVE UP TO THAT EVER SINCE.
UNCLE ALAN?
I LOVE YOU, TOO...

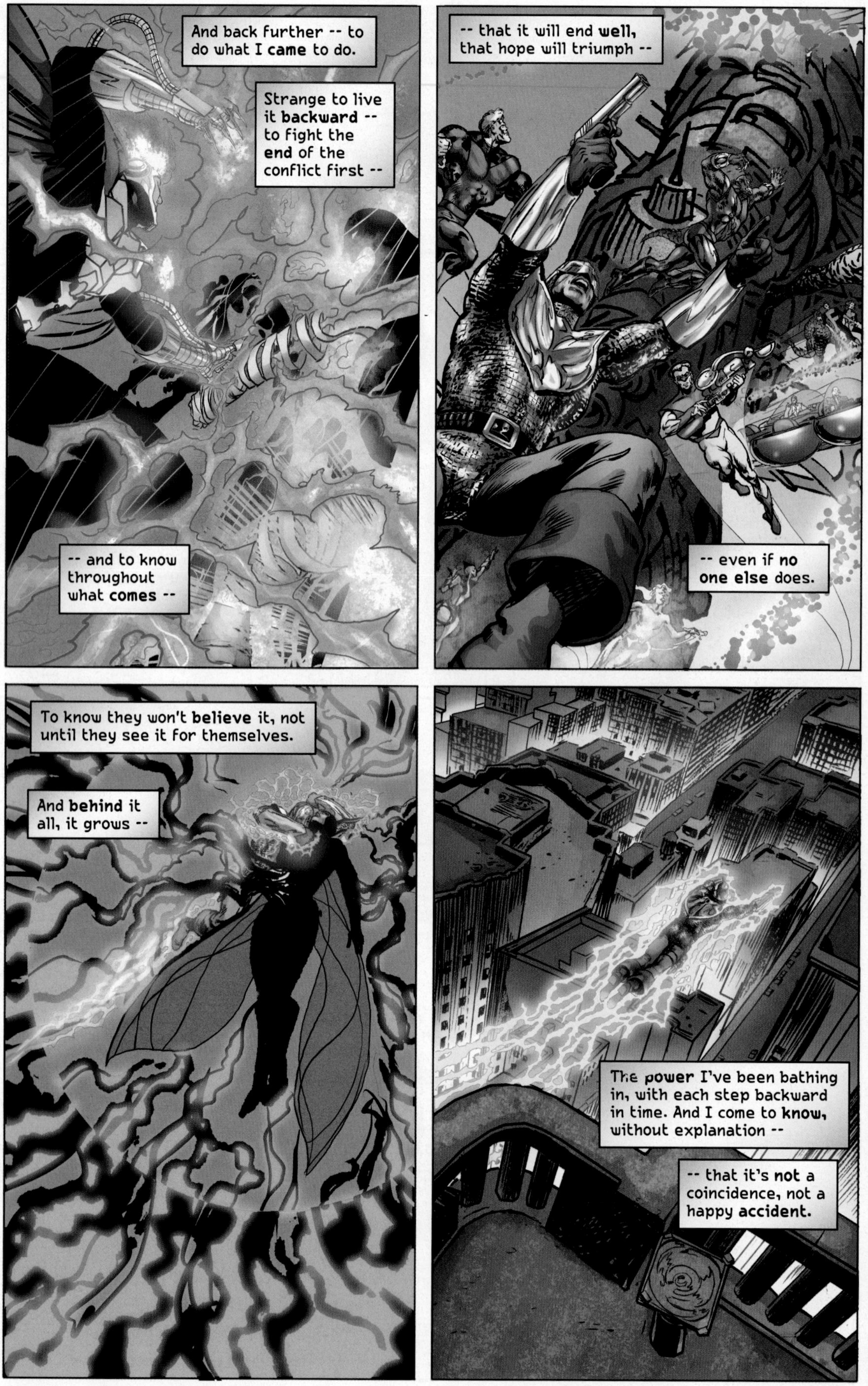
And back further -- to do what I came to do.
Strange to live it backward -- to fight the end of the conflict first --
-- and to know throughout what comes --
-- that it will end well, that hope will triumph --
-- even if no one else does.
To know they won't believe it, not until they see it for themselves.
And behind it all, it grows --
The power I've been bathing in, with each step backward in time. And I come to know, without explanation --
-- that it's not a coincidence, not a happy accident.

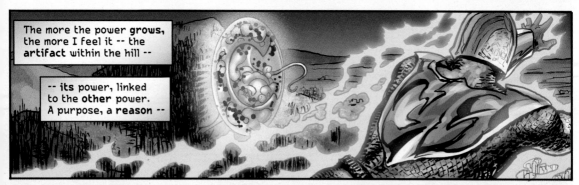

The more the power **grows**, the more I feel it -- the **artifact** within the hill --

-- its power, linked to the **other** power. A purpose, a reason --

And I may not know, not **yet**, what the purpose is.

But I know who it's meant to **serve**.

AS I NEAR THE END, I **EDIT** MY JOURNALS. MAKE SURE THE INFORMATION IN THEM IS **HELPFUL**, BUT NOT ENOUGH TO BREED OVERCONFIDENCE.

OR **TERROR** AT WHAT WILL COME.

I USE TECHNOLOGY ØMNIX GAVE ME, TO CONVERT THEM TO A FORMAT THAT'LL BE READABLE, WHEN THE WORLD **NEEDS** THEM --

AND BACK I **GO**, ALONE WITH MY THOUGHTS --

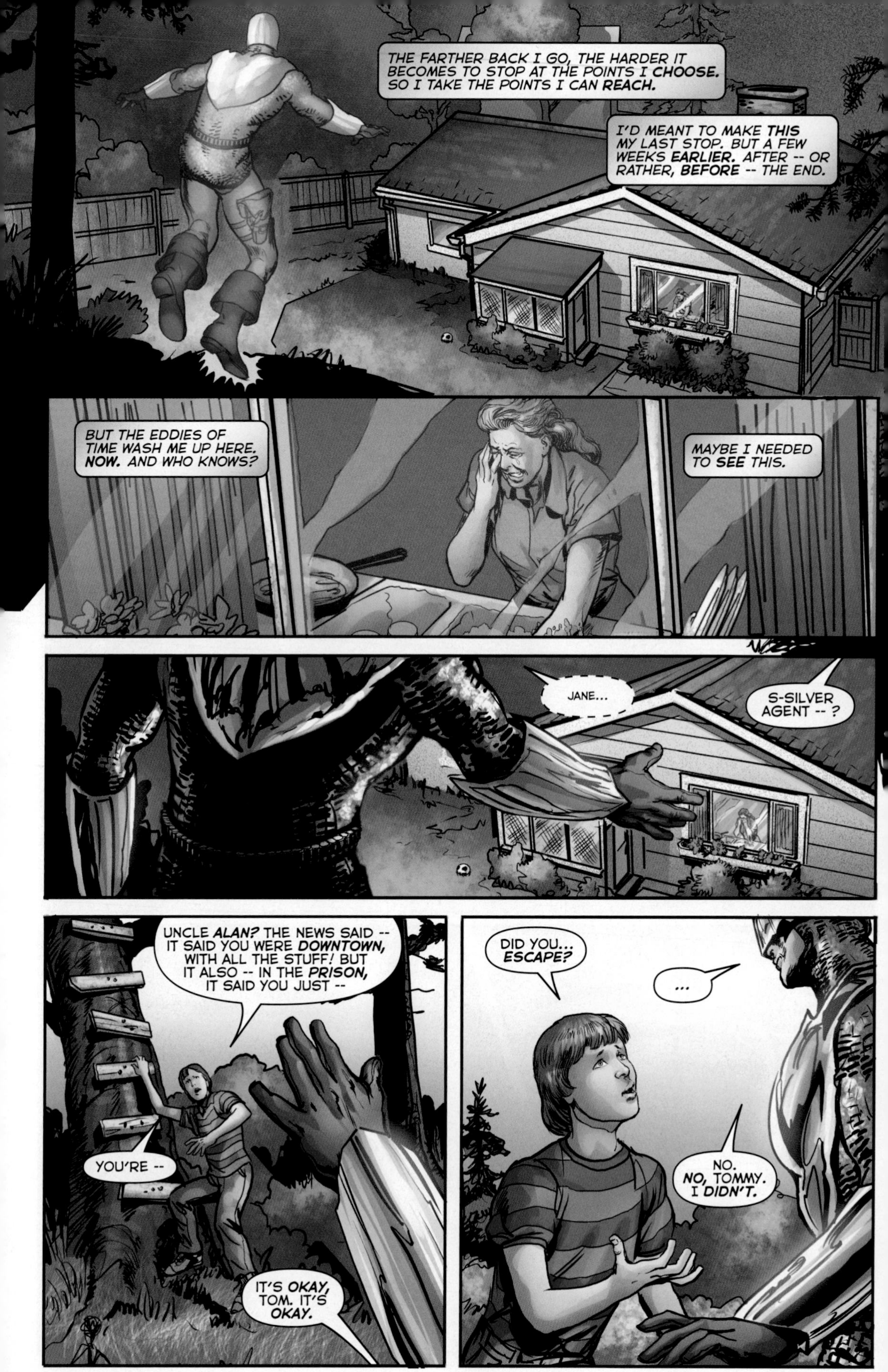
THE FARTHER BACK I GO, THE HARDER IT BECOMES TO STOP AT THE POINTS I CHOOSE. SO I TAKE THE POINTS I CAN REACH.
I'D MEANT TO MAKE THIS MY LAST STOP. BUT A FEW WEEKS EARLIER. AFTER -- OR RATHER, BEFORE -- THE END.
BUT THE EDDIES OF TIME WASH ME UP HERE. NOW. AND WHO KNOWS?
MAYBE I NEEDED TO SEE THIS.
JANE...
S-SILVER AGENT -- ?
UNCLE ALAN? THE NEWS SAID -- IT SAID YOU WERE DOWNTOWN, WITH ALL THE STUFF! BUT IT ALSO -- IN THE PRISON, IT SAID YOU JUST --
YOU'RE --
IT'S OKAY, TOM. IT'S OKAY.
DID YOU... ESCAPE?
...
NO. NO, TOMMY. I DIDN'T.

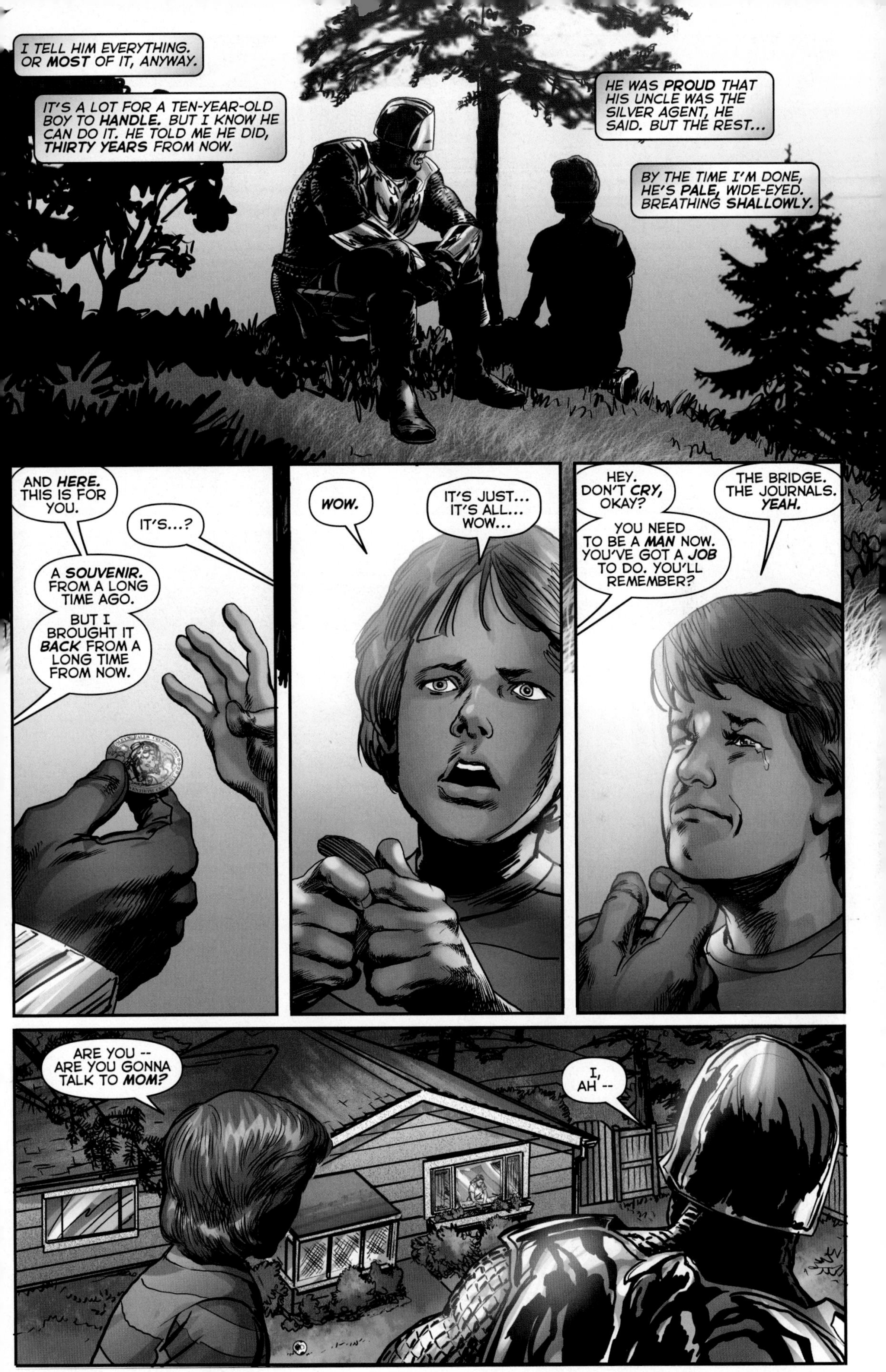
I TELL HIM EVERYTHING. OR MOST OF IT, ANYWAY.
IT'S A LOT FOR A TEN-YEAR-OLD BOY TO HANDLE. BUT I KNOW HE CAN DO IT. HE TOLD ME HE DID, THIRTY YEARS FROM NOW.
HE WAS PROUD THAT HIS UNCLE WAS THE SILVER AGENT, HE SAID. BUT THE REST...
BY THE TIME I'M DONE, HE'S PALE, WIDE-EYED. BREATHING SHALLOWLY.
AND HERE. THIS IS FOR YOU.
IT'S...?
A SOUVENIR. FROM A LONG TIME AGO.
BUT I BROUGHT IT BACK FROM A LONG TIME FROM NOW.
WOW.
IT'S JUST... IT'S ALL... WOW...
HEY. DON'T CRY, OKAY?
YOU NEED TO BE A MAN NOW. YOU'VE GOT A JOB TO DO. YOU'LL REMEMBER?
THE BRIDGE. THE JOURNALS. YEAH.
ARE YOU -- ARE YOU GONNA TALK TO MOM?
I, AH --

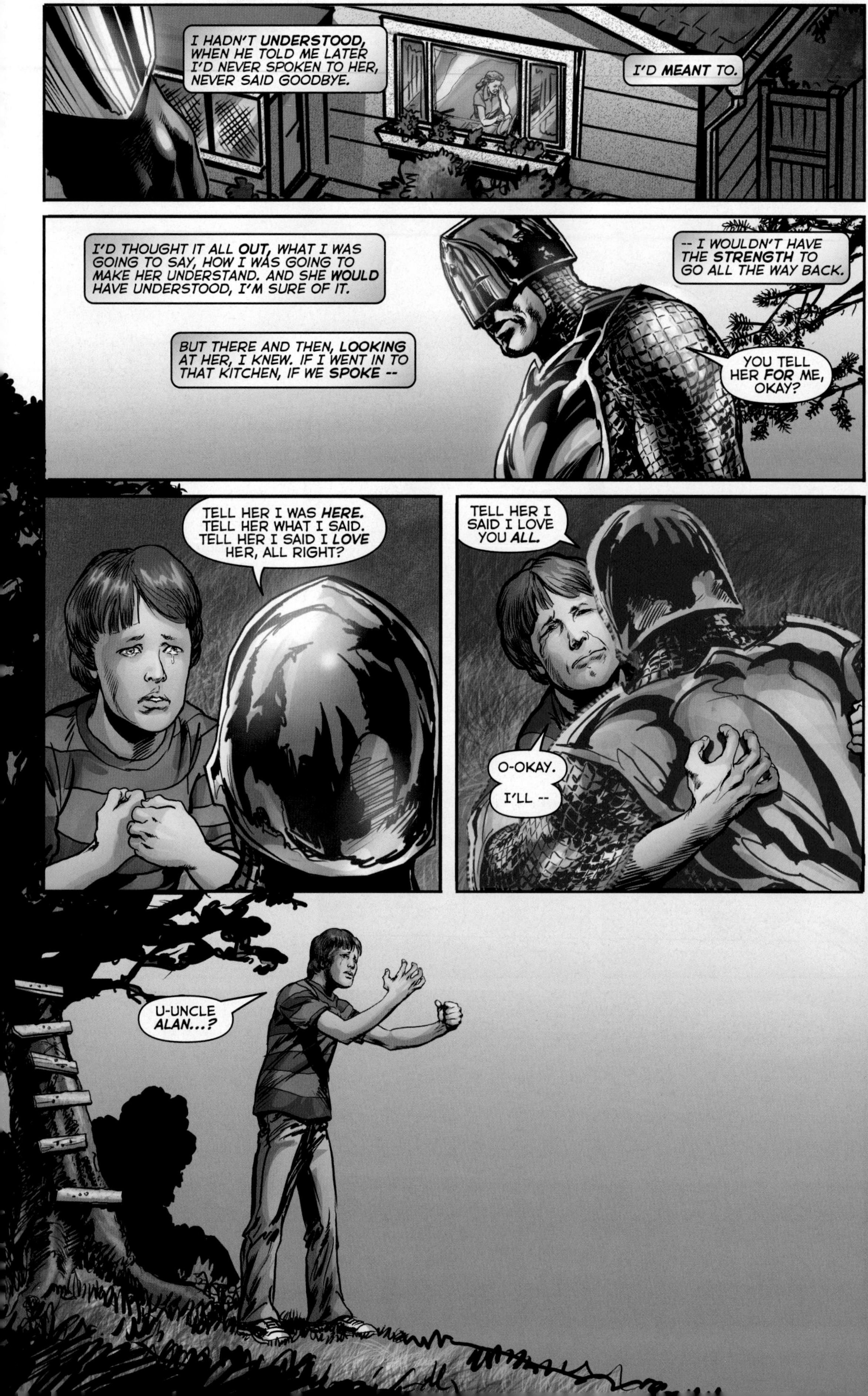
I HADN'T UNDERSTOOD, WHEN HE TOLD ME LATER I'D NEVER SPOKEN TO HER, NEVER SAID GOODBYE.
I'D MEANT TO.
I'D THOUGHT IT ALL OUT, WHAT I WAS GOING TO SAY, HOW I WAS GOING TO MAKE HER UNDERSTAND. AND SHE WOULD HAVE UNDERSTOOD, I'M SURE OF IT.
BUT THERE AND THEN, LOOKING AT HER, I KNEW. IF I WENT IN TO THAT KITCHEN, IF WE SPOKE --
-- I WOULDN'T HAVE THE STRENGTH TO GO ALL THE WAY BACK.
YOU TELL HER FOR ME, OKAY?
TELL HER I WAS HERE. TELL HER WHAT I SAID. TELL HER I SAID I LOVE HER, ALL RIGHT?
TELL HER I SAID I LOVE YOU ALL.
O-OKAY.
I'LL --
U-UNCLE ALAN...?

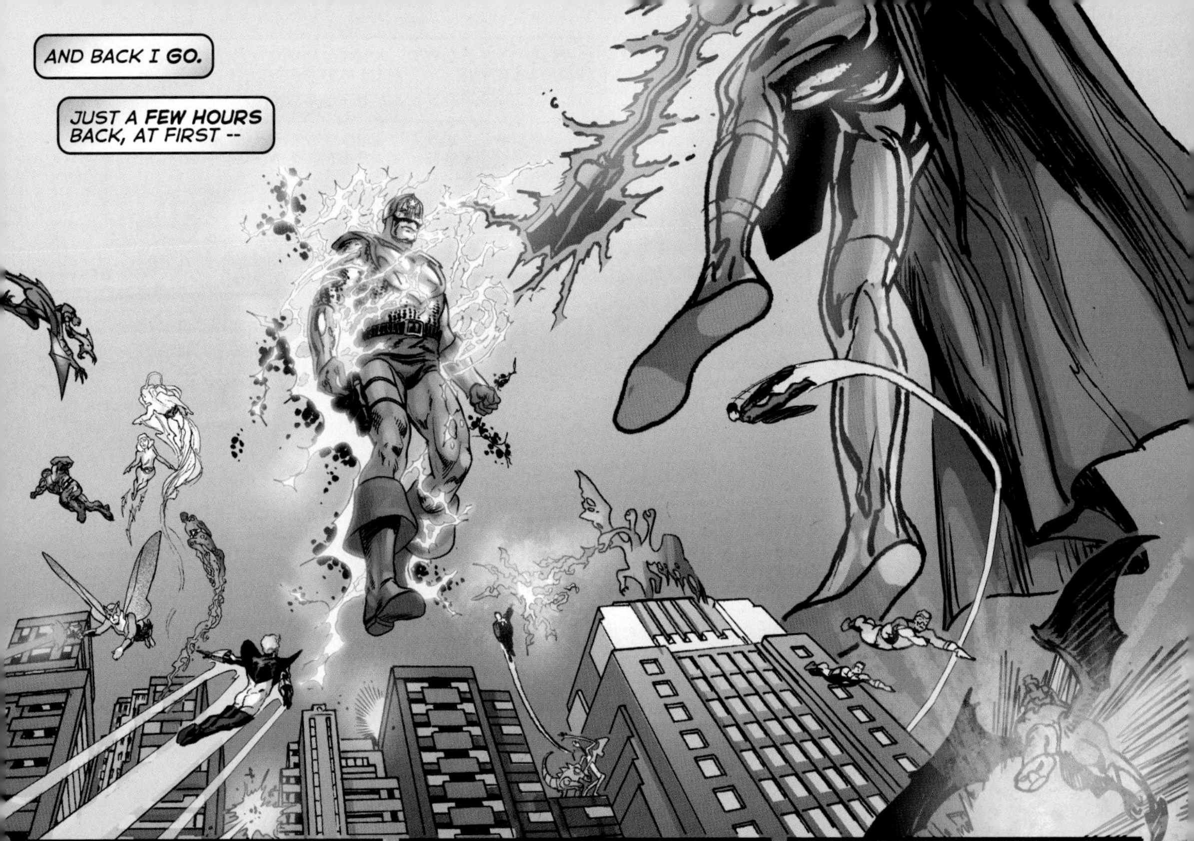
AND BACK I GO.
JUST A FEW HOURS BACK, AT FIRST --

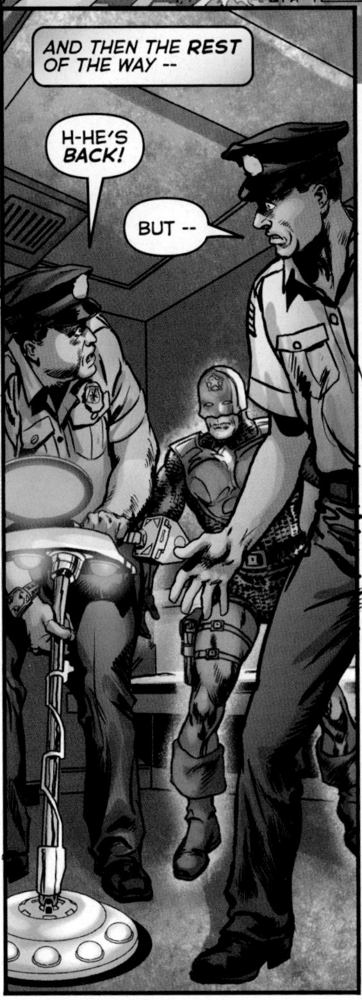
AND THEN THE REST OF THE WAY --
H-HE'S BACK!
BUT --

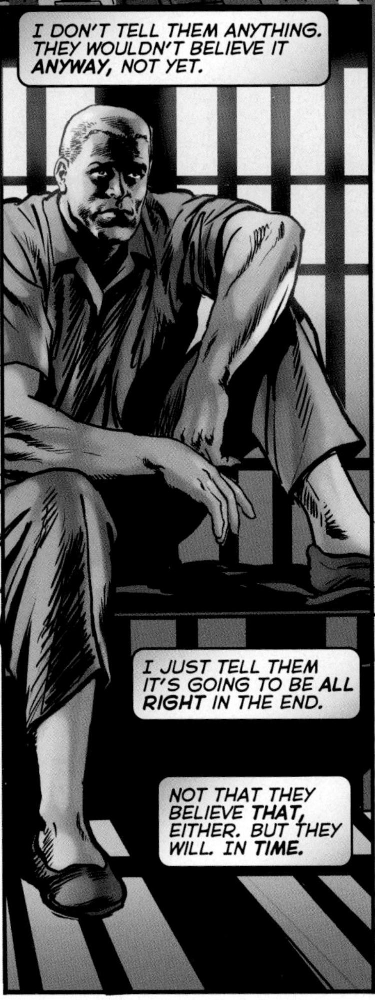
I DON'T TELL THEM ANYTHING. THEY WOULDN'T BELIEVE IT ANYWAY, NOT YET.
I JUST TELL THEM IT'S GOING TO BE ALL RIGHT IN THE END.
NOT THAT THEY BELIEVE THAT, EITHER. BUT THEY WILL. IN TIME.

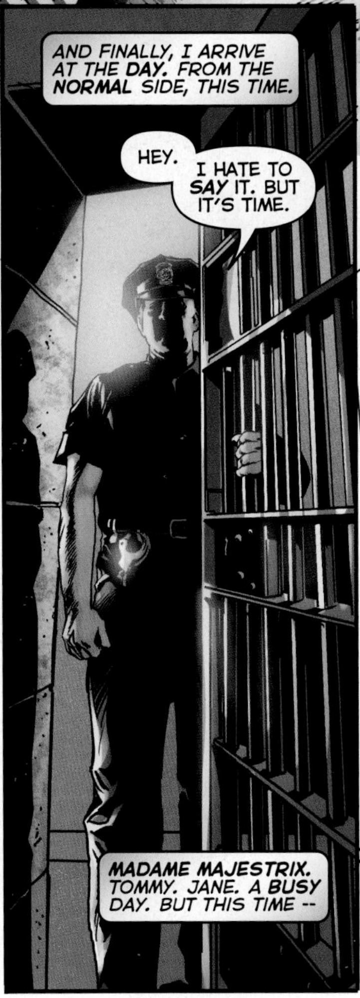
AND FINALLY, I ARRIVE AT THE DAY. FROM THE NORMAL SIDE, THIS TIME.
HEY.
I HATE TO SAY IT. BUT IT'S TIME.
MADAME MAJESTRIX. TOMMY. JANE. A BUSY DAY. BUT THIS TIME --

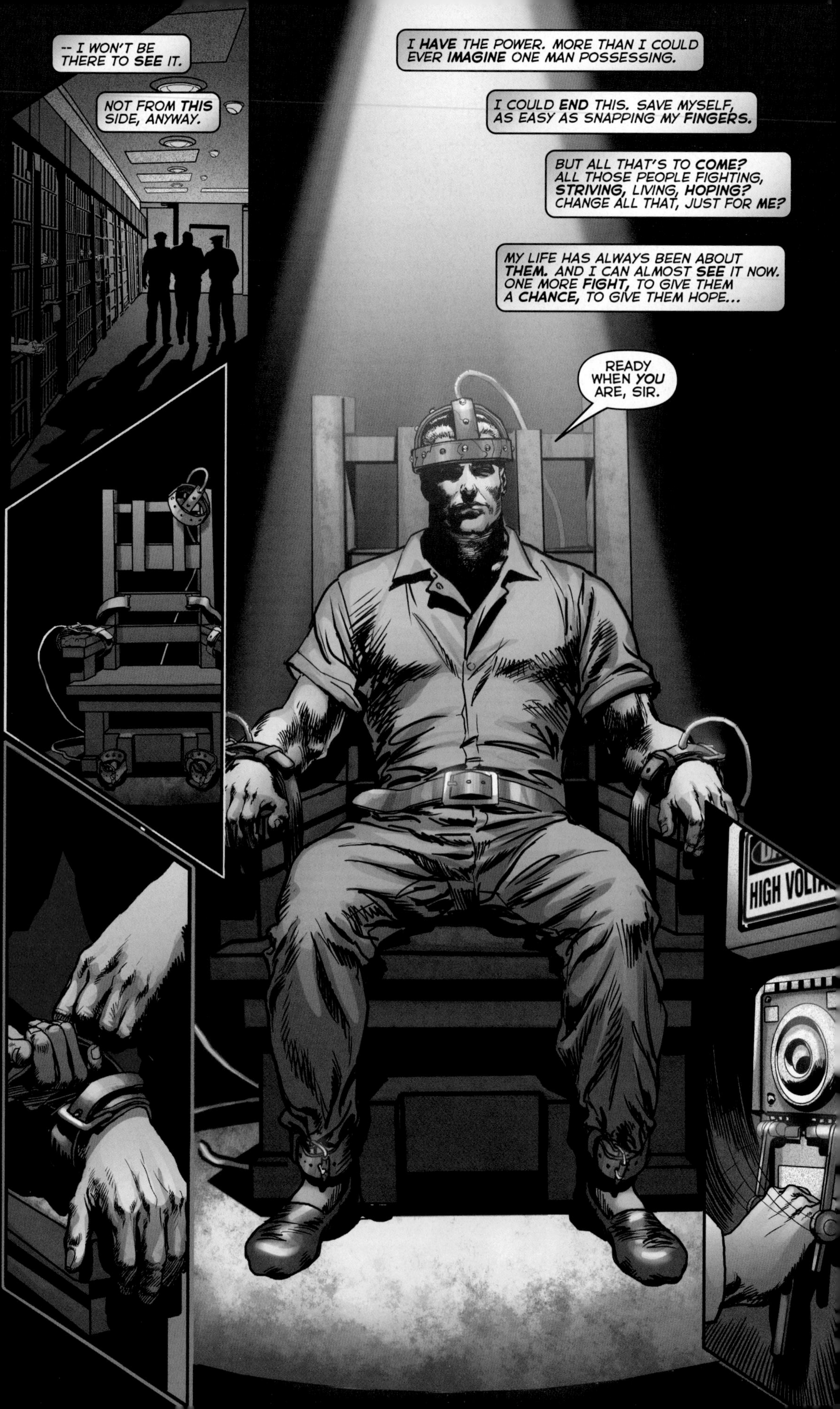
-- I WON'T BE THERE TO SEE IT.
NOT FROM THIS SIDE, ANYWAY.
I HAVE THE POWER. MORE THAN I COULD EVER IMAGINE ONE MAN POSSESSING.
I COULD END THIS. SAVE MYSELF, AS EASY AS SNAPPING MY FINGERS.
BUT ALL THAT'S TO COME? ALL THOSE PEOPLE FIGHTING, STRIVING, LIVING, HOPING? CHANGE ALL THAT, JUST FOR ME?
MY LIFE HAS ALWAYS BEEN ABOUT THEM. AND I CAN ALMOST SEE IT NOW. ONE MORE FIGHT, TO GIVE THEM A CHANCE, TO GIVE THEM HOPE...
READY WHEN YOU ARE, SIR.
HIGH VOLTA

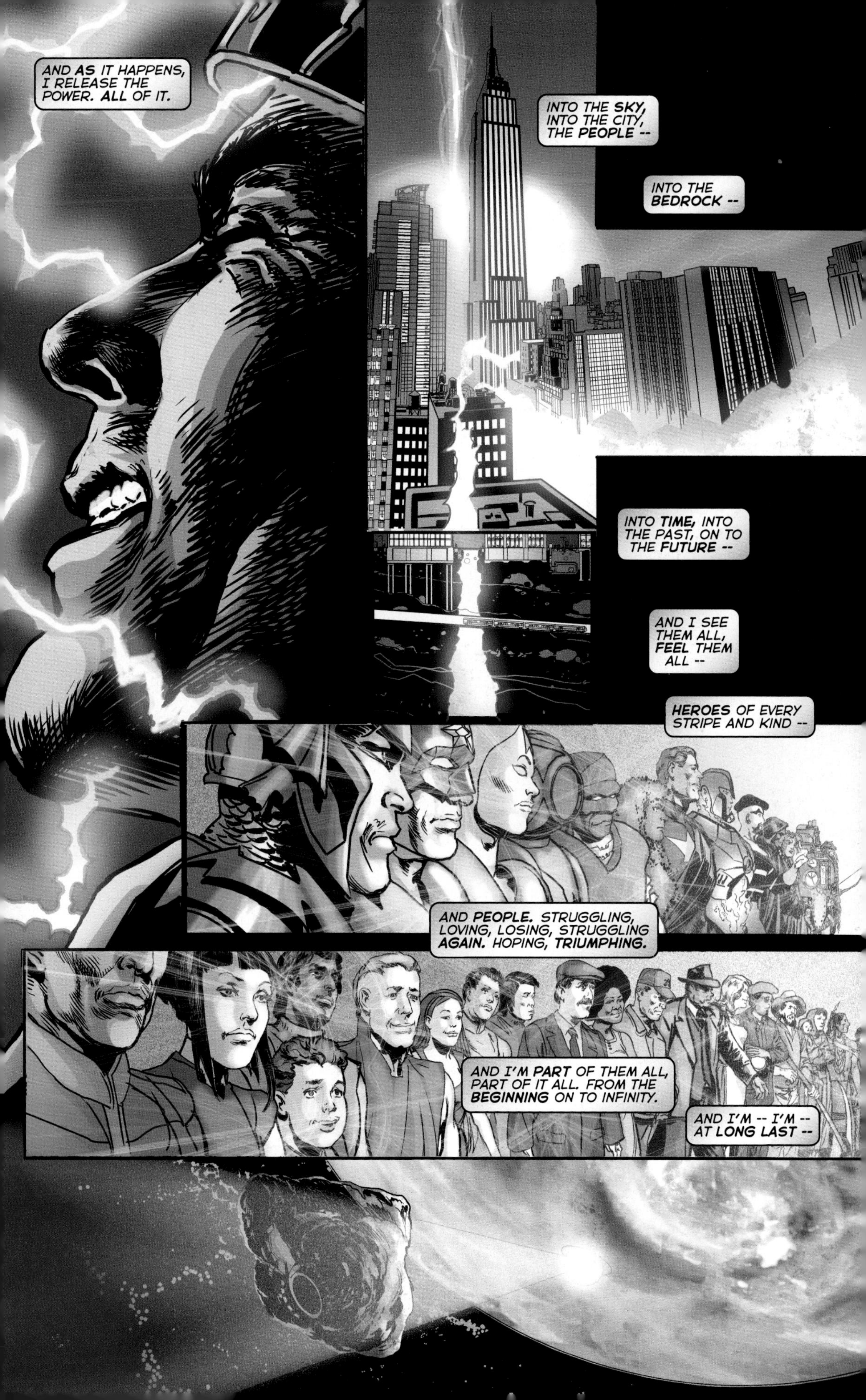
AND AS IT HAPPENS, I RELEASE THE POWER. ALL OF IT.
INTO THE SKY, INTO THE CITY, THE PEOPLE --
INTO THE BEDROCK --
INTO TIME, INTO THE PAST, ON TO THE FUTURE --
AND I SEE THEM ALL, FEEL THEM ALL --
HEROES OF EVERY STRIPE AND KIND --
AND PEOPLE. STRUGGLING, LOVING, LOSING, STRUGGLING AGAIN. HOPING, TRIUMPHING.
AND I'M PART OF THEM ALL, PART OF IT ALL. FROM THE BEGINNING ON TO INFINITY.
AND I'M -- I'M -- AT LONG LAST --

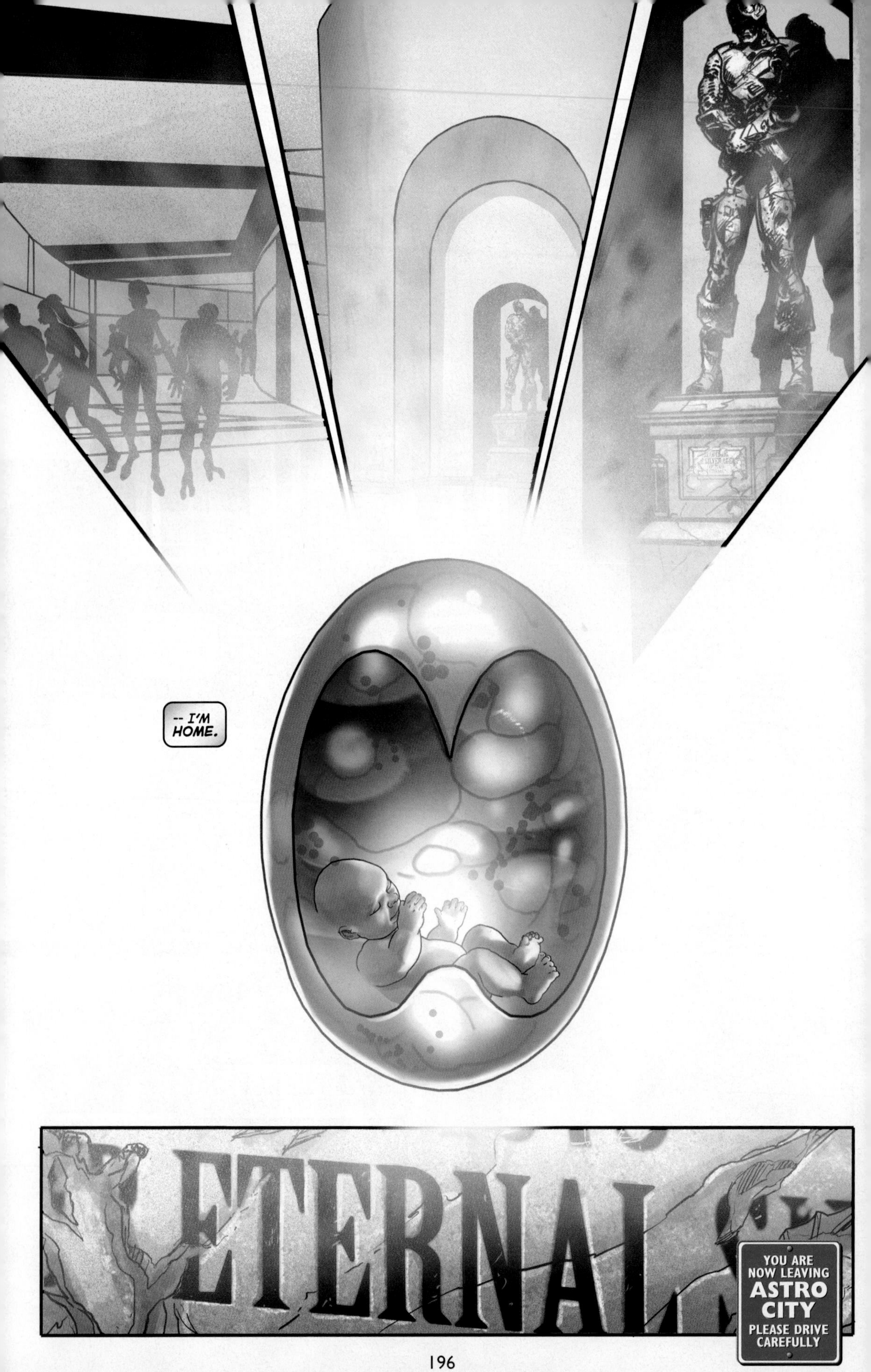
-- I'M HOME.
ETERNAL
YOU ARE NOW LEAVING
ASTRO CITY
PLEASE DRIVE CAREFULLY

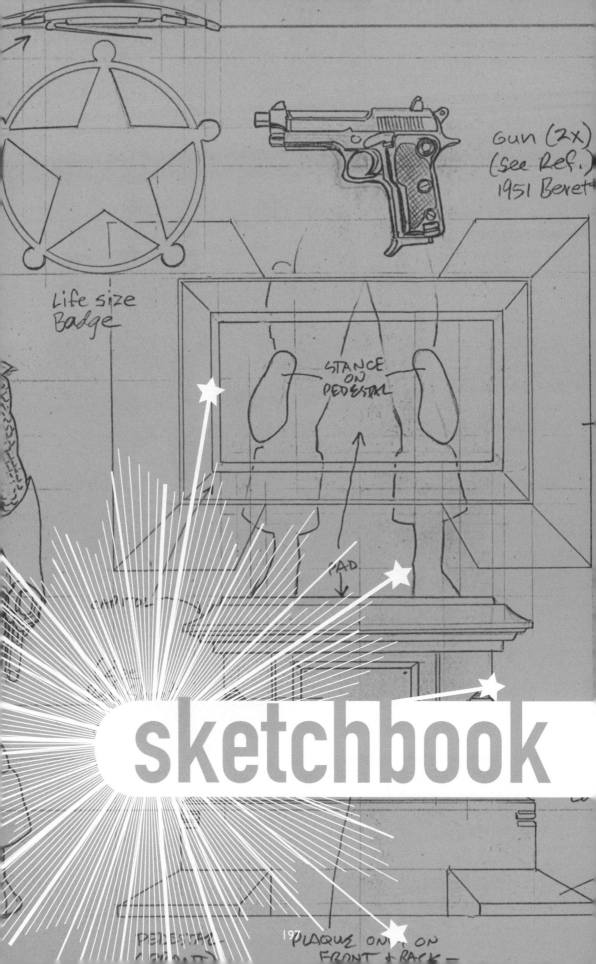

Gun (2x)
(see Ref.)
1951 Beretta

Life size
Badge

STANCE
ON
PEDESTAL

PAD

sketchbook

PEDESTAL
197 PLAQUE ON?? ON
FRONT + BACK —

Wizard Magazine asked Alex and me to walk readers through the creation of a villain, for the WIZARD DARK BOOK '98 SPECIAL. Infidel was the result.

He was a study in contrasts with Samaritan: from the past rather than the future, using alchemy instead of superscience, a tyrant rather than a hero—but still a time-traveler, powered by the same "empyrean fire" that powers Samaritan.

Creating him was a very enjoyable process—the only problem was, we didn't have a story to feature him in.

It took eight years, but eventually, we had the perfect tale for his debut.

— KURT BUSIEK

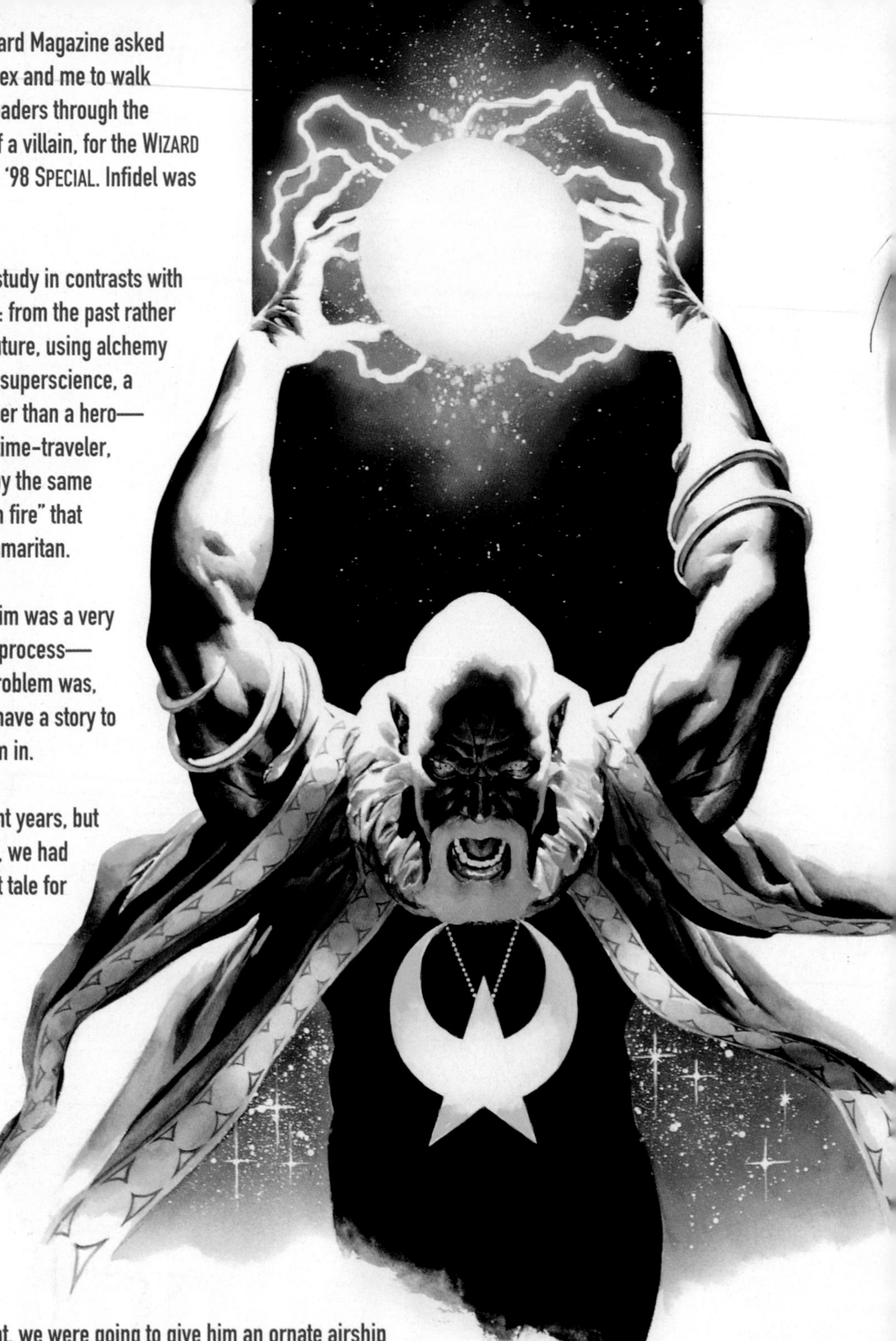

At one point, we were going to give him an ornate airship with a complex wicker gondola. But then someone said "flying carpet," and of course he had to have a flying carpet.

So he got an ornate wicker castle instead.

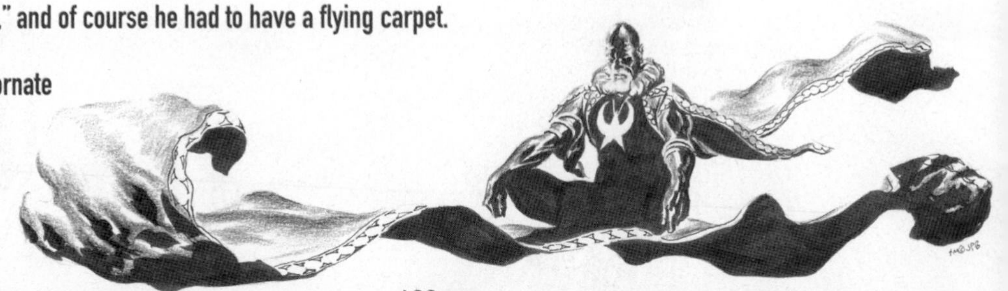

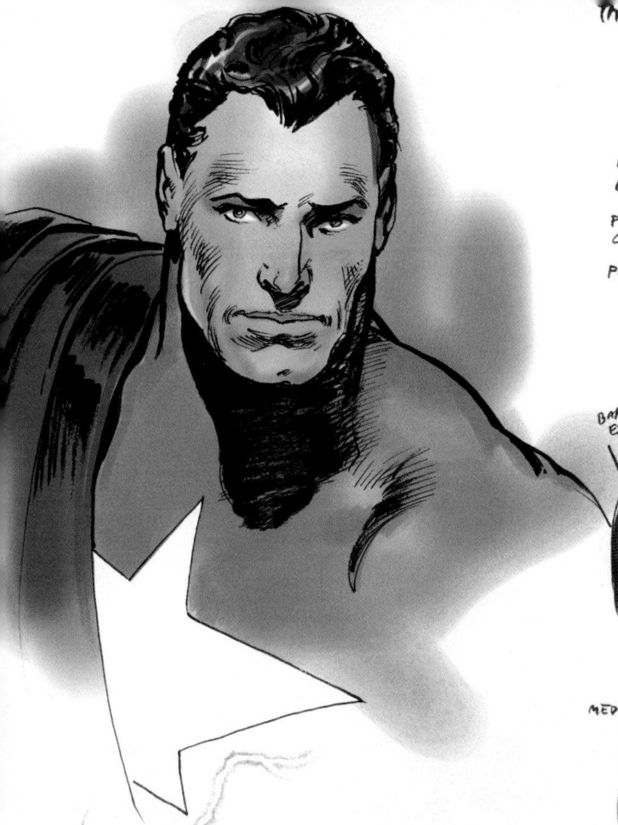

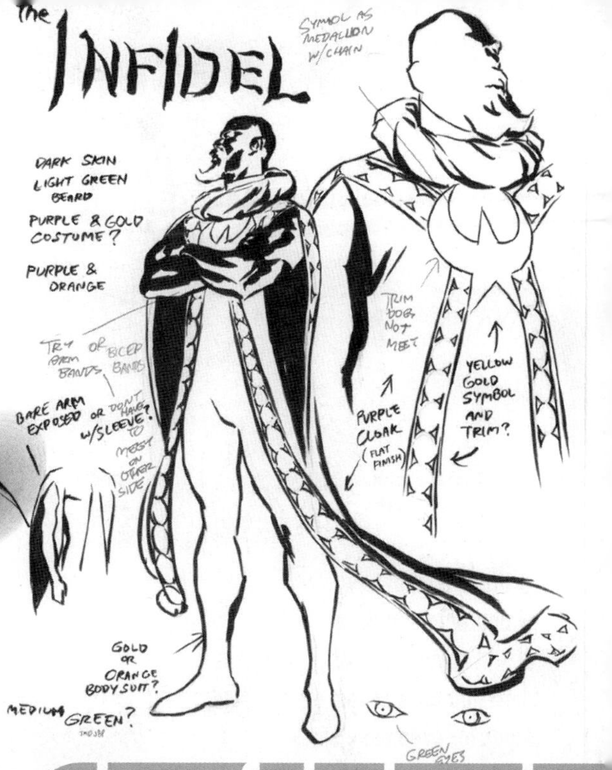
the INFIDEL
SYMBOL AS MEDALLION W/CHAIN
DARK SKIN
LIGHT GREEN BEARD
PURPLE & GOLD COSTUME?
PURPLE & ORANGE
TRY ARM BANDS OR BICEP BANDS
BARE ARM EXPOSED OR DON'T HAVE W/SLEEVE? TO MESSY ON OTHER SIDE
TRIM DOES NOT MEET
YELLOW GOLD SYMBOL AND TRIM?
PURPLE CLOAK (FLAT FINISH)
GOLD OR ORANGE BODYSUIT?
MEDIUM GREEN?
GREEN EYES

infidel

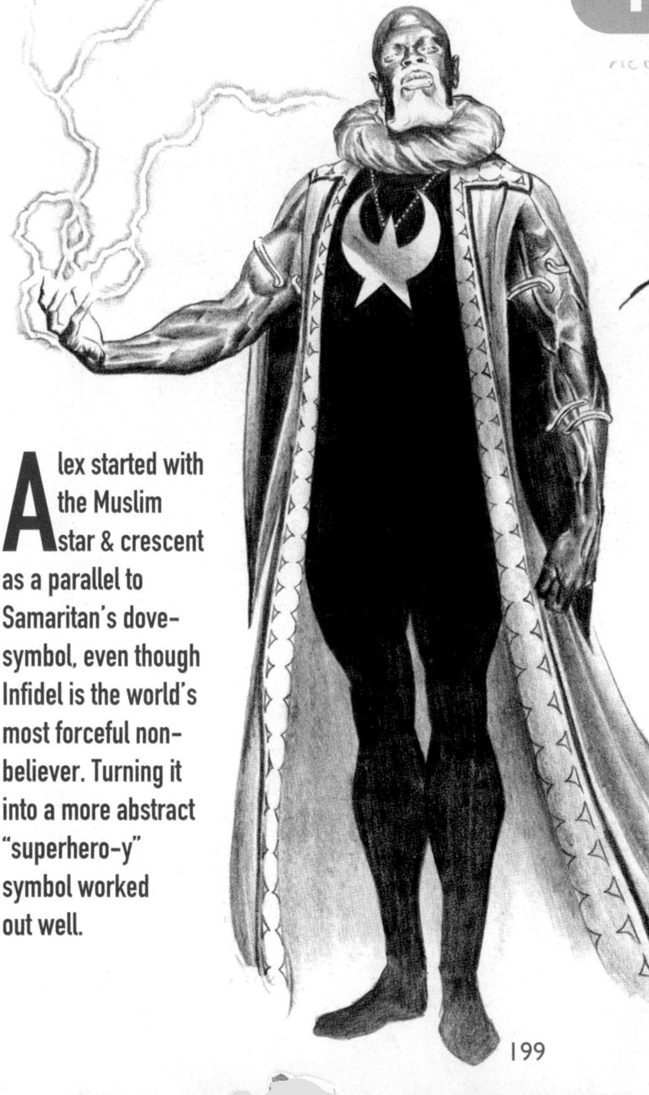

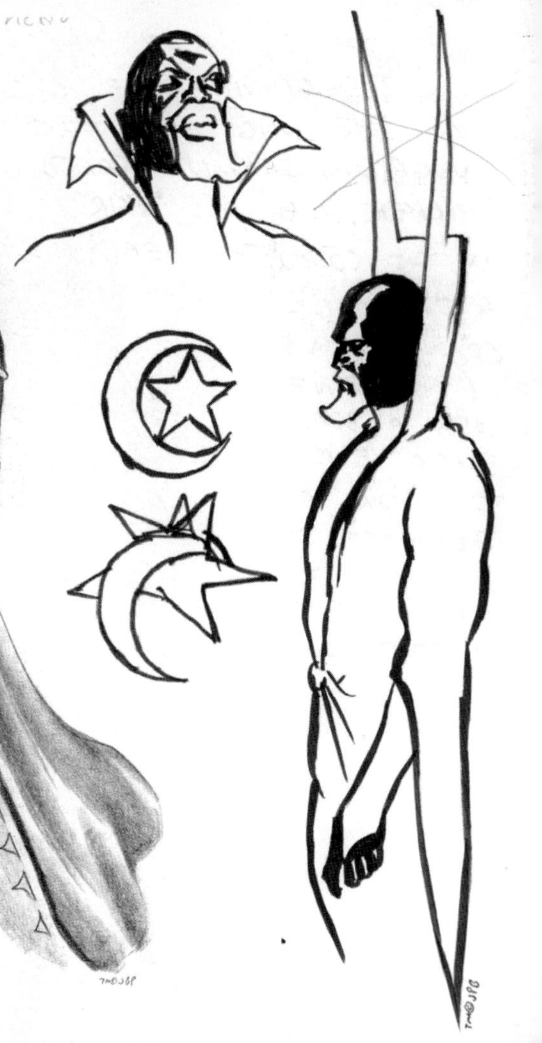

Alex started with the Muslim star & crescent as a parallel to Samaritan's dove-symbol, even though Infidel is the world's most forceful non-believer. Turning it into a more abstract "superhero-y" symbol worked out well.

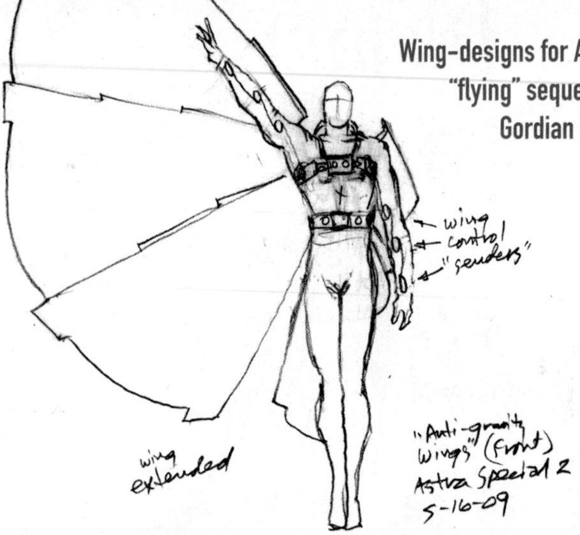

wing
control
"senders"
wing extended
"Anti-gravity wings" (Front)
Astra Special 2
5-16-09

Wing-designs for Astra and Matt's "flying" sequence in the Gordian Knot.

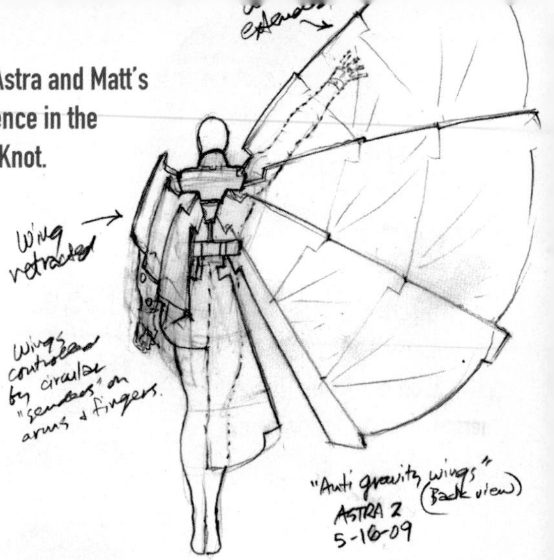

Wing retracted
Wings controlled by circular "senders" on arms & fingers.
"Anti gravity wings" (Back view)
ASTRA 2
5-16-09

I throw a lot of new characters at Brent, and someone who shows up for a couple of pages (or even panels) needs designing just as much as someone who get a whole arc.

You never know when they'll be appearing again, after all!

SKYSWEEPER (the former Kid Jackdaw): my suggestion to Brent was that he have hi-tech elements that looked like they were made of molded high-density plastic, the Apple Macintosh to most armored heroes' Cadillac.

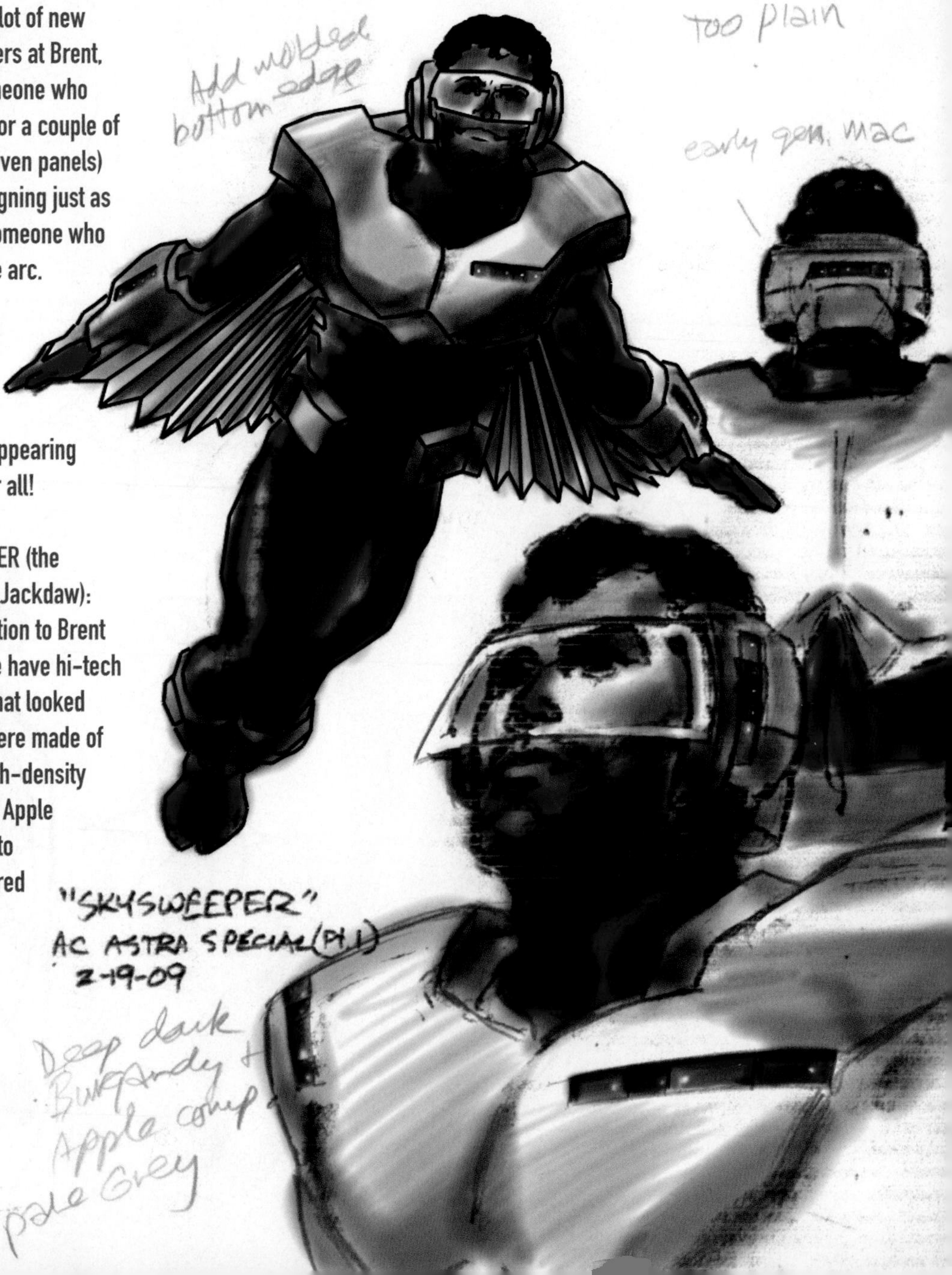

Too plain
Add molded bottom edge
early gen. mac
"SKYSWEEPER"
AC ASTRA SPECIAL (Pt.1)
2-19-09
Deep dark Burgundy +
Apple comp
pale Grey

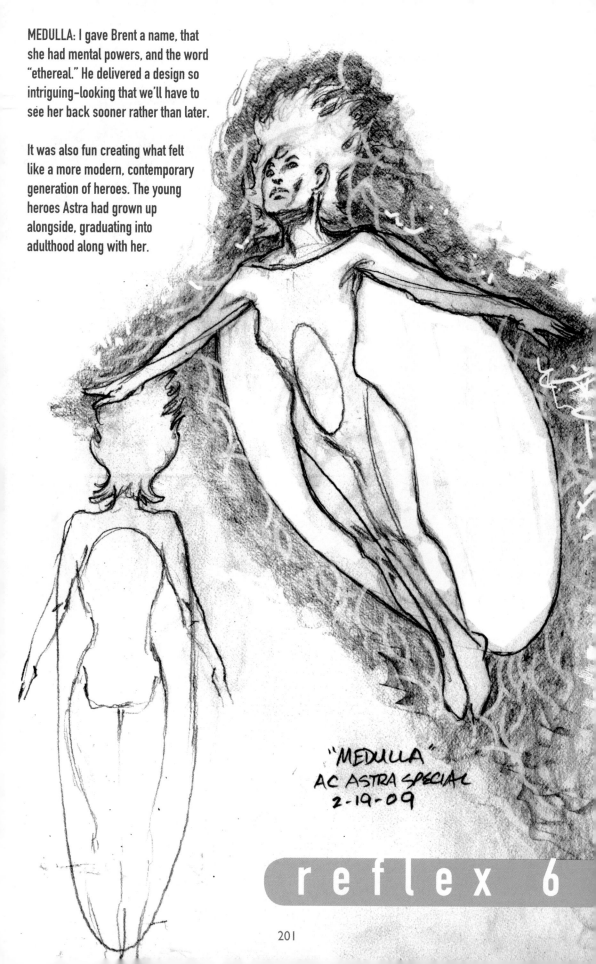

MEDULLA: I gave Brent a name, that she had mental powers, and the word "ethereal." He delivered a design so intriguing-looking that we'll have to see her back sooner rather than later.

It was also fun creating what felt like a more modern, contemporary generation of heroes. The young heroes Astra had grown up alongside, graduating into adulthood along with her.

"MEDULLA"
AC ASTRA SPECIAL
2-19-09

reflex 6

TEARAWAY: The final member of Reflex 6. Or Firewall. (But not Wildrogues). If you don't count the not-yet-seen Gorgon and Jimmy Shade.

He's the kind of guy where powers, personality and codename are all wrapped up in a single word.

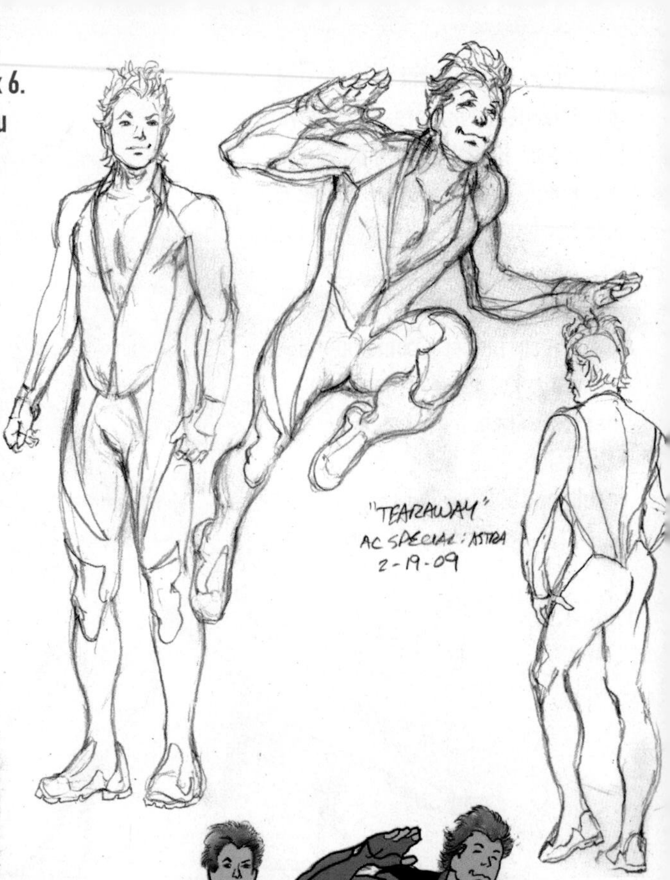

"TEARAWAY"
AC SPECIAL: ASTRA
2-19-09

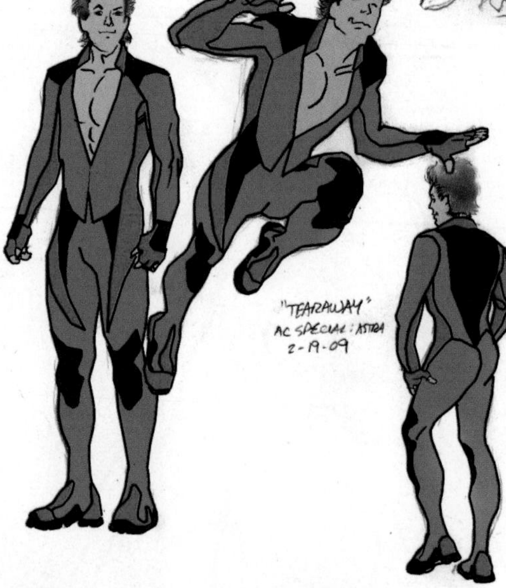

"TEARAWAY"
AC SPECIAL: ASTRA
2-19-09

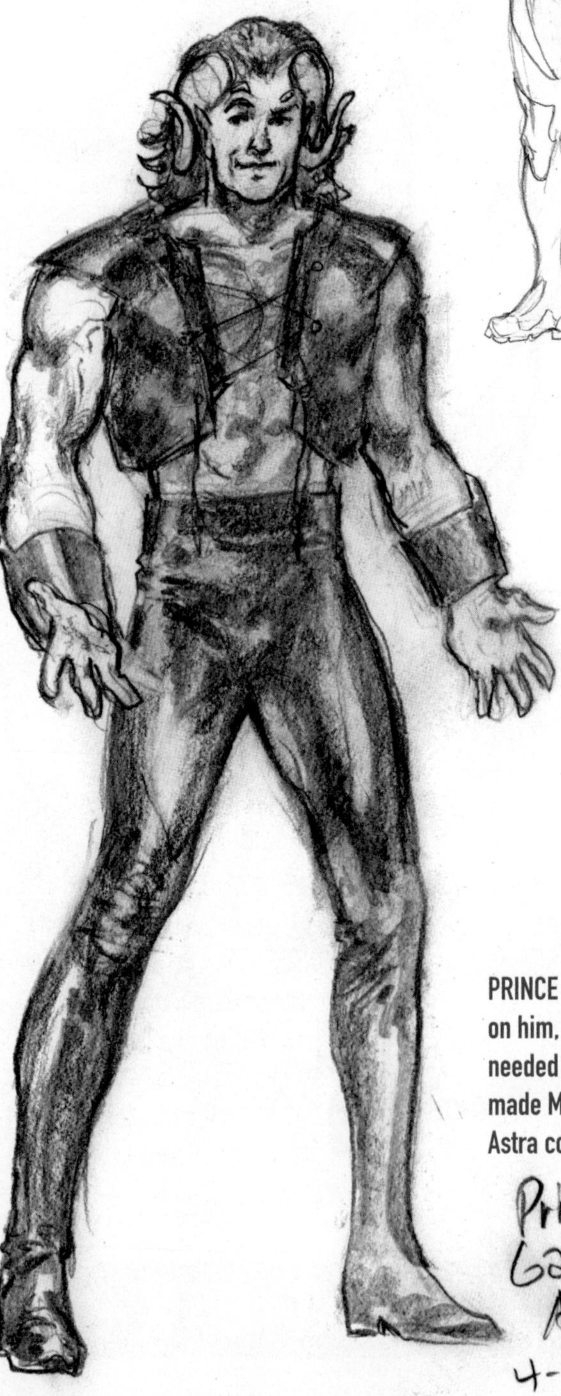

Prince
Gavrad
Astra Sp. 2
4-24-09

PRINCE GAVRAD: We went through a lot of revisions on him, this being one that was close to finished. He needed to be overtly masculine and sexual in a way that made Matt instantly jealous, But not so overstated that Astra couldn't seem relaxed around him.

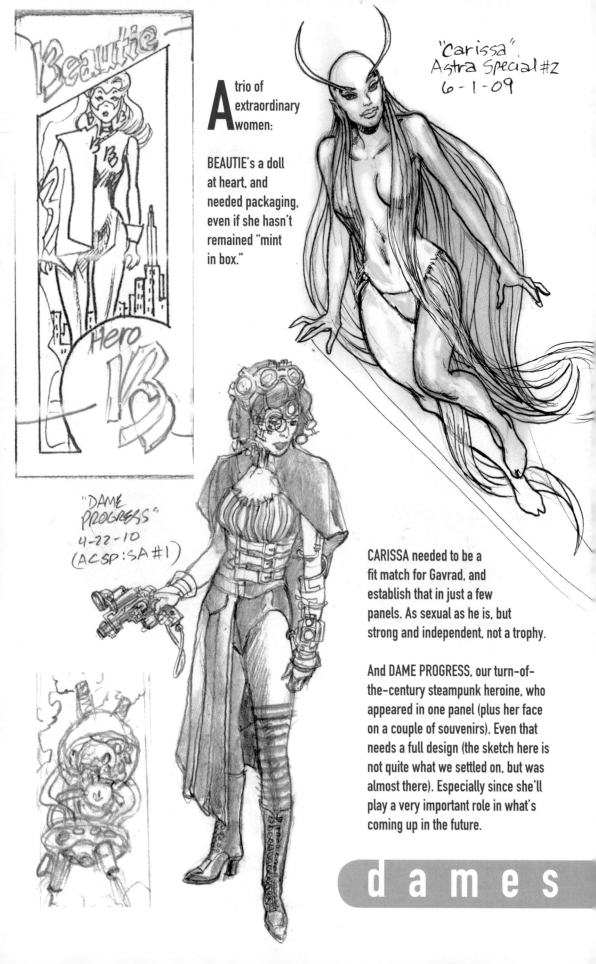

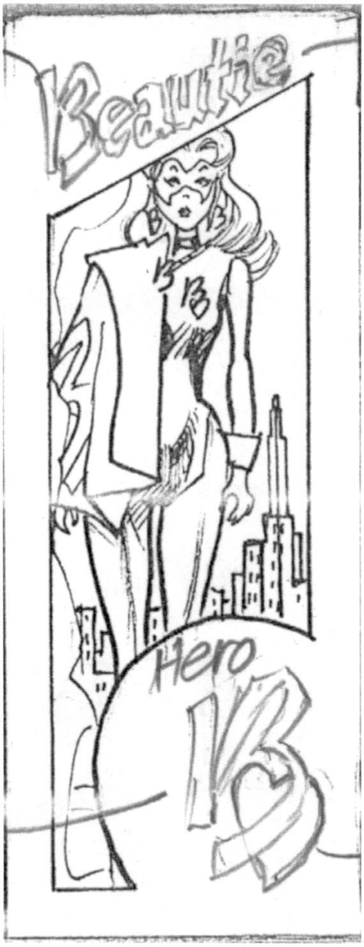
Beautie
Hero

A trio of extraordinary women:

BEAUTIE's a doll at heart, and needed packaging, even if she hasn't remained "mint in box."

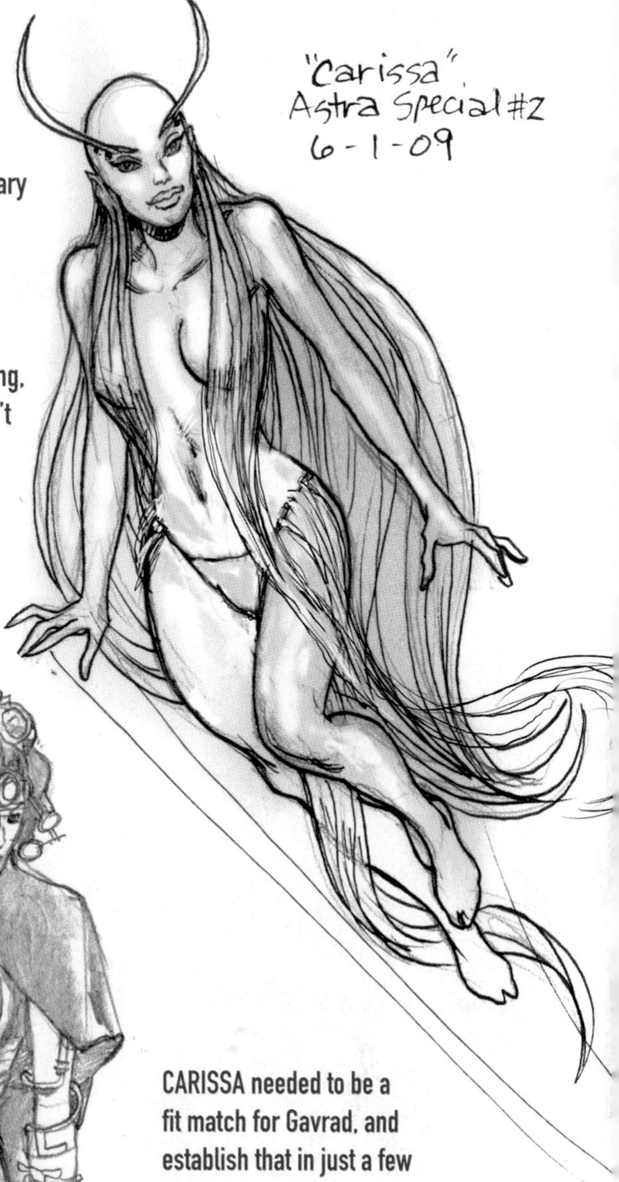
"Carissa"
Astra Special #2
6-1-09

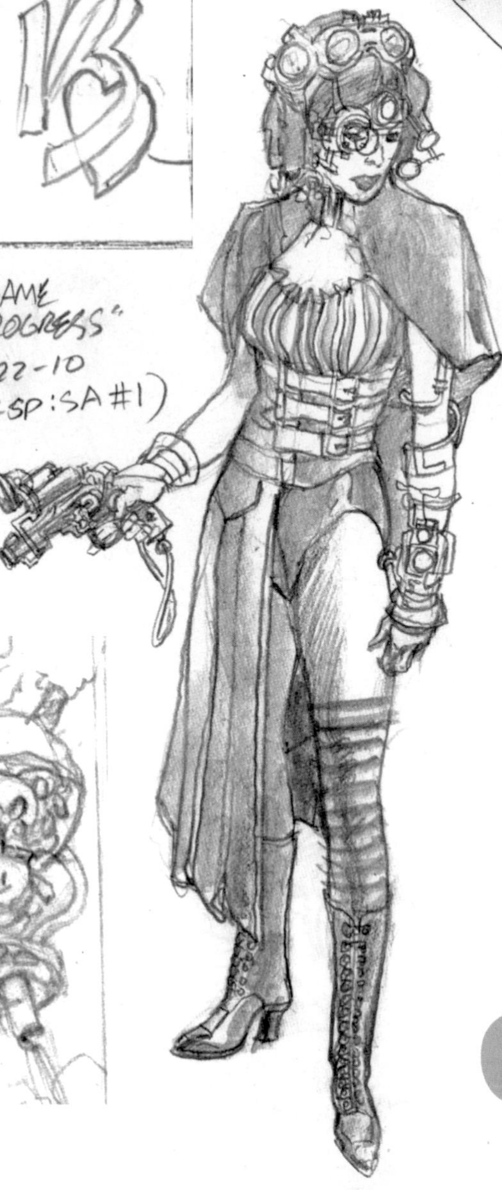
"DAME PROGRESS"
4-22-10
(ACSP:SA #1)

CARISSA needed to be a fit match for Gavrad, and establish that in just a few panels. As sexual as he is, but strong and independent, not a trophy.

And DAME PROGRESS, our turn-of-the-century steampunk heroine, who appeared in one panel (plus her face on a couple of souvenirs). Even that needs a full design (the sketch here is not quite what we settled on, but was almost there). Especially since she'll play a very important role in what's coming up in the future.

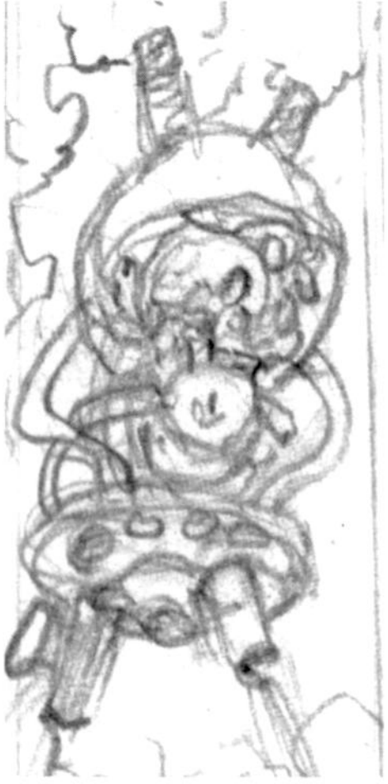

dames

THE SILVER CENTURIONS: They needed a costume design that'd unify them, even though the team featured wildly-diverse members, some not even humanoid.

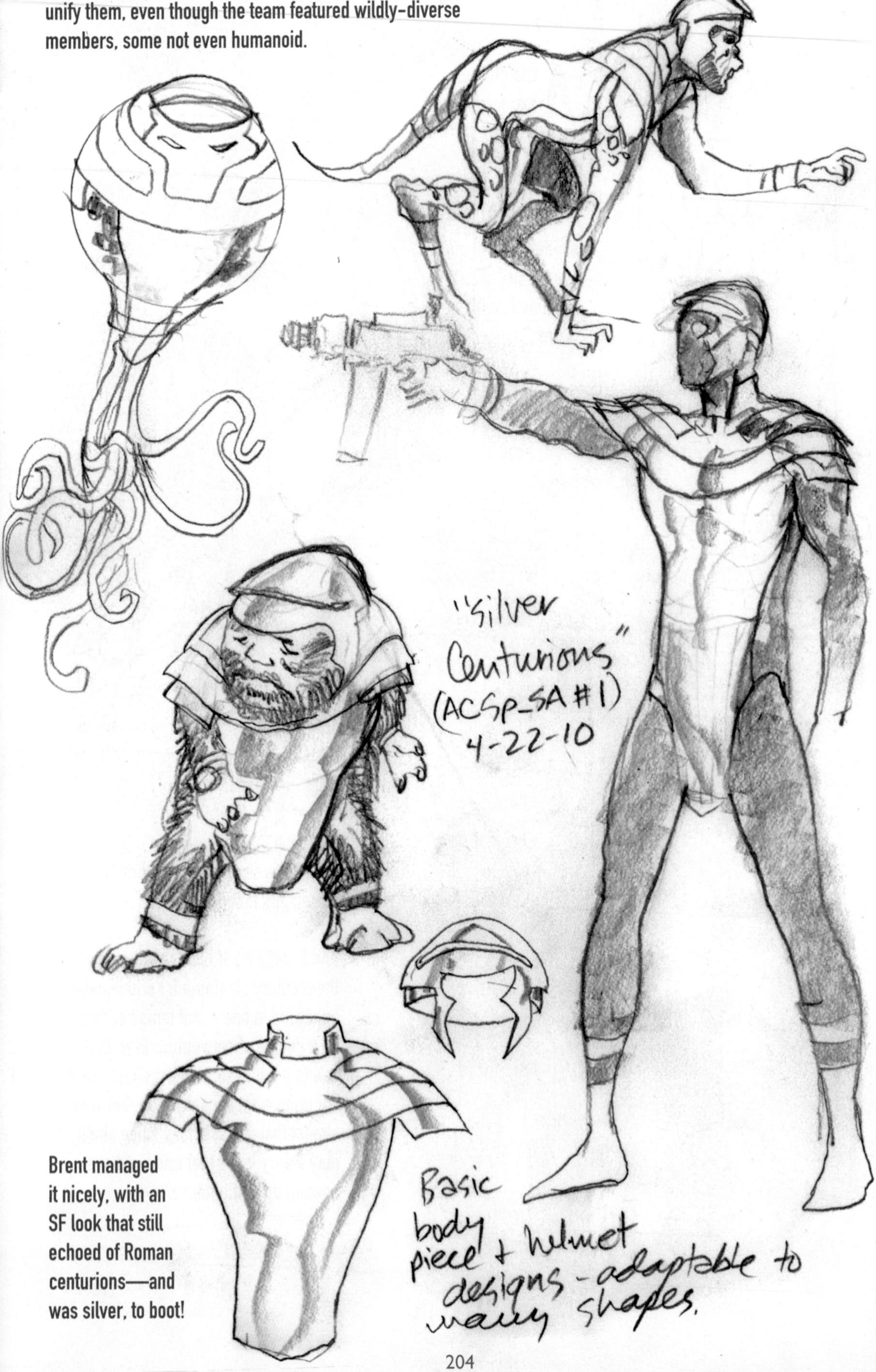
"Silver Centurions" (ACSP-SA #1) 4-22-10
Basic body piece + helmet designs - adaptable to many shapes.

Brent managed it nicely, with an SF look that still echoed of Roman centurions—and was silver, to boot!

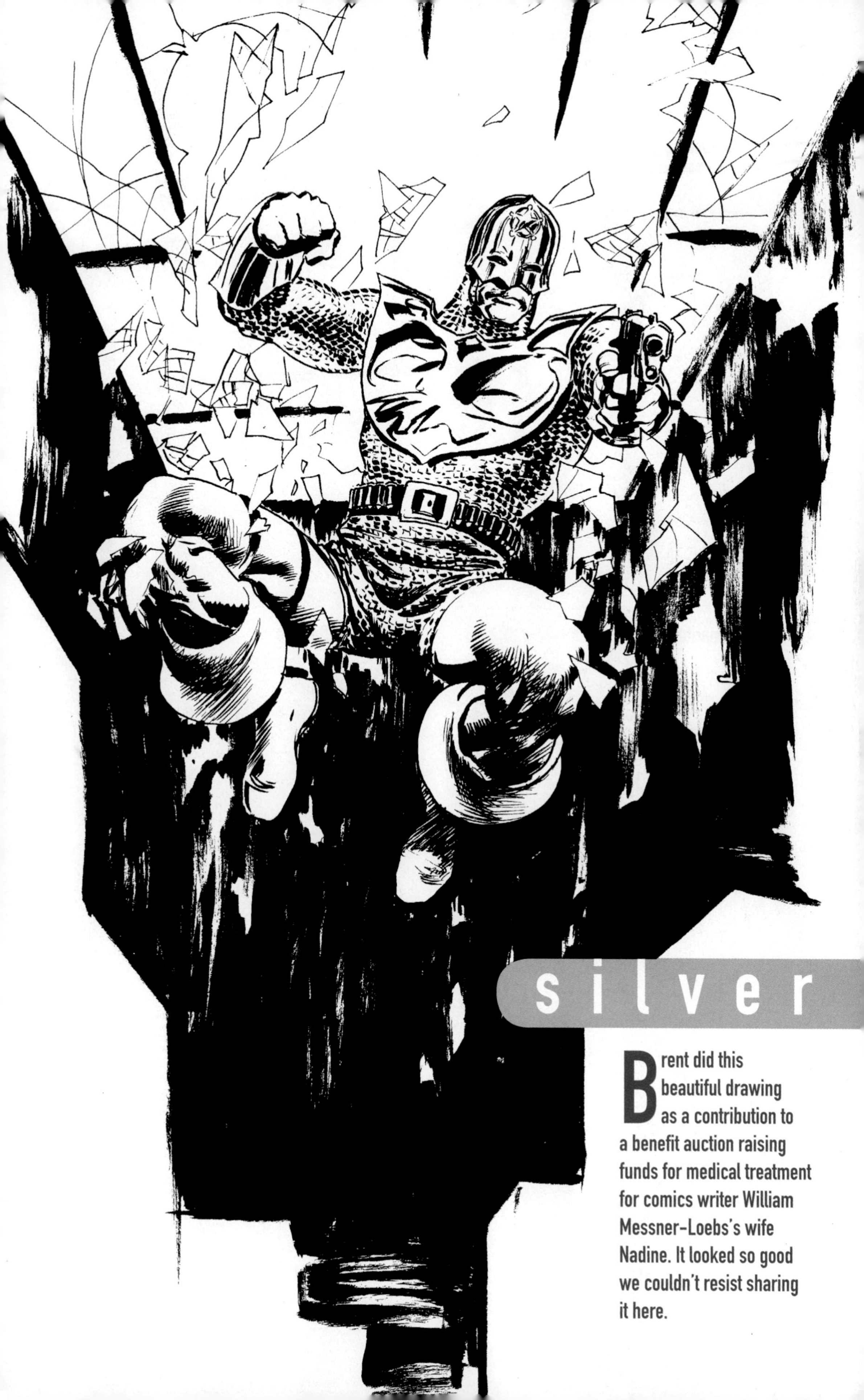

silver

Brent did this beautiful drawing as a contribution to a benefit auction raising funds for medical treatment for comics writer William Messner-Loebs's wife Nadine. It looked so good we couldn't resist sharing it here.

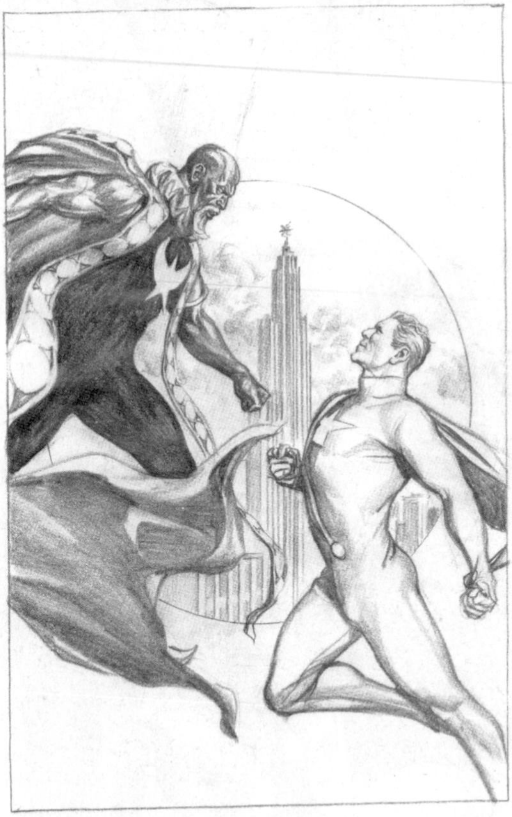

Astro City: Samaritan

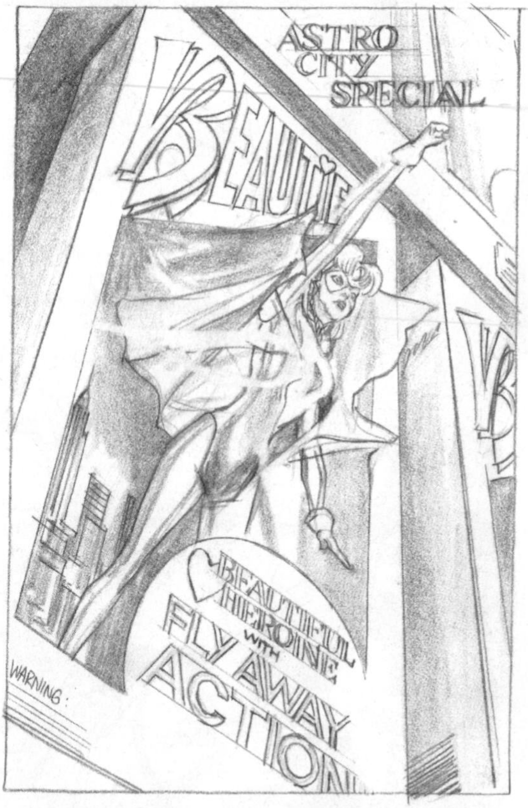

ASTRO CITY SPECIAL
BEAUTIE
BEAUTIFUL HEROINE WITH FLY AWAY ACTION
WARNING:

Astro City: Beautie

PREVIOUS LOGO

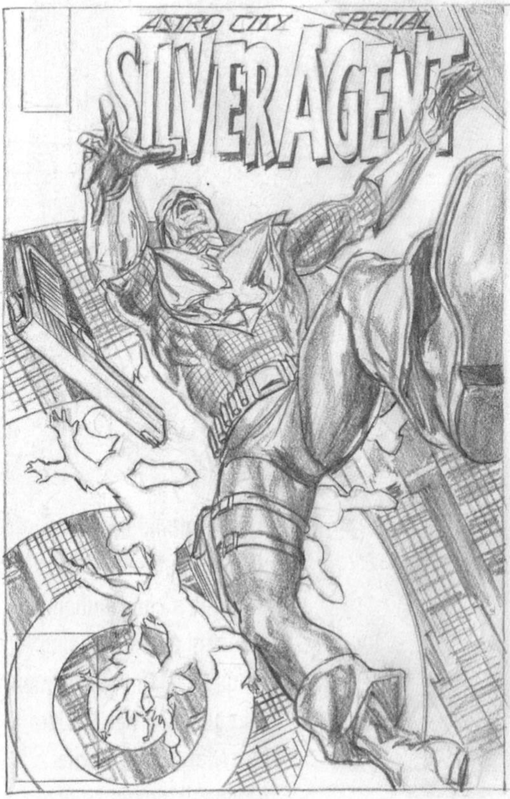

ASTRO CITY SPECIAL
SILVER AGEN

Astro City: Silver Agent #1

LOGO ALTERNATIVE

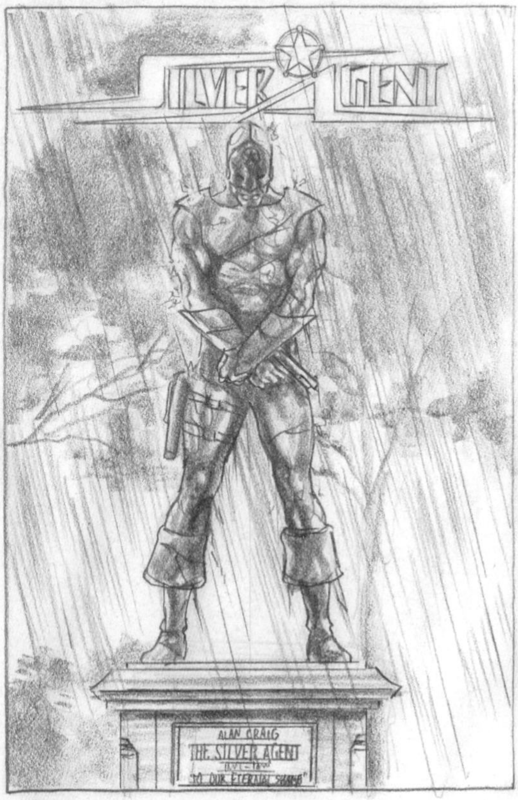

SILVER AGENT
ALAN CRAIG
THE SILVER AGENT
TO OUR ETERNAL SHAME

Astro City: Silver Agent #2

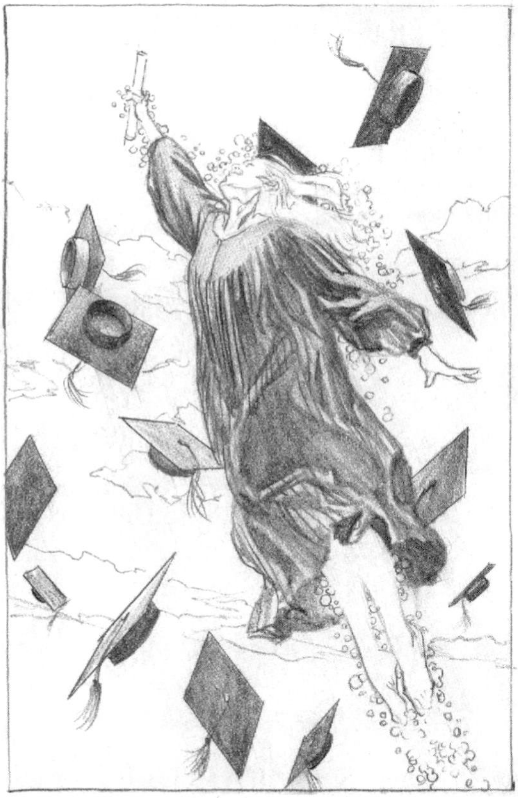

Astro City: Astra #1 (this one changed a bit)

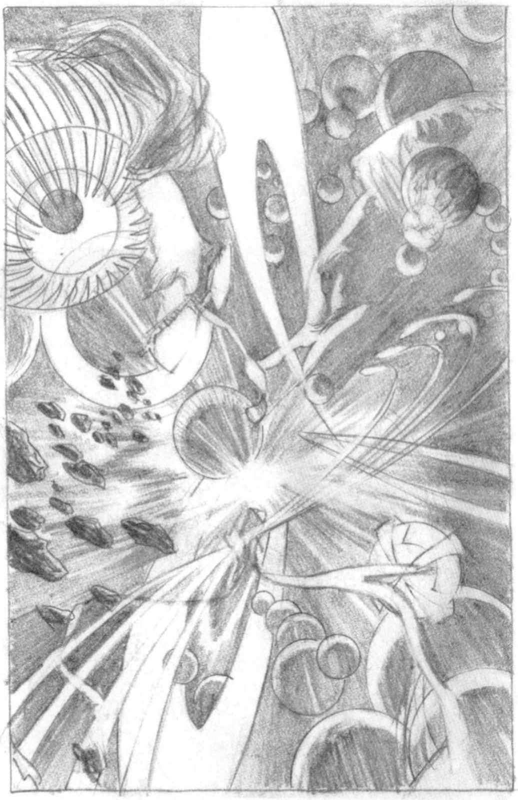

Astro City: Astra #2

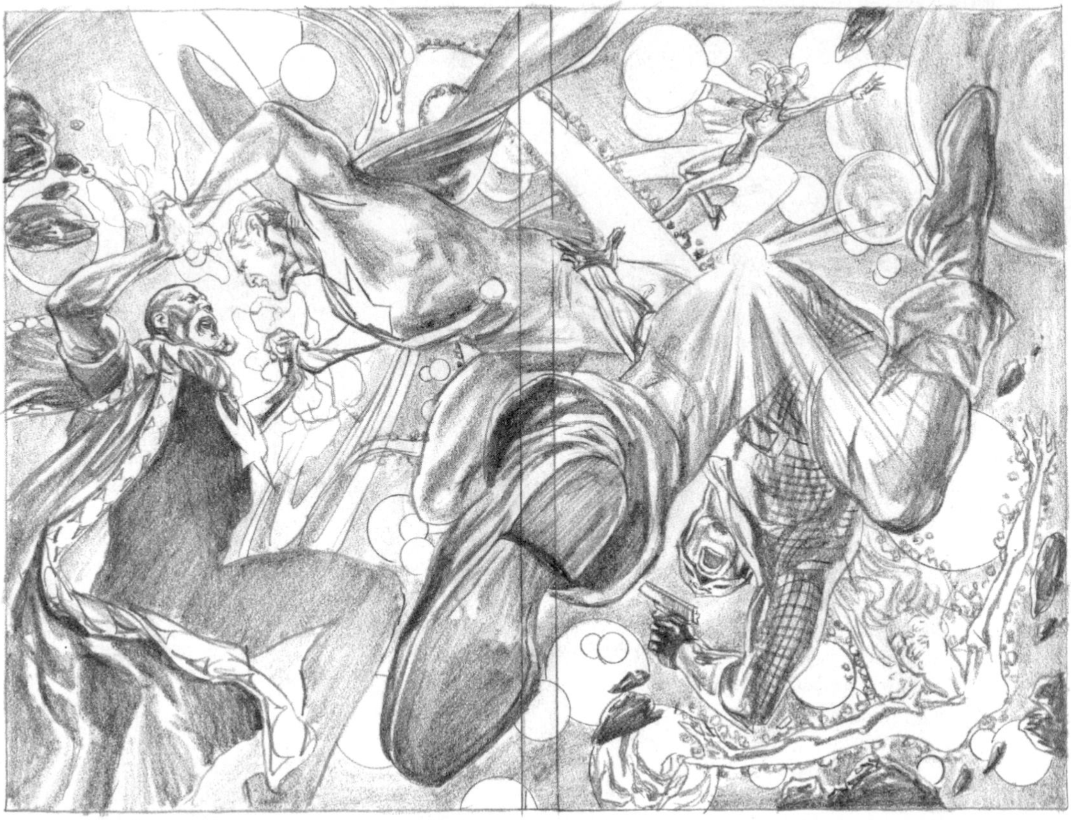

The wraparound cover for the hardcover edition of this volume.
(We flopped the design to put Samaritan and Infidel up front.)

DON'T MISS THE REST OF THE ASTRO CITY SERIES:

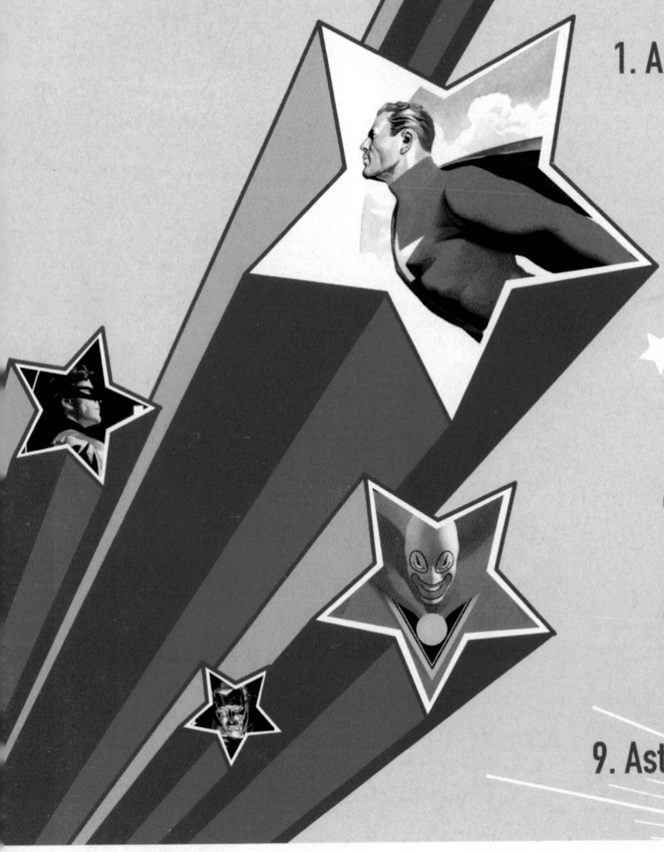

1. Astro City: Life In The Big City
2. Astro City: Confession
3. Astro City: Family Album
4. Astro City: The Tarnished Angel
5. Astro City: Local Heroes
6. Astro City The Dark Age 1: Brothers & Other Strangers
7. Astro City The Dark Age 2: Brothers in Arms
9. Astro City: Through Open Doors

about the creators

KURT BUSIEK broke into comics in 1982, selling stories to both DC and Marvel within weeks of finishing college. Since then, he's been an editor, a literary agent, a sales manager and more, but is best known as the multiple-award-winning writer of ASTRO CITY, MARVELS, SUPERMAN, CONAN, ARROWSMITH, SUPERSTAR, SHOCKROCKETS and many others. He lives in the Pacific Northwest with his family.

BRENT ANDERSON began writing and drawing his own comics in junior high school, and graduated to professional work less than a decade later. He's drawn such projects as KA-ZAR THE SAVAGE, X-MEN: GOD LOVES MAN KILLS, STRIKEFORCE: MORITURI, SOMERSET HOLMES, RISING STARS and, of course, ASTRO CITY, for which he's won multiple Eisner and Harvey Awards. He makes his home in Northern California.

ALEX ROSS worked on TERMINATOR: THE BURNING EARTH and Clive Barker's HELLRAISER before his breakout series, MARVELS, made him an overnight superstar. Since then, he's painted, plotted and/or written such series as KINGDOM COME, SUPERMAN: PEACE ON EARTH, JUSTICE, EARTH X, AVENGERS/INVADERS and PROJECT SUPERPOWERS, and won over two dozen industry awards.

ALEX SINCLAIR has colored virtually every DC Comics character in existence, and more besides. Best known for his award-winning work with Jim Lee and Scott Williams, he's worked on such books as BATMAN: HUSH, SUPERMAN: FOR TOMORROW, BLACKEST NIGHT, BATMAN & ROBIN, ASTRO CITY, JLA, IDENTITY CRISIS, ARROWSMITH and more.

JOHN G. ROSHELL joined Comicraft in 1992, helping propel the lettering/design studio to its dominant position in the industry. As Senior Design Wizard, he's lettered thousands of comics pages, along with creating logos and fonts, designing book editions and more. He also writes the series CHARLEY LOVES ROBOTS, which appears in ELEPHANTMEN.

WENDY BROOME was a longtime member of the coloring staff at WildStorm Studios, before going freelance in 2004. She's made a specialty of coloring large-cast books, including WILDCATS 3.0, THE AUTHORITY, GEN13, THE END LEAGUE, THUNDERCATS, WETWORKS and TOP10 as well as pitching in as needed on ASTRO CITY.

RICHARD STARKINGS dimly remembers working on some BATMAN project... THE KILLING JOKE? People insist that he did letter it with a tool not unlike a computer... but too many lattes and British chocolate has wiped his recollections of anything prior to Illustrator 5. He currently writes ELEPHANTMEN.